SHAKESPEARE SURVEY

ADVISORY BOARD

Aspects of *Macbeth*
Aspects of *Othello*
Aspects of *Hamlet*
Aspects of *King Lear*
Aspects of Shakespeare's 'Problem Plays'

SHAKESPEARE SURVEY

AN ANNUAL SURVEY OF

SHAKESPEARE STUDIES AND PRODUCTION

42

EDITED BY

STANLEY WELLS

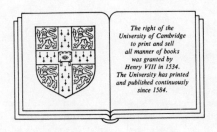

The right of the
University of Cambridge
to print and sell
all manner of books
was granted by
Henry VIII in 1534.
The University has printed
and published continuously
since 1584.

CAMBRIDGE UNIVERSITY PRESS

CAMBRIDGE

NEW YORK   PORT CHESTER   MELBOURNE   SYDNEY

Published by the Press Syndicate of the University of Cambridge
The Pitt Building, Trumpington Street, Cambridge CB2 1RP
40 West 20th Street, New York, NY 10011, USA
10 Stamford Road, Oakleigh, Melbourne 3166, Australia

First published 1990

Printed in Great Britain at The Bath Press, Avon

British Library cataloguing in publication data

Shakespeare survey: an annual survey of
Shakespeare studies and production. – 42:
[Shakespeare and the Elizabethans].
1. Drama in English. Shakespeare, William –
Critical studies – Serials
822'.3'3

Library of Congress catalogue card number: 49–1639

ISBN 0 521 38034 0

Shakespeare Survey was first published in 1948. Its first
eighteen volumes were edited by Allardyce Nicoll. Kenneth
Muir edited volumes 19 to 33.

CE

EDITOR'S NOTE

Volume 43 of *Shakespeare Survey*, which will be at press by the time this volume appears, will focus on '*The Tempest* and After', Volume 44 on 'Politics and Shakespeare', and Volume 45 on '*Hamlet* and Its Afterlife'. Topics for Volume 45 may include the afterlife of *Hamlet* in production, adaptation, and influence up to our own time.

Submissions should be addressed to the Editor at The Shakespeare Institute, Church Street, Stratford-upon-Avon, Warwickshire CV37 6HP, to arrive at the latest by 1 September 1990 for Volume 44 and 1 September 1991 for Volume 45. Pressures on space are heavy; many articles are considered before the deadline, so those that arrive earlier stand a better chance of acceptance. Please either enclose return postage (overseas, in International Reply coupons) or send a copy you do not wish to have returned. A style sheet is available on request. All articles submitted are read by the Editor and at least one member of the Editorial Board, whose indispensable assistance the Editor gratefully acknowledges.

Unless otherwise indicated, Shakespeare quotations and references are keyed to the modern-spelling Complete Oxford Shakespeare (1986).

In attempting to survey the ever-increasing bulk of Shakespeare publications our reviewers inevitably have to exercise some selection. Review copies of books should be addressed to the Editor, as above. We are also pleased to receive offprints of articles which help to draw our reviewers' attention to relevant material.

S.W.W.

CONTRIBUTORS

Jonathan Bate, *Trinity Hall, Cambridge*
David Bevington, *University of Chicago*
Giles E. Dawson, *Washington, D.C.*
Richard Dutton, *University of Lancaster*
Juliet Dusinberre, *Girton College, Cambridge*
Charles Edelman, *Dulwich, South Australia*
Richard F. Hardin, *University of Kansas, Lawrence*
E. A. J. Honigmann, *University of Newcastle-upon-Tyne*
G. K. Hunter, *Yale University*
MacDonald P. Jackson, *University of Auckland*
P. H. Parry, *University of St Andrews*
Lois Potter, *University of Leicester*
N. Rathbone, *Birmingham Shakespeare Library*
Anthony Brian Taylor, *West Glamorgan Institute of Higher Education, Swansea*
Stanley Wells, *The Shakespeare Institute, University of Birmingham*
R. S. White, *University of Western Australia, Nedlands*

CONTENTS

ILLUSTRATIONS

ILLUSTRATIONS

'JACK HATH NOT JILL': FAILED COURTSHIP IN LYLY AND SHAKESPEARE

DAVID BEVINGTON

I begin with two perceptions: first, the observation of Robert Y. Turner that English comedy did not really find a successful way to dramatize love in any psychological sense before Lyly began his career as a playwright, and second, that of Alfred Harbage and others that *Love's Labour's Lost* is the most Lylyan of Shakespeare's plays.[1] The Lyly play that immediately invites attention in this regard is *Sappho and Phao*, written in 1584, since, like Shakespeare's *Love's Labour's Lost*, it ends in a lack of romantic completion for the young lovers.[2] Without wishing to argue that Shakespeare turned directly to *Sappho and Phao* as a kind of source, I should like to ask what we can learn from examining these two plays together. They are both centred on the experience of young men and women as they meet one another for the first time in amorous encounter, and in both plays the experience is a difficult one, evoking in the men sensations of apprehension, curiosity, fascination of course but also diminished self-regard and humiliation, all leading ultimately to a collapse or at least postponement of the negotiations in love. Both plays feature a princess or queen whose independence and regal self-assurance inspire an outspokenness in the women around her that the men find, in varying degrees, threatening.[3]

Shakespeare's ending does to be sure leave open the possibility of a resumption of love relations and even eventual marriage while Lyly's portrayal of wooing ends in separation,

1 Robert Y. Turner, 'Some Dialogues of Love in Lyly's Comedies', *ELH*, 29 (1962), 276–88; Alfred Harbage, '*Love's Labour's Lost* and the Early Shakespeare', *Philological Quarterly*, 41 (1962), 18–36; G. K. Hunter, *John Lyly: The Humanist as Courtier* (London, 1962), pp. 298–349, especially pp. 330–5 and 339–42; T. W. Baldwin, *Shakespere's Five-Act Structure* (Urbana, Illinois, 1947), pp. 618–29; and Louis Adrian Montrose, '*Curious-Knotted Garden': The Form, Themes, and Contexts of Shakespeare's 'Love's Labour's Lost'* (Salzburg, 1977), p. 38.
2 John Wilders, in 'The Unresolved Conflicts of *Love's Labour's Lost*', *Essays in Criticism*, 27 (1977), 20–33, discusses the irresolutions of Shakespeare's play as compared with Lyly's dramaturgy, though he does not mention *Sappho and Phao*. Blaze Odell Bonazza, *Shakespeare's Early Comedies: A Structural Analysis* (The Hague, 1966), pp. 44–75, compares *Love's Labour's Lost* structurally with *Endymion* and *Gallathea*, citing R. Warwick Bond, ed., *The Complete Works of John Lyly*, 3 vols. (Oxford, 1902), vol. 2, pp. 276 and 297. (All quotations from *Sappho and Phao* in this essay are from my forthcoming edition of the play, to be published in the Revels Series; the line references here are to Bond's edition, vol. 2, pp. 369–415.) The *Gallathea* connection, described also by G. K. Hunter, *John Lyly*, p. 340, is pursued in Peter Berek, 'Artifice and Realism in Lyly, Nashe, and *Love's Labor's Lost*', *Studies in English Literature*, 23 (1983), 207–21. Oscar James Campbell, *Studies in Shakespeare, Milton, and Donne*, University of Michigan Publications in Language and Literature, vol. 1 (Ann Arbor, Michigan, 1925), pp. 3–45, sees an indebtedness in *Love's Labour's Lost* to *Sappho and Phao* and other Lyly plays in terms of wit and badinage. Barry Thorne, '*Love's Labour's Lost*: The Lyly Gilded', *The Humanities Association Bulletin*, 21 (1970), 32–7, focuses on the debt to *Endymion*.
3 See Irene Dash, *Wooing, Wedding, and Power: Women in Shakespeare's Plays* (New York, 1981), pp. 9–30.

but this is only to say, as Mary Beth Rose has argued, that Lyly and Shakespeare are dealing with the 'dualizing, idealizing Petrarchan sensibility' to which both were heir, but that Shakespeare's theatre also postulates a more pragmatic view of marriage in which the greater moral prestige accorded to love and marriage makes eventual resolution more possible.[4] More possible, yes, but my emphasis is on the extent to which Lyly and Shakespeare are alike in dramatizing not so much the success of courtship as its hazards and uncertainties. The comedy in both playwrights is directed chiefly at the sweet, hapless absurdity of the young person (especially the young man) as he postures defensively, seeks advice and precedent, idealizes, and collapses in embarrassment. What he eventually gains is a sobering knowledge of self, but it is a knowledge paradoxically achieved through a process of self-delusion and of being scorned and rejected by the young woman. Part of my argument, then, is that in both plays the male point of view is central to the dramatists' uncomfortable vision of the female as the attractive yet baffling prize that seemingly cannot be attained or controlled. The misogyny implicit in this point of view, marked especially in Lyly, is something of which the dramatist may have been only partially aware.

When we examine *Sappho and Phao* in these terms, focusing on the experience of Phao, we see the story of a young man, a common ferryman, who is at first perfectly content because he desires nothing beyond what he presently has. Venus' gift to him of supreme beauty is paradoxically the beginning of his misfortune, for, although he becomes enormously attractive to the ladies of Sappho's court and eventually to Sappho herself, when he himself falls in love with Sappho he is doomed to realize that she is impossibly above his reach. Of course the play is concerned as well with Sappho's unhappy experience in love, as she confronts the fact of social and

political disparity between her and Phao, wrestles with her affections, behaves rather moodily for a time, and eventually gains control of herself. Her triumph over Venus as the new queen of love gives the play its nominally comic ending. Yet the final scene is devoted to Phao, who finally has no choice but to leave Syracuse in bitter disappointment, aware that he has been lifted out of the humble station in which he once found contentment, and that he has no place to go. For all the play's ostensible purpose of flattering Sappho and, by extension, Queen Elizabeth, as the object of her subjects' veneration, *Sappho and Phao* begins and ends as the story of the rejected male.

This encounter of Phao with Sappho, princess of Syracuse, is traditionally seen in the 'old' historicism as a political allegory of the Duc d'Alençon's unsuccessful courtship of Queen Elizabeth in the 1580s.[5] Even if that particular topical application is chronologically impossible and too officious in its implied message to have served Lyly's purposes, on a broader topical level the play is certainly intended as a gracious compliment to Elizabeth, one that stresses (as do *Campaspe*, written earlier in 1584, and *Endymion*, 1588) the noble choice a monarch must often make between personal happiness through love and the higher demands of public office. At the same time, the social discrepancy separating

---

4 Mary Beth Rose, 'Moral Conceptions of Sexual Love in Elizabethan Comedy', *Renaissance Drama*, NS 15 (1984), 1–29, and *The Expense of Spirit: Love and Sexuality in English Renaissance Drama* (Ithaca, New York, 1988), pp. 22ff.

5 For example, Frederick Gard Fleay, *A Biographical Chronicle of the English Drama*, 2 vols. (London, 1891), vol. 2, p. 40; Bond, ed., *Complete Works of John Lyly*, vol. 2, p. 366; Felix Schelling, *Elizabethan Drama, 1558–1642*, 2 vols. (Boston, 1908), vol. 2, p. 127; Albert Feuillerat, *John Lyly* (Cambridge, 1910), pp. 108–18. See David Bevington, 'John Lyly and Queen Elizabeth: Royal Flattery in *Campaspe* and *Sappho and Phao*', *Renaissance Papers 1966* (1967), 57–67.

the two lovers can be read in terms of a more universal love allegory as well.[6]

It is on this level that I should like to explore a reading of the play I have not seen attempted before, one that examines the disparity in rank as indicative of psychological tensions as well as political and social ones. Here the gap separates the self-abnegating male from his idealized love-object; his idealization is strongly mingled with resentment and even misogyny. The conflict is one in which the male is sure to lose. The subtext that gives the play its peculiar energy is a male sense of betrayal by the goddess and motherly figure whom he finds himself indebted to for his very being. Sappho is, in these terms, not merely an allegory of Queen Elizabeth or even a portrait of womanhood, but even more a male projection of fears of rejection – fears that are abundantly confirmed by the play's ending, and, what is worse, made inevitable and justified by the political and social necessity of Sappho's choice. Sappho may be 'right' to reject Phao, but that fact doesn't make matters any easier for the discomfited male whose only future is to be a useless appendage. (The political and psychological readings come together, of course, if we imagine that Queen Elizabeth's flirtatious ways of holding her courtiers at bay simply exacerbated the dualizing Petrarchan sensibility that was already there in the courtly attitudes of the governing class.)

In *Sappho and Phao*, in these terms, Phao is a young man who has not known love, and whose awakening to sexual curiosity is one of self-abasement because he finds himself in love with a goddesslike creature impossibly above his reach. It is Venus who awakens Phao's sexual curiosity. Sappho's women are of the opinion that Phao has been made 'disdainful' and 'imperious' by his sudden gift of beauty from Venus (1.4.8), but Ismena at least knows that men in love are mere compounds of weakness: 'I cannot but oftentimes smile to myself to hear men call us weak vessels when they prove themselves broken-hearted, us frail when their thoughts cannot hang together, studying with words to flatter and with bribes to allure when we commonly wish their tongues in their purses, they speak so simply, and their offers in their bellies, they do it so peevishly' (1.4.28–33). Mileta readily agrees: 'It is good sport', she says, 'to see them want matter, for then fall they to good manners, having nothing in their mouths but "Sweet mistress", wearing our hands out with courtly kissings when their wits fail in courtly discourses – now ruffling their hairs, now setting their ruffs, then gazing with their eyes, then sighing with a privy wring by the hand, thinking us like to be wooed by signs and ceremonies' (lines 34–40). Phao is himself not yet in love when these things are being said, but if he is like other young males he will be comically absurd in his vacillations between vanity and vulnerability, self-awareness and stuttering incompetence as a wooer. We as spectators to the play can see that Lyly objectivizes the plight of the male to a significant degree by bestowing on women a cutting wit and an ironic sense of what is so discrepant about male behaviour. Because Sappho's ladies are almost choric in their function of analysing male weakness, we are invited to look through their eyes and come to the conclusion that young women understand these matters – and themselves – far better than do males.

---

6 See, for example, Bernard F. Huppé, 'Allegory of Love in Lyly's Court Comedies', *ELH*, 14 (1947), 93–113, and Marco Mincoff, 'Shakespeare and Lyly', *Shakespeare Survey 14* (1961), 15–24. Muriel Bradbrook points out to me that oarsmen on the Thames were often great favourites with court ladies; particular oarsmen were in demand as ferrymen. As George Hunter observes, there may well have been a contemporary class dimension, distantly anticipatory of D. H. Lawrence, in Lyly's portrayal of a mutual attraction between a great lady and a handsome but distinctly lower-class waterman. Compare what Ferdinand says about 'some strong-thighed bargeman' with whom the Duchess, his sister, might engage in 'the shameful act of sin' (John Webster, *The Duchess of Malfi*, ed. Elizabeth M. Brennan, New Mermaids (London, 1964), 2.5.43–6).

When Phao goes to visit the ancient Sibylla for counselling in love, the folly of adding 'to a poor estate a proud heart and to a disdained man a disdaining mind' (2.1.4–5) emphasizes still further the paradox of the divided male sensibility. The Ovidian source of Sibylla's tale about her own seduction, and the no less Ovidian point of view in Sibylla's sardonic advice about the art of wooing, come together in an ironic portrait of male amorousness that is at once self-assured and helplessly ingenuous. Sibylla's age and experience portray her not only as one who has suffered all that men do to women, but as one who personifies the dark mystery that men so desperately seek and fail to know. She is an oracle, offering a key to success, but the formula turns out to be so trite and self-mocking that the young man ends up knowing no more than he did before. Beauty is a flower that must be seized before it fades. Be diligent as a servant in love. Flatter; 'it is unpossible for the brittle metal of women to withstand the flattering attempts of men' (2.4.63–4). Persevere, and choose a time when women are weakest, especially when they have drunk some wine: 'The wooden horse entered Troy when the soldiers were quaffing, and Penelope, forsooth, whom fables make so coy, among the pots wrung her wooers by the fists when she loured on their faces' (lines 77–80). Write love letters. Dress pleasantly but not too 'curiously'. Laugh when she smiles, stand when she stands, dance, play upon any instrument. Be assured that women are coy when they 'would be overcome' (lines 93–4). Ply her with gifts. Be patient, and be secret.

All these hoary formulas from the *Ars Amatoria*, as applicable to the Petrarchan as to the Ovidian wooer, seem to counsel self-assurance. But, as in unsavoury love-advice even today in the advertisements of men's magazines, Sibylla's seeming reassurances only betray the self-evident anxiety of the male looking for the secret to success. The way to the woman's secret place is at once so sure and so unachievable, so easily devalued and so inestimably beyond the man's worth, that Phao can only resolve to end it all: 'Die, Phao, Phao, die . . . the more thou seekest to suppress those mounting affections, they soar the loftier, and the more thou wrestlest with them, the stronger they wax – not unlike unto a ball which, the harder it is thrown against the earth, the higher it boundeth into the air; or our Sicilian stone, which groweth hardest by hammering' (2.4.8–14). This splendid euphuistic sentence depends for its energy on images of the frightening consequences of uncontrolled erection. The divinity of love confronts Phao with the sad perception that he is 'committing idolatry' with that very god whom he has most cause to 'blaspheme' (lines 18–19). Sibylla's wry Ovidian advice captures the ambivalent sense in which she appears to be unlocking feminine mystery and yet is instead mocking the male with a caricature of his own depraved imagination; the advice to the lovelorn male does not really unveil what women know and feel, perhaps, but is instead a self-serving and ludicrous male fantasy of irresistibility with which Phao can temporarily prop up his withered male self-esteem but which the facts of Phao's case too plainly contradict.

The play's strategy in dealing with this bifurcated vision of male anxiety is to objectivize the duality of women to which the male imagination is so prone. That is, *Sappho and Phao* actually presents us with two kinds of women, with Sappho and with her pert, saucy, and flirtatious ladies-in-waiting. This is not to say that these ladies-in-waiting are shown to be promiscuous, but they certainly manifest the feminine wiles that Phao and, I suspect, the male members of Lyly's audience are meant to find daunting: they engage in sharp repartee; reveal through their dreams a range of love fantasies extending through the various permutations of infatuation and surrender, and know how to put men down. Sappho meantime is regal, goddesslike, impossibly above Phao's head. If she too falls in love and shows human frailty in her passionate moods, if she is in fact enough like Phao for the play to tease us with the possibility of a love that might have succeeded, the love is also presented as unworthy of Sappho and imposed on her by the arbitrary whim of Venus and Cupid.

Setting to one side the political allegory directed at Queen Elizabeth, we can see that Lyly's portrait of Sappho embodies a view of womanly grace too noble for the flawed importunity of male desire. By craving woman, the male (as Lyly represents him) simultaneously devalues her into an attainable though polluted commodity and elevates her into a beatific vision he cannot hope to deserve. Phao's coming of age in *Sappho and Phao* is a process of discovering that he is fallen simply because he is male. His new consciousness of amorous desire brings no euphoria, not even briefly; instead, it brings shame, dissatisfaction with his lot, self-hatred, and most of all resentment towards the sex that has imposed upon him the sense of guilt and failure. His choices at this point are equally unsatisfactory. When he imagines that women (notably Sappho's flirtatious ladies-in-waiting) are fallen like him into sensuality, he is punished by the seeming confirmation that women are carnal and false, with the resulting loss of an idealization of women on which his spiritual life depends. When he concludes at last that some women, or one woman at any rate, are free of his unhappy accusations, he thereupon validates the justice of his own rejection by that woman and his resulting loss of identity. Phao, at the end of the play, is a person without identity: no occupation or determinable rank, no place of residence, no friend or lover. Sappho's triumph over Venus and her ascending the throne as the new goddess of love preserve the image of womanhood from the dark insinuations that have never left Phao's mind, abetted as those insinuations seem to be by Sibylla's riddling revelations, but these achievements on Sappho's part do not carry Phao along to share in the resolution.

This elevation of ideal womanhood and its objectivization in an Eliza figure are achieved, then, at a fearful price for Phao, since he can now find no way to understand his debased imaginings about women other than that they are a product of his male aggressiveness or that women are indeed unknowable. If *Sappho and Phao* appears to portray a happily concluding political world in which matriarchy has taken the place of patriarchy in the best interests of all the courtiers and philosophers who will be nurtured by this wise Elizabethan princess of Syracuse, the consequences for the central male figure of the play are distressing. Phao accepts his fate because he must, but he has lost the contentment he knew as an oarsman, has failed to achieve any definable masculine status, and can look forward to nothing other than a life of banishment, wandering, superfluousness, and absence of role. Phao has become a drone. His impotent anger at women is barely contained within the play's polite formalities of farewell to the audience.

The young men in *Love's Labour's Lost* are conditionally promised a happiness exceeding that of Phao, but in the play itself their misery and comic discomfiture are hardly less acute. *Love's Labour's Lost* is one of Shakespeare's earliest comedies (*The Two Gentlemen of Verona* is another) in which the young men and women are sharply differentiated in terms of self-knowing and discovery of self through experience. The women know from the start not only who they are but by whom they are being courted. In their first scene onstage, Act 2 Scene 1, Maria, Catherine, and Rosaline answer the Princess's questions about the 'vow-fellows' of the young King of Navarre with a series of crisp *curricula vitae*. Maria, having seen Longueville at a marriage feast in Normandy, knows him to be 'A man of sovereign parts', 'Well fitted in arts, glorious in arms'. She also knows his salient defect: 'a sharp wit matched with too blunt a will' (lines

44–9). The appraisal is balanced, coolly judicious, generous and yet unsentimental. Catherine and Rosaline follow suit with résumés of Dumaine and Biron that combine firsthand observation and awareness of the men's social accomplishments with a somewhat distanced, even ironic perception of the young men's naïveté and need for maturation. Dumaine, for example, is characterized by Catherine as having 'Most power to do most harm, least knowing ill' (line 58).

The ladies know already, though the men apparently do not, which young man is attracted to which lady (and the reverse); the men, conversely, lack self-knowledge and are a potential menace, most of all to themselves. It is very hard to say when the young ladies fall in love, if they ever do; the term is not descriptive, since the ladies have long since appraised the young men and have essentially made their choice. By the play's end they can scarcely be said to have evinced much deeper emotion or loss of control than that with which they began. Meantime we savour the irony that the young men proceed to fall in love, choosing among the eligible ladies as though by their own volition when we know that the women have quietly chosen for them long ago. The young women do not change much as dramatic characters because they are not portrayed as in need of change; the dramatic interest is instead in the men's changing attitudes towards them.

The women are the goal, the prize. For all their self-possessed candour in their first scene, they remain as enigmatic and unknowable as when they first speak. If the form of comedy suggests that their ultimate wish is to secure the young men as lovers and husbands, they never let on to such a wish or betray any ungovernable desire. Essentially complete in themselves, the women remain a mystery.

Meantime the men dramatize in hyperbolical leaps and falls the uncertain trajectories of male encounters with the other sex.[7] Their first response to their own instinctual tugs is to band together as young males and assert the prior necessity of accomplishment in the arts. Sounding a theme to be developed in Shakespeare's Sonnets,[8] they vow to conquer 'cormorant devouring time' by making war against their own affections 'And the huge army of the world's desires' (1.1.1–10). Their unannounced aim is, as Louis Montrose points out, 'to transcend the limits of mortality'[9] through lasting fame and honour. Despite the abstract quality of this talk about time and the world's desires, we soon discover what the real problem is for them: it is sexuality. The stipulation of seeing no women in their three-year term is at once the centrepiece of their resolution and its Achilles' heel. Erotic love is for them symbolic of worldly pleasure of all sorts, and stands opposed not to contemplative withdrawal (despite their resolve to see that the flesh is 'mortified': line 28), but to fame (line 1) and to those accomplishments through which 'Navarre shall be the wonder of the world' (line 12). Like Jack Tanner in Shaw's *Man and*

---

7 E. M. W. Tillyard, *Shakespeare's Early Comedies* (New York, 1966), p. 145, speaks of the young men as 'plunging from one crude male immaturity to another'. Hugh Richmond, in *Shakespeare's Sexual Comedy: A Mirror for Lovers* (Indianapolis, Indiana, 1971), p. 83, quotes Leslie Fiedler's *Love and Death in the American Novel* to the effect that American novelists are like the male lovers in *Love's Labour's Lost* in their inability to handle a mature sexual relationship.

8 Gates K. Agnew, 'Berowne and the Progress of *Love's Labour's Lost*', *Shakespeare Studies*, 4 (1968), 40–72, notes 'an anxious preoccupation with death' in the young men's masochistic self-assertion of a devotion to renown (p. 43). See also Bobbyann Roesen (Anne Barton), '*Love's Labour's Lost*', *Shakespeare Quarterly*, 4 (1953), 411–26, and Robert G. Hunter, 'The Songs at the end of *Love's Labour's Lost*', *Shakespeare Studies*, 7 (1974), 55–64, for whom the battle the young men encounter is one of Carnival and Lent. Ruth Nevo, *Comic Transformations in Shakespeare* (London, 1980), pp. 69–91, appropriately cites Ernest Becker's *The Denial of Death* (New York, 1973).

9 Montrose, '*Curious-Knotted Garden*', p. 28.

Superman,[10] these young men see eros as potentially sapping the vital strength men must devote to their careers. They seek male companionship both to reinforce their resolve (admitted by the most self-aware of them, Biron, to be shaky) through safety in numbers, and to provide a better kind of loving companionship, one in which intellect and fondness can be unreservedly mixed. The King's 'forgetting' that they are about to be visited by a delegation of ladies, a prospect that offers the central comic complication and the first demonstration of the frailty of their vows, can be read simply as evidence that the King and his fellows (excepting the more sceptical Biron) have not thought about the sheer practicalities of such an impending visit, but surely it is also the kind of 'forgetting' that Freud talks about; that is, a sign that the young men partly wish that women would go away and that male pursuit of excellence were more simple. With no Eve in the garden of Eden, what might not Adam accomplish in the way of dutiful self-improvement? And Navarre's park is, in many ways, a garden of Eden, a land like that described in *The Winter's Tale* (1.2.67ff) where twinned male lambs frisk in the sun and bleat the one at the other, knowing not the doctrine of ill-doing until temptation is born to them in the shape of young females who are no longer girls.

This ironic view of the young men's professions of seriousness is forced upon us by the comedy of their unselfknowing,[11] but it should not take away entirely from the worth of their project. The young men are viewed as silly not because they want to make something of themselves nor because they are enamoured of learning and the arts, but because they gauge so poorly their own weakness. From the first, they are discomfited by the women. Their embarrassment at having to choose between their oaths and the obligations of hospitality to a princess of the royal blood is, I hope to show, suggestive of a deeper embarrassment, the feeling of male inadequacy

before such an exalted and goddesslike creature as a woman. (Here the Princess's rank functions much like that of Sappho in Lyly's play, even if the male's sense of inferiority and inadequacy is conveyed by Shakespeare not through lesser social rank but by inexperience and clumsiness.)

The young men first reveal their inexperience and unselfknowing by their need to ask who the young women are. 'I beseech you a word, what is she in the white?' asks Longueville of Boyet (2.1.197), only to be rewarded with a witticism suggesting a play on lightness and wantonness: 'A woman sometimes, an you saw her in the light'. To the question, 'Pray you, sir, whose daughter?', Longueville is playfully informed, 'Her mother's, I have heard' (lines 201-2). The answer suggests that the object of Longueville's curiosity is, to borrow Don Armado's phrase, 'a child of our grandmother Eve' (1.1.255). When Biron asks if the lady 'in the cap' – Rosaline – is wedded, he is informed that she is wedded 'To her will' (2.1.211-12). The questions the men ask, and the features by which they distinguish one woman from another, suggest a kind of vulnerability and reliance on surface appearances. Young men who know only that young ladies are their mothers' wilful daughters and that they can be distinguished by a white dress or cap know very little about the inner person, and are ripe targets for a satirical plot in which they will mistake their lovers' identities by means of an easily exchanged diamond, pearl necklace, pair of gloves, or other such 'favours' or outward tokens. Anyone who loves through the eyes is justly punished by the eyes' deception.

10 For the analogy to Shaw, see Catherine M. McLay, 'The Dialogue of Spring and Winter: A Key to the Unity of *Love's Labour's Lost*', *Shakespeare Quarterly*, 18 (1967), 119-27; p. 122.
11 See Rolf Söellner, '*Love's Labour's Lost*: Seeking Oneself', in *Shakespeare's Patterns of Self-Knowledge* (Columbus, Ohio, 1972), pp. 78-96.

The young men's attitude towards the women is at once aggressive and anxious. Boyet describes their preparations for meeting the ladies in the metaphors of military adventurism – 'I was as willing to grapple as he was to board', he says of Biron (2.1.218) – but also reverses the usual male ascendancy in the warfare of the sexes by describing the men as under siege: the King, says Boyet, is lodging the Princess in the field 'Like one that comes here to besiege his court' (line 86).

The image of woman as besieger is only the beginning of what the men find so dismaying. When Biron begins to discover that he is in love, he realizes that he is putting himself at the mercy of an enemy whose most dangerous weapon is that she cannot be controlled by him. A woman, Biron jests painfully, is like a German clock, 'Still a-repairing, ever out of frame, / And never going aright, being a watch, / But being watched that it may still go right' (3.1.186–8). The reason that a man must try to keep a woman under surveillance is that she will prove faithless to him at the slightest opportunity, and indeed is so gifted at deception that the man's watchfulness will be of no avail: she is 'one that will do the deed / Though Argus were her eunuch and her guard' (lines 193–4). She is a 'whitely wanton', a pure-seeming slut, whose 'velvet brow' and 'two pitch-balls stuck in her face for eyes' (lines 191–2) suggest a carnal nature like that of the Dark Lady of the Sonnets. Much of the jesting among the men about the women whom they now admire has to do with complexion, especially the dark complexion of Rosaline.

To love a lady, according to this view, is to enslave oneself to a creature who seeks domination over the male and whose ultimate weapon is the threat of shameful betrayal through cuckoldry. Boyet asks rhetorically, 'Do not curst wives hold that self-sovereignty / Only for praise' sake when they strive to be / Lords o'er their lords?' (4.1.36–8). When the Princess turns huntress of the deer, the joking about the deers' horns makes the point that

another kind of horn will not be in short supply if any of these ladies marry (lines 110–11). We sense that the threat of cuckoldry is not very real in this play, of course, any more than in *The Merchant of Venice* or *As You Like It*, where the heroines similarly jest about woman's infidelity, but that does not lessen the pointedness of the wit about this potential source of feminine power. Romantic women in Shakespeare who have no real intention of cheating on their men are not averse to reminding those men of the options available to women. The bawdry of pricks and rubbing and 'cleaving the pin' in this same scene (lines 131–5) extends the image of the Amazonian huntress and her unequal power in the battle of the sexes. That foolhardy man who takes aim at the woman, in a phallic image of male aggression, will find that he has met his match; as an intrepid bowman aiming at the feminine anatomy he 'must shoot nearer, or he'll ne'er hit the clout' (line 132). The male's attempt to prove his masculinity in sexual conquest is destined to be greeted by the jeering of his intended target:

> Thou canst not hit it, hit it, hit it,
> Thou canst not hit it, my good man

and the even more threatening consequences of his own sexual inadequacy:

> An I cannot, cannot, cannot,
> An I cannot, another can.   (lines 124–7)

The men are driven into love, then, by a desire that at once makes them anxious. They devalue the women with whom they are infatuated by speaking of them as debased beauties wielding the power to cuckold men. This sexual anxiety by which the men are driven manifests itself in one of the play's most bizarre images: a street paved with male eyes on which women tread with their dainty feet. It is Biron who introduces the metaphor: 'O, if the streets were pavèd with thine eyes', he tells Longueville, 'Her feet were much too dainty for such tread'. Dumaine cannot resist the prurient consequences of Biron's fanciful image: 'O vile! Then as she goes, what upward lies / The street should see as she walked overhead' (4.3.278–9). Together, as Tom Greene has noted,[12] the men construct a voyeuristic fantasy in which their eyes, trodden on for their presumption (and *tread* is often a sexual verb in Shakespeare, describing the copulation of fowl), look upward to catch a glimpse of the forbidden woman's part. 'O vile!' Is it the voyeuristic image itself that is vile, or the male imagination that presumes so; or is it the thing they would see and yet punish themselves for desiring?

Accordingly, the scene in which the young men expose one another's perjuries in love is a paradoxical one of shame and release.[13] They are bound by feelings of shame to deplore their own sexual longings, and hang on to the exclusively male credo of their academy as support for their failing resolve. What we today call peer pressure seems to forbid an interest in the opposite sex, as it does also with Mercutio and his friends in *Romeo and Juliet*. Yet the undeniable feeling of relief also becomes a part of the young men's experience of being caught out as lovers. If one's peers are also in love, then one is free to make a fool of oneself; the ribbing one takes is tolerable so long as one can find safety and precedent in numbers. Biron is of course the last to be caught out, the one who comes nearest to being able to maintain his pose of moral superiority – a pose that he would be able to maintain only at the huge cost of having to continue in that role of censor and hypocrite. Once he too is released, he becomes the new spokesman for a companionship in service to love.

> Sweet lords, sweet lovers! – O, let us embrace.
> As true we are as flesh and blood can be.
> The sea will ebb and flow, heaven show his face.
> Young blood doth not obey an old decree.
> We cannot cross the cause why we were born,
> Therefore of all hands must we be forsworn.
>
> (lines 212–17)

And at this point Biron becomes the leader in a new competition, one that seems ineffably male: that of boasting about one's woman, of competing not only for her but offering her in competition with the women of one's friends. This motif of parading a woman's virtue leads to such disaster in *The Rape of Lucrece*, *Cymbeline*, and elsewhere in Shakespeare, and betrays such a host of masculine and patriarchal obsessions – possessiveness, the need to affirm one's masculinity by insisting on the woman's chastity, and the like – that we are hardly surprised to discover in this instance that trouble is looming for the men. Male bonding and peer pressure, used before to validate a rejection of eros, now serve the cause of competition to see who can be more amorous. The men preen themselves on having overcome their scruples and, in a series of aggressively male metaphors, make plain that they assume conquest to be a simple matter. 'Advance your standards, and upon them, lords. / Pell-mell, down with them; but be first advised / In conflict that you get the sun of them' (lines 343–5). The hard thing is to have overcome one's own reticence and anxiety; once the male offers himself as the desired prize to the grateful woman, victory is a matter of course.

The play's famous 'unfinished' ending is thus expressive in part of prolonged male reluctance, but it is even more suggestive of the comeuppance men deserve for their fatuous assumption that the final conquest will be easy once they have overcome their own reserve.[14] These young men still know the women scarcely at all, and thereby deliver into

---

12 Thomas M. Greene, '*Love's Labour's Lost*: The Grace of Society', *Shakespeare Quarterly*, 22 (1971), 315–28; p. 320.

13 C. L. Barber, in *Shakespeare's Festive Comedy* (Princeton, 1959), p. 89, speaks tellingly of 'the folly of release taking over from the folly of resistance'.

14 Greene, '*Love's Labour's Lost*: The Grace of Society', p. 324, speaks of the young lords' comic punishments as a 'final prodding toward maturation'.

the women's hands a comic weapon of disguise and interchanged love tokens through which to enforce the lesson that the men still love only outwardly and without sufficient constancy. Male perjury is subjected to playful parody in a plot skilfully manipulated by the women, a plot in which perjury can lead to no lasting or harmful consequences since women play the role of playwright and forgiver (much as Portia later does in the episode of the rings in *The Merchant of Venice*).

In the process, the women begin to show what they are perhaps really like in this play.[15] They look forward pleasurably to torturing the men (5.2.60); Rosaline longs to make Biron 'fawn, and beg, and seek, / And wait the season, and observe the times, / And spend his prodigal wits in bootless rhymes, / And shape his service wholly to my hests'. She will 'make him proud to make me proud that jests' (lines 62–6). The women put down the men through 'mockery-merriment' (line 138), counter mock with mock, offer such 'sport' as to make the men's 'sport o'erthrown' (lines 139–52), teasingly refuse to dance, laugh at the pain they inflict, and impose a penance that requires a long postponement of desire – for them, of course, as for the men, but they at least control the game as the objects of desire. There is more than a suggestion of sexual withering in their witty scenes of one-upping the men. Their power is ultimately that of sexual denial, though they do all this with grace and cleverness.

Their method is justified in any event by what the men must learn. Male assumptions about ease of conquest, the play seems to suggest, are not healthy for the men themselves, not realistic. As in *As You Like It* and in Lyly's *Sappho and Phao*, the women seem to feel they must help men understand that women are neither unattainably perfect nor attainably corrupt. Women can be waspish and mercurial of mood (as Sappho shows herself to be at the height of her lovesickness), but they are not ordinarily insatiable or inconstant.

Men must be disabused of their hyperbole in sexual imagining just as in their use of language.[16] The male nightmare of womanly infidelity and appetite is exposed as a chimera, one that women can parody by making it a game of disguises. Reassurance takes the form for the audience of the realization that infidelity is only a dramatic illusion – or is it? In *Love's Labour's Lost*, as in *Sappho and Phao*, the women are presented as unknowable from a male point of view. The 'imperfect' ending offers hope, more so in Shakespeare than in Lyly, but it provides uncertainty as well. Will the women's promises be kept, as the men's promises were not? The dramatist keeps the ultimate power in women's hands so long as no sexual resolution is provided. In Peter Erickson's view, the conventions of female domination and male humility manifested in the men's love poems shape the dramatic action accordingly, creating a situation in which the women remain ascendant over the men, with the result that a genial solution is impossible; marital bonds, male bonds, and female bonds are all sources of vague discomfort in a three-way stalemate.[17] As Romeo

---

[15] Agnew, 'Berowne and the Progress of *Love's Labour's Lost*', p. 59, argues that the women are no more idealized than the men, in that they are vivacious 'to a fault', bright, shrewish, and competitive, even if they enjoy the advantage of superior self-knowledge. Alexander Leggatt, in *Shakespeare's Comedy of Love* (London, 1974), pp. 80–1, similarly makes the point that although it would be pleasant to believe the women are using ridicule as a loving way to educate their men, they in fact never say so; the ridicule is exercised 'for its own sake'.

[16] William C. Carroll, *The Great Feast of Language in 'Love's Labour's Lost'* (Princeton, 1976).

[17] Peter Erickson, 'The Failure of Relationship Between Men and Women in *Love's Labour's Lost*', *Women's Studies*, 9 (1981), 65–81, and *Patriarchal Structures in Shakespeare's Drama* (Berkeley, 1985), pp. 9, 16–21, 178–9. See also Richard Wheeler, *Shakespeare's Development and the Problem Comedies* (Berkeley, 1981), pp. 170–1, where Wheeler argues that the men 'are unable . . . to negotiate the transition from strong bonds linking them with each other to bonds of men and

says in *Romeo and Juliet*, 'Wilt thou leave me so unsatisfied?' Only in *Love's Labour's Won* will the answer be known, and it has been conveniently lost, no doubt forever.

The secondary comic characters of *Love's Labour's Lost* offer a comically exaggerated perspective on the difficulties of the male in attempting to deal with the female and to come to terms with his own ambivalent desire. Costard is the perfectly assured male, one who feels no shame (other than the inconvenience of arrest) in confessing that he was taken 'with a wench', and who turns even his interrogation by the King to his advantage in the exchange of wit. By repeatedly evading and varying the terminology of what he is charged with, Costard manages to assert again and again his sexual success: 'Sir, I confess the wench', 'I was taken with a damsel', 'I was taken with a maid.' And, when the King tries to use this admission against him by objecting that 'This "maid" will not serve your turn, sir', Costard has the last word in his role as successful male (which of course the King is not as yet): 'This maid will serve my turn, sir' (1.1.272–87).[18]

Costard is put down by no woman, neither, and gives as good as he takes even in sparring verbally with the Princess. When he comes seeking the Princess in Act 4 Scene 1, for example, and encounters nothing but choplogic wit in response to his straightforward request to know who is the 'head' lady ('Thou shalt know her, fellow, by the rest that have no heads', the Princess replies) and 'the greatest lady, the highest' ('The thickest and the tallest', the Princess quips), he gives the Princess the answer her pertness deserves by taking her literally at her word:

The thickest and the tallest – it is so, truth is truth.
An your waist, mistress, were as slender as my
    wit
One o' these maids' girdles for your waist should
    be fit.
Are you not the chief woman? You are the
    thickest here.   (4.1.48–51)

The Princess, annoyed no doubt that her own word play has led directly to this candid observation that she is not petite, can do no more than huff and change the subject: 'What's your will, sir? What's your will?' (lines 42–52). It is perhaps the one time in the play that she is rattled, and by a man.

Armado conversely is a parodic version of male insecurity and compulsive desire. He envies Costard's suave success with 'a child of our grandmother, Eve', with 'the weaker vessel' (1.1.255–62), and expresses that envy in his puritanical arrest of Costard for the very thing Armado himself desires. 'I do affect the very ground – which is base – where her shoe – which is baser – guided by her foot – which is basest – doth tread', he confesses in soliloquy. 'I shall be forsworn' (1.2.159–61). He describes his love and his love object in hyperbolically debased terms. Love is 'a devil' (line 164). Jaquenetta is a 'country girl' (line 112) while he is a magnifico, a Spanish soldier: 'and as it is base for a soldier to love, so am I in love with a base wench' (lines 56–8). Like the young lords of Navarre's court he seeks safety in precedent and in numbers: if Samson and Hercules have succumbed to women, the shame of his doing so is more bearable.

The young men of the court, vastly amused by Armado's style, as has been often noted, are also drawn, I suggest, to Armado by a satirical picture of their own debilitating attitudes towards love, for in his example they can laugh at what they find painful in themselves and can eventually exorcise that painfulness by transferring its worst qualities to a scapegoat. As Armado takes on the role of Hector in the

---

women united in marriage . . . The love plot ends with the young women bound together by mutual grief and with the young men united in mutual frustration.'

18 Stanley Wells, 'Shakespeare without Sources', in *Shakespearean Comedy*, ed. Malcolm Bradbury and David Palmer, Stratford-upon-Avon Studies 14 (London, 1972), pp. 58–74, makes a related point: Costard and Jaquenetta 'represent a simplification of the lords' (and ladies') baser selves, the all-too-natural instincts that they are over-anxious to quell' (p. 60).

spectacle of the Seven Worthies, he becomes the object of mirthful attack by the young men and young women alike, the young men eager to show their awareness of their own folly by joining in the ladies' laughter. The men are especially aggressive in their wit at the expense of the Seven Worthies, as Anne Barton notes,[19] so much so that we wonder if their overreaction is not occasioned by a sense of humiliation that is not yet healed. 'Though my mocks come home by me', says Dumaine, 'I will now be merry' (5.2.628–9). Armado is bested in this show by his nemesis, the confident Costard, whose very stage name, Pompey the Huge, suggests the part of him that Armado finds awesome. These two are joined in the show by the old men, Nathaniel and Holofernes, whose functions as curate and pedant parody the ambitious young men in their futile attempts at male bonding and the sterile pursuit of learning.

The antithetical vision of the final song restates the polarities found by the young men in their comic quest for male identity, and offers some hope of an uneasy accommodation, but the threat of anxiety is not allowed to dissipate even in this closing moment. Spring's song is one of variations on the theme of cuckoldry, of desire unpleasantly awakened by maidens bleaching 'their summer smocks' to the accompaniment of a refrain 'Unpleasing to a married ear', while 'greasy Joan' presides over the pot in the wintry world of frozen longing. It is in this sense that the ending of *Love's Labour's Lost* is, despite its promise of future merger, more like that of *Sappho and Phao* than unlike. Whatever women come to represent in these two plays, the male experience is one of admonishment and something close to failure, while the vision of what is to be achieved even in a successful courtship is enough to make one wonder. As Biron concludes, granting to the women the power to decide whether men will succeed or not:

> Our wooing doth not end like an old play.
> Jack hath not Jill. These ladies' courtesy

> Might well have made our sport a comedy.
>
> (5.2.861–3)

These two comedies, by Lyly and Shakespeare, can thus be seen in terms of a larger pattern of patriarchal control, male bonding and maturation, and tentative explorations towards mutuality as analysed by Peter Erickson, Mary Beth Rose, Coppélia Kahn, and Richard Wheeler, among others.[20] The polarization of Petrarchan sensibility and cynicism is fairly extreme in *Sappho and Phao*, as it is in *Euphues*, where we also find rapturous idealism about women juxtaposed with blatant misogyny. If worship and lust are the sole possible alternatives, the protagonist of *Sappho and Phao*, like Euphues, can only see love as a compulsive, impersonal, and ridiculous passion. The polarization, reflected in the conflict of Venus and Sappho, is an intolerable one that can end only with the exclusion of sexual desire from the dénouement. Lyly seems to betray himself, in the words of Hereward Price, as someone who 'does not like women'.[21] Even if the play gives little place in its resolution for male-to-male bonding and patriarchal structures, and seems to insist instead on the glories of chaste matriarchal rule, it does so at the tremendous expense of banishing the erotic from noble human relationships – an impossible condition at the end of a romantic comedy.

With acknowledgement of a new moral prestige in love and marriage, and greater acceptance of a kind of equality in the marital relationship as portrayed on the English stage, as Mary Beth Rose has argued, the popular romantic comedy of the 1590s, including Shakespeare's, found itself in a position to

---

[19] Roesen (Barton), '*Love's Labour's Lost*', p. 422.

[20] In addition to the critical studies by Erickson, Rose, and Wheeler already cited, see also Coppélia Kahn, *Man's Estate: Masculine Identity in Shakespeare* (Berkeley, 1981).

[21] Hereward T. Price, 'Shakespeare and His Young Contemporaries', *Philological Quarterly*, 41 (1962), 37–57.

move increasingly towards accommodation and mutuality. Shakespeare controls the impulse towards misogyny; he seems both more amusedly aware of it than Lyly and more ready to find a resolution of sexual conflict through the male discovery that most of the male's misogynistic feeling is chimerically in himself rather than in the women. Even so, we can see in *Love's Labour's Lost* the kind of Lylyan resistance that must be overcome. In Erickson's and Wheeler's terms, women are indeed given a strong role in this play, but it is a role that threatens comic resolution. *Love's Labour's Lost* and *Sappho and Phao* are alike in providing women with a matriarchal power structure in which the authority of affirmation or denial remains in women's hands, even though in both cases this matriarchal authority does not coexist easily with the comic structure.

Moreover, even if the women come into their own in terms of power, we need to question whether they are fully realized in human terms. Many readers and viewers, especially women, have come to Shakespeare for insight into female nature only to sense disappointedly that too often Shakespeare's women are projections of male attitudes. Certainly the dramatic action in *Love's Labour's Lost*, the comic revelations, the changes in behaviour, are more eventful and understandable in the men than in the women, as the men come partly to terms with what they suppose women to be. Even though the play does move towards some genuine accommodation and mutuality, towards some hint of softening in the women and self-knowledge in the men, this comedy shows its Lylyan and early Shakespearian characteristics in ways that relate it to the more overt impositions of patriarchal control we see in *The Taming of the Shrew*, *A Midsummer Night's Dream*, and the Henry VI plays.

TRUTH AND ART IN HISTORY PLAYS

G. K. HUNTER

Since the First Folio says that Shakespeare wrote history plays I think there is a great deal to be said for assuming not only that he did so but did so in the plays thus designated and no others; let evidence precede definition. It is true of course that the evidence available is mixed; Elizabethan generic vocabulary is notoriously spongy: contemporary title pages give us such hybrids as *The Tragedy of Richard II, The Tragedy of Richard III, The History of Troilus and Cressida, The True Chronicle History of King Lear, A Pleasant Conceited History called The Taming of a Shrew*. The Folio's generic divisions seem to belong, however, to a different mode of discourse: F1 is a company volume, and I have no doubt that its division of plays into Comedies, Histories, and Tragedies reflects company understanding of the repertory, and so, I take it, the understanding of that good company man, William Shakespeare.

Academic critics inevitably prefer definitions to be less blandly empirical, for what space for dazzling reinventions, for pulling rabbits out of hats, not to mention a name in lights, is left available by so preconditioning an acceptance? As professional systematizers we like to be seen to generate our definitions from general principles and our first chapters from titles such as 'What is a history play? Some problems and answers'. Irving Ribner, for example, in what remains by far the most thorough treatment of the Elizabethan genre, starts by asking how the purposes of history

were understood in the period and then calls any play that fulfils any of these purposes a 'history play', and so includes under the rubric such works as *Gorboduc, Cambyses*, and *Tamburlaine* – plays that can make no claim to appear in the Heminges and Condell list.

Heminges and Condell offer us no formal definition; what one can derive from their list is the sense that this genre must be defined, above all, by its subject matter: a history play is a play about English dynastic politics of the feudal and immediately post-feudal period – is, you might say, 'a play about barons'. No doubt they had noticed that the audience in a theatre has a relationship to stories about its own national identity in the intelligible past which is different from its relationship to other stories.[1] Several much-quoted testimonies of the period confirm this view of the role of history plays in the culture of the time.[2] But

---

[1] Coleridge, I find, has made the same point in an uncharacteristically succinct manner: 'In order that a drama may be properly historical it is necessary that it should be the history of the people to whom it is addressed' (*Coleridge's Shakespearean Criticism*, 2 vols. (Cambridge, Mass., 1930), vol. 1, p. 138).

[2] Nashe praises historical subject matter 'wherein our forefathers' valiant acts ... are revived, and they themselves raised from the grave of oblivion and brought to plead their aged honours in open presence: than which, what can be a sharper reproof to these degenerate effeminate days of ours?' (*The Works of Thomas Nashe*, ed. R. B. McKerrow, vol. 1 (Oxford, 1904), p. 212). Heywood says: 'What English blood, seeing the person of any bold Englishman presented, and doth not hug his

little attempt has been made to interrelate the emotional effect on the Elizabethan or other self-consciously English audience, thus described, to the aesthetic structures of the plays themselves. The usual point made is that these are plays of patriotism – a patriotism that can be linked historically to a national mood following the defeat of the Armada in 1588. But the point would be more convincing if the plays were more than occasionally jingoistic and xenophobic, were not so largely concerned with the malignities and incompetences of English governments; patriotism is part of the story but it cannot be the whole story. A more satisfactory answer to the problem can be derived, I believe, from the general thought (contemporary and modern) that such historical narratives must be 'true', as against other kinds of plays which can be acknowledged and responded to as feigned or fictive.

The paradoxical idea of an invented true history is one that is difficult to get into focus, and there is some evidence from the sixteenth century of the unease that was generated by a genre that undoubtedly existed but could not be fitted into the categories or vocabulary available. The Induction to the anonymous *A Warning for Fair Women* (printed 1599) shows us Comedy, History, and Tragedy in dispute for the possession of the stage. History enters the scene as if he has a role to perform, armed with the accoutrements of war (a drum and an ensign), but no space is provided in the play for the deployment of these signifiers. The axis of the dispute remains stolidly binary: to Tragedy the opponent is 'slight and childish' Comedy; for Comedy it is extremist and hysterical Tragedy. History is relegated to the unfortunate role of a neuter in a family quarrel; between the alternative trajectories of death and happiness no third possibility is allowed.[3] The one Induction of the period which tackles the status of History in a more positive vein is, unsurprisingly, the one attached to an early history play, the anonymous *True Tragedy of Richard III* (printed 1594). This play begins

with a conversation between Poetry and Truth:

POETRY. Truth, well met!
TRUTH. Thanks, Poetry. What makes thou upon a
 stage?
POETRY. Shadows
TRUTH. Then will I add bodies to the shadows.
 Therefore depart and give Truth leave
 To show her pageant.
POETRY. Why, will Truth be a player?
TRUTH. No, but Tragedia-like for to present
 A tragedy in England done but late
 That will revive the hearts of drooping minds.[4]

What we seem to see here is a degree of self-consciousness about the claim that this history play is a 'true tragedy'. Poetry can only (as in Plato) offer 'shadows', but Truth can give substance to poetic shadows by showing things that actually happened, what 'the Chronicles make manifest' (line 21). As a player or fictionalizer, Truth has to allow herself to appear 'Tragedia-like' in order to secure the effects described in the last line quoted, but the recentness of the events and faithfulness to the chronicles may serve to counteract the danger that poetry necessarily means lies.

The sense, clearly expressed in the Induction

---

fame and honey at his valour ... as if the personator were the man personated? ... What coward, to see his countrymen valiant would not be ashamed of his own cowardice? What English prince, should he behold the true portraiture of that famous king Edward the Third ... would not be suddenly inflamed with so royal a spectacle, being made apt and fit for the like achievement?' (E. K. Chambers, *The Elizabethan Stage*, 4 vols. (Oxford, 1923), vol. 4, p. 251).

[3] In many ways this Induction can be seen to pick up and sharpen the generic implications of an earlier Induction – that to the anonymous *Soliman and Perseda* (1590) – where Death, Fortune, and Love conduct a very similar dispute, Death demanding a tragic conclusion, Love demanding comic happiness and Fortune (the process of change) appearing as an unstable intermediary between the other two.

[4] Malone Society Reprint, ed. W. W. Greg (Oxford, 1929), lines 7–16.

to *The True Tragedy of Richard III*, that truth has to be invoked to justify history plays, appears as a recurrent feature of the word as it turns up among Elizabethan play titles. I have discovered thirteen uses of the word 'true' among titles of plays published between 1573 and 1616, four times attached to plays about English history, four times to plays about Ancient British history (always as 'true chronicle history'), three times to plays about Roman history, and twice to plays about recent notorious murders (both called 'lamentable and true').[5] Of course the word 'true' found in such contexts is, like other words in title pages, a piece of advertising copy, not a scientific description; what I take to be significant is therefore only the fact that *this* was the word found recurrently appropriate for advertising plays about history. The word is significant only because it designates a set of claims against a set of received expectations. 'Truth' in these terms may be said to be a word that indicates the rhetorical precondition or mode of history.

A reader today, given the anti-positivist slant of modern thought, might expect that truth of this kind would require a characteristic formal structure before the plays involved could impose their values on the audience. If the Heminges and Condell implication of a third genre is to be sustained in terms of a particular theatrical effect, then the cause ('truth') of that effect can hardly be left as an inert slice of chronicle subject matter unaffected by the shaping process which alone will allow it to achieve the *telos* proposed. Setting the genre side-by-side with Tragedy and Comedy makes this issue particularly hard to avoid. For these others are genres marked by well-known and recurrent formal characteristics. Can the history play justify its place in this row by its possession of comparable qualities requisite to convey its claim to 'truth', its particular hold on an audience's attention, its mode of catharsis?

Most twentieth-century criticism has

sought to deal with such questions by allegorizing both history and the mimetic process. The Tudor understanding of history, we are often told, turned individual reigns and individual successes and failures into exemplary instances of the intervention of God (or of the Capitalist System – God under another name) in the daily affairs of men. In particular, the eight plays of Shakespeare that run a continuous course from *Richard II* to *Richard III* are said to present a pattern of divine punishment for national apostasy in which the Tudor audience could identify itself as the final inheritor of God's forgiveness once the pattern had been completed. Inside the plays of the sequence, consequently, we must look *through* individual lives and personal relations so that

---

[5] The relevant title-pages are as follows:

1592 *The Lamentable and True Tragedy of M. Arden of Feversham in Kent.*

1594 *The Wounds of Civil War. Lively set forth in the true tragedies of Marius and Sylla.*

1594 *The True Tragedy of Richard, Duke of York.*

1594 *The True Tragedy of Richard III.*

1600 *The First Part of the True and Honourable History of the Life of Sir John Oldcastle.*

1602 *The True Chronicle History of the Whole Life and Death of Thomas, Lord Cromwell.*

1605 *The True Chronicle History of King Leir and his Three Daughters.*

1606 *Nobody and Somebody: with the true chronicle history of Elydure.*

1607 *The Tragedy of Claudius Tiberius Nero . . . Truly represented out of the purest records of those times.*

1608 *M. William Shakespeare: His True Chronicle History of the Life and Death of King Lear and his Three Daughters.*

1608 *A Yorkshire Tragedy. Not so new as lamentable and true.*

1608 *The Rape of Lucrece. A true Roman tragedy.*

1615 *The Valiant Welshman, or the true chronicle history of . . . Caradoc the Great.*

One may add to these two later history plays where the word has a continuing but somewhat more oblique function:

(1) Shakespeare's *Henry VIII* – apparently known when first performed (1613) as *All Is True*.

(2) Ford's *The Chronicle of Perkin Warbeck: A Strange Truth* (1634).

we may understand their places on the giant wheel of historical necessity (Jan Kott's 'Grand Mechanism').[6] 'Truth' in these terms is identified as the shape of the divine purpose. That there is something of this in the plays need not be denied; but the experience of seeing or reading Shakespeare's history plays, or (more pertinently) of being deeply moved by them, owes very little to this mode of conceptual organization. And this is not, incidentally, what Elizabethan title pages mean when they use the word 'true', which refers there rather to the 'truth' of factual detail, authenticated by the witness of the Chronicles.[7]

Modern scholars usually tell us that the Chronicles (particularly Edward Hall's) are marked by an overall design that controls their presentation of detail. But to read continuously in the Chronicles is to discover that they exemplify less the grand historical design than the complexity, dispersal, randomness, even incomprehensibility of actual happenings. We are regularly told about the genealogical tree on the title-page to Hall's Chronicle as a kind of aerial map of the dynastic conflict that 'explains' the history of this period. But when we turn over the page and actually begin to read in Hall (or better still in Holinshed) word by word and page by page, then we must descend from the hot-air balloon of theory that floats *above* history and see events from the level of the human eye, share in the bemusement and mistakennness that characterizes the 'truth' of historical experience as here retailed. In his dedication to Burghley Holinshed says that the reading of his volumes will 'daunt the vicious' – I find that the reading daunts nearly everyone – and 'encourage worthy citizens'. But in telling his story Holinshed fails to show that history points a moral in either of these directions. And when he does risk causal moralization, that too appears random and particular rather than generally explanatory. Thus when Edward IV arrives at York and swears on the sacrament that he has invaded England only to claim his rightful dukedom of York, Holinshed comments as follows:

For this wilful perjury (as has been thought) the issue of this king suffered (for the father's offence) ... And it may well be. For it is not likely that God, in whose hands is the bestowing of all sovereignty, will suffer such an indignity to be done to his sacred majesty and will suffer the same to pass with impunity.[8]

The tentativeness of the judgement here, as well as the limitation imposed on the connection made, are both entirely characteristic of the author. What Holinshed wrote was, in his own phrase, a 'collection of histories'; the pluralism attaches both to the variety of sources drawn on and to the collaborative effort that went into the production, and both these point away from explanatory clarity. We are much indebted to all these authors for the legal documents that they report *in extenso*, giving the actual statements drawn up for Humphrey of Gloucester or Jack Cade (for example). But the authentic words given represent only what these men wanted to be believed, tendentious opinions contradicted by the equally 'true' or authentic documents prepared in rebuttal by Henry Beaufort or the government of Henry VI. The *wie es eigentlich gewesen ist* is nowhere invoked as a unifying perspective, and indeed one might say that the closer the chroniclers bring us to the documentation of the past the more obscured becomes the overview.

The chroniclers' annalistic method of year-by-year accounting further reinforces the general effect of one-thing-after-another randomness. In this mode the idea of an individual's purposive career is difficult to sustain;

---

[6] See *Shakespeare Our Contemporary*, translated by Boleslaw Taborski (New York, 1964).

[7] See particularly the title-page of *The Tragedy of Claudius Tiberius Nero* cited in note 5 above.

[8] *The Third Volume of Chronicles* [London, 1587], p. 680.a.65ff.

even though Holinshed sometimes signals ahead with 'as will hereafter appear' and similar locutions, his 'hereafter' is, like God's, mostly invisible. What is entirely and continuously obvious is that life in feudal England is most adequately represented as a series of individual raids on the inarticulable: a castle is besieged here or there and then retired from when a larger army appears on the horizon; the Scots do their annual thing, try to burn Carlisle or Berwick, drive away cattle, then give up when the weather gets too bad (or too good); the price of wheat rises and falls, a high wind destroys houses, people try to avoid taxes and get hanged, drawn, quartered, beheaded, burned, massacred – random events suffered by individuals continually trying to derandomize them, including Holinshed himself, who offers us the guidance of 'some say', 'others allege', 'it is reported that', but makes little or no sustained effort to assess accuracy or probability. And when the absence of explanatory connection is particularly blatant he throws up his hands in a gesture that might be despair or might be piety, as when he says of the usurpation of Bolingbroke that he cannot make sense of it: 'But ... the providence of God is to be respected and his secret will to be wondered at ... For as in His hands standeth the donation of kingdoms, so likewise the disposing of them consisteth in His pleasure.'[9] Or again when, after the second battle of St. Albans, he notes that all the advantages seemed to lie with the Lancastrians: 'But what Man proposeth God disposeth'.[10] In such cases a providential pattern emerges, but not as an overall explanation, only as a justification for the humanly inexplicable.

A dramatist who makes his way through such actual chronicles – and we should remember that Shakespeare could not lay his hands on a copy of *Shakespeare's Holinshed* – has to achieve his design by means of rigorous exclusion and reshaping. But if I am right in assuming that the ideal of truth to the experience of life in the past remains a defining quality of the Elizabethan history play, then the process of streamlining a watertight cause-and-effect kind of structure can easily carry the history play beyond its *telos*, for the demonstration of Art inevitably diminishes our acceptance of Truth.[11] And this takes us back to the comparison between Comedy, History, and Tragedy with which I started. Tragedies and Comedies operate inside efficient and well-tested modes of artful unification. It has sometimes seemed as if the history play could not achieve such unity unless it fell into the artful mode of one or the other of its siblings. This was an agreed and probably an inevitable view among neoclassical critics, whose respect for Art allowed variations from the canon of Tragedy and Comedy only as consequences of ignorance or boorishness ('common ... among our rude ancestors', Dr Johnson assumed).[12] The earliest systematic critic of Shakespeare, Charles Gildon, is interestingly specific on this issue.[13] He calls history plays 'draughts of the lives of princes, brought into dialogue', and goes on to note that 'since these plays are histories, there can be no manner of

---

9 Holinshed, p. 499.b.64ff.

10 Holinshed, p. 661.a.31.

11 For a general discussion of this issue see Philip Edwards, *Shakespeare and the Confines of Art* (London and New York, 1968).

12 *Selections from Johnson on Shakespeare*, ed. Bertrand Bronson and Jean M. O'Meara (New Haven, Conn., 1986), p. 226.

13 'Remarks on the Plays of Shakespeare', printed in vol. 9 of Rowe's edition of Shakespeare (London, 1710), pp. 302–3. He further remarks that it is 'the misfortune of all the characters of plays of this nature that they are directed to no end, and therefore are of little use; for the manners cannot be necessary, and by consequence must lose half their beauty. The violence, grief, rage and motherly love and despair of Constance [in *King John*] produce not one incident, and are of no manner of use; whereas if there had been a just design, a tragic imitation of some one grave action of just extent, both these characters being formed by the poet [Constance and Falconbridge] must have had their manners directed to that certain end, and the production of these incidents which must beget that end.'

Fable or Design in them'. Dr Johnson seems to defend history plays from the full rigour of such neoclassical rules: 'his histories, being neither comedies nor tragedies are not subject to any of their laws'; but by agreeing with the principles of the neoclassical position he leaves little or nothing worth defending. He calls the history plays 'a series of actions with no other than chronological succession and without any tendency to introduce or regulate the conclusion . . . a history might be continued through many plays; as it had no plan it had no limits . . . Nothing more is necessary . . . than that the change of action be so prepared as to be understood . . . no other unity is intended, and therefore none is to be sought.'[14] In the jargon of the Russian Formalists and their acolytes, such plays exhibit *fabula* but no *sjužet*: they are mere transcripts of chronology, and chronology provides the only articulation they possess.

It takes very little reading in Shakespeare's historical sources to learn what nonsense this is. But the general issue is not so easily disposed of. History plays are not shaped by the formal closures of death or marriage; they allow the open-endedness of history itself to appear – when one king dies another king emerges; time and politics grind on with a degree of indifference to the life-cycles of individuals. But to say that *Richard II*, *Richard III* or *King John* are simply tragedies that are poorly unified because open-ended is clearly inadequate as a description. The dialectical relation between Art and Truth seems central enough to require a further effort to define the conditions of history plays, preferably in their simplest and most unsophisticated forms, whether as Shakespeare employed them or as Shakespeare inherited them.

F. P. Wilson has famously remarked that 'there is no certain evidence that any popular dramatist before Shakespeare wrote a play based on English history'.[15] If that is to be believed, then *Henry VI* is, however sophisticated in itself, the great originating event in the history of the history play. But should one believe it? There are in fact two extant Elizabethan history plays with a powerful claim to anticipate *Henry VI* – one (Dr Legge's *Richardus Tertius*) clearly dated 1579, the other (the anonymous *Famous Victories of Henry V*) probably to be dated before 1588; and it seems reasonable to argue (I intend to do so) that these plays give us a glimpse of dramaturgical control of history in the process of formation. Legge's play is not, of course, that of a 'popular dramatist' and so by definition may be excluded from Wilson's chronology, but the idea that it cannot therefore tell us anything about popular drama seems much too categorical. As for *The Famous Victories of Henry V*, Wilson does refer to it but seems to be denying it a place in the story by the curious argument that it is too bad a play to count. He calls it 'a play of incredible meanness in the form in which it has come down to us, written in bad prose, one imagines, because the compiler could not rise to bad verse'.[16] Even bad plays, one is bound to respond, can influence good dramatists. And as for 'certain evidence' in the matter of Elizabethan theatrical chronology, if this is our criterion we had better cede the territory as quickly as possible, for there is no 'certain' way of defending it.

My aim here is not, however, to argue for or against chronology or to specify influences on Shakespeare or even to deny Shakespeare's originating power, but only to question his power to originate *ex nihilo* – a question, I note in passing, that even God cannot always avoid. In what follows I wish to use these plays only to illustrate the conditions attached to history playwriting outside the Shakespearian orbit, to exemplify what I have called the central dilemma in the genre – the contradiction (or at least tension) between truth to the experience

---

[14] Rowe, 'Remarks on the Plays', pp. 16, 22.

[15] *Marlowe and the Early Shakespeare* (Oxford, 1953), p. 106.

[16] Wilson, *Marlowe and the Early Shakespeare*, p. 106.

of the past and the fictional or artful means by which such material can be unified and so given general significance.

Dr Legge, unsurprisingly, given his status as Master of Caius and Vice-Chancellor of Cambridge University, undoubtedly found his material (the reign of Richard III) convenient on at least two counts. The reign of Richard III was one of the few reigns that could be presented in political detail without offending the Queen: and Vice-Chancellors, as we all know, have to be very tender of the susceptibilities of their political mistresses. More important from our point of view is the fact that this material lent itself very easily to the formal literary organization that current scholarly opinion most heartily approved. Tyrant-tragedy provided the staple of the Senecan and Italian Humanist tragic repertory. Both the pseudo-Senecan *Octavia Praetexta* (then accepted as genuine) and the *Ecerinus* of Albertino Mussato (usually called 'the first modern tragedy')[17] deal with the careers of recently dead tyrants (Nero and Ezzelino da Romano) seen from the point of view of the subsequent administration, in modes of formal and political organization that could easily be adapted to fit the case of Richard of Gloucester. Indeed this process of aestheticization or adaptation had begun to be applied to Richard soon after his reign ended. Sir Thomas More, in his Suetonian history of the English Nero copied by all the chroniclers, presents a system of explanation for the events of Richard's kingship that Legge did not have to modify. In More he could find that everything in Richard's reign happened as it did because of the kind of person Richard was. His will, or rather his obsession, his manipulative drive, undiverted by social loyalties to brother, mother, wife, benefactor, comrade-in-arms, can be shown directing the passive world around him to the ends he alone foresees. All the others, Hastings, Brackenbury, the Queen Mother, Buckingham, are cajoled, bribed, terrified, deceived, magnetized into compliance; in themselves they seem to lack positive aims or understandings and therefore must be destined to be victims. In these terms we have a quasi-Senecan scenario already in place.

Yet in dealing even with so well digested a tract of modern history Legge faced methodological problems. Evidently he found it impossible to ignore the un-Senecan modernity of the political forces present in Richard's reign, the complex of voices, resistancies, uncertainties that More reveals. The Senecan form is not only static but also heavily retrospective; it is this that gives emotional density to the exchanges of the small family groups, whose shared life together stretches back through history into myth and legend, accumulating the crimes and resentments that eventually explode in the present. But Legge's history must be prospective. His play cannot end in Senecan mayhem and Stoic acceptance of a malign universe but must carry us through the complex web of English political life and show how it slips out of Richard's manipulative control, so leaving space for Henry Tudor, the Christian deliverer, to descend from the flies and take over the system.

In rendering modern political conditions with a degree of documentary truth Legge is, in fact, obliged to betray the unifying formalism of classical tragedy. The vast extent of his three-part play, the mass of its characters, its geographical range across the English landscape, the continual improvisation the protagonist has to engage in to answer new unexpected resistances – all these factors point away from the form he sought to imitate. The play thus becomes significant in the context I am sketching less as an achievement than as a model of the tensions and contradictions inherent in the genre, especially that contradiction between desire to fulfil the trajectory of the protagonist's plot (in the classical manner)

---

17 Edited by L. Padrin (Bologna, 1900). There is a serviceable translation by Joseph R. Berrigan: *Mussato's 'Ecerinus' and Loschi's 'Achilles'* (Munich, 1975).

and acceptance of the random points of resistance and diversion that his drive was bound to find in any 'true' picture of modern politics.

My second model play – *The Famous Victories of Henry V* – deals with the same issues from a totally different angle. In *Richardus Tertius* the *chorus civium* is shown as disbelieving, reluctant, sullen, and needing to be manipulated, in this *de haut en bas* treatment, by dazzling displays of rhetoric and chicanery. In *The Famous Victories* on the other hand the ruler's power is seen as operating not from above but from below; it is presented as a natural outgrowth from the life of the Folk, so that his rhetoric is simply their rhetoric played back to them, with appropriate magnification. The Cambridge play invites its audience to a distanced observation and analysis of political techniques. The popular play offers no such distance: it invites *its* audience to identify with a man like themselves, with the same emotions and values, though with more space to deploy them. To make this point the author, in a move that must remind us of Shakespeare, shows us Henry V first of all as a down-to-earth Hal, as a bully-boy gang leader who eventually becomes a bully-boy national leader, not too much change of attitude being required. The famous 'conversion' of Hal into Henry, his embracing of the Lord Chief Justice and turning away his riotous companions suggests that here, as in Shakespeare, the action is divided by a change of viewpoint and a new set of values into two distinct and differentiated parts, and critics often tell us that this is how we ought to look at *The Famous Victories*. But a reading of the play in its own terms rather than those of Shakespeare gives us a different profile. It is true that the newly crowned king turns away his evidently well-born boon companions, Ned, Tom, and Jocky Oldcastle. But these are not the figures who represent the 'true' underworld of *The Famous Victories*, which is carried not by deboshed gentlemen but by the genuine proletariat of Dericke, John Cobler, and Cuthbert Cutter (usually known

as 'The Thief'). Ned, Tom, and Jocky disappear from the play after Henry comes to the throne, but for Dericke and company the underworld ethos has never represented a holiday in the slums that can be put behind one, but is life itself. Their inevitable mode of existence is simply transferred, when Henry becomes king, from petty criminality in London to the equally criminal milieu of the private soldier in a foreign war (shades of Brecht!). It is true that the Lord Chief Justice is established in England; but the rest of the cast meanwhile removes to France, and there king and commoners carry on with the old populist pleasure of exploiting the formalistic, the smug and self-satisfied, the self-important, by a witty if brutal realism. The exploitables are now French aristocrats rather than London moneybags, but the attitude of the exploiters remains the same. Dericke and the Cobler end their war by retailing their Schweik-like capacity to minimize fighting while maximizing booty. They share with us their ingenious plan to use the funeral procession of the heroic Duke of York as a foolproof method of getting their stolen goods back home. Clearly we are not meant to be shocked but rather amused by their cynical exploitations of convention. When they get home, they tell us, they will show what they have learned in France by burning down Dericke's house, preferably with his wife inside. At the same time, and in a not altogether different vein, we see a ferociously genial King Henry backslap his 'good brother' the French king, his nobles, and his daughter into surrender and matrimony. This is overhand, not underhand; but the same sense that it all grows out of the anti-formalist or 'realist' English way pervades both social levels.

In spite of the coming and going of its large cast of characters, the indeterminacy of the many social levels it contains, the disjointed and episodic nature of its action, *The Famous Victories of Henry V* is, tonally speaking, a remarkably unified play. We may not like the tone – F. P. Wilson has eloquently registered his distaste for it – but we must allow that by assimilating the king and the national destiny to the life of the Folk this play solves the contradiction that appears in *Richardus Tertius* between the personal career of the monarch (dramatic) and the political life of the nation (historical). For the public life of the country is treated in *The Famous Victories* as a simple extension of the (shared) private life of camp and tavern. On the other hand we may well feel that the unification of *muthos* and *ethos* has been bought here at too high a price. And it is true that political life, as presented in this version, has not enough complexity to challenge our imagination or to represent the problems that a real politician must face.

In their startlingly different ways then, one clinging to the mode of high tragedy, the other to that of low comedy, both *Richardus Tertius* and *The Famous Victories of Henry V* show the problem of linking historical 'truth' to a seriously unified plot, in both cases one controlled by a dominant monarch whose will and ambition create the context within which historical development is to be understood. But neither author can be said to have secured that very delicate balance between such opposites in a history play – a balance that may be as much social as aesthetic – where the potentials for tragedy and comedy are combined in a manner that transcends both. What both plays can convey to the modern reader is rather the nature of the coordinates within which a history play must exist (and will exist), vectors moving on one axis through the 'truth' of content towards formlessness, and on the other axis moving through the necessities of form and order towards unhistorical fictional closure. Like other kinds of art, the history play advances by playing 'true' disorder against the promise of an order that can only emerge as fiction.[18] Where the history play differs from more traditional forms, such as tragedy and comedy, is mainly in the nature of the balance it sets up between these two opposed forces. In comedy and tragedy the knowledge that the life depicted does not exactly fit into the artful pattern, is not resolved by the artful closure, is only a minor though recurrent counterpoint, an enrichment of the dominant harmony. In the history play, however, the awareness that life cannot be resolved by art is much more powerful. Here in consequence the power to control and complete that pattern is held at a much more tentative level; the authorial or interpretative stance must be more heavily infected by irony, as has been pointed out by David Riggs in his admirable account of the *Henry VI* plays.[19]

And so we reach Shakespeare. What I take to be genuinely creative and originating in the *Henry VI* plays (creative, that is, in generating all the other weak-king plays of the early nineties) is the perception that only by placing an inadequate monarch in the centre of the play can this ironic or detached viewpoint be used to fulfil the tragicomic potential of modern history's indeterminate and destabilized worlds. Only so can an audience enjoy both a detached analysis of political activity (as in *Richardus Tertius*) and the pleasure of participating in the world of *The Famous Victories* where (as a recognizable truth) things are liable to happen without anyone anticipating them.

---

[18] Compare Philip Edwards's *Threshold of a Nation* (Cambridge, 1979), pp. 112–13, where, discussing the Epilogue to *Henry V*, he speaks of the dramatic resolution of the play's tensions as 'belonging to the experience of art', concluding 'Shakespeare reminds us of the existence of the two worlds, art and history, without compromising either.'

[19] *Shakespeare's Heroical Histories: 'Henry VI' and Its Literary Tradition* (Cambridge, Mass., 1971). Riggs notes: 'What finally distinguishes the early histories from their antecedents is the fact that only Shakespeare manages to accept the contradictions between individual aspiration and ethical convention in a spirit of conscious irony' (p. 29); and again (speaking of the episodic structure of *Henry VI*), 'the sequence of episodes provides us not with a conventional plot based on historical materials, but rather with a continuous commentary on an irreducible set of historical facts' (p. 95).

And having reached Shakespeare it is time to stop. My purpose has been to set out the generic conditions within which the texts that Heminges and Condell call history plays can exist. To show how these conditions are exploited is a larger task which belongs to another time and no doubt to another person.

CHRONICLES AND MYTHMAKING IN SHAKESPEARE'S JOAN OF ARC

RICHARD F. HARDIN

Like many characters of historical fiction, Joan of Arc in Shakespeare's *First Part of Henry the Sixth* is largely a creation of other texts, and some would have the dramatist (perhaps in his late twenties) powerless to consolidate her amid the passions and contradictions that beset these texts. Noting the contrasts between Joan at the beginning and end of the play, Shaw supposed that Shakespeare

having begun by an attempt to make Joan a beautiful and romantic figure, was told by his scandalized company that English patriotism would never stand a sympathetic representation of a French conqueror of English troops, and that unless he at once introduced all the old charges against Joan of being a sorceress and a harlot, and assumed her to be guilty of all of them, his play could not be produced.[1]

Nowadays scholars usually concede that Shakespeare wrote this uneven play, though a noteworthy case has been made for returning it to the composite authorship that was widely accepted, if on tenuous grounds, fifty years ago.[2] 'Shakespeare's Joan', then – and inverted commas are implicit in everything that follows – refers to a literary character who is perhaps not the property of any author, who came to Shakespeare already 'created' by a century of chronicle writers, and whose devising, there is a good chance, may not have been Shakespeare's at all. For that matter, Shakespeare's reputed source, Raphael Holinshed, probably did not write the account of Joan usually attributed to him. And the actual author would not have found unanimity about Joan among

his predecessors. Her inconsistencies as a figure of history are owing in part to her dual status, for she also belongs in the domain of myth, though Shakespeare's position and purpose in her mythography remain to be seen.

I

For one thing, there seems little truth behind Shaw's (and others') assumption that there was a popular image of Joan in England around 1590. Fifty years ago a British historian, W. T. Waugh, demonstrated that the actual Joan of

---

[1] Bernard Shaw, Preface to *Saint Joan*, in *Complete Plays with Prefaces*, 2 vols. (New York, 1962), vol. 2, p. 286. Cf. Andrew Lang, 'The Voices of Jeanne D'Arc', in *The Valet's Tragedy and Other Studies* (New York, 1903), p. 194: 'Are these two authors, and is Shakespeare one of them, with his understanding of the human heart?'.

[2] See Andrew S. Cairncross, ed., *I Henry VI*, new Arden edition (London, 1962), p. liii; Dennis H. Burden, 'Shakespeare's History Plays: 1952–1983', *Shakespeare Survey 38* (1985), 12. In opposition, see Gary Taylor's case for co-authorship and a date of 1592 (*following* Parts Two and Three) in Stanley Wells, Gary Taylor, John Jowett, and William Montgomery, *William Shakespeare: A Textual Companion* (Oxford, 1987), p. 217; Taylor further develops his argument in his 'Shakespeare and Others: The Authorship of *I Henry VI*', forthcoming in the journal *Medieval and Renaissance Drama in England*. John Dover Wilson, ed., *The First Part of King Henry VI* (Cambridge, 1952), proposes that the play was written in 1592 with Shakespeare as collaborator, later reviser. Neither Wilson nor Taylor imputes to Shakespeare the scenes that most denigrate Joan.

Arc 'made no great impression on the popular mind in England' during her own century, and that even in the sixteenth century there was no specifically English legend hostile to Joan, since almost all the derogatory details about her were elaborated from Burgundian writers hostile to Charles VII.[3] Still earlier, C. L. Kingsford could find only one contemporary allusion to Joan in an English chronicle (the *London Chronicle*), and that called her a 'false witch' and false prophetess, but gave no further hint of what was to come in later histories. 'Hall, and after him Stow and Holinshed, introduced her history, taken from [the Burgundian chronicler] Monstrelet, as something that would be novel to their readers and required explanation.' In this seeming lack of a clear tradition about Joan, Kingsford believed, lies the 'chaotic uncertainty' about her manifested in Shakespeare's play.[4] Some English historians whom Shakespeare could have read show, if not sympathy for Joan, at least no hostility to her. Polydore Vergil goes so far as to say that she was 'endowed both with a singular witt, and could also foreshewe thinges to come' – though not once does he impute this to witchcraft. It was 'the common sorte', he says, who made this charge. He objects to the English execution of Joan, comparing her to the heroic Roman virgin Cloelia, who received mercy from King Porsenna despite her opposition to him.[5] The influential *St Alban's Chronicle*, written somewhat earlier than Polydore's text, surprisingly says nothing about Joan's supposed sorcery, giving no reason why she was 'brent'. If anything it praises her, saying, 'This mayde rode lyke a man & was a valyaunt Capytayne amonge them & toke upon hyr many greete enterpryses.'[6] It is not quite right to lay the blame entirely on Hall and his successors for the defamation of Joan, however. Robert Fabyan, an earlier patriotic Londoner and no francophile, used the *Compendium* of 'Gaguynus', a rather brief French chronicle by Robert Gaguin (d. 1501/2), which later English

writers also consulted. Fabyan cites Gaguin, who revered the maid as a saint, on her miraculous recognition of the Dauphin and her equally miraculous finding of her armour and sword, 'whereof', sniffs the old alderman, 'the processe to me appereth so darke and fantastycall, yt therewyth me lyst not to blot my booke, but suffre it to passe by'.[7] Like his later English counterparts, Fabyan chose the most convenient explanation for Joan's marvellous powers, namely that 'God for a season sufferyth suche sorcery and develysshe wayes to prospere & regne, to the correcion of synners' (p. 642).

The Reformation brought the expected animosity towards the French heroine. John Bale took the occasion of a tribute to the amazon-like British warrior Boadicea ('Bunduica') to draw a contrast with Joan, saying, 'This famous scourge of France surpasses by the farthest measure that Joan of Dampreme, a leaderess first of pigs then of Frenchmen, of whom their chroniclers so recently boast as their liberator from the English yoke – though not from the exceptional dishonor of their princes.'[8] Quieter voices are still heard. Although the Elizabethan bishop Thomas

---

[3] W. T. Waugh, 'Joan of Arc in English Sources of the Fifteenth Century', in J. G. Edwards and V. H. Galbraith, eds., *Historical Essays in Honour of James Tait* (Manchester, 1933), pp. 387–98.

[4] C. L. Kingsford, *English Historical Literature in the Fifteenth Century* (1913; reprinted New York, 1962), p. 264.

[5] *Three Books of Polydore Vergil's English History*, ed. Sir Henry Ellis, Camden Society, vol. 29 (London, 1844), p. 38.

[6] *St. Alban's Chronicle* (Westminster, 1497), f. G3ᵛ.

[7] Robert Fabyan, *The New Chronicles of England and France* (1516), ed. Henry Ellis (London, 1811), p. 641.

[8] John Bale, *Illustrium Maioris Britanniae Scriptorum* (Wesel, 1548), f. 16ᵛ: 'Haec Gallomastix inclyta, Joannam illam Dampremam, porcorum primo, postea Gallorum ductricem, longissimo intervallo exuperat, quam eorum Chronographi tam crebro ab Anglorum jugo liberatricem non absque insigni suorum principum ignominia jactitant.'

Cooper, contemporary with Hall, Holinshed, and Shakespeare, reports that Joan was a sorceress, in his later mention of her death he says simply, 'Joan the holy woman of Fraunce, in whom the Dolphine had put all his truste, was taken by one Sir John Luxenburge, and adjudged to be brent.'[9] In the phrase 'holy woman of Fraunce' no irony is apparent.

A more illustrious historian of the age, John Stow, wavered on the subject of Joan. Stow wrote two histories of England, the first being the skeletal *A Summarie of Englyshe Chronicles*, gradually expanded and much read over the next half-century. The editions of 1565 and 1566 do not mention Joan, scarcely attending to the wars in France. The next edition, in 1570, contains a matter-of-fact entry for the year 1430: 'The xxiii. daye of May before the Towne of Champaigne was taken a woman armed with many other Captaines, ye Frenchmen called this woman La pucell de Dieu, through whom the Dolphin and al oure adversaries trusted to have conquered againe all Fraunce' (fo. 269ᵛ). With slight variations, this continues to be the only mention of Joan in later editions of the *Summarie*. Stow also wrote a more expansive history, called *Chronicles of England* in 1580, and after that, *Annals*, a book that again held its readership well into the next century. In the first edition of this work, under the year 1430, Stow says that in their battles, 'the *Frenchmen* prevayled greatly by the helpe of a Woman which they named The Mayden of God'; however, at Champaigne 'by the manhoode of a *Burgonian* Knight named sir John Luxenborough, she was taken alive'. After her captivity, 'she fained her selfe to be with child, but when the contrarie was known, she was condemned & brent' (p. 600). Stow alludes to a story invented, as will be seen, by the English in the fifteenth century. Still missing from Stow's account is any mention of Joan's supposed devil-worship or witchcraft, though this may be implied in the more vituperative passage Stow wrote for the next edition of his *Annals* in 1592, the year some

think marks the first performance of Shakespeare's play. This passage appears a few pages before the preceding one and mentions that the 'French histories' report Joan's first appearance at Charles's court: 'And even at this time, a monstrous woman, named Joan la pucell de dieu, was presented to him at Chinon', adding that later Joan 'was honoured as a saint' (p. 597 – she was not, of course, canonized until this century). That opening sentence, as will be seen, also appeared in Holinshed's 1577 text. Still, it is possible that Stow's addition, bringing his figure more into line with Shakespeare's, stands as evidence contemporary with Nashe's famous Talbot allusion that Londoners were stirred by Shakespeare's early play.[10]

Edward Hall was the first English historian to develop a full-scale assassination of Joan's character. Richard Grafton's *Chronicle* (1569) printed Hall on Joan almost verbatim, providing a secondary channel for this myth of Joan the monster. The Henrician Reformation is clearly the main 'source' for Hall's arguments, but they depend on the contemporary account of Enguerand de Monstrelet (d. 1453), an enemy of Charles VII who served at the siege of Compiègne when Joan was captured. Three editions of Monstrelet's chronicle had been printed in the sixteenth century when Hall wrote his, and others were to come. Monstrelet is gentle with Joan compared to Hall. He writes, 'This Joan, the Maid, had for some time been chambermaid in an inn; she was thoroughly used to riding horses and taking

---

[9] Thomas Lanquet, *Coopers Chronicle* (London, 1560), p. 259.

[10] The *Summarie* text appears in 1573, 1574, 1587, 1598, and 1607, while the 1590 edition, since it omits mention of Joan, may have been set from a pre-1570 copy. The text of the 1580 *Chronicles* (= *Annals*) reappears in 1600, but other later editions of the *Annals* (1601–2 and 1605) contain the 1592 derogatory passage. The passage seems to have been a hasty insertion, since Joan is mentioned later (reproducing the 1580 text) as if being introduced for the first time.

them to water and could do other feats which girls do not usually do.'[11] In Hall's colouring (and this typifies what he does with Monstrelet) Joan is 'a rampe of suche boldnesse, that she would course horses and ride them to water, and do thynges, that other yong maidens both abhorred & were ashamed to do'.[12] Joan is called a 'monster' (fo. 107), a disgrace to her sex, an oracle, a soothsayer, and a witch, terms Monstrelet never uses. Worst of all she was French. A point of some importance, for Shakespeare's handling of the story is that Hall, like Monstrelet, nowhere questions Joan's virginity. Hall may have known that Joan's virginity was proven during her examination.

One indication that Shakespeare read about Joan in Holinshed is that the story of Joan's pretending pregnancy appears there and not in Hall. That Hall would omit this detail is strange, since it is a dandy smear and the one original English contribution to folklore about Joan. Waugh found the earliest version of this story in a chronicle called 'Continuation G' of Brut, written between 1464 and 1470, an account that does not, by the way, accuse Joan of witchcraft: 'And then she said that she was with childe, whereby she was respited A while; but in conclusion it was found that she was not with child, and then she was brent in Roane' (p. 394). The origin of this story seems unknown, perhaps being invented to account for the long period between her capture and execution – just over a year. Caxton's chronicle picked up this detail, his account of Joan being otherwise impartial.

In 1577 came the first edition of Holinshed's Chronicles, with Joan appearing much more briefly than in the second edition of 1587, the one Shakespeare used. Despite the tradition of 'Shakespeare's Holinshed', the 1587 text, at least on Joan, is almost certainly not the work of Holinshed, who died in 1580, leaving the expansion to John Hooker, Francis Thynne, Abraham Fleming, and Stow. The editor in charge of the English chronicle was probably

Fleming, who in turn may have solicited work from still others.[13] Any reader of the 1587 edition can see that some of the entries on Joan are marked off by square brackets, with the initials 'W.P.' beside them in the margins among the names of sources. Since this probably identifies the author of these passages, it would be useful to know W.P.'s name.[14] In 1577 Holinshed had introduced Joan with the sentence, 'And even at the same time [as the siege of Orléans] that mo[n]strous woman named Joan la Pucell de Dieu, was presented unto him at Chinon where as then he sojourned, of which woman yee maye finde more written in the French Histories, touching her birth, estate, and qualitie' (p. 1241). The paragraph on Joan, a bit over a hundred words, gives way in 1587 to one over five hundred words long. Very little is said of Joan in 1577 between this point and her capture, but in 1587 W.P. adds the story of her killing the Burgundian Franquet, as found (like most of his additions) in Monstrelet. Finally, Joan's fate, told in three sentences in 1577, is magnified into two pages (in the Ellis edition) later on. It adds these important details: Joan was examined and found a virgin; she pretended

---

11 Contemporary Chronicles of the Hundred Years War, translated by Peter E. Thompson (London, 1966), p. 298. This selection from three French chroniclers translates every word of Monstrelet concerning Joan (pp. 298–316).

12 Edward Hall, The Union of the Two Noble and Illustre Famelies of Lancastre & Yorke (London, 1548), ff. 107–115ᵛ.

13 Citations from the 1587 edition are to Raphael Holinshed, Chronicles of England, Scotland, and Ireland, ed. Henry Ellis, 6 vols. (London, 1808), vol. 3, pp. 166–72. See William E. Miller, 'Abraham Fleming: Editor of Shakespeare's Holinshed', Texas Studies in Literature and Language, 1 (1959), 89–100.

14 The likeliest candidate, I think, is William Patten, a teller of the exchequer at Westminster who flourished 1548–80 (DNB). Earlier in his history (vol. 3, p. 61) Holinshed identifies a 'W.P.' writing on Scottish affairs as 'Wil. Patten'. Patten's only known writing is an account of a 1548 expedition into Scotland.

pregnancy to avoid execution and got a stay of nine months; in 1456 the Church found the sentence in error and declared her a 'damsell divine' (pp. 170–2). These pages concluding the 1587 account constitute a speciously researched, highly charged attack on the martyr – strangely coming long after the events and issues of 1431 had ceased to matter.

The most notable difference between Holinshed and his predecessors, says F. J. Levy, lies in the number of sources he cites.[15] Though Levy doesn't acknowledge the committee-like status of 'Holinshed', the point holds true in regard to Joan's story. The authors note, and had probably read, the anonymous *Le Rozier Historial de France* (1522 and later), a Stow-like chronicle that has the French historians' usual praise for Joan (see 1522 edition, pp. CXII–CXV); *Les Grandes Chroniques de France*, an official history begun under the Valois Charles V; an unidentified 'Chroniques de Britaigne', which the authors resent as pro-Joan (p. 170); Jean du Tillet's *Commentariorum et disquisitionum de rebus Gallicis*, whose comparison of Joan with Deborah and Judith (Frankfurt, 1574 ed., p. 91) they roundly condemn (p. 172). They mention Monstrelet elsewhere, and clearly used him in this section.

Shakespeare (i.e. 'Shakespeare') recognized 'Holinshed's methods of defamation and simply followed the leader, sometimes adding still more colour to the already exaggerated picture. To emphasize her villainous role as a satanic 'angell of light' (p. 171), Holinshed represents Joan as no chambermaid but the handsome daughter of a shepherd. Shakespeare gives her the same pastoral innocent beauty. Holinshed says that on her seemingly miraculous detection of Charles at court the two held a long, secret conference, but does not say the Duke d'Alençon was on hand for this (evidence, perhaps, that Shakespeare found this point in Monstrelet or one of the other French sources). The mention of Charles's 'hour in secret and private talke, that

of his privie chamber was thought verie long' (p. 164) may have led Shakespeare to write the odd, historically groundless love scene that follows the dauphin's demand for single combat with her. When they duel and Charles loses, he utters a love-pledge redolent of medieval courtly Frauendienst:

> Impatiently I burn with thy desire.
> My heart and hands thou hast at once
>   subdued...
> Let me thy servant, and not sovereign be.
>
> (1.3.87–8, 90)

The scene parodies the romance motif of the lovestruck knight conquered by a female in battle, as when Spenser's Artegall falls to Britomart's magic spear. Bawdy asides by René and Alençon counterpoint this interlude, pointing up Charles's folly and foreshadowing Joan's later exposure as a fraud. The effect is to collaborate with the historians' agenda of defamation in establishing uneasiness if not revulsion towards Joan, the foolish Charles, and the cynical French courtiers.

Joan's next important moment in the play, the siege of Orléans (1.7–2.1) abandons both history and Holinshed, but it does follow certain cues. Holinshed counters the loss of Orléans with Talbot's repulse of the French when they sally out from the city. Shakespeare simply makes Talbot and his allies victorious when they remount the walls of Orléans, a feat that almost destroys Charles's confidence in Joan. Joan next appears in the play at the wholly fictitious (or anachronistic) siege of Rouen (3.2–7), where once more the French win only to lose again. Joan's and Charles's success in winning Burgundy to their side is again unfounded, being derived from a mere hint in Holinshed that 'the French king sought by all meanes possible to breake the amitie betwixt the realme of England, and the house of Burgognie' (p. 168). Talbot's and his son's

---

15 F. J. Levy, *Tudor Historical Thought* (San Marino, Calif., 1967), p. 183.

deaths in 4.7 are, of course, wholly anachronistic (the old man survived Joan by more than twenty years, and the son lived seven years after his father). Finally, Holinshed has the captive Joan charged with witchcraft at her trial, but never questions her virginity. (Hall does not doubt Joan on this point either.) Indeed, Holinshed thinks it shameful of her to have pretended she wasn't a virgin. Shakespeare, then, goes out of his way to invent the most unpleasant part of his portrayal of Joan, the scene where she debases herself into a camp whore (5.6).

By the late sixteenth century, then, English historians had so increased their vilification of Joan that the Burgundians and English who actually took part in her ordeal would probably not recognize the character and her story. And far from merely 'following his sources', as Shakespeare's defenders sometimes say, the playwright enthusiastically compounded the felony. In John Dover Wilson's words, he 'blackened her character beyond anything he found in his sources'.[16] Joan occasionally does win the audience to her side, but that is mainly a studied effect of the 'angel of light' tradition. If there are 'two Joans', there are also two Macbeths and two Claudiuses.

II

Shakespeare develops a notable chronicle theme about Joan's villainy in addition to her witchcraft. Edward Berry has observed that Shakespeare's Joan is an 'extended parody' of the chivalric ideal epitomized in the English hero Lord Talbot.[17] This parody begins in Joan's first scene when Charles worships her, continuing in recurrent contrasts between the idol and the real thing, Talbot. The chroniclers, too, present Joan as a travesty of the chivalric hero. Hall scolds the French for honouring her:

O Lorde, what dispraise is this to the nobilitie of Fraunce? What blotte is this to the Frenche nacion? What more rebuke can be imputed to a renowmed

region, then to affirme, write and confesse, that all notable victories, and honorable conquestes, which neither the kyng with his power, nor the nobilitie with their valiauntnesse, nor the counsaill with their wit, nor the commonaltie with their strength, could compasse or obtain, were gotten and achived by a shepherdes daughter, a chamberlein in an hostrie, and a beggars brat.   (fo. 113ᵛ)

Holinshed, though preoccupied with the religious (satanic) side of the story, accentuates the chivalric element by recounting Joan's treacherous killing of the Burgundian knight Franquet, called 'a vailaunt man in feates of armes'. Against the code of arms Joan dishonourably subdued Franquet by sheer weight of numbers. Then 'she had his head stroken off: contrarie to all manhood (but she was a woman, if she were that) & contrarie to common right and law of armes. The man for his merits was verie much lamented, and she by hir malice then found of what spirit she was' (p. 169). The only source of this story, Monstrelet, merely observes, 'The Maid finally ordered Franquet's head to be cut off; his death was much lamented by his followers, because he was a most courageous man in battle' (p. 311). Holinshed ends with a pun on Joan's offence against gentry – 'And thus much of this gentle Jone' (p. 172) – much as Shakespeare has her shepherd father do in the line, 'Deny me not I prithee, gentle Joan' (5.6.20).

The prominent theme of waning chivalry in this play helps explain the aptness of Edward Berry's seemingly odd comparison of Joan with Falstaff. Joan, he says, 'foreshadows Falstaff' partly in her 'indifference to honor in the face of physical reality' (p. 17). He refers here to Joan's sudden recantation when confronting death. In 5.6 Joan renounces her real father when the old shepherd comes to plead

---

[16] *I Henry VI*, p. xxxiii.
[17] Edward I. Berry, *Patterns of Decay: Shakespeare's Early Histories* (Charlottesville, Va., 1975), p. 20; David Riggs, *Shakespeare's Heroical Histories: 'Henry VI' and Its Literary Tradition* (Cambridge, Mass., 1971), p. 104.

for her life, claiming that she really descends from 'the progeny of kings' (line 38). Finding the English unimpressed by her boast, she says she is pregnant by the dauphin. With soldierly bluntness Warwick replies, 'we will have no bastards live, / Especially since Charles must father it' (lines 70–1). Joan then switches the blame for paternity to Alençon, then to René, only to find that these names merely increase her enemies' resolution to kill her. This scene would have greatly amused a mostly male audience. She effectively loses the last shred of her honour, her virginal reputation, much as Sir John Fastolf had compromised his honour in an act of cowardice that led Talbot to publicly degrade him.

The chivalric theme helps to reconcile the monster Joan with the worldly wise figure in Act 4, who speaks over Talbot's dead body much as Falstaff does over the corpses of Hotspur and Blunt. Taken by itself the scene appears to demythologize aristocracy. When Sir William Lucy enters to ask for Talbot's body he needs twelve lines to get through all of Talbot's titles (if we include 'Alcides'). All those dukedoms and lordships for one man! Joan's reply has a certain appeal:

> Here's a silly, stately style indeed.
> The Turk, that two-and-fifty kingdoms hath,
> Writes not so tedious a style as this.
> Him that thou magnifi'st with all these titles
> Stinking and flyblown lies here at our feet.
>
> (4.7.72–6)

The problem of interpreting these lines resembles that of Falstaff's catechism speeches in *I Henry IV*, because, taken alone, they could be a populist sneer at aristocratic ceremonialism and honour-seeking. Yet Falstaff undermines his position by proving his own thirst for honour when he stabs Hotspur's corpse. Similarly, Joan's scoffing at Talbot's honours conflicts with her later boasting of royal birth while refusing to acknowledge her true father. In addition, still vivid at this point is the pathos of Talbot's death as he holds the body of his son (4.7.32). The message is that all those titles

and more are owed to the man who made such sacrifices. Knowing how to speak fair, to debase virtue as pretence, is a requisite talent of the morality vice, a character-type that went into Joan's making. Joan speaks fair elsewhere in the play, but her motives and motivating forces will be mercilessly exposed when next she appears, in the scene with her diabolic accomplices.

This lurid moment captures the witchcraft mythology of the chroniclers, who took far more pleasure in discussing this sin than her affront to chivalry. The peculiar logic of the day classed her sorcery, since it entailed devil-worship, with the great sin of idolatry. No Puritan tract could set forth quite as effectively as 5.3 the dark truth of Catholic superstition. The courtly love parody between Joan and Charles obtains its effectiveness partly by fusing idolatry with Frauendienst, as indicated in Charles's 'Bright star of Venus, fall'n down on the earth, / How may I reverently worship thee enough?' (1.3.123–4). Charles has a similar moment of pagan frenzy when promising Joan that for her victories,

> all the priests and friars in my realm
> Shall in procession sing her endless praise.
> A statelier pyramid to her I'll rear
> Than Rhodope's of Memphis ever was.
>
> (1.8.19–22)

And so on. Shakespeare could not escape Hall's and Holinshed's naming Joan the 'great Idol' of the French, and he plays this for all it is worth before an audience likely to be as anti-Catholic as it was Francophobic. Compounding this sin, of course, is Joan's daring, as a woman, to assume a man's role. Even the French poets who celebrated Joan's heroism during her life sometimes balked at this point.[18] The lawyer Hall, as if summing up to

---

[18] Deborah Fraioli, 'The Literary Image of Joan of Arc: Prior Influences', *Speculum*, 56 (1981), 811–30, says that while Christine de Pizan acclaimed Joan in 1429 as a female warrior, Jean Gerson downplayed this role in a poem of the same time.

a jury, seems to find this a hanging offence in her case: she violated three of the chief 'womanly virtues' – first, shamefastness ('which the Romain Ladies so kept, that seldome or never thei wer seen openly talkyng with a man'), second pity, and third 'womanly behavior' (by which he means avoiding not only shameful actions but even the occasions that might give rise to slander). 'She was no good woman', Hall concludes, 'then it must nedes, consequently folowe, that she was no sainct' (fo. 115ᵛ).

III

Joan's mythological dimension emerges fully in Act 5, first in her desertion by the diabolic spirits to whom she has sold her soul, then in the degrading scene before her execution. Neither scene is 'historical', and both appeal strongly to certain epidemic passions and convictions, even the worst prejudices of the audience. This handling of Joan is perhaps best understood in the light of René Girard's ideas on the scapegoat, that 'other' whom people choose to attack when they themselves cannot resolve conflict. Girard believes scapegoating to be a perennial reflex in human nature, virtually defining human culture:

The preceding analyses force us to conclude that human culture is predisposed to permanent conceal-ment of its origins in collective violence. Such a definition of culture enables us to understand the successive stages of an entire culture as well as the transition from one stage to the next by means of a crisis similar to those we have traced in myths [his favourite instances are Oedipus and Pentheus] and to those we have traced in history during periods of frequent persecutions.[19]

The Hobbesian view of humanity is not at issue here, so much as the theory's applica-bility to the world of *Henry VI*, and more explicitly to that of the play's first audiences. In these instances the situation matches won-derfully well with the kind of crisis Girard discusses. Religious upheavals, plagues, civil wars, and other disasters cause a loss of identity, whereby relations of family, institu-tions, the state, and religion are no longer differentiated. People see the cause of this breakdown of differentiation not for what it is (a plague or whatever) but in terms of religious suppositions. A monstrous 'criminal' is exposed through the concerted effort of the mob. Once the black rapist is lynched or the well-poisoning Jew has been burned, differ-ence is re-established and for the time being the crisis is alleviated.

Anthropological investigations of scape-goats indicate that they must be like us in some ways, yet possess differences that will readily allow them to be punished while the guilty often go free. They thus resemble the figure of the 'stranger' in Leslie Fiedler's book on Shakespeare, though Girard's viewpoint cor-rects some of the biographical and psycho-analytical idiosyncrasies of that study.[20] The surrogate victim's differences from the major-ity powerfully stimulate hatreds and fears

---

[19] René Girard, *The Scapegoat* (Baltimore, 1986), p. 100. For a recent application of Girard's ideas to Shake-speare, see Derek Cohen, 'The Rite of Violence in *I Henry IV*', *Shakespeare Survey 38* (1985), 77–84.

[20] Leslie A. Fiedler, *The Stranger in Shakespeare* (New York, 1972), pp. 56–81, discusses Joan as symptomatic of Shakespeare's problems with women, also as an avatar of 'the Great Goddess' (p. 78). Nevertheless, Fiedler's chapter contains the most stimulating discuss-ion of Joan in print. Shakespeare's Joan appears alongside others in Ingvald Raknem, *Joan of Arc in History, Legend and Literature* (Oslo, 1971). Feminist scholars have curiously neglected Joan. Irene Dash explicitly omits her in the chapter on the first tetralogy in *Wooing, Wedding, and Power* (New York, 1981), p. 156; Juliet Dusinberre, *Shakespeare and the Nature of Women* (London, 1975), does not mention her; neither does Diane Elizabeth Dreher, *Domination and Defiance: Fathers and Daughters in Shakespeare* (Lexington, Ky., 1986), despite a notable father–daughter conflict. Angella Pitt, *Shakespeare's Women* (London, 1981), summarizes Joan's actions and makes the same error Shaw did in saying that 'As a legendary figure she needed no introduction' (p. 148). See, however, Phyllis Rackin, 'Anti-Historians: Women's Role in Shake-speare's Histories', *Theatre Journal*, 37 (1985), 329–44.

lying deep in the social psychology of the crowd (Joan would have had this effect on the late Elizabethan clientele of the Rose Theatre). Some of the older criticism implicitly recognizes this mob influence on the play, as when F. S. Boas remarks that the 'representation of Joan, however crude and harsh it may seem today, won hearty plaudits from the groundlings of the Rose Theatre'.[21] It is this mob that, projecting itself into the English heroes, is really closing in for the kill in Act 5. Shakespeare has collaborated with them in rewriting Joan's history. Her crime lies with their prejudices. She is French, and her devotion to this traditional enemy so intense that she gives both her honour and her soul for France. And it is crucial to an understanding of this play that France, not only in its past conflicts but in its current, late-Elizabethan turmoil, shapes the world of this play. Despite the received date for this play of 1590,[22] there is much to be said for Wilson's and Taylor's dating of 1592. Wilson (p. xix) suggests that the made-up siege of Rouen in Act 3 is intended to parallel the real siege commanded by Henry IV and Essex at Rouen from November 1591 to April 1592, also that Lucy alludes to Essex in saying that from the Talbots' ashes 'shall be reared / A phoenix that shall make all France afeard' (4.7.92–3).[23] If so, perhaps the famous line, 'Done like a Frenchman – [aside] turn and turn again' (3.7.85), found its way into the play after Henry IV's abjuring Protestantism in 1593. Like a play of about the same vintage, Marlowe's *Massacre at Paris*, this play excoriates French perfidy and pride in such characters as René and Alençon, but it also focuses this evil in a character rich in archetypal potential.

These crimes against the implied sacred are every bit as serious as those like sorcery listed in the chronicles. A renegade daughter, Joan violates the cherished patriarchalism of the age. She also offends prejudice in adopting a male role, in pretending to the virginity so prized in a male-dominated culture, and in

being a Catholic at a time when Catholics were associated with outrages like the Inquisition and the St Bartholomew's Day Massacre. Some of these traits, of course, she shares with Mary Stuart, the woman Elizabethans loved to hate, executed perhaps five years earlier and execrated by Spenser in the character of Duessa. Finally, Joan offends in being a low-born person pretending to aristocratic rank and meddling with the aristocracy's mysteries of love, honour, and war. At the deepest level, as she has been recently described, Joan subverts the 'logocentric, masculine historical record', one of three women in this play to do so.[24]

Yet there is no denying the contrasts between Joan in Act 5 and the first three acts of the play. Some earlier readers (Boas, p. 39) found evidence of several hands in the play largely because of Joan's seemingly inconsistent characterization. Earlier scenes, with such ringing lines as 'Glory is like a circle in the water' or the speech urging Burgundy to join the French, seem to make her a genuinely heroic figure, not unlike the heroine of the remarkably long (20,529 lines) *Mystère du siège d'Orléans*, a pageant play first performed at Orléans a few years after Joan's death. But the tactics are the same ones used so much more effectively in Macbeth's characterization, concealing the truth with shows of fair speech. Holinshed had perhaps suggested this ambiguity in Joan when he described her as proof that 'satan (after S. Paule) can change himselfe into an angell of light, the deeplier to deceive' (p. 171). At the start of Act 5 Joan's evil spirits help bring about the change from patriot to monster, and they effect that ultimate dehumanization needed if the scapegoat mechanism is to work effectively. In his essays Girard

---

21 F. S. Boas, 'Joan of Arc in Shakespeare, Schiller, and Shaw', *Shakespeare Quarterly*, 2 (1951), 35.

22 *I Henry VI*, p. xxxviii.

23 *I Henry VI*, p. xix.

24 Rackin, 'Anti-Historians', p. 329.

takes the view that scapegoat is always a matter of theme, not structure, in Shakespeare. *The Merchant of Venice*, for example, aims not to make Shylock a scapegoat, but to reveal a characteristically debased human effort to change one person into a monster so as to exonerate the group from its sins (i.e. the avarice and wrath of Venice).[25] Yet it seems doubtful that the author has so distanced himself in this play, perhaps further evidence against Shakespeare's responsibility for this character. At best one could say that the trade-off at the end of the play, when Margaret of Anjou replaces Joan, presents Joan as a surrogate victim who is guiltless only in relative terms. Both Margaret and Joan are female, French, Catholic, and pretenders; but Henry's tigress queen will inflict far deeper wounds on England than Joan ever did.

Writing on Tudor nostalgia for chivalry, Diane Bornstein has observed that during the sixteenth century 'Rituals and symbols of chivalry were part of an attempt to keep up an appearance of stability in the face of change.'[26] Of rituals in general Girard writes that their 'sole purpose' is 'to ensure total immobility, or failing that, a minimum of disturbance'.[27] Shakespeare's play conveys this stasis through characters like Talbot and Bedford, who lend a mythical aura to the world of old England. In that era of chivalry, a time eclipsed by monsters like Joan, traitors like Suffolk, and cowards like Fastolf, the purity and unselfishness of the Golden Age still existed. Whether Shakespeare intends it or not, we come to think of Talbot and Bedford as spokesmen for an ideal order now passing. The later history plays subject the old order to critical scrutiny. Not so *I Henry VI*. Perhaps this is because it is a 'history' created by the moment. As recent historians like Lawrence Stone and R. B. Wernham have shown, the last twenty years of the Elizabethan period were especially burdened by change. Recall that Stow's language about Joan becomes most abusive in 1592, with relatively innocuous entries in editions

before and even after that date. It could be said that Stow is simply responding to the popular dramatic treatment of this figure, but that is merely another way of saying that Stow was led by Shakespeare to make himself part of the mob. After the execution of Mary Stuart and the narrow escape of the Armada, not to mention the ongoing self-doubts among the English about their Catholicism or Protestantism; after the social rank-jumping that rendered it increasingly difficult to tell the ruling class by its clothes or family name; after the joining of the religious wars in France by a good number of English soldiers, many of whom must have guessed that their Protestant champion was less than reliable – after so many episodes conducive to collective uncertainty, it was useful to have such a character.

On stage the factionalized English seem momentarily united as they join against France and Joan. Among the audience watching them the same false sense of union occurred. Girard reminds us of a point that becomes increasingly discernible in the other *Henry VI* plays; that 'the basic function of foreign wars, and of the more or less spectacular rites that generally accompany them, is to avert the threat of internal dissension by adopting a form of violence that can be openly endorsed and fervently acted upon by all'.[28] If chivalric rites lay at the heart of war's mystery, then they celebrated an illusion of unity in community, creating an illusion of triumph over the threat of change.

25 René Girard, '"To Entrap the Wisest": A Reading of *The Merchant of Venice*', in *Literature and Society: Selected Papers of the English Institute, 1978*, ed. Edward Said (Baltimore, 1980), pp. 100–19. See also Girard, 'Shakespeare's Theory of Mythology', in *Classical Mythology in Twentieth-Century Thought and Literature*, ed. Wendell M. Aycock and Theodore M. Klein, Proceedings of the Comparative Literature Symposium, vol. 11 (Lubbock, Texas, 1980), pp. 107–24.
26 Diane Bornstein, *Mirrors of Courtesy* (Hamden, Conn., 1975), p. 125.
27 *Violence and the Sacred*, p. 284.
28 *Violence and the Sacred*, p. 280.

The critical, and therefore directorial, problem of Joan's character can never be solved to everyone's satisfaction, in part because modern audiences cannot mount the enthusiasm for the historical moment. Gareth Lloyd Evans rightly says that in Joan's character, 'what seemed despicable to the Elizabethans has for us much that is wryly attractive', recounting some of the comments on her role as played in twentieth-century theatres. In 1906 she was 'unexceptionably ... a brave warrior', while in 1959 she had 'an obvious sincerity ... one was almost persuaded of her innocence'. Five years later she was 'a charming but coquettish exemplar of feminine emancipation'.[29] If there is any way to smooth over the contradictions in her, it may be to project a sense of irony rather than 'obvious sincerity', an expedient that may have shaped the performance at the Oregon Shakespeare Festival in 1975, where Joan was marked by 'energy, humor, and even self-mockery'.[30] Probably the most notable attempt to assimilate conflicting qualities in recent years came with the Royal Shakespeare Company's production of all three *Henry VI* plays in 1977–8. Joan became, according to one witness, 'a fascinating mixture of saint, witch, naïve girl, clever woman, audacious warrior, and sensual tart'.[31] In the scene with Talbot's body, she was made to gaze on the English hero as if foretelling her own death in his. The production obviously convinced many sceptics, but some who did not enjoy it will remain sceptical. In theoretical terms one problem with Joan is that she inhabits a mimetic drama as a symbolic, mythic character, the sort who transcends mimesis. It is as if Spenser's Busirane showed up on the battlefield at Agincourt. Evans goes so far as to say that all of this play may generally be termed allegorical, in contrast to the 'naturalistic' Part Two: 'Within the depths of the play's meaning Talbot and Joan meet in an allegorical dance' (pp. 40–1). Yet every shade of allegorical colouring, at least in Joan, originates in the 'true' histories of the Tudor age.

Twenty years after Joan and Talbot's first dance, John Speed published his history of 'Great Britain'. By 1611 the reigning monarch, now a man of sorts, no longer favoured chivalric games, and the French had outwardly settled their religious shambles, if to the dissatisfaction of Protestants. Joan's picture could now be painted in more subdued colours. Speed seems to admire the spirit with which Joan writes her letter to Suffolk and the bravado of her speech on being wounded at Orléans: 'This is a favour, let us goe on; they cannot escape the hand of God.'[32] His account shows no awareness of Shakespeare's play – indication, perhaps, that the 'popular image' had a life span not much longer than 1587 (the date of the defamatory additions to Holinshed) to 1592 (the date of Stow's last additions). Yet Speed agrees with the English-sponsored verdict against Joan. He resurrects Polydore's comparison of Joan with the brave Roman virgin fighting against Porsenna, but adds that the English could not indulge in Porsenna's magnanimity once they had captured her because they 'found it necessary to deface the opinion which the *French* even with superstition had conceived of her' (p. 655). A gentlemanly detachment pervades this account, devoid of the earlier historians' rage and vindictiveness. Speed is something of a politic historian here, and it never occurs to him that he is saying the English created a myth by destroying one. But then myths, saints, and devils are often the farthest thing from the minds of politic historians.[33]

---

29 Gareth Lloyd Evans, *Shakespeare I: 1564–1592*, Writers and Critics (Edinburgh, 1969), p. 36.

30 Alan C. Dessen, 'The Oregon Shakespeare Festival, 1975', *Shakespeare Quarterly*, 27 (1976), 90.

31 Homer D. Swander, 'The Rediscovery of *Henry VI*', *Shakespeare Quarterly*, 29 (1978), 158.

32 John Speed, *The Theatre of the Empire of Great Britaine* (London, 1611), p. 655.

33 An earlier version of this paper was read at the Joan of Arc session of the 1987 International Medieval Congress in Kalamazoo, Mich.

KING JOHN AND EMBARRASSING WOMEN

JULIET DUSINBERRE

Compared with almost any other play of Shakespeare's, *King John* has had a poor press both in quantity of what is written about it and also in the faint praise accorded to it. This lack of interest has been reflected in its stage history. Arthur Colby Sprague wrote in 1945 that the play is 'now almost unknown as an acting play'.[1] When it was put on in the Old Vic season of 1953–4 the editors of a commemorative volume (Roger Wood and Mary Clarke) record that 'it only just maintained a 75 per cent attendance record', and that 'this was in spite of good reviews and first-rate acting' (by a cast which included Fay Compton as Constance, Richard Burton as Falconbridge, and Michael Hordern as John). They conclude that this lukewarm reception 'must be attributed to the play's own comparative unpopularity'. Wood and Clarke consider *King John* to be 'purely medieval', and add that 'a play of such mixed fabric, where every man is for himself and no common purpose or theme emerges, presents many problems to the producer'.[2] In 1988 one might feel less confident in declaring that a drama in which every man is out for himself represents the medieval rather than the modern world. Perhaps Garrick's idea for a production which was 'half old English and half modern' both identifies and solves the problem.[3] In the later twentieth century *King John* has not – at least until the advent of Deborah Warner's excellent 1988 production at The Other Place in Stratford-upon-Avon – shared notably in the revival of enthusiasm about Shakespeare's other history plays set in motion by John Barton's adaptations and productions. Standing alone where the other histories support each other in two tetralogies, *King John* remains to some extent odd man out. Or should one say, odd woman out? There are certainly enough odd women in it, or at least, men have often thought so.

In the early nineteenth century the play came into its own when in John Philip Kemble's production of 1804 Sarah Siddons (his sister) played Constance. Many actresses followed Mrs Siddons's lead in making Constance the first major part in the tragic repertoire. Leigh Hunt described Siddons's performance in *The Examiner* for 3 June 1810:

The Constance of Mrs. Siddons is an excellent study for young actresses, to whom it will shew the great though difficult distinction between rant and tragic vehemence. In an inferior performer, the loudness of Constance's grief would be mere noise; but

---

[1] Arthur Colby Sprague, *Shakespeare and the Actors: The Stage Business in His Plays (1660–1905)* (Cambridge, Mass., 1945), p. 108. After the Restoration the play was not a favourite; it appears not to have been performed until 1737.

[2] Roger Wood and Mary Clarke, *Shakespeare at the Old Vic* (London, 1954), p. 61. The production ran for only thirty-six performances.

[3] Cecil Price, *Theatre in the Age of Garrick* (Oxford, 1973), p. 59.

tempered and broken as it is by the natural looks and gestures of Mrs. Siddons, by her varieties of tone and pauses full of meaning, it becomes as grand as it is petrifying.[4]

According to Leigh Hunt, the refinement of Mrs Siddons's rendering of the part tempered its potential for alienating the audience through its excesses, emotional and verbal. However, Constance's vehemence touched throughout the Romantic period a responsive chord in critics, and presumably in audiences, of the play. Hazlitt observes in *Characters of Shakespear's Plays* (1817) that 'the excess of maternal tenderness, rendered desperate by the fickleness of friends and the injustice of fortune, and made stronger in will, in proportion to the want of all other power, was never more finely expressed than in Constance', and he quotes (without delineation) the lines: 'To me and to the state of my great grief, let kings assemble' (2.2.70).[5] Constance becomes in this speech the locus for the conflict of power and powerlessness which shapes the whole play.

The play of *King John* thus became for the mid-nineteenth-century actress and audience the play of Constance and Arthur. Both Ellen Terry and her elder sister Kate appeared as Arthur with Charles and Ellen Kean when the play was produced in the 1850s under Kean's direction at the Princess's Theatre, London. Terry recalls vividly the stir she made in Arthur's scene with Hubert. She also remembers that

Another night I got into trouble for not catching Mrs. Kean, when, as Constance, in 'King John', she sank down on to the ground.

'Here is my throne, bid kings come bow to it!'

I was, for my sins, looking at the audience, and Mrs. Kean went down with a *run*, and was naturally very angry with me![6]

The anger is easy to understand. Dr Johnson noted in his edition of Shakespeare (1765) that in Constance despair creates power over, and independence from, those who have afflicted her:

III.i.70. *Constance.* To me and to the state of my great grief / Let kings assemble.] In *Much Ado about Nothing*, the father of Hero, depressed by her disgrace, declares himself so subdued by grief that *a thread may lead him.* How is it that grief in Leonato and Lady Constance produces effects directly opposite, and yet both agreeable to nature? Sorrow softens the mind while it is yet warmed by hope, but hardens it when it is congealed by despair. Distress, while there remains any prospect of relief, is weak and flexible, but when no succor remains, is fearless and stubborn; angry alike at those that injure and at those that do not help; careless to please where nothing can be gained and fearless to offend when there is nothing further to be dreaded. Such was this writer's knowledge of the passions.[7]

---

4 Quoted in Gāmini Salgādo, *Eyewitnesses of Shakespeare: First Hand Accounts of Performances, 1590–1890* (London, 1975), p. 107. In *Shakespeare's Histories: Plays for the Stage* (London, 1964), Arthur Colby Sprague quotes (from Campbell's biography) Mrs Siddons's own comments on Constance: 'Whether the majestic, the passionate, the tender *Constance*, has ever yet been, or ever will be, personated to the entire satisfaction of sound judgment and fine taste, I believe to be doubtful; for I believe it to be nearly impossible' (p. 20). Siddons's performance also seems to have inaugurated a tradition of artistic representation of Constance: Salgādo (p. 108) reproduces Thomas Rowlandson's sketch of the actress rehearsing with her father, Roger Kemble.

5 William Hazlitt, *Characters of Shakespear's Plays* (1817; reprinted London, 1906), p. 191.

6 Ellen Terry, *The Story of my Life* (1908; reprinted Woodbridge, Suffolk, 1982), p. 17.

7 W. K. Wimsatt, Jr, *Samuel Johnson on Shakespeare* (London, 1960), p. 85. David Bevington, *Action is Eloquence: Shakespeare's Language of Gesture* (Cambridge, Mass., 1984), observes that Constance's 'binding and unbinding of her hair express her powerlessness at the hands of the King of France and Cardinal Pandulph. The only authority such women enjoy is that of prophecy' (p. 85). However, Alan C. Dessen, *Elizabethan Stage Conventions and Modern Interpreters* (Cambridge, 1984), pp. 36–8, demonstrates that although the loosening of hair in Elizabethan drama usually signified, for the benefit of both the boy actor and his audience, female distraction, the convention was also used for mourning. Constance insists that the vehemence of her grief is evidence of her sanity (3.4.44–60) and defies male control, thus appropriating the scene to her purposes.

Dr Johnson identifies with acuity the psychological truth behind the theatrical reality of Constance's domination not only of the princes and potentates on the stage, but of the audience itself, who must salute her even as her world casts her aside. It requires, says Leigh Hunt, fine discrimination on the part of the actress for this dominion over the audience not to become aggression at the expense of true feeling. And the arbiter of true feeling? As Herschel Baker remarks in his introduction to the edition of the play in the Riverside Shakespeare: 'Philip's comment on this appalling woman's rhetoric (which has endeared the role to many actresses) is one every reader will endorse: "You are as fond of grief as your own child"'.[8] But will every audience, that motley multitude of potentially equally appalling women and equally appalled men, endorse that judgement?'[9] Kenneth Muir points out that Shakespeare has amplified Constance's part (if one takes *The Troublesome Raigne of King John* as precursor to the play). The playwright gives her 'some 140 lines', and Muir adds: 'An impressive vehicle for great actresses, no doubt, although in my experience most audiences feel that the lady doth protest too much'.[10]

It is intriguing to consider why Shakespeare expanded Constance's part. He had, after all, no great actresses eager to cut their teeth on tragic rhetoric, and it could be argued that the advent of the great actress to the stage may have radically changed the balance of the play as first conceived. There is no knowing whether Shakespeare wanted in 1596 to train up a particular boy for the parts of tragic heroines. *King John* is usually dated within the same two-year period as *Romeo and Juliet*,[11] and it is possible that the boy actor who played Constance would also have acted Juliet.[12] By the time that there were women actresses, the two parts do seem to have gone in harness, for on 8 December 1816 Hazlitt saw Constance performed by Eliza O'Neill, an actress who had already achieved fame as Juliet.[13] For a late

[8] Edited by G. Blakemore Evans (Boston, Mass., 1974), p. 766.

[9] Ann Jennalie Cook, *The Privileged Playgoers of Shakespeare's London, 1576–1642* (Princeton, 1981), warns that 'modern accounts of the audience suffer from the bias of the writer fully as much as did the contemporary accounts' (p. 3). In discussing bias in past critics I make no claim to an 'unbiassed' position in the present, but only to a recognition of bias.

[10] Kenneth Muir, *The Sources of Shakespeare's Plays* (London, 1977), p. 83. The quotation is an apt reminder that men and women may differ in their responses to characters on stage; in *Hamlet* the audience member who disliked the lady's vehemence was herself a lady.

[11] The *Textual Companion* to the Oxford edition suggests the following order for the plays: (1) *Richard II* (1595), (2) *Romeo and Juliet* (1595), (3) *King John* (1596), with *A Midsummer Night's Dream* (1595) intervening between *Romeo* and *King John*. The Riverside edition (pp. 50–1) suggests another order: (1) *King John* (1594–6), (2) *Richard II* (1595), (3) *Romeo and Juliet* (1595–6). E. A. J. Honigmann in the new Arden edition (London, 1954, p. lviii) dates *King John* as early as 1590.

[12] Scholars are now sceptical of the theory, developed by T. W. Baldwin in *The Organisation and Personnel of the Shakespearean Company* (Princeton, 1927), that Shakespeare used 'lines' of boy actors (pp. 416, 418): see Gerald Eades Bentley, *The Profession of Player in Shakespeare's Time 1590–1642* (Princeton, 1984), pp. 119, 233. Baldwin does not in any case link Constance and Juliet. The part of Juliet is perhaps the more difficult of the two because of its length, and it may therefore have followed rather than preceded Constance in the boy actor's repertoire; on the other hand the role of Constance requires the sustaining of mature maternal feeling to a degree not demanded of the boy actor until Gertrude in *Hamlet*.

[13] Salgādo, *Eyewitnesses of Shakespeare*, p. 107. Russell Jackson, 'Shakespeare on the Stage from 1660 to 1900', in *The Cambridge Companion to Shakespeare Studies*, ed. Stanley Wells (Cambridge, 1986), p. 201, notes that the twenty-one-year-old Macready, when he came to the stage, 'noticed a new emphasis in the treatment of women's roles that foreshadows later, more sentimental treatment of Shakespeare's heroines:

> The noble pathos of Mrs Siddons's transcendent genius no longer served as the ground commentary and living exponent of Shakespeare's text, but in the native elegance, the feminine sweetness, the unaffected earnestness and gushing passion of Miss O'Neill the stage had received a worthy successor to her.'

Under the guise of gushing passion perhaps Miss O'Neill did manage to make Constance and Juliet a

twentieth-century audience the conjunction seems bizarre, not only because of the ages of the two women, but because *Romeo and Juliet* has remained at the centre of the Shakespearian repertoire while *King John* is still a curiosity. Perhaps the decline of the 'star' in the modern directors' theatre has operated against the play's popularity in the same way that its ostensible subject matter – the triumph of England over her Catholic enemies – when untempered by the romantic image of a charismatic central figure, as in *Henry V*, has seemed out of tune with the temper of our times. Whatever the case, the modern theatre is no longer as committed to establishing stars as it was in 1941 when Sybil Thorndike played Constance.

Nor is Constance the kind of woman character who might immediately appeal either to modern actresses or audiences, not because of her ranting but because she is, as Dr Johnson pointed out, the epitome of powerlessness. Dr Johnson concluded blandly that 'the lady's grief is very affecting'.[14] But Constance stands for aspects of patriarchal power which might affect women rather differently from the way in which Dr Johnson was affected. Her very impotence seems to cry out against her, and throughout the play alienation might seem more likely to accompany the sallies of the main women characters, Eleanor and Constance, than any great sympathy with their wrongs. They are, for the modern feminist, too palpably acquiescent in the values which have created these wrongs. Indeed some kind of male directorial embarrassment has often accompanied productions of *King John*, resulting in the cutting of the scolding between Eleanor and Constance. Sprague records a judgement in the *Monthly Mirror* for 1810, that it was a relief that the 'Billingsgate scene' between Eleanor and Constance had been cut. Sprague himself thinks the scene best understood in terms of 'the formal defiances before battle, so frequent on the Elizabethan stage', and declares that the homely interchanges

between the women which appeal to a modern audience 'would certainly have been embarrassing to spectators brought up on the neoclassical ideas of decorum'.[15] Honigmann, the Arden editor, draws attention to other possibilities of imbalance in the play: 'Often the principal actor played Faulconbridge, not John, which must also have distorted the play. The custom of casting girls to play Arthur seems quite as dangerous' (p. lxxv). It is not immediately clear who or what was in danger, any more than it is immediately obvious who decides what a distortion is. And this is where *King John* is, conversely, a play of intense interest to feminists.[16] Where does its central drive lie: where the great actress located it, in the figure of Constance? Where Hazlitt saw it, in the pathos of Arthur and the comedy of the Bastard? In the title role of John himself? Or, as some critics have claimed, in the identity of England, a nation emerging from papal domination? What is clear from reading the play – and Deborah Warner's 1988 production reinforced this impression – is that up till the end of Act 3 the dramatic action is dominated by the women characters, and this is a cause of extreme embarrassment to the men on stage, while it also provides a pretext for their own determination to create embarrassment for those women.

It is now considered somewhat oldfashioned to think of Shakespeare's plays as primarily 'reading' texts, or of the recipient of them as 'the reader'. How does the audience, that collective body to whom the collective energy of the theatrical performance is addressed and who themselves constitute an

---

more congruent pair for the tragic actress than might be imagined if one had bracketed Constance with Margaret in *Richard III*.

[14] Wimsatt, *Johnson on Shakespeare*, p. 85.

[15] Sprague, *Shakespeare's Histories*, p. 14.

[16] Phyllis Rackin discusses the significance of Shakespeare's treatment of women in *King John* in 'Anti-Historians: Women's Roles in Shakespeare's Histories', *Theatre Journal*, 37 (1985), 329–44.

essential part of that performance,[17] in 1988 respond to the embarrassment of women which is so large a part of the first three acts of *King John*? The people in it often seem to challenge the audience to declare its presence, and the audience's implied reaction sometimes speaks as eloquently as anything that is actually said upon the stage. This is nowhere more evident than in the scenes which feature the play's embarrassing and embarrassed women.

The first few lines of the opening scene of *King John* show Shakespeare using a technique more familiar from the second scene of *Hamlet*, in which Claudius' smooth official discourse is punctured by a dissenting voice: 'A little more than kin and less than kind' (1.2.65). *King John* opens with the arrival of the French ambassador and the challenge to John to give up his throne in favour of Arthur:

KING JOHN
    Now say, Châtillon, what would France with
    us?
CHÂTILLON
    Thus, after greeting, speaks the King of France,
    In my behaviour, to the majesty –
    The borrowed majesty – of England here.
QUEEN ELEANOR
    A strange beginning: 'borrowed majesty'?
KING JOHN
    Silence, good mother, hear the embassy.

                                           (1.1.1–6)

Châtillon's strange beginning, couched in the formal language of diplomatic challenge, is not half so strange to the audience as Eleanor's intervention protesting against it and John's attempt to quell her protest. The conventional hostile interchange between the representatives of two centres of power is displaced by a new contender for power, the woman. She immediately forces the monarch into a subservient role, that of son, in which he has to plead with her, with the traditional courtesies of the dependent – 'Good mother' – to allow him to carry on with his business, not only as ruler but as independent adult. How is this to be staged? Does Châtillon totally ignore the inter-

ruption as his next speech implies? Or does the actor's mien express any of the astonishment which the audience feels at seeing a man so tied to his mother's apron-strings? Or does the French ambassador acknowledge the reality behind the interruption, which is that to address John is to address Eleanor, and that his next speech must be made to her as much as to John himself?[18] The question is to some extent a feminist one, because the status of Eleanor's intervention has yet to be determined. Is this an example of subversion contained within the discourses of power, the thesis which Greenblatt argues so ably, which then allows authority to control and order apparent threats to that authority? In other words, does Eleanor's attempt to enter the discourse of power between the two states demonstrate the impotence of that attempt? Or is the intervention a *real* subversion of power, whatever that might mean?

One of the problems of analysing theatre in terms of discourses of power which contain their own antitheses is that according to this hypothesis subversion can never really subvert anything at all, and one is left wondering whether there can be a form of protest which truly does undermine authority structures. Surprisingly enough, Eleanor's interruption,

---

17 Stephen Greenblatt, *Shakespearean Negotiations: The Circulation of Social Energy in Renaissance England* (Oxford, 1988), is one of many critics who have emphasized that the theatre is 'the product of collective intentions' and that it 'manifestly addresses its audience as collectivity' (p. 5).

18 In Warner's production the actor playing Châtillon turned slightly after Eleanor's outburst so that his next speech was directed both to John, centre stage, and to Eleanor, who was placed stage right behind him. But although Eleanor's power thus received a modicum of official acknowledgement, her intrusion was not startlingly disruptive of the political *status quo*, because Eleanor herself was somewhat underplayed, while John, finely acted by Nicholas Woodeson, came over as a strong and complex figure whose authority, certainly at this point in the play, was capable of containing challenges to it.

which protests against Châtillon's slur on John's legitimacy as monarch, has the effect not of reinforcing his right to the throne, but, by giving the slur a primal place in everyone's thoughts, of undermining it. The question of legitimacy is summarily removed from the anodyne of diplomatic discourse into an arena which challenges that discourse, despite the fact that what is actually said ought logically to underline rather than undermine John's authority.

Eleanor does not speak again until after Châtillon's exit at line 30, when she breaks out into a flurry of pent up feeling:

QUEEN ELEANOR
    What now, my son? Have I not ever said
    How that ambitious Constance would not cease
    Till she had kindled France and all the world
    Upon the right and party of her son?
    This might have been prevented and made
        whole
    With very easy arguments of love,
    Which now the manage of two kingdoms must
    With fearful-bloody issue arbitrate.
KING JOHN
    Our strong possession and our right for us.
QUEEN ELEANOR (aside to King John)
    Your strong possession much more than your
        right,
    Or else it must go wrong with you and me:
    So much my conscience whispers in your ear,
    Which none but heaven and you and I shall
        hear.   (1.1.31–43)

Here Eleanor not only assumes authority within a man's universe, the right to declare that John has mismanaged his diplomacy and brought on his head a war which could have been avoided, but she also takes on herself the role of divine authority in becoming the secret voice of conscience, of a higher judgement on the actions not only of John but also of herself. Curiously, she seems to feel that the subversive instincts of the divine in challenging their joint power can be contained by her own recognition of that heavenly subversion. The problem is the audience. No one, says Eleanor, will hear this whisper of dissent. As Falstaff

himself says in a different context: 'Nothing confutes me but eyes, and nobody sees me' (1 Henry IV, 5.4.125). But Eleanor's assertion draws the silent audience whose existence she denies into the action of the play, giving it divine authority to judge both her and her world. Ironically, she herself becomes the mouthpiece of the higher authority of heaven, whose presence she secretly recognizes – thus also perhaps secretly acknowledging the presence of the audience – at the very moment in which she disavows its power over herself and her son.

A glance at Shakespeare's adaptation of source material for these opening lines casts light on the realities of Eleanor's power in relation to John. Holinshed declares that at the death of Richard Coeur-de-lion, John travelled in France in order to procure the allegiance of his French subjects in those parts subdued by Richard, and that meanwhile Elianor performed the same office in England. Elianor, remarks Holinshed:

Being bent to prefer hir sonne John, left no stone unturned to establish him in the throne, comparing oftentimes the difference of government betweene a king that is a man, and a king that is but a child. For as John was 32 yeares old, so Arthur duke of Britaine was but a babe to speak of. In the end, winning all the nobilitie wholie unto hir will, and seeing the coast to be cleare on everie side, without any doubt of tempestuous weather likelie to arise, she signified the whole matter unto K. John, who foorthwith framed all his indevours to the accomplishment of his business.

Her motive, claims Holinshed, was not any dislike of Arthur himself but her rivalry with another woman, Constance, his mother: 'For that she saw if he were king, how his mother Constance would looke to beare most rule within the realme of England, till hir sonne should come to lawfull age, to governe of himself.'[19] This account would prompt the

---

[19] Geoffrey Bullough, *Narrative and Dramatic Sources of Shakespeare*, vol. 4 (London and New York, 1975), p. 26.

interpretation that Eleanor's determination to speak on John's behalf at the beginning of Shakespeare's play derives from the fact that she has done the major part of the work in getting him accepted as ruler in his own country. This reading is certainly reinforced if one compares that troublesome play *The Troublesome Raigne of King John* (1591), in which the opening speech is given not to John but to Elinor, who thus has control of the language of official political discourse:

> Barons of *England*, and my noble Lords;
> Though God and Fortune have bereft from us
> Victorious *Richard* scourge of Infidels,
> And clad this Land in stole of dismall hieu:
> Yet give me leave to joy, and joy you all,
> That from this wombe hath sprung a second hope,
> A King that may in rule and vertue both
> Succeede his brother in his Emperie.

John graciously acknowledges both his mother and his nobles and sends for the French Ambassador. Elinor's next speech presupposes the reason for the Embassy:

> Dare lay my hand that *Elinor* can gesse
> Whereto this weightie Embassade doth tend:
> If of my Nephew *Arthur* and his claime,
> Then say my Sonne I have not mist my aime.

When Châtillon enters, the diplomatic interchanges are entirely between him and John, with John adopting the language of disruption – 'I wonder what he means to leave for me' – which in Shakespeare's play is associated with Eleanor's utterances. Elinor herself then directly addresses Châtillon, commending herself to Arthur and charging him that he 'leave his Armes / Whereto his head-strong Mother pricks him so', thus bringing into the open the power-struggle between herself and Constance:

> Her pride we know, and know her for a Dame
> That will not sticke to bring him to his ende,
> So she may bring her self to rule a Realme.[20]

If one assumes, as on the evidence of the opening alone one probably must, that *The Troublesome Raigne* precedes Shakespeare's *King John*,[21] then Shakespeare's version infinitely complicates the source material. The focus of that complexity is the figure of Eleanor herself. In *The Troublesome Raigne* Elinor enjoys parity with or indeed supremacy over John; she speaks as the primal authority in the realm, and his remarks are pointed with the petty defiance of an underling. In this early play, however, the complexity of the relationship between mother and son is totally subsumed in the concentration – prompted by Holinshed's account – on the rivalry between the two women and on Elinor's fear of Constance's seizing of power through the person of her son Arthur. There is no hint in *The Troublesome Raigne* of the competition between Eleanor and John for the centre of the stage, which Shakespeare creates in the first scene and which he would have found only in the subtext of Holinshed's story, where Elianor harangues the English nobles on the 'difference of government betweene a king that is a man, and a king that is but a child'.[22] In Shakespeare's version John himself is forced into the role of mere child ('good mother') by his mother's manifestly unseemly assertion of power: that is, unseemly within the prevailing discourse, which belongs not to her, as in *The Troublesome Raigne*, but to her son (despite the fact that she has done all the work establishing that power). Must feminists then prefer *The Troublesome Raigne*? Well, maybe. And maybe not. For Shakespeare's Eleanor reaches out to the perceptions of the audience in a way which is entirely debarred from Elinor in the earlier play, who remains contained within the power

---

[20] Bullough, *Sources*, vol. 4, pp. 73, 74.

[21] MacD. P. Jackson, 'The Transmission of Shakespeare's Text', in Wells, *The Cambridge Companion*, observes that 'E. A. J. Honigmann's theory that *The Troublesome Reign of John King of England* (1591) ... derives from *King John* has not supplanted the traditional view that Shakespeare was indebted to an anonymous predecessor' (p. 175).

[22] Bullough, *Sources*, vol. 4, p. 26.

structure of which she is a part. Shakespeare's Eleanor challenges that structure by creating first of all an alternative discourse even as she seems to underwrite her son's legitimate claims, but also by proposing an alternative judgement on that legitimacy, because she hears the whisper of heaven which her son is too dull to apprehend. In hearing it she speaks to an audience which registers both the illegitimacy of John's claim and the superior intelligence, moral and political, of his mother.

Eleanor's statements are an embarrassment to her son, but interestingly enough, they also embarrass the audience because it is given the role of divine judge by a character whose disregard of the potency of that Judge and scorn of His values is patent. Hamlet has only to open his mouth, only to appear, for him to be our man, dissociating himself, as we dissociate ourselves, from the political rhetoric of all the other characters on the stage. It is far from obvious that Eleanor is going to be our woman, despite the evident weakness of those whose authority she challenges. If she is, we must apparently align ourselves against heaven and conscience. How difficult that the person who defies those forces should be the only one capable of defining them. If there is no choice between the discourse of diplomacy with its patent hypocrisies, and the subversion of it, with its deliberate disregard of conscience and integrity, how is the audience to find its own space in language in which to relate to its knowledge of the play world and the people in it?

Having created the question, the scene immediately offers a possible answer in the person of a real bastard,[23] a man ready to shame his own mother in public. A surprising ally, indeed: remember the fate meted out to Joan of Arc for such perfidy to parental honour. Even Eleanor is shocked when Philip of Falconbridge doubts that he and his brother own the same father:

> Out on thee, rude man! Thou dost shame thy
> mother

And wound her honour with this diffidence.
>
> (1.1.64–5)

The Bastard protests that the suit against his legitimacy is his brother's, not his; but this hardly bears investigation, as in his next speech he exclaims:

> Compare our faces and be judge yourself.
> If old Sir Robert did beget us both
> And were our father, and this son like him,
> O old Sir Robert, father, on my knee
> I give heaven thanks I was not like to thee.
>
> (1.1.79–83)

Eleanor's aristocratic nose sniffs the air:

> He hath a trick of Cœur-de-lion's face;
> The accent of his tongue affecteth him.
> Do you not read some tokens of my son
> In the large composition of this man?
>
> (1.1.85–8)

Blood will out, is the clear message, even if it means blushes all round. Eleanor and the Bastard are delighted with each other. He is to be her man, and she is to be his grandam. As the legitimate Robert and the court leave the stage the Bastard speeds them on their way with an irreverent riposte:

> Brother, adieu. Good fortune come to thee,
> For thou wast got i'th' way of honesty.
>
> (1.1.180–1)

There is no mistaking the contemptuous tone with which the word 'honesty' – meaning chastity within marriage – is uttered. Another blow to heaven. We have found our man, but he does not appear to be on the side of the angels any more than Eleanor is, and the long soliloquy in which he rejoices in his new fortunes: 'Well, now can I make any Joan a lady' (1.1.184), culminates in a doctrine of unashamed self-interest:

---

23 R. L. Smallwood, 'Shakespeare's Use of History', in Wells, *The Cambridge Companion*, observes: 'The role of the Bastard in *King John*, altogether unhistorical, acts rather as the audience's window on the events of history' (p. 155).

But this is worshipful society,
And fits the mounting spirit like myself;
For he is but a bastard to the time
That doth not smack of observation.

(1.1.205–8)

The practice of deceit 'shall strew the footsteps of my rising' (1.1.216). Meanwhile, he espies, with a swift transition worthy of *The Faerie Queene*, a damsel in distress:

What woman-post is this? Hath she no husband
That will take pains to blow a horn before her?

(1.1.218–19)

Disconcertingly late, he recognizes the author of his being: 'O me, 'tis my mother!' (1.1.220). This good lady is in a right royal state of rage:

LADY FALCONBRIDGE
Where is that slave thy brother? Where is he
That holds in chase mine honour up and down?
BASTARD
My brother Robert, old Sir Robert's son?
Colbrand the Giant, that same mighty man?
Is it Sir Robert's son that you seek so?
LADY FALCONBRIDGE
Sir Robert's son, ay, thou unreverent boy,
Sir Robert's son. Why scorn'st thou at Sir
    Robert?
He is Sir Robert's son, and so art thou.
BASTARD
James Gurney, wilt thou give us leave awhile?

(1.1.222–30)

The Bastard dismisses the company so as not to embarrass his mother. The audience is not so easily dismissed, and it remains as silent but enthralled witness to their interchanges. He begs Lady Falconbridge to admit that he is none of Sir Robert's:

We know his handiwork. Therefore, good
    mother,
To whom am I beholden for these limbs?
Sir Robert never holp to make this leg.

(1.1.238–40)

But his mother is by no means easily persuaded to give up her honour. It is only when she finds that he has already denied his Falconbridge inheritance that she comes clean, so to speak:

LADY FALCONBRIDGE
Hast thou denied thyself a Falconbridge?
BASTARD
As faithfully as I deny the devil.
LADY FALCONBRIDGE
King Richard Cœur-de-lion was thy father.
By long and vehement suit I was seduced
To make room for him in my husband's bed.
Heaven lay not my transgression to my charge!
Thou art the issue of my dear offence,
Which was so strongly urged past my defence.
BASTARD
Now by this light, were I to get again,
Madam, I would not wish a better father.
Some sins do bear their privilege on earth,
And so doth yours ...
                    Ay, my mother,
With all my heart I thank thee for my father.
Who lives and dares but say thou didst not well
When I was got, I'll send his soul to hell.

(1.1.251–62, 269–72)

With a glare over his shoulder at the befuddled audience, the Bastard escorts his mother from the stage. Yet the moment which might have been the most embarrassing for everyone, when a woman is called to confess her infidelity in public – think of Hermione, think of Desdemona's shrinking from the word whore, think of dear Lucrece seizing up the dagger – is the first moment of genuine emotional force in the whole play. In invoking Heaven to her aid Lady Falconbridge calls more on the human than the divine, urging her child not to lay her sin to her charge. The Bastard proves his royalty in a championing of Una, *truth*, more startling than any offered by Spenser's Redcrosse Knight. And the audience, dazed by its own acquiescence in unconventionality, is forced to honour her – and does so freely – for an act which has created the son who exemplifies a new world. Without the woman's perfidy neither he nor it could have been born. If Eleanor dominates the action of the opening part of the scene, Lady Falconbridge, a real sinner in a society where everyone pretends to virtue, both embarrasses the world of the play and in a literal sense has created, in the person of the Bastard, its potential for action.

The part of Lady Falconbridge is such a small one and so little discussed that it seems worth pausing to consider it further. The Falconbridge story appears in *The Troublesome Raigne*, but in none of Shakespeare's historical sources.[24] The story of the Bastard of Orléans rejecting his legitimate kindred in favour of the nobility of the Duke of Orléans is told in Hall's *The Union of the Two Noble and Illustre Famelies of Lancastre and York* (1548),[25] but the mother herself plays no part in the scene Hall describes. With Lady Falconbridge and the Bastard, Shakespeare completed the triad of mothers and sons in *King John*: Eleanor with the legitimate John whose claim to the throne is illegitimate, as she herself knows; Constance whose son Arthur's claim is the best in terms of lineage but who had been disinherited by Richard Cœur-de-lion on his death-bed;[26] and now the unknown Lady Falconbridge. This lady disappears from the play as swiftly as she entered it to acknowledge to her own son – whom the audience must be tempted to take to its heart as the true hero of the play – that he really is a bastard and she herself no better than she should be. Yet in that brief interchange a new language is born, and a new range of feeling is released. Here at last is a language of honesty, from a woman to a man, which is not related to chastity. Lady Falconbridge's short confession liberates warmth and love into the frigid world of this play:

> Heauen lay not my transgression to my charge,
> That art the issue of my deere offence
> Which was so strongly vrgd past my defence.
> (TLN 269–71; 1.1.256–8)[27]

The First Folio reading allows a felicitous ambiguity to accompany the placing of the word 'Heauen', which calls into the audience's consciousness Eleanor's previous use of the word: 'So much my conscience whispers in your ear, / Which none but heaven and you and I shall hear' (1.1.42–3). The heaven

Eleanor invokes is distant and unavailing. In Lady Falconbridge's mouth the word is a strong asseveration, both oath and supplication, not to higher powers and arbiters of human behaviour, but to the son who stands as living witness to her sin, that he should not blame her for his being. But it is also simultaneously a plea to heaven itself to extenuate the fault, the issue of it being so proper. How wildly different those words sound when associated with Gloucester and his bastard son. Falconbridge's reply to this plea is both tender and courteous. This is no Hamlet berating his mother for not being able to control her own

---

[24] Honigmann, who argues that *The Troublesome Raigne* follows rather than precedes Shakespeare's *King John*, thought that Shakespeare invented the Falconbridge story, and lists the parallels in Shakespeare's other plays: see new Arden edition of *King John*, pp. xxii–xxv. A. R. Braunmuller discusses the Bastard's role in relation to the 'factual' and the 'fictive' in the play in '*King John* and Historiography', *ELH*, 55 (1988), 309–65; pp. 312–16.

[25] Bullough, *Sources*, vol. 4, pp. 54–5.

[26] Marie Axton, *The Queen's Two Bodies: Drama and the Elizabethan Succession* (London, 1977), p. ix, points out that in the view of some Elizabethans, Arthur would have been disqualified for the English crown through his French connections.

[27] In the First Folio (the first published edition of the play) there is no punctuation after 'Heauen' (TLN 269). Most editors now follow Knight's emendation of adding an exclamation mark (or, as in Honigmann's new Arden edition, a comma) to direct and accentuate the oath. The Oxford editor, John Jowett, restores the Folio reading in removing the added punctuation mark after 'Heaven', but at the end of the line, where the Folio has only a comma, he places an exclamation mark, so that the first line quoted above becomes a separate clause. For the second line he adopts the F4 reading of 'Thou' instead of 'That', thus creating another new clause:
> Heaven lay not my transgression to my charge!
> Thou art the issue of my dear offence,
> Which was so strongly urged past my defence.
> (1.1.256–8)
The first line becomes a simple invocation to the Almighty and the second a statement of the obvious; that the Bastard is the issue of his mother's offence. But these changes obscure the real subtlety of the lines.

sexuality; how touchingly the Bastard alights on the salutation for a great lady whose world would have called her the word Desdemona could not utter: '*Madam, I would not wish a better father*' (my italics). Charles Kemble's performance is recalled by Mrs Cowden Clarke: 'In the scene with his mother ... his manly tenderness, his filial coaxing way of speaking and putting his arm round her as he thanks her for having made Richard Coeur de Lion his father, was something to be grateful for having witnessed.'[28]

It must be said that not all audiences or all societies were grateful for having witnessed this scene. In Cibber's adaptation of 1745 the whole of Shakespeare's first act was cut, with loss of this episode as well as of the entire character of Eleanor and the comedy of the Bastard's encounter with Austria.[29] Sprague records that the *Monthly Mirror* which took exception to the Billingsgate scene protested strongly against John Philip Kemble's restoration of the Falconbridge episode following its excision from Dr Valpy's adaptation, declaring that its 'indecencies ... render it almost infamous for a modest family to be present at the performance' (February 1804). The *Dramatic Magazine* in January 1831 claimed that 'the scene between Falconbridge and his mother would have been "hooted off the stage" had the author not been Shakespeare'. In the late nineteenth century Charles Flower expunged the interchanges between the Bastard and his mother from the Memorial Theatre Edition, declaring that the encounter was 'unnecessary as well as disagreeable'.[30] Even more surprisingly, Odell, describing in 1920 Cibber's version of the play, refers himself to the 'unpleasing matter of the washing of the Falconbridge family linen'.[31] Ellen Terry remarked truly: 'Has there ever been a dramatist, I wonder, whose parts admit of as many different interpretations as do Shakespeare's? There lies his immortality as an acting force. For times change, and parts have to be acted differently for different generations.'[32] A late

twentieth-century audience can feel, at the end of Act 1 of *King John*, suddenly at home in the Shakespearian world, having heard in Lady Falconbridge's speech and her son's response to it the register of real emotion. The emotion is, surprisingly enough, one which releases sexual energy, that energy which surrounds the figure of the Bastard until he becomes John's man in Act 4.

The part of Lady Falconbridge was probably doubled in Shakespeare's theatre – as it may have been in later productions – with that of Blanche.[33] The fearful frigidity of the political

---

[28] Quoted in Sprague, *Shakespeare and the Actors*, p. 109. In Deborah Warner's 1988 production Lady Falconbridge was hoydenish, and the moment consequently comic rather than poignant.

[29] George C. D. Odell, *Shakespeare – From Betterton to Irving*, 2 vols. (New York and London, 1920), vol. 1, p. 349.

[30] Sprague, *Shakespeare's Histories*, p. 14.

[31] Odell, *Shakespeare – From Betterton to Irving*, vol. 1, p. 349.

[32] Terry, *The Story of my Life*, p. 67.

[33] Bentley, *The Profession of Player in Shakespeare's Time 1590–1642*, pp. 228–33, 242, remarks on the 'universal doubling' in Shakespeare's theatre. William Ringler, Jr, 'The Number of Actors in Shakespeare's Early Plays', in Gerald Eades Bentley, ed., *The Seventeenth-Century Stage* (Chicago and London, 1968), p. 126, argues that 'between 1594 and 1599, Shakespeare *never* wrote a play for more than 16 actors including mutes, [and] that the composition of his company during that period appears to have remained stable with 12 adults and 4 boys'. He believes that *King John* would have required in all fourteen actors (p. 126n). Eleanor, Constance, Lady Falconbridge, Blanche, Arthur, and Prince Henry would have been boys' parts. Since proposing the doubling of Lady Falconbridge and Blanche, I have found the same suggestion in the pioneer work of Julia Engelen, 'Die Schauspielen-Ökonomie in Shakespeares Dramen', *Shakespeare Jahrbuch*, 62 (Leipzig, 1926), 36–97; pp. 94–5. Engelen believes that Prince Henry would have been doubled with Prince Arthur. Her comprehensive survey of doubling in Shakespeare's plays was completed in a second article in the *Shakespeare Jahrbuch*, 63 (Leipzig, 1927), 75–158. However, Engelen's suggestion that *King John* could have been staged with a total of eleven actors, four of whom were boys, seems to me less convincing than Ringler's more moderate fourteen.

marriage with Louis, Blanche's attempts to wrest an expression of love from him, and her own naïve claims to love a man offered her in the name of diplomacy[34] form an amazing contrast with this earlier interchange. Blanche's agonies are as embarrassing to the audience as Octavia's are in *Antony and Cleopatra*, in which the audience is deeply ashamed of its own longing to escape from this virtuous Roman lady and boot it back to Egypt with Antony. Blanche is, in her own words, dismembered by the men on the stage:

> The sun's o'er cast with blood; fair day, adieu!
> Which is the side that I must go withal?
> I am with both, each army hath a hand,
> And in their rage, I having hold of both,
> They whirl asunder and dismember me.
>
> (3.1.252–6)

While the audience pities her they are also alienated from her suffering because she speaks a language which lies in the level of her own dreams. In that first scene the warmth which created the Bastard in the seduction of his mother by Richard Cœur-de-lion is recreated in her son's wooing her to confess and affirm the act which has made him what he is. Through this interchange the audience can discover its own centre of gravity, and for the next two acts this rests in the person of the Bastard, the one genuine being on stage. But where does that leave Constance and Arthur?

The answer must be that they are both located deep in the heart of that embarrassment which the play is so adept at arousing both on stage and in the auditorium. Act 2 opens with King Philip of France, Louis the Dauphin, and Limoges Duke of Austria all paying court to Arthur, whose responses sound as pathetically inopportune as Blanche's: 'I give you welcome with a powerless hand, / But with a heart full of unstainèd love' (2.1.15–16). The word 'unstainèd' strikes a peculiar note coming so soon after the discovery of that welcome stain on Lady Falconbridge's honour, and the audience is too new to its revelation of alternative

values, Bastard as hero, seduction as salvation, to readjust to the concept of unstainèd love without a painful sense of incongruity. This discomfort is aggravated by an awareness of the blatant hypocrisies of the men who surround Arthur and of his powerlessness in an environment where power is everything and purity nothing at all. Constance's first speech of gratitude to Austria distances the audience: the presage of disaster hangs on her lips even while she utters her gratitude:

CONSTANCE
> O, take his mother's thanks, a widow's thanks,
> Till your strong hand shall help to give him strength
> To make a more requital to your love.

AUSTRIA
> The peace of heaven is theirs that lift their swords
> In such a just and charitable war.   (2.1.32–6)

The word 'heaven' is again replete with irony. Then follows an extraordinary replay of the opening scene. Enter Châtillon, with bad news from England. King John is in arms at the behest of his mother: 'With him along is come the Mother-Queen, / An Ate stirring him to blood and strife' (2.1.62–3). The Ambassador had apparently noticed who held the reins in John's kingdom. The news is barely given before the English forces enter, complete with Eleanor, Blanche, and the Bastard. John's claim to France is brief and well rehearsed, and his mother does not interrupt him. Philip retorts with a long accusation of John's illegitimacy:

> But thou from loving England art so far
> That thou hast underwrought his lawful king,
> Cut off the sequence of posterity,
> Outfacèd infant state, and done a rape
> Upon the maiden virtue of the crown.
>
> (2.1.94–8)

---

[34] In Warner's 1988 production, Ralph Fiennes delivered Louis's stylized Petrarchan wooing speech with a chilling admixture of cynicism and affectation.

It seems impossible to escape the seduction image,[35] and the child Arthur is brought forward as proof of the illegitimacy of John's claim:

Look here upon thy brother Geoffrey's face.
These eyes, these brows, were moulded out of
his.   (2.1.99–100)

Philip calls on heaven to witness his right to guard Arthur, and at this point another voice enters the dialogue: 'Who is it thou dost call usurper, France?' The answer is not from France, but from another embattled female voice: 'Let me make answer: thy usurping son' (2.1.120–1). And off they go, Eleanor and Constance, into the biggest slanging match Shakespeare ever wrote for women. The smooth blank verse is as much in pieces as the dignity of the participants, and in there at the centre, urging on the two women, is the Bastard. The other men are left gawping:

AUSTRIA
What cracker is this same that deafs our ears
With this abundance of superfluous breath? –
King Philip, determine what we shall do
straight.
[KING PHILIP]
Women and fools, break off your conference. –
                              (2.1.147–50)[36]

Easier said than done, however, and where Austria and France had previously made Arthur the centre of their discourse, Eleanor and Constance now focus on the child. Arthur tries to silence Constance just as John had tried to silence Eleanor earlier in the play:

Good my mother, peace.
I would that I were low laid in my grave.
I am not worth this coil that's made for me.
                              (2.1.163–5)

What is one to make of it? Male critic: appalling women, must be cut. Women in audience: cathartic moment, go it, Constance. But in Shakespeare's theatre the most remarkable thing about the scene is the brilliant way it is conceived for the talents not of women but of boys.

In this scene Shakespeare shows the boy actor in his element in a fine old scrap with another boy actor, and surely the truth about the casting of Arthur as a girl in later productions recognizes along the pulse the boy actor's presence in the encounters between Eleanor and Constance, which make Arthur into an archetypal 'feminine' figure[37] in the

---

[35] Ralph Berry, *The Shakespearean Metaphor* (London, 1978), pp. 26–36, discusses the relation between sexual and political legitimacy in the play.

[36] Honigmann in the new Arden edition gives the last line of Austria's speech – which in the Folio reads 'King Lewis' – to Philip, assuming 'King' as speech prefix: 'Lewis, determine what we shall do straight.' Lewis responds, as in the Folio: 'Women and fools, break off your conference.' Lewis's next line in the Folio, 'King *Iohn*, this is the very summe of all', reverts to Philip in Honigmann's edition; Jowett, in the Complete Oxford edition, gives both lines to Philip (see Honigmann's Arden edition, pp. xxiv–xxv, for a full discussion of this textual crux). Honigmann's reading is appealing in the present context because all three men are then enlisted in an attempt to silence the two women and the Bastard (here cast as a professional fool).

[37] Honigmann, in his Arden edition, p. 171, points out that Arthur in Shakespeare's play is much more of a child than in either Holinshed or *The Troublesome Raigne*, where he is about sixteen. It was a pity that in Warner's production Arthur's voice had already broken, as the 'feminine' character of the part demands an unbroken voice. That Arthur is, in the modern theatre, an exacting part for the age of boy whose voice would still be unbroken is no doubt another reason why the part came to be played by a girl. When Ellen Terry played Arthur in 1858 she was eleven years old (Nina Auerbach, *Ellen Terry, Player in Her Time* (London, 1987), pp. 31, 42); English law requires in 1988 that a child performer must be at least twelve. The voices of Shakespeare's boy actors certainly broke much later than is now customary, so that boys playing demanding parts, such as Arthur's, could have seemed very young without necessarily being so. Nevertheless, the difficulty of finding in the modern period a boy with an unbroken voice skilled enough to act Arthur – or indeed any of Shakespeare's juvenile parts, which are more often than not travestied by child actors on the twentieth-century stage – demonstrates yet again the vast gap which separates children and youths in our culture from the highly trained boys of Shakespeare's theatre.

way that poor Blanche is to be later in the scene. It would be possible to argue that Shakespeare had two major sources of worry in his utilizing of the boy actor: one, that he would ruin the scene with overacting, and two, that he would be as dumb as a post. In *King John* Shakespeare gave the boy actors parts in which they might overact to their heart's content, stealing the stage from their betters, who are forced to stand around wondering how to quell them.[38] The problem must have been to reconcile Arthur to playing such a wet part, and Shakespeare gave the boy as a reward the finest dramatic scene in the play, with Hubert. For the boy who played Blanche, equally disconsolate under a thankless role, he dreamed up the real heroine of the whole piece, Lady Falconbridge, who upturns the entire world of conventional morality and gets away with it rather better than Anne Boleyn.[39] On the boys' side of total theatrical subversion he placed one man, another disrupter of official discourse, as he was also of official lineage, the Bastard himself: 'Zounds! I was never so bethumped with words / Since I first called my brother's father Dad' (2.1.467–8). The climax of 2.1 shows the Bastard rededicating himself to the ways of the world:

> Since kings break faith upon commodity,
> Gain, be my lord, for I will worship thee.
>
> (2.1.598–9)

But this astonishing scene is followed by one as different in tone as Lady Falconbridge's speeches to her son are from Eleanor's to John. Constance, from the eye-scratching with Eleanor, is suddenly transformed into the great tragic figure of Mrs Siddons's performances:

> Gone to be married? Gone to swear a peace?
> False blood to false blood joined! Gone to be
>   friends?
> Shall Louis have Blanche, and Blanche those
>   provinces?
> It is not so, thou hast misspoke, misheard.

> Be well advised, tell o'er thy tale again.
> It cannot be, thou dost but say 'tis so.
>
> (2.2.1–6)[40]

Once again the audience is caught totally on the hop and experiences much the same emotions as Mrs Bennet on hearing that Elizabeth is to marry Darcy: 'Oh, my dear Lizzy! pray apologise for my having disliked him so much before.' The ranting boy is suddenly one of us, 'A woman naturally born to fears' (2.2.15), and even her child a source of irritation in his calm beholding of sufferings whose implications he is too inexperienced to understand: 'I do beseech you, madam, be content' (2.2.42). The word 'madam', so chill and so unchildlike, recalls the warmth with which the Bastard had used the same word to his mother. Constance, deprived of everything, is suddenly everything in the world of the play: 'Here is my throne; bid kings come bow to it' (2.2.74).

That power is by no means dissipated in Act 3, which shows Constance in the same relation to official discourse as Eleanor was in Act 1 and the Bastard in Act 2. Philip begins by blessing the wedding of Blanche and Louis:

> The yearly course that brings this day about
> Shall never see it but a holy day.

---

38 Steven R. Smith, 'The London Apprentices as Seventeenth-Century Adolescents', *Past and Present*, 61 (1973), 149–61, discusses the existence of a corporate sense of identity amongst adolescent apprentices in London in the early to mid-seventeenth century, reinforcing some of the conclusions about the challenging of authority by adolescents in the Renaissance period drawn by Natalie Zemon Davis in 'The Reasons of Misrule: Youth Groups and Charivaris in Sixteenth-century France', *Past and Present*, 50 (1971), 40–75. While neither writer deals with the boy actor, the work of both stimulates further enquiry into the relation between the boy apprentices and adult actors in Shakespeare's company.

39 Axton, *The Queen's Two Bodies*, pp. 108–11, discusses the importance of *King John* as a play about the succession of Elizabeth I, and there is probably more to be said on this subject.

40 In Warner's 1988 production this speech was delivered by Susan Engel in tones of laughing disbelief.

CONSTANCE (*rising*)

> A wicked day, and not a holy day! (3.1.7–9)

Her attack on Austria brings the audience (or at least, the women in the audience) totally to her side:

> Thou little valiant, great in villainy;
> Thou ever strong upon the stronger side . . .
> Thou wear a lion's hide! Doff it, for shame,
> And hang a calf's-skin on those recreant limbs.
> AUSTRIA
> O, that a man should speak those words to me!
> BASTARD
> And hang a calf's-skin on those recreant limbs.
> AUSTRIA
> Thou dar'st not say so, villain, for thy life.
> BASTARD
> And hang a calf's-skin on those recreant limbs.
> KING JOHN (*to the Bastard*)
> We like not this. Thou dost forget thyself.
>
> (3.1.42–3, 54–60)

There spoke our man, smoking out the pretended chivalry of the male world. And there spoke Eleanor's little John, desperately trying to assume a royalty which really belongs to his mother. And there spoke a woman who has at last plumbed the depths of what the male world has to offer her and found it a bottomless well of treacle: 'Thou ever strong upon the stronger side' (3.1.43). At this moment when the entire stage is energized, enter the representative of the Church of Rome to announce that the marriage is off. Eleanor is going to find a backer after all: has Heaven finally entered on her side? How embarrassing for that original Elizabethan Protestant audience, assembled for a play about the first English king on record as defying the authority of the Pope, that the Almighty (or should one say Shakespeare?) should choose for Constance's champion a representative of the Church of Rome. John, to add to the confusion, is now getting off a good deal about meddling priests:

> Yet I alone, alone do me oppose
> Against the Pope, and count his friends my
>   foes. (3.1.96–7)

The climax of what is dignified by the name of debate is Pandulph's speech: 'All form is formless, order orderless, / Save what is opposite to England's love' (3.1.179–80), and the rhetorical figure of polyptoton, the changing of forms, is wonderfully suited to the shifting conditions of the world Pandulph describes and which we as audience observe with increasing bafflement. The whole thing begins to sound more like *Love's Labour's Lost* than a momentous passage in British history; as Pandulph remarks:

> It is religion that doth make vows kept;
> But thou hast sworn against religion.
>
> (3.1.205–6)

It is hardly surprising that later on in the act the Roman prelate should declare to Louis: 'How green you are, and fresh in this old world' (3.4.145). The play makes us all look green. At the end of Act 3 we assent almost languidly to Louis's closing words: 'Strong reasons makes strange actions' (3.4.182), and wonder how long our dramatist, Constance, Eleanor, Arthur, Blanche, the Bastard or anyone else can keep it up.

The greatest peculiarity of all is that they make no attempt to keep it up. With the great grief speech – 'Grief fills the room up of my absent child' (3.4.93) – Constance's part is played. Eleanor is to be snuffed out in France – 'What, Mother dead?' (4.2.127) – Arthur throws himself off the battlements, John is poisoned, and the Bastard becomes a yes-man. Some would say, discovers integrity; others, that England has emerged as hero. But what is really the case is that the play goes to pieces once the women leave the stage, or, once the boys leave it, and whether one thinks of a theatre peopled by boy actors, or by girls playing Arthur, that seems to include the scene between Arthur and Hubert. Nevertheless in that scene a kind of death-wish[41] begins to

---

[41] This seems to me to be true even though Prince Henry is present in the final scene to witness his father's death

pervade the play, and it never recovers the energy associated with the new world of the Bastard and the new generation: the boys. Or, in our terms, and certainly in Elizabethan terms, the women. For what did the Elizabethans have to comfort them once they allowed Gloriana to leave the great stage she had dominated so long? Shakespeare seems to lose interest in the official world once it is no longer challenged by the subversive discourses of that triad of mothers and once the Bastard has been annexed into official discourse. And if one says that the subversiveness was always contained within authority and was a part of its maintenance, then one must also say that the most subversive thing of all occurs when that subversion is removed, because without it the hollowness of male power structures can only bore, confuse, and embarrass the reluctant witnesses of them.

and receive the allegiance of his nobles. Henry remains a choric figure whose speeches comment on mortality:

Even so must I run on, and even so stop.
What surety of the world, what hope, what stay,
When this was now a king and now is clay?

(5.7.67–9)

GOLDING'S OVID, SHAKESPEARE'S 'SMALL LATIN', AND THE REAL OBJECT OF MOCKERY IN 'PYRAMUS AND THISBE'

ANTHONY BRIAN TAYLOR

I

In an influential article some years ago on Shakespeare's method in 'Pyramus and Thisbe', Kenneth Muir claimed it was the playwright's purpose to mock earlier Elizabethan writers who had treated the story awkwardly and clumsily.[1] Muir saw Thomas Mouffet as Shakespeare's main quarry, but prominent among the other writers to whom he referred was Arthur Golding. Since Muir wrote, editors of *A Midsummer Night's Dream*, sceptical about Mouffet's part in the proceedings, have increasingly tended to read the burlesque as a parody of Golding's translation:[2] R. A. Foakes in his New Cambridge edition, for example, is convinced that it is based on 'the story as told in Golding',[3] and Harold Brooks, the Arden editor of the play, also has no doubt that '"Pyramus and Thisbe" is patently from Golding's version in his translation of Ovid's *Metamorphoses*.'[4]

Yet there is reason for unease with this situation. Although constantly referred to incidentally by editors and critics, Shakespeare's use of Golding has never received specific attention and is itself somewhat problematic.[5] Neither the extent nor the precise nature of the debt to the translator has ever been accurately gauged, a point emphasized recently by the case of *Titus Andronicus*.[6] The background to Shakespeare's use of the translation is obscure, the circumstances in which he first read it continuing to be befogged in some quarters by the 'myth' that it

1. 'Pyramus and Thisbe: A Study in Shakespeare's Method', *Shakespeare Quarterly*, 5 (1954), 141–53.
2. In 'Pyramus and Thisbe: Shakespeare's Debt to Moffet Cancelled', *Review of English Studies*, NS 32 (1981), 296–301, Katherine Duncan-Jones convincingly argues that Mouffet is not involved at all.
3. Cambridge, 1984, p. 10.
4. London, 1979; reprinted with corrections, 1983, p. lix.
5. There have been no studies of Shakespeare's use of Golding, only incidental examinations in discussions of his general use of Ovid such as that by T. W. Baldwin, *Shakspere's Small Latine and Lesse Greeke*, 2 vols. (Urbana, Illinois, 1950), vol. 2, pp. 417–55, J. A. K. Thomson, *Shakespeare and the Classics* (London, 1952), pp. 35ff., and J. Dover Wilson, 'Shakespeare's "Small Latin" – How Much?', *Shakespeare Survey 10* (1957), 12–26.

   There have been only two brief studies of Golding's translation *per se*: 'Golding's Ovid', by Gordon Braden, in *The Classics and English Renaissance Poetry: Three Case Studies* (New Haven, 1978), pp. 1–52, and the Introduction to *Ovid's Metamorphoses: The Arthur Golding Translation 1567* (New York, 1965), by the volume's editor, J. F. Nims, pp. xiii–xxxv. Quotation from Golding is from *The xv. Bookes of P. Ovidius Naso, entytuled Metamorphosis* (London, 1567), ed. W. H. D. Rouse (London, 1904, reprinted London, 1961).
6. It has always been assumed that *Titus* contained no debt to Golding. But evidence has now come to light that Shakespeare used the translation for the story from Ovid's poem that was one of his main sources, that he took from it the play's dominant image of the tiger, that he echoed it consistently in incidental references to myth, and that Golding is a significant influence on the concept of metamorphosis which is at the heart of the play. (See my 'Golding's Translation of *Metamorphoses* as Source for *Titus Andronicus*', *Notes and Queries*, 233 (1988), 449–51; 'Golding's *Metamorphoses* and *Titus Andronicus*', *Notes and Queries*, 223 (1978), 117–20; 'Shakespeare, Studley, and Golding', *Review of English Studies*, 39 (1988), 522–7; and my forthcoming book, *Shakespeare's Ovid and Arthur Golding*.)

was used in the Elizabethan grammar school.[7] And the question of Shakespeare's attitude to Golding is a particular cause for concern.

Influential modern scholars see Golding's translation as a second-rate, stop-gap work which Shakespeare did not like but was forced to use because of his 'small Latin'.[8] T. W. Baldwin speaks of it, for example, as 'a necessary evil in the background of Shakespeare';[9] Dover Wilson, alluding to Ezra Pound's eccentric proclamation of it as the most beautiful book in the language, is confident that if Pound 'admires Golding's verse: I am very sure Shakespeare, a different kind of poet, did not';[10] and J. A. K. Thomson writes of Shakespeare's use of it in exasperation,

I ask this question: how could a man, who could read Ovid's Latin with ease and pleasure, bear to read Golding instead?[11]

But the Elizabethans took a very different view. Shakespeare's contemporaries used Golding whether they were able to read the original or not.[12] As we now know, Spenser,

Yet writers like Shakespeare and Marlowe, who knew Golding well, give no sign of having known Phaer when using heavily Vergilian material.

Assumptions about the possible use of Golding's Ovid, which its expansive, paraphrastic nature makes totally unsuitable for the close work required in the grammar-school classroom, are based on a single recommendation in a work written in 1622 by John Brinsley, *A Consolation for Our Grammar Schooles* (p. 64).

However, Brinsley himself shows in an earlier work, *Ludus Literarius*, that the use of translations such as Golding's was regarded as bad practice; they were not allowed into their schools by the 'best and wisest' teachers (p. 115), were not used by average teachers who are represented in this work by Spoudaeus (p. 91), and were widely regarded as unsuitable for use in school (pp. 115–16). (In *A Consolation for Our Grammar Schooles*, he remarks that they were 'generally in disgrace' in schools (p. 45).) He recommends them only as part of an advanced stage of a careful system built upon his 'grammaticall translations', which are nicely geared to the needs of the pupils (see, for example, *Ludus Literarius*, pp. 89–125).

Quotations are from *Ludus Literarius: or, The Grammar Schoole* (1612), ed. E. T. Campagnac (London, 1917), and from *A Consolation for Our Grammar Schooles* (1622), reprinted in *The English Experience*, vol. 203 (New York, 1969).

[8] From Ben Jonson's 'To the memory of my beloved', first printed among the preliminaries of the Shakespeare First Folio; it appears in the Complete Oxford Shakespeare among the 'Commendatory Poems and Prefaces (1599–1640)', p. xliii, line 31.

[9] T. W. Baldwin, review of *Ovid's Metamorphoses: The Arthur Golding Translation 1567*, ed. J. F. Nims (New York, 1965), *Journal of English and Germanic Philology*, 66 (1967), 125.

[10] Dover Wilson, 'Shakespeare's "Small Latin" – How Much?', p. 18.

[11] Thomson, *Shakespeare and the Classics*, p. 154.

[12] We know, of course, that Shakespeare used Latin texts, but that like other Elizabethan writers, such as Marlowe and Spenser, he also used contemporary translations; for *Metamorphoses*, for instance, he used the original or Golding or, upon occasion, the partial translation of Ovid's poem by Abraham Fraunce in *Amintas Dale* (London, 1592; STC 11341). In his case, however, a comparative lack of facility in reading Latin probably accentuated the use of a favoured translation like Golding.

For examples of Shakespeare's use of Fraunce, see 'O brave new world: Abraham Fraunce and *The Tempest*', *English Language Notes*, 23 (1986), 18–24, and 'Two Notes on Shakespeare and the Translators', *Review of English Studies*, NS 38 (1987), 523–6.

---

[7] Nims, the only editor of Golding's translation in recent times, states in his Introduction that 'Shakespeare quite possibly used Golding in the Stratford school along with the Latin' (p. xx). In 'Ovid in the Sixteenth Century' (*Ovid*, ed. J. W. Binns (London, 1973), pp. 210–42), Caroline Jameson also states that, in view of the fact that 'the use of translations, especially versified ones was not frowned on for school use ... it is quite possible that major translations such as Golding's, Turbervile's and Churchyard's became interwoven with the original in the pupil's mind' (p. 213), and later that 'if translations such as Golding's were used as an aid to study, it would be most likely that Shakespeare used, and remembered, Golding and Ovid together as a composite source' (p. 217).

Such an hypothesis throws up anomalies large and small. There is the heavy use of Golding by Elizabethan writers who were too old to have possibly used him in school, such as George Gascoigne, Barnabe Riche, Lodowicke Loyd, and, above all, Edmund Spenser. If Golding was used in grammar schools, then Phaer's *Aeneid* would have most certainly also been used, forming with the original, like Golding and Ovid's poem, another 'composite source' in any pupil's mind.

Gabriel Harvey, Marlowe, George Peele, and others who were university men and whose general competence in Latin is beyond question, not only could 'bear' to read Golding but also, as the borrowings in their work show, found doing so an impressive experience.[13]

In fact, far from being a second-rate, stop-gap work, Golding's Ovid was highly regarded by the Elizabethans. Consider the excitement at the universities and Inns of Court at its first appearance. Published in partial form in 1565,[14] it was immediately hailed at Cambridge as a 'thoondrynge' work,[15] and such was the enthusiasm of one young student of Trinity College for this new translation of Ovid that he incorporated favourite moments from it into his translations of Seneca.[16] It caused such a stir in London that before 1565 had drawn to a close a young member of the Middle Temple tried to steal some of Golding's glory by hurriedly and rather dishonestly publishing a heavily imitative translation of a fragment of *Metamorphoses*.[17] And Golding continued to be popular reading with the young Elizabethan intelligentsia in the years that followed. In the seventies at Oxford when William Gager, the Latin dramatist, praised English translators in a poem to George Peele, only Golding was singled out by name;[18] at Cambridge, the translation was being read by Gabriel Harvey, who was later to rate Golding among the 'excellent and singular good Poets in this our age';[19] and it was almost certainly during his time at Pembroke Hall (1569–77) that Edmund Spenser, who is second only to Shakespeare in his use of the translation, first read the work.[20] Nor was enthusiasm confined to young men at the universities and Inns of Court. Critics who took stock of the Elizabethan poetic scene had nothing but praise for the work. George Puttenham applauded Golding, praising the translator of Ovid for 'very faithfully answering the authors intent'.[21] And William Webbe, who was of the opinion that it 'beautified' the English language with its 'majesty' and

'grace', thought Golding's Ovid a work for which 'our Country hath for many respects to gyve God thankes'.[22]

Whereas modern readers find the ungainliness and occasional coarseness of the work hard to digest, the Elizabethans delighted in it for its stirring dramatic character. Its dynamic imagery and graphic detail, vividly exemplified in the great set pieces of Ovid's poem such as the Phaethon story, Cadmus' fight with the Snake of Mars, Actaeon and Diana,

---

[13] For Spenser, see my 'Spenser and Golding', *Notes and Queries*, 230 (1985), 18–21; 'Spenser and Golding: Further Debts in *The Faerie Queene*', *Notes and Queries*, 231 (1986), 342–4; 'Debts to Golding in Spenser's Minor Poems', *Notes and Queries*, 231 (1986), 345–7; and '*The Faerie Queene* Bk 1 and Golding's Translation of *Metamorphoses*', *Notes and Queries*, 232 (1987), 197–9; for Gabriel Harvey, see my 'When Did Spenser Read Golding?', *Notes and Queries*, 233 (1988), 38–40; for Marlowe, see M. M. Wills, 'Marlowe's Role in Borrowed Lines', *PMLA*, 52 (1937), 902–5, and my 'Notes on Marlowe and Golding', *Notes and Queries*, 232 (1987), 191–3; and for Peele, my 'George Peele and Golding's *Metamorphoses*', *Notes and Queries*, 214 (1969), 286–7, and 'Arthur Golding and George Peele's *Polyhymnia*', *Notes and Queries*, 230 (1985), 17–18.

[14] The first four books of Golding's translation were published in 1565, the full version in 1567.

[15] T.B. (Thomas Blundeville?), in commendatory verses to John Studley's translation of Seneca's *Agamemnon* (London, 1566).

[16] See my 'Echoes of Golding's Ovid in John Studley's Translations of Seneca', *Notes and Queries*, 232 (1987), 185–8.

[17] See my 'Thomas Peend and Arthur Golding', *Notes and Queries*, 214 (1969), 18–19.

[18] For Gager's tribute, see my 'Arthur Golding and George Peele's *Polyhymnia*'.

[19] Harvey quotes Golding in a poem he wrote in November 1573; for details of this, of other debts to Golding in Harvey's works, and his high opinion of the translator, see my 'When did Spenser read Golding?'

[20] See my 'When did Spenser read Golding?'

[21] George Puttenham, *The Arte of English Poesie* (London, 1589); reprinted in *Elizabethan Critical Essays*, ed. G. Gregory Smith, 2 vols. (Oxford, 1904), vol. 2, pp. 1–193; p. 65.

[22] William Webbe, 'A Discourse of English Poetrie' (London, 1586); reprinted in *Elizabethan Critical Essays*, vol. 1, pp. 226–302; pp. 257, 256, 243.

the Hunt for the Calydonian Boar, reverberate through Elizabethan literature. At crucial moments in their work, the greatest Elizabethan writers reflect Golding's impact: in Book One of *The Faerie Queene* when the Redcrosse Knight succumbs in the Cave of Despair, Spenser recalls the abject terror of Golding's Achemenides before the Cyclops 'trembling like an aspen leafe ... sad and bloodlesse quyght' (14.245), and how when 'the cruell feend' cried out for Ulysses and his 'mates' to be delivered into his hands so that as he devoured them, their 'flesh might pant betweene' his 'jawes', 'before myne eyes then death the smallest sorrow stood' (236);[23] when Edward II curses Mortimer in 'Killingworth castell', Marlowe has in mind the moment when Jove strikes down Phaethon, 'with fire he quencht fire', and the boy falls to earth 'blasing' (2.414), and the memorable entry of Tisiphone 'girded about ... with wreathed Snakes', sent from hell to inflict insanity upon Ino and Athamas,

> There stoode the Fiend, and stopt their
> passage out,
> And splaying forth hir filthie armes beknit
> with Snake about,
> Did tosse and wave hir hatefull heade.
>
> (4.606–8)[24]

And there is nothing other than the burlesque in Shakespeare's work that suggests that he did not share the general admiration for Golding. Debts to the translator in his work remind us that he was as impressed as his contemporaries by the dramatic character of the translation; he recalls, for example, moments such as the predicament of one 'uppon the hatches', who has been brought 'too utter perill through fond toyes' and 'soothsayres prophecies', fated to be cast into 'the tumbling billowes' below and 'strangled in the gulf' of the sea (11.648),[25] or the 'crack' of the 'sinews' of an heroic figure enduring 'labours' imposed by a god who is purging his nature of its 'earthly drosse' before lifting him to 'heaven' (9.213),[26] or the way a

murderous boar, 'the sturdie bristles on his backe ... like a front of armed Pikes set close in battell ray' (8.379–80), sinks 'his tushes' into the groin '(the speeding place of death)', of one foolhardy enough to oppose him and 'rippeth up his paunche'.[27] Consider the response to Golding's dramatic feel for action in the debts to his favourite episode in the translation, the story of Phaethon. Among the first are allusions to the boy as 'the wagoner ... whirling' about the globe and 'reeling' in the heavens in

---

23 Compare the Redcrosse Knight's reaction to the sight of 'damned ghosts that doe in torrents waile',

> The sight whereof so throughly him dismaid,
> That nought but death before his eies he saw
>
> (1.9.1–2)

and, when Despair gives him the dagger to end his life,

> his hand did quake
> And tremble like a leafe of Aspin greene,
> And troubled blood through his pale face was seene
> To come and goe.
>
> (i.51.3–6)

(Quotation is from *The Works of Edmund Spenser*, ed. R. Morris (London, 1902).)

24 Compare:

> if proud Mortimer do weare this crowne,
> Heavens turne it to a blaze of quenchlesse fire
> Or like the snakie wreathe of Tisiphon,
> Engirt the temples of his hateful head.
>
> (*Edward II*, lines 2031–4)

(Quotation is from *The Works of Christopher Marlowe*, ed. C. F. Tucker Brooke (Oxford, 1910; reprinted 1962).)

25 Compare Clarence, who is put in mortal danger by 'prophecy' and 'suchlike toys' (1.1.39, 60), and in his dream is walking 'Upon ... the hatches', when 'Struck ... overboard / Into the tumbling billows of the main' and 'smothered ... in the envious flood' (*Richard III*, 1.4.17–20, 40, 37).

26 Compare Ferdinand, 'I had rather crack my sinews' (*Tempest*, 3.1.26), when he is about the 'labours' set by Prospero in the log-bearing scene and what is 'dead' in him is quickened (3.1.6–7).

27 Compare the description of the boar who will give the imprudent Adonis his death wound by sheathing his 'tusk in his soft groin':

> On his bow-back he hath a battle set
> Of bristly pikes that ever threat his foes.
>
> (*Venus*, 1116, 619–20)

weariness as the reins slip from his grasp,[28] and among the last, the moment when as the sun god 'gathered up his steedes ... that yit for feare did run / Like flaighted fiends' after the death of his son, Golding has him seize the first solid object he can lay his hands on and 'beate his whipstocke on their pates' (2.501).[29] And Shakespeare also went beyond his contemporaries in his appreciation of Golding. There is evidence on a small and large scale that he was much taken with the prospect of 'Jove in a thatched house' (*As You Like It*, 3.3.7–8), the way the translator transposes the world of Ovidian myth to the more humble and earthy surroundings of the English landscape. And his treatment of myth both in incidental references and in more significant features in his work reminds us that he had been deeply impressed by the Calvinistic translator's strong moral and spiritual vision of Ovid's poem.[30]

As for 'Pyramus and Thisbe', it seems to have been a favourite episode in Golding which Shakespeare found moving for its pathos and romance. In Lysander's proposal to Hermia, he recalled the lovers' 'covenant' that they 'steale out of their father's house ... to meete without the towne' (4.106–8); for Juliet's passionate enquiry about her parents' grief over the dead Tybalt, he is indebted to the moving line when Thisbe discovers the dying boy,

> And taking him betweene hir armes did
>   wash his wounds with teares.   (169)

And he is thinking of it in the loveliest of all references to the lovers' story in his work when,

> In such a night
> Did Thisbe fearfully o'ertrip the dew
> (*Merchant of Venice*, 5.1.6–7)[31]

For Shakespeare to have paused in mid-career, therefore, to direct ridicule of 'a rather scornful and mocking nature'[32] at Golding's Ovid in 'Pyramus and Thisbe' appears to be out of character. Evidence found in his work, outside the burlesque, indicates that he not only shared his age's general admiration for the work but was rather fond of the translator's version of the lovers' story. However, the idea of his ridiculing Golding in the burlesque is curiously in keeping with the irritation and impatience which has been felt by influential twentieth-century readers of the translation but of which there is no trace in the Elizabethan response to the work. It is also suspiciously in line with the climate of opinion generated by mistaken assumptions about Shakespeare's attitude to it. In these circumstances, it seems worthwhile re-examining the case for Golding's involvement in the burlesque.

---

[28] Compare:
> And then I'll come and be thy wagoner,
> And whirl along with thee about the globe
> (*Titus*, 5.2.48–9)

and Sonnet 7, lines 9–10: 'when from highmost pitch, with weary car' ... 'he reeleth'. (For further details of these particular debts to Golding's Phaethon episode, see my 'Shakespeare, Studley, and Golding'.)

[29] Compare Valerius' warning of the King's anger to Palamon and Arcite:
> yet be leaden-footed
> Till his great rage be off him. Phoebus, when
> He broke his whipstock and exclaimed against
> The horses of the sun, but whispered to
> The loudness of his fury.
> (*The Two Noble Kinsmen*, 1.2.84–8)

[30] For further discussion of both these points, see my forthcoming *Shakespeare's Ovid and Arthur Golding*.

[31] Compare:
> Steal forth thy father's house tomorrow night,
> And in the wood, a league without the town,
> Where I did meet thee once ...
> There will I stay for thee.
> (*A Midsummer Night's Dream*, 1.1.164–6, 168)

and
> Wash they his wounds with tears; mine shall be
>   spent
> When theirs are dry.
> (*Romeo and Juliet*, 3.2.130–1)

In Golding Thisbe meets with Pyramus as soon as 'the deawie grasse had dride' (4.102).

[32] Caroline Jameson, 'Ovid in the Sixteenth Century', p. 217.

II

It was Kenneth Muir who assembled the significant evidence.[33] He saw this as Shakespeare's use of a number of words that are distinctive to Golding; 'cranny' for the fissure in the wall separating the lovers, Thisbe's 'tarrying' beneath the mulberry tree, the reference to the girl's upper garment as a 'mantle', the lovers' thanking the 'courteous' wall, and what he took to be a parody of Golding's style, the translator's habit of padding out his lines with the use of the auxiliary 'did'.[34]

Others besides Muir[35] have placed particular store on 'cranny' on the grounds that 'No other version uses this word'.[36] However, a source has been entirely overlooked which makes it extremely probable that every Elizabethan schoolboy would have had both the words Shakespeare uses for the gap in the wall separating Pyramus and Thisbe drilled into him: the dictionaries specifically designed for use in schools.[37] In one of these, Richard Huloet's *Abcedarium Anglico Latinum* (London, 1552; revised edition 1572), for example, one finds *rima*, the word used in Ovid's text, defined as '*Chinck, clyft, crany*' (italics mine);[38] and the first English–Latin dictionary, *Promptorium Parvulorum* (London, 1449; five times reprinted), suggests that 'cranny' had long been the traditional translation of the word in English schools.[39] The dictionaries show that schoolboys would have also been familiar with the notion of Thisbe 'tarrying' beneath the mulberry tree. Ovid says that when she is waiting for Pyramus, Thisbe 'sub arbore sedit' (*Metamorphoses*, 4.95),[40] and in Cooper's *Thesaurus*, for example, we find *sedere* as 'to tarie or abyde';[41] so, in the girl's circumstances, an Elizabethan would naturally translate Ovid's text at this point as Thisbe '*tarries* beneath the tree'.

As for Thisbe's 'mantle', there is clear textual evidence that this was taken not from Golding, but from a source which supplied Shakespeare with various other details as well as with part of the metre for the burlesque, the ballad on Pyramus and Thisbe by I. Thomson in *A Handful of Pleasant Delightes*. This is Thomson:

---

33 Since Muir wrote (1954), the assumption that the burlesque is a parody of the translator has led to the production of some rather dubious evidence by editors and critics who forget about Ovid in their preoccupation with Golding. R. A. Foakes, for instance, cites not only 'the general alignment of the "tedious brief scene" of Pyramus and Thisbe with the story as told in Golding' but also 'the correspondence of a number of details which are different in other versions, such as the mantle dropped by Thisbe (5.1.141; iv.125); the "crannied hole" (5.i.156; iv.83); the "Ninus' tomb" (5.i.137; iv.108); and the mulberry tree (5.i.147; iv.110)' (Foakes, *Dream*, p. 10). But Shakespeare would have surely known the story line from his schoolboy study of Ovid and also that the lovers meet at 'Ninus tomb' ('ad busta Nini', *Metamorphoses*, 4.88) under 'the mulberry tree' ('Arbor ... morus', 89–90); in addition, 'crannied hole' is not an expression used in Golding, and, as Muir points out, Thisbe wears a 'mantle' in Thomson's ballad on Pyramus and Thisbe.

34 Muir, 'Pyramus and Thisbe', pp. 143–4.

35 See, for example, Brooks, *Dream*, p. lix.

36 Muir, 'Pyramus and Thisbe', p. 143.

37 John Brinsley speaks of these as 'the Dictionaries, which they ought to have ever at hand' (*Ludus Literarius: or, The Grammar Schoole* (London, 1612), ed. E. T. Campagnac (London, 1917), p. 123). In addition, there would be a large dictionary such as Cooper's available to them, kept permanently in the school, chained to some convenient point in the schoolroom.

38 Reference is to a copy of the 1575 edition of Huloet. There were two editions of Huloet's dictionary (1552 and 1575). In *Shakspere's Small Latine*, vol. 1, p. 715, Baldwin discusses Shakespeare's possible use of Huloet.

39 This was produced in the fifteenth century but continued to be used in the sixteenth. For 'crany', see the Early English Text society edition by A. L. Mayhew (London, 1908), p. 100.
The use of 'chink' was also well established; see, for example, Peter Levins, *Manipulus Vocabulorum* (London, 1570), ed. H. B. Wheatley, Camden Society (London, 1867), p. 138.

40 Quotations are from a Regius edition, *Metamorphoseos* (Lyon, 1518), ed. Stephen Orgel (New York, 1976).

41 Thomas Cooper, *Thesaurus Linguae Romanæ & Britannicæ* (London, 1565).

And as in haste she fled awaie,
Her *Mantle* fine:
The *Lion* tare in stead of praie.[42]

And here is the first reference to the garment in Shakespeare:

her *mantle* she did fall,
Which *Lion* vile *with bloody mouth* did stain.
(5.1.141–2, italics mine)

What shows Shakespeare is recalling Thomson and not Golding at this point is the reference to the 'Lion'. There is no 'lion' in Ovid's (or Golding's) 'Pyramus and Thisbe'. Ovid identifies the beast that frightens Thisbe as *Lea* or *Leaena* and Golding follows him, referring in his translation to a 'Lionesse'. Thomson is unusual in referring to the beast as a 'lion'.[43] Shakespeare is also thinking of Thomson in the other reference to Thisbe's 'mantle' in Quince's Prologue:

Anon comes Pyramus, sweet youth and tall,
And finds his trusty Thisbe's *mantle* slain;
Whereat with *blade* – with bloody, blameful
blade –
He bravely broached his boiling bloody
breast   (5.1.143–6, italics mine)

Golding follows Ovid, referring to Pyramus' weapon as a 'sword' and locating the boy's self-inflicted wound in the stomach. But in Thomson, as in Shakespeare, one finds the weapon described as a 'blade' and the wound inflicted not in the stomach but higher on the boy's person, in the 'hart',

The *Mantle* this of Thisbie his,
he desperately doth fare . . .
Then from his sheath he drew his *blade*,
and to his *hart*
He thrust the point.   (p. 37, italics mine)

The lines in which Muir detects mockery of one of Golding's methods for padding out his fourteeners are in the Prologue, where Quince tells how the lion Thisbe:

Did scare away, or rather *did* affright;
And as she fled, her mantle she *did* fall,

Which Lion vile with bloody mouth *did*
stain.   (5.1.140–2, italics mine)[44]

This, allowing for the variations caused by Thomson's influence, is Shakespeare's translation of Ovid's text, which reads at the relevant point:

timido pede fugit . . .
Dumque fugit; tergo velamina lapsa reliquit . . .
Ut Lea . . .
Ore cruentato tenues laniavit amictus.
(*Metamorphoses*, 4.99–104)

But compare a translation of the same lines in a very familiar Elizabethan work, Thomas Cooper's *Thesaurus Linguae Romanae & Britannicae*; in the *Dictionarium Historicum & Poeticum*, in an account of the lovers' story, one finds Thisbe, 'in greate feare of a Lyonesse',

for haste *dyd* lette fall hir upper garmente,
which the
beaste *dyd* rente and teare in peeces.
(italics mine)

Elizabethans were generally fonder of the pleonastic 'did' than we are and, as Cooper reminds us, would be very liable to use it several times when faced by lines of Latin which contained, as these do, four verbs in the perfect tense. Shakespeare's lines are thus a slightly comic elaboration of a stock Eliza-

---

[42] *A Handful of Pleasant Delights* (London, 1584; STC 21105), ed. Clement Robinson (Manchester, 1871), p. 36 (italics mine).

[43] A lioness appears, for example, in the account of the lovers' story in Cooper's *Thesaurus* which is discussed below. And it was the traditional identification of the beast: Chaucer, for example, refers to 'a wyld lyonesse' in *The Legend of Thisbe* (805), and in Sandys's translation (1626), one finds 'a *Lyonesse*, smear'd with blood'.

[44] He cites these lines from the translation of 'Pyramus and Thisbe', but they are rather exceptional:
This neighbrod bred acquaintance first, this
neighbrod first *did* stirre
The secret sparkes, this neighbrod first an entrance
in *did* showe,
For love to come to that which afterward *did*
growe.   (4.74–6, italics mine)

bethan habit which arises because of Quince's verbose rhetoric. As for the more general notion that Shakespeare is satirizing Golding's metre, this is puzzling on the face of it, for none of the burlesque is written in Golding's long fourteener.[45] However, the conviction that Golding is Shakespeare's target has produced the theory that his metre is present in 'disguise', although explanations of why Shakespeare should bother to go to such ingenious lengths have not been forthcoming. Thus Brooks, for example, argues that the extremely short rhyming couplet of the lovers' laments 'is a variation, *with internal rhyme* [italics mine], of the fourteener used by Golding',[46] and R. A. Foakes, while allowing that Pyramus' lament is directly based on the metre in Thomson's poem on Pyramus and Thisbe, will not discount his involvement for 'Golding's fourteen-syllable line *breaks down into* [italics mine] the measure of part' of Thomson's poem.[47]

Close examination, therefore, leaves the impression that there is scarcely a trace of Golding in the burlesque.[48] And collation of the text of the mechanicals' 'play' with that of the original confirms that Shakespeare's favourite translation of *Metamorphoses* had no part in his plans. Indeed, the confusion of Golding's translation with the burlesque has only served totally to obscure its most intriguing feature, which only becomes apparent once it is realized that 'Pyramus and Thisbe' is, in fact, based on an incompetent reading of the Latin text. This is the root cause of much of the humour in the burlesque, as well as the only explanation for some of its more eccentric features.

III

To understand Shakespeare's real satirical purpose in the burlesque one needs to fix one's attention on the 'author' of 'Pyramus and Thisbe' *within the context of A Midsummer Night's Dream.*

It is Peter Quince the Carpenter who is the writer amongst the tradesmen, as Bottom reminds us when waking from his dream: 'I will get Peter Quince to write a ballad of this dream' (4.1.11–12), and the implication of the 'company's' discussions is that it is Quince who is the 'author' of the play. Hence Snug's enquiry to him, 'Have you the lion's part written?' (1.2.62), and the unquestioned assumption by the others that it is Quince who will rewrite and reshape the play where necessary: there are Bottom's instructions addressed to him, 'Write me a prologue . . . tell them that I, Pyramus, am not Pyramus' (3.1.16.19), and again, 'you must name his name . . . and tell them plainly he is Snug the joiner' (3.1.33, 41–2). It is Quince who immediately decides on the metre for the prologue, although apparently later changing his mind; and despite giving them written parts as Pyramus' father and Thisbe's mother, it is Quince who pre-

---

[45] When the prologue is proposed, Quince does say, 'it shall be written in eight and six', but this proves of little significance; it is immediately contradicted by Bottom, 'let it be written in eight and eight' (3.1.18–20), and when it does appear, it is in iambic pentameter.

[46] *Dream*, p. lxxxvii.

[47] *Dream*, p. 11.

    Compare the metre of the lovers' lament,

        Thy mantle good,
        What, stained with blood?
    Approach, ye Furies fell.
        O Fates, come, come,
        Cut thread and thrum,
    Quail, crush, conclude, and quell.
                                        (5.1.277–82)

with that of Golding,

    And as she knew right well the place and faction of
        the tree
    (As whych she saw so late before:) even so when
        she did see
    The colour of the Berries turnde, shee was
        uncertain whither
    It were the tree at which they both agreed to meete
        togither.   (4.157–60)

[48] Golding's involvement is limited to a single word, 'Thanks, *courteous* wall' (5.1.176, italics mine), which echoes 'we think ourselves in debt / For this same piece of *courtesy*' (4.96, italics mine).

sumably rapidly rewrites the play and recasts Snout and Starveling because of his concern that 'Wall' and 'Moonshine' be represented.

A pointer to Quince's method in composing 'Pyramus and Thisbe' is the Latinate reference to Pyramus as a 'juvenal' (3.1.89)[49] and the joke on the 'cranny' which is 'right and *sinister*' (5.1.162, italics mine). It is evident that he has some Latin and is rather proud of the fact, which probably explains why he has gone directly to Ovid's text for his source. At times, he recalls it word for word, as in 'And as she fled, her mantle she did fall' (5.1.141) ('Dumque fugit ... velamina lapsa reliquit', *Metamorphoses*, 4.101), and his play is strewn with phrases and words taken directly from the Latin. Some examples are the lovers' agreement 'To meet at Ninus' tomb' (5.1.137) ('Conveniant ad busta Nini', 4.88), Thisbe's 'mantle ... stained with blood' (5.1.278) ('tinctam sanguine', 4.107),[50] the lion tearing it 'with bloody mouth' (5.1.142) ('cruentato ore', 4.104),[51] and the lovers 'making moan' (5.1.329) ('questi', 4.84).[52]

However, his confidence in going back to the original is misplaced; his Latin is so poor that he repeatedly stumbles over the most elementary words and phrases. There is, for example, that small, problematic feature of *A Midsummer Night's Dream*, the perplexing description of Pyramus as 'most lovely *Jew*' (3.1.89, italics mine); the suggestion that has been made from time to time – that this should be read as 'most lovely *Juv*'[53] – should be accepted by editors of the play for it is, in fact, a strained attempt to translate the phrase Ovid uses to introduce the boy, '*iuvenum pulcherrimus*' (4.55, italics mine), 'the most lovely of young men'.[54] There is also the unforgettable moment when his hero, in a magnanimous mood, declares,

Sweet moon, I thank thee for *thy sunny beams*.
(5.1.67, italics mine)

In Ovid's text Quince had found 'lunae radios' (iv.99), 'the rays of the moon', but the phrase

presented him with a problem because he knew *radius* only by the stock definition he found in dictionaries like Cooper's *Thesaurus*,

---

49 The Oxford editors, who follow Q in their original-spelling text and print 'Iuuenall' (line 876), modernize this to 'juvenile' in their modern-spelling text, commenting in the *Textual Companion* to the edition that 'The -*al* spelling is early (twice in Shakespeare and once in 1607), superseded by the -*ile* alternative (1625+). Here there seems no reason *not* to modernize' (p. 282). I believe that the more widely adopted Latinate 'juvenal' is the preferable modern-spelling form, for it does not so obscure what I believe and here argue to be Quince's struggle with Latin.

50 Golding does not refer to blood 'staining' the garment at all; 'vestem quoque sanguine tinctam', for example, appears in his translation as 'the bloudie cloke' (4.132). (For '*tinctus*' as 'stained', see Cooper, *Thesaurus Linguae*.)

51 Golding has the more dramatic phrase, 'with bloudie teeth' (129). Muir, 'Pyramus and Thisbe', described 'with bloody mouth' as a debt to Chaucer and has recently been followed by Anne Thompson in *Shakespeare's Chaucer* (Liverpool, 1978), p. 93. But Chaucer, like Shakespeare, took the phrase from the Latin.

Chaucer is not involved in the burlesque; the other 'debt' Muir refers to, the '*wicked* wall', is taken, as textual evidence shows, from 'The History of Pyramus and Thisbe', the anonymous poem in *A Gorgeous Gallery of Gallant Inventions* (London, 1578). For detailed discussion of this and E. Talbot Donaldson's recent claim that *Sir Thopas* is a source for the burlesque (*The Swan at the Well: Shakespeare Reading Chaucer* (New Haven, 1985), pp. 5–20), see my 'Chaucer's Non-Involvement in "Pyramus and Thisbe" in *A Midsummer Night's Dream*', scheduled for publication in *Notes and Queries*, Sept. 1989.

52 'To make moan' is the meaning given for *queror.questus* in Cooper's *Thesaurus Linguae*. (Golding at this point has 'after much complaint' (4.104).) In addition to the other terms taken from the Latin, it is a probability that the expression, 'poor soules' (5.1.132), although referring to both lovers, was suggested by 'anima ... miseranda' (4.110) in Ovid's text; in Sandys at the relevant point, for instance, one finds ''twas I (poore soule) that slew thee', and Mouffet also describes Thisbe as 'poor soul'.

53 See, for example, R. A. Foakes's footnote to 3.1.77 in his edition of *Dream*.

54 The epithet Ovid uses to introduce Pyramus (*pulcherrimus*) also accounts for his being referred to as 'most lovely' earlier (1.2.69). (Golding does not translate *pulcherrimus* as a superlative.)

as 'A beame of the sunne'. He therefore has settled for what seems to him a sensible compromise and, in the process, afforded audiences amusement ever since. And then there is his biggest gaffe of all. He mistranslates the word Ovid uses in his initial reference to the story of the lovers. Ovid introduces it in *Metamorphoses* as a 'fable' not commonly known ('vulgaris fabula non est', *Metamorphoses*, 4.53). For the Elizabethans, *fabula* had two meanings. It meant 'a tale', but, as Cooper's *Thesaurus* tells us, it could also mean 'an interlude or a comedie'; and somehow Quince arrives at the secondary meaning of *fabula*. Hence his constant reference to his dramatization of the lovers' story as an 'interlude' (1.2.5 and 5.1.154) and as a 'comedie', despite its obviously tragic content, as in its title, 'The Most Lamentable *Comedy* and Most Cruel Death of Pyramus and Thisbe' (1.2.11–12, italics mine), is an attempt in his own muddled way to be true to what he thinks he has found in Ovid's text.

Indeed, his understanding of the Latin text is strained and confused throughout. Although he refers to Pyramus as a 'sweet youth' (5.1.143), 'young' (5.1.56), and a 'juvenal', he has no real grasp of one of the central features of the story, the extreme youth of the lovers; in Ovid, they are little more than children. He raises no objection to Bottom's ludicrous suggestion that he play Pyramus in a beard, and also refers to Pyramus as a 'man' (5.1.128), a 'gentlemanlike man' (1.2.81), and, in his play, as a 'poor knight' (5.1.72). Thisbe similarly is a 'lady' (5.1.129) and 'the fairest dame' (288), possibly a mistranslation of 'praelata puellis', 'the loveliest of girls'. His instruction to Flute that Thisbe's part must be played 'in a mask' (1.2.45) is also the result of his misreading the Latin.[55] In the play itself, he muddles details, transferring them from one lover to the other with unintentionally hilarious results. For example, in Pyramus' celebrated *apostrophe ad leones*, the detail of the lions 'devouring' the boy ('consumite viscera', 4.113), which is part

of his despairing request to them when he thinks Thisbe dead, is transferred to the girl in the equally impassioned address to the beasts by the hero of the 'play' (5.1.286ff) and, either through Quince's occasionally unhappy way with words or through a particularly infelicitous slip of the tongue on Nick Bottom's part, becomes the grossly unnatural, 'Since lion vile hath here *deflowered* my dear' (5.1.287, italics mine). In addition, the exact manner of Thisbe's death, by the sword after it has been placed carefully to the heart ('aptato pectus mucrone sub imum', 4.162), is transferred to Pyramus who actually dies of a *stomach* wound in Ovid, yet 'pectus' is still translated when applied to the boy as if it referred to a woman's breast. Hence the swordthrust into the gallant hero's 'left *pap*' (5.1.293, italics mine).[56]

Peter Quince is bedevilled by other afflictions. He is liable to stumble over his English: 'Thisbe's mantle slain' (5.1.144), kissing 'the wall's hole' (5.1.200); his cultural references go hopelessly astray: linking 'Lemander' and 'Helen' (5.1.195–6), 'Shafalus and Procris' (5.1.197); and he is constantly at odds with poetic decorum. But it is his running battle with the Latin text of Ovid's original that is at the root of most of the unintentional and hilarious humour of his 'Pyramus and Thisbe'.

---

55 Thisbe is not masked throughout Ovid's story, as Quince suggests; he is confused by the fact that during the course of the story, when she leaves her father's house to meet Pyramus at Ninus' tomb, wishing to conceal her identity, she has her face covered: 'adopertaque vultum' (4.94). (In Sandys's translation at this point, one finds Thisbe coming 'maskt to Ninus tomb'; Golding has 'muffling hir with clothes about hir chin' (116).)

56 The anonymous writer of 'The History of Pyramus and Thisbe' provides an interesting parallel. At the relevant moment in his poem, he, too, has the line from the Latin text in mind, and, echoing Ovid's phrase, 'pectus ... sub imum', he describes the death of Thisbe as, 'Wherewith *beneath her pap* (alas) into her brest shee strake': *The Gorgeous Gallery of Gallant Inventions* (London, 1578), ed. D. E. L. Crane (Menston, Yorkshire, 1972), p. iiv (italics mine).

IV

In *A Midsummer Night's Dream*, therefore, one finds among the tradesmen, that 'crew of patches' who have brought their 'company' to court to entertain the nobility, a playwright with small Latin. The quiet and conscientious Peter Quince has always seemed peripheral, overshadowed by his irrepressible leading man, but if one turns one's attention to this retiring figure one will see that his other features are not without significance. One notes, for example, that he is both playwright and player taking a supporting role in his own work. And, together with its leading actor, he is one of the leaders of the company, involved in its management; he assigns parts, deals diplomatically with egotistical leading men, discusses suggestions for re-writing and costume, draws up the 'bill of properties' (1.2.97–8), and arranges rehearsals and the location of the 'tiring-house' (3.1.4). (It is very noticeable that, besides being literate in an age when the majority of his class could not sign their names, Peter Quince is also surprisingly knowledgeable about theatrical detail and requirements.) In addition, when it comes to the matter of his writing, this hempen homespun is notable for his facility; he works under pressure and, whatever the dubious quality of his work may be, he works quickly, producing rapid and quite extensive rewrites at short notice. Moreover, as his play vividly illustrates, he has a weakness for romantic and tragic verse, and a fondness for Ovid.

Among another 'crew of patches' who often took their company to court to entertain the nobility on festive occasions, the Lord Chamberlain's Men, there was also, of course, a playwright with 'small Latin', Shakespeare himself. And if one allows for the exaggerated dimensions and mockery of his picture, Peter Quince bears a quite striking resemblance to his creator. Shakespeare, for instance, was unique among Elizabethan playwrights in both writing and performing in his own plays,

taking, like Peter Quince, a supporting role. His versatility is alluded to in the first known reference to him by a contemporary, Robert Greene's scorn of him in 1592 as 'an absolute Johannes Factotum'. A few years later, and before *A Midsummer Night's Dream* was written, his influence and activities had increased still more; he had become both a shareholder (a 'housekeeper') and, along with Kempe and Burbage, one of the leaders of his company. Moreover, as far as his writing was concerned, like Quince, Shakespeare had remarkable facility; as well as Ben Jonson's reference to this, Heminges and Condell noted in the First Folio that 'His mind and hand went together, and what he thought he uttered with that easiness that we have scarse received from him a blot in his papers'.[57] His taste for romantic and tragic verse had been made apparent by this date in *Venus and Adonis*, and, significantly, elements of self-mockery have been detected in the parody of the poem in the burlesque.[58] His fondness for Ovid was, of course, well known; it occasioned Francis Meres' tribute that 'the soule' of the Latin poet lives on in 'mellifluous & honey-tongued Shakespeare'. Which takes one back to his 'small Latin'.

In stories which have come down to us such as that of the 'Lattin Spoones', it seems that his limited Latin was something of a joke between Shakespeare and his friends.[59] The climate created by mistaken assumptions about his

---

57 John Heminges and Henry Condell, 'To the Great Variety of Readers', first printed among the preliminaries of the Shakespeare First Folio; it appears in the Complete Oxford Shakespeare among the 'Commendatory Poems and Prefaces (1599–1640)', p. xliii, lines 33–6.

58 See Walter Staton Jr, 'Ovidian Elements in *A Midsummer Night's Dream*', *Huntington Library Quarterly*, 26 (1962–3), 177, and my forthcoming 'Chaucer's Non-Involvement in *Pyramus and Thisbe*'.

59 For this particular story, see S. Schoenbaum, *William Shakespeare: A Documentary Life* (Oxford, 1975), p. 207.

attitude to the translation, combined with apparent resemblances to the translator's version of the lovers' story has led to the burlesque's being misread as a satiric attack on Golding. But it is Shakespeare himself with his 'small Latin' who is the central target for its mockery. By creating his humble *alter ego* in Peter Quince and installing him at the heart of the 'company' of the 'rude mechanicals' to provide a stuttering and hilarious treatment of the Latin source of their 'play', the great poet, who could refer to himself elsewhere as 'dumb' (Sonnet 83, line 10), 'unletter'd' (Sonnet 85, line 6), and as one who made himself 'a motley to the view' (Sonnet 110, line 2), and sold 'cheap what is most dear' (Sonnet 110, line 3), has contrived to send up his 'fault'[60] gloriously by his own hand.

---

[60] But it is noticeable that even while mocking this 'fault' in himself in the burlesque, he not only handles the Latin text but also knowingly mishandles it, which suggests a degree of competence and confidence on his part. Nevertheless, as he shows quite delightfully here, he was self-conscious about his Latin, moving as he did among acquaintances who, if they had been at university, would be much more competent in the language; but the truth of the matter seems to lie with what was reported to Aubrey by William Beeston, whose father had belonged to the Lord Chamberlain's men and worked with Shakespeare: 'Though as Ben: Johnson sayes of him, that he had but little Latine and lesse Greeke, He understood Latine pretty well' (Schoenbaum, *Documentary Life*, p. 88).

OVID AND THE SONNETS; OR, DID SHAKESPEARE FEEL THE ANXIETY OF INFLUENCE?

JONATHAN BATE

Early in *The Anxiety of Influence*, Harold Bloom announces that 'the greatest poet in our language is excluded from the argument of this book'. He gives three reasons for this exclusion, one historical, one generic, and one individual. Historically, Bloom states, 'Shakespeare belongs to the giant age before the flood, before the anxiety of influence became central to poetic consciousness'; only with eighteenth-century and Romantic notions of genius and originality does 'the burden of the past' become the poet's overriding problem. Generically, Bloom thinks, drama is less susceptible to anxiety than is lyric: 'As poetry has become more subjective, the shadow cast by the precursors has become more dominant.' But for Bloom – and this accords with the essentially Freudian mode of his criticism – the most important cause is the individual one: 'Shakespeare's prime precursor was Marlowe, a poet very much smaller than his inheritor . . . Shakespeare is the largest instance in the language of a phenomenon that stands outside the concern of this book: the absolute absorption of the precursor. Battle between strong equals, father and son as mighty opposites, Laius and Oedipus at the crossroads; only this is my subject here.'[1]

I think that all three of these arguments are wrong. I believe that we *can* talk about Shakespeare and the anxiety of influence, though the dynamics of anxiety and confidence in his relationship with his precursors differ in certain respects from the Bloomian pattern.

To be fair to Bloom, it should be acknowledged that he has changed his mind about the historical argument concerning the giant race before the flood: he now thinks that the anxiety of influence 'is crucial in Euripides confronting Aeschylus or in Petrarch dreaming about Dante'.[2] As usual, Bloom boldly asserts rather than scrupulously demonstrates; I would like to historicize the matter and consider certain symptoms of anxiety in Renaissance imitation theory. As for the generic argument, Bloom has forgotten about the Sonnets, which have precisely the self-consciousness about themselves as poems in relation to other poems and poetic conventions that makes them readable in terms of what he calls the aboriginal poetic self. I do not wish to argue the case about Marlowe here, though it does seem to me that his influence needs to be thought about afresh in the light of Bloom. *Did* Shakespeare absolutely absorb Marlowe? How complete is the revision of *Hero and Leander* in *Venus and Adonis*, *Edward II* in *Richard II*, *The Jew of Malta* in *The Merchant of Venice*, and *Dido Queen of Carthage* in *Hamlet*? Might not Pistol's parodies be a symptom of anxiety? Did Shakespeare think of Laius at the crossroads when he heard that Marlowe had been stabbed to death in Deptford? After all, when Francis Meres sought a classical prece-

---

[1] Harold Bloom, *The Anxiety of Influence* (New York, 1973; reprinted 1975), p. 11.
[2] *The Breaking of the Vessels* (Chicago, 1982), p. 15.

dent for Marlowe's death, he remembered the poet Lycophron shot to death by a rival.[3] Bloom now thinks that Marlowe was Shakespeare's 'prime' precursor, but not the only one; I understand that in a Norton lecture at Harvard this year he added two others, Chaucer and the English Bible. Perhaps because he is a Hebraist and not a Latinist, he still has not seen that in fact Shakespeare's prime precursor was Ovid.

The Bloomian rhetorical ploy is to announce that x is the precursor of y and that poem B is a creative revision of poem A. By virtue of such bold juxtapositions, Francis Meres may be reclaimed as a kind of Elizabethan Yale critic. Thus he reads the civil war poems of Daniel and Drayton as revisions of Lucan's *Pharsalia*, proclaims Ausonius to be the precursor of William Warner, and so on.[4] Such associations as these are Bloomian in that they profess some affinity other than overt imitation. As in Bloom 'the profundities of poetic influence cannot be reduced to source-study' (*Anxiety*, p. 7), so in Meres the *Fasti* of Ausonius are not a source but a precedent for Warner's *Albion's Englande*. The trope used by Meres is that which Puttenham in his *Arte of English Poesie* denominated 'Paradigma, or a resemblance by example':

if in matter of counsell or perswasion we will seeme to liken one case to another . . . and doe compare the past with the present, gathering probabilitie of like successe to come in the things wee have presently in hand: or if ye will draw the judgements precedent and authorized by antiquitie as veritable, and peradventure fayned and imagined for some purpose, into similitude or dissimilitude with our present actions and affaires, it is called resemblance by example: as if one should say thus, *Alexander* the great in his expedition to Asia did thus, so did *Hanniball* coming into Spaine, so did *Caesar* in Egypt, therfore all great Captains & Generals ought to doe it.[5]

Antiquity, then, offers a paradigm or an example which, by serving as a precedent, authorizes 'the things wee have presently in hand'. The purpose of Meres's 'Comparative Discourse of our English Poets with the Greeke, Latine, and Italian Poets' is to dignify the poetry that is presently in hand in Elizabethan England by bringing paradigms to bear upon it. The structure with which he works is Puttenham's 'as . . . so . . .' formulation: 'As Virgil doth imitate Catullus in the like matter of *Ariadne* for his story of Queene *Dido*: so Michael Drayton doth imitate Ovid in his *England's Heroical Epistles*'; 'As the soule of Euphorbus was thought to live in Pythagoras: so the sweete wittie soule of Ovid lives in mellifluous and hony-tongued Shakespeare, witnes his *Venus and Adonis*, his *Lucrece*, his sugred *Sonnets* among his private friends, &c.' (Meres, pp. 316–17). Here, *paradigma* is both a figure of speech and a design for the construction of literary history.

Meres articulates two different kinds of relationship between English poets and their forebears, the specifically imitative and the grandly paradigmatic. *Imitatio* is a symptom of *paradigma*, but *paradigma* is not dependent on recognizable *imitatio* (Caesar's Egyptian expedition cannot really be described as an *imitation* of Alexander's Asian one). Thus *Englands Heroical Epistles* is an imitation of Ovid's *Heroides*, as *The Shepheardes Calender* is of Theocritus' *Idylls* and Virgil's *Eclogues*, whereas the affiliation of Shakespeare to Ovid

---

[3] Meres derived his information about Lycophron, as he did most of his classical allusions, from a popular handbook, the *Officina* of J. Ravisius Textor: see Don Cameron Allen, *Francis Meres's Treatise 'Poetrie': A Critical Edition* (Urbana, Illinois, 1933). Allen castigates Meres for lack of originality, failing to see that his value lies precisely in his status as a purveyor of Elizabethan *commonplaces*.

[4] Meres, 'A Comparative Discourse of our English Poets with the Greeke, Latine, and Italian Poets', in his *Palladis Tamia, Wits Treasury* (1598), reprinted in *Elizabethan Critical Essays*, ed. G. Gregory Smith, 2 vols. (Oxford and London, 1904), vol. 2, pp. 316–17.

[5] George Puttenham, *The Arte of English Poesie* (1589), ed. G. D. Willcock and Alice Walker (Cambridge, 1936), p. 245.

is more broadly paradigmatic. Meres cites not only *Venus and Adonis* and *Lucrece*, which may be seen as imitations of parts of the *Metamorphoses* and the *Fasti*, but also the Sonnets, which, being in a genre unknown to Ovid, cannot be so directly imitative. The metaphor used for this relationship is suggestively self-performing: the metamorphosis of Ovid into Shakespeare is imaged in an allusion to the fifteenth book of the *Metamorphoses*, where Pythagoras supports his theory of metempsychosis by claiming that he is a reincarnation of the soul of Euphorbus (*Metamorphoses*, 15.161). Meres, writing in 1598, lists *The Merchant of Venice* as Shakespeare's most recent comedy, and he may well be remembering Graziano's allusion in that play to the metempsychotic opinions of Pythagoras (4.1.130); whether or not this is the case, the comparison is an inspired one, for the fifteenth book of the *Metamorphoses* is the prime *paradigma* for the Sonnets. The principle of metempsychosis which book fifteen articulates is enacted in the metempsychosis of book fifteen into the Sonnets.[6]

Puttenham's figure of paradigm provides an Elizabethan equivalent for Bloom's concept of a precursor; Meres provides an instance of an Elizabethan reader of the Sonnets who believed that their paradigm was the *Metamorphoses*. This model offers an Elizabethan version of 'influence', but what about 'anxiety'? Here, I would suggest, Bloom's sixteenth-century precursor is Erasmus.[7] Indeed, Erasmus is far more of a Bloom than is Meres, since he writes a form of criticism that is itself creative: Bloom conjures up 'a theory of poetry that presents itself as a severe poem' (*Anxiety*, p. 13), and he would not admit that criticism is a secondary activity – 'all criticism is prose poetry' (p. 95). So too with Erasmus: his dialogues are severe poems, not mere critical diagnoses. The point about both Erasmus and Bloom is that they should never be taken entirely seriously; the strength of their criticism lies in its scandalous excess.

Here is the opening of the *Dialogus Ciceronianus*, first published in 1528:

BULEPHORUS
Who's that I see strolling about down there at the end of the arcade? Unless my eyes have lost their sharpness, it's our old friend and fellow student, Nosoponus.
HYPOLOGUS
Nosoponus? the fellow who once used to be the life and soul of our set, rosy-cheeked, a bit on the plump side, diffusing charm and amiability in every direction?
BULEPHORUS
The very same.
HYPOLOGUS
But whatever has made him look so different? He's more like a ghost than a human being. Is he suffering from some disease?
BULEPHORUS
Yes, a very serious one.
HYPOLOGUS
Whatever is it? Surely not dropsy?
BULEPHORUS
No, it's a malady that goes deeper than the skin.
HYPOLOGUS
You don't mean that new sort of ulcerating disease, the scab, as people euphemistically call it nowadays?
BULEPHORUS
No, this is eating him away deeper than that.

---

[6] The aim of this essay is to reread the relationship between Ovid and the Sonnets in the light of sixteenth-century imitation theory and late twentieth-century influence theory. It is not to enumerate Shakespeare's 'debt' in detail: there are accounts of Ovid as a 'source' for the Sonnets in Sidney Lee, 'Ovid and Shakespeare's Sonnets', *The Quarterly Review*, 210 (1910), 455–76, T. W. Baldwin, *On the Literary Genetics of Shakspere's Poems and Sonnets* (Urbana, Illinois, 1950), J. W. Lever, *The Elizabethan Love Sonnet* (London, 1956), pp. 248–72, and the commentary and appendix 2 of Stephen Booth's edition of *Shakespeare's Sonnets* (New Haven and London, 1977).

[7] The best account of Erasmus, and the *Ciceronianus* in particular, in relation to sixteenth-century imitation theory, is that of Terence Cave in chapter 2 of his *The Cornucopian Text: Problems of Writing in the French Renaissance* (Oxford, 1979). For the broader Renaissance context, Thomas M. Greene's *The Light in Troy: Imitation and Discovery in Renaissance Poetry* (New Haven and London, 1982) is indispensable.

HYPOLOGUS

He's not spitting blood?

BULEPHORUS

This illness has got a hold somewhere further in than the lungs.

HYPOLOGUS

Not tuberculosis or jaundice?

BULEPHORUS

It's something more deep-seated than the liver.

HYPOLOGUS

Perhaps he's got a fever affecting his veins and heart?

BULEPHORUS

Yes, it is a fever, but then it isn't: it's something that burns deeper down than any fever raging in the veins and heart – something with its source in the brain, in the depths of the mind. But stop making wrong guesses, it's a new sort of illness.

HYPOLOGUS

Hasn't it got a name yet then?

BULEPHORUS

Not a Latin one; the Greeks call it *zelodulea*, 'style-addiction'.

HYPOLOGUS

Did he catch it recently, or has he had it a long time?

BULEPHORUS

It's had the poor fellow in its grip for more than seven years. I say, we've been spotted. It looks as if he's coming this way. You'll get a better idea what's wrong from the man himself.[8]

Bulephorus cannot find a Latin name for this peculiarly nasty illness which the Greeks call *zelodulea*. But we now have an English one: Nosoponus is suffering from the anxiety of influence. However, as is the way with literary diseases, its symptoms in the sixteenth and seventeenth centuries are precisely the opposite of what they become in the nineteenth and twentieth centuries. Romantic influenza springs from the poet's realization that he has failed to create himself, whereas *zelodulea* is the melancholy that grows from the realization that one cannot succeed in being created by one's precursor. Romantic influenza is a form of manic-depression, *zelodulea* of obsessional-neurosis. Keats veers between triumph and despair as he wrestles with Milton; Nosoponus

is ground down by a compulsion to imitate Cicero.

Zelodulea is an obsessive desire not to be original, or rather to find one's every origin in a paradigm.[9] The paradigm for prose is Cicero. Thus Nosoponus desires that every word, phrase, clause, period, verbal inflection, rhythmical pattern, and rhetorical structure he uses should have a precedent somewhere in the works of Cicero. If *amo*, *amas*, and *amat* are in Cicero, but *amamus* is not, then *amamus* cannot be used. Nosoponus is ill because he sits up all night every night reading, analysing, indexing, and cataloguing his Cicero. Erasmus' witty dialogue is an intervention in the celebrated debate about whether one should imitate a single authority or range more widely, taking choice morsels from a variety of models; Nosoponus is a parody of the extreme Ciceronianism of such humanists as Christophe de Longueil and Pietro Bembo. Bulephorus, the Erasmian voice, goes on to make a number of distinctions that are traditional in classical and Renaissance imitation theory: the ape is contrasted to the true son; the bee gathering honey from many flowers is set up as an ideal. But what is distinctive about the *Ciceronianus* is its metaphor of illness, its sense that influence is something profoundly problematic. 'Ben Jonson has no anxiety as to imitation', says Bloom, adopting the traditional view that influence was not problematized prior to 'the post-Enlightenment passion for Genius and the Sublime' (*Anxiety*, p. 27). Yet in the *Ciceronianus* anxiety is a key term:

---

8 *The Ciceronian: A Dialogue on the Ideal Latin Style*, translated by Betty I. Knott, in *Collected Works of Erasmus*, vol. 28; *Literary and Educational Writings 6*, ed. A. H. T. Levi (Toronto, Buffalo, and London, 1986), p. 342.

9 For the shift from Renaissance quests for origins in an authoritative, ultimately a divine, 'source' to the Enlightenment desire for originality, and Milton's pivotal position in this development, see David Quint, *Origin and Originality in Renaissance Literature: Versions of the Source* (New Haven and London, 1983).

'that carping anxious concern [*anxiam sollicitu-dinem*] for imitating Cicero'; 'this very anxiety [*haec anxietas*] makes one less likely to reach the goal one is aiming for' (*Ciceronianus*, p. 444).

In Erasmus, Nosoponus cannot write anything because he worries so much about finding a style that is answerable to Cicero: in Bloom, the post-Miltonic poet is inhibited because he worries so much about finding a style that is not answerable to Milton. In both Erasmus and Bloom, *revision* offers the only release from this stranglehold. Thus Bloom: 'Oedipus, blind, was on the path to oracular godhood, and the strong poets have followed him by transforming their blindness towards their precursors into the revisionary insights of their own work' (*Anxiety*, p. 10). And Erasmus: 'It may well be that the most Ciceronian person is the one least like Cicero' (*Ciceronianus*, p. 399). Both Bloom's 'blindness'/'insights' turn (itself a shameless revision of Paul de Man) and Erasmus' 'most'/'least like' paradox are riddling solutions to the problem of influence. Oedipus' cleverness, as well as his paternity, hovers over both texts: as Hypologus puts it in the *Ciceronianus*, 'Now you're producing a riddle fit for the Sphinx, if a person is to be unlike someone else at the very point where he is like him' (p. 399). The proposition which I want to test is that among Elizabethan sonneteers weak poets are obsessive imitators like Nosoponus, while strong poets are those who are unlike their paradigm at the very point where they are like him.

At this juncture one needs a bridge between the theory and the poetry. It must be demonstrated that Elizabethan sonnets did invite their readers to think about imitation and paradigm. One does not have to look very far to find such a bridge, for Thomas Watson actually built one into the first Elizabethan sonnet-cycle, the *Hekatompathia* of 1582. Probably working under the influence of E.K.'s marginal glosses to *The Shepheardes Calender*, he prefaced each poem with a brief critical account of its own imitative practices. In the headnote to 'Harke

you that list to heare what sainte I serve', the blazon of which 'My mistress' eyes are nothing like the sun' is a direct or indirect parody, he proclaims that he is proud to be a parasite:

This passion of love is lively expressed by the Authour, in that he lavishlie praiseth the person and beautifull ornamentes of his love, one after an other as they lie in order. He partly imitateth here in *Aeneas Silvius*, who setteth downe the like in describing *Lucretia* the love of *Euryalus*; & partly he followeth *Ariosto cant. 7.* where he describeth *Alcina*: & partly borroweth from some others where they describe the famous *Helen* of *Greece*: you may therefore, if you please aptlie call this sonnet as a Scholler of good judgement hath already Christened it *ainë parasitikë*.[10]

Further assistance is provided for the reader in the form of learned marginal references along the lines of 'Vide Chiliad. I. cent. 5 adag. 74. vbi. Erasm. ex Philostrati ad uxorem epistola mutuatur'. Watson is an eclectic rather than a Ciceronian in his imitative predilections, but these signpostings mark him out as a Nosoponus.

In Erasmus' dialogue, Bulephorus attacks those who 'over-anxiously' try to emulate their idols: 'The industrious but incautious imitator risks finishing up with a style that is flashy and overdone instead ... I have known men who attempted to reproduce that wonderful fluency of Ovid's and merely spouted verses devoid of any substance and force' (*Ciceronianus*, p. 378). The criticism applies perfectly to the sonnet in *Hekatompathia* that immediately follows 'Harke you that list to heare what sainte I serve.' Watson's headnote includes a quotation from Ovid's *Tristia* (2.103–6) and an explication: 'The Author alluding in al this Passion unto the fault of *Actaeon*, and to the hurte, which hee susteined, setteth downe his owne amorous infelicitie; as *Ovid* did after his banishmente, when in an

---

[10] Thomas Watson, *The Hekatompathia or Passionate Centurie of Love* (London, 1582), sonnet 7, p. 21. Greek transliterated in both title and quotation.

other sense hee applied this fiction unto him-selfe, being exiled (as it should seeme) for having at unawares taken *Caesar* in some great fault'. The ensuing verses set down the poet's own amorous inficility through the same allusion:

> Actaeon lost in middle of his sport
> Both shape and life, for looking but a wry,
> Diana was afraid he would report
> What secretes he had seene in passing by:
> To tell but trueth, the selfe same hurt have I
> By viewing her, for whome I dayly die.

(*Hekatompathia*, sonnet 8, p. 22)

But the allusion is vapid, since there is no element of prohibition in the viewing of his mistress. Whether the 'error' (*Tristia*, 2.207) for which Ovid was exiled was something he saw in the imperial household or an actual involvement with the emperor's grand-daughter, the figure of Actaeon is a perfect image in which to convey it. Watson, however, alludes to Actaeon solely out of a desire to imitate Ovid's wit, and his lines are accordingly empty of substance and force.

Shakespeare did not parade the imitativeness of his sonnets in the Watsonian manner, but on one occasion he did write a piece of literary criticism of his own work. It suggests, as Meres does, that Ovid is the sonneteer's para-digm. The sonnet 'If love make me forsworn, how shall I swear to love?', later published by William Jaggard in *The Passionate Pilgrim*, is subjected to the astringent scrutiny of Holo-fernes: 'Here are only numbers ratified, but for the elegancy, facility, and golden cadence of poesy – *caret*. Ovidius Naso was the man. And why indeed "Naso" but for smelling out the odoriferous flowers of fancy, the jerks of invention? *Imitari* is nothing. So doth the hound his master, the ape his keeper, the tired horse his rider' (*Love's Labour's Lost*, 4.2.121–7). Holofernes may be a pedant, but he is not a fool: he sees that Berowne's sonnet is a catalogue of commonplaces and that these verses are, to follow Bulephorus again, spouted without any substance or force. Holo-

fernes also knows his imitation theory. He has been reading in the tenth book of Quintilian: 'imitatio per se ipsa non sufficit'; 'invenire primum fuit estque praecipuum' [imitation by itself is not sufficient; invention came first and is all-important].[11] Contained within Holo-fernes' analysis is Quintilian's distinction between imitation and emulation, which had also been picked up by Erasmus in the *Cicer-onianus*. The business of poesy is not ape-like imitation à-la-Watson but the emulation of Ovid's elegance and facility. Like Puttenham's figure of *paradigma*, emulation leaves room for dissimilitude as well as similitude.

The distinction may be made by contrasting the handling of Ovidian mythology in a repre-sentative piece by a weak Elizabethan and in a Shakespearian sonnet. Sonnet 63 of Barnabe Barnes's *Parthenophil and Parthenophe* begins as follows:

> JOVE for EUROPA's love, took shape of Bull;
> And for CALISTO, played DIANA's part:
> And in a golden shower, he filled full
> The lap of DANAE, with celestial art.
> Would I were changed but to my Mistress'
>   gloves,
> That those white lovely fingers I might hide!
> That I might kiss those hands, which mine
>   heart loves![12]

Thereafter the poet expresses the desire to be metamorphosed into his mistress's necklace or belt, or the wine that she is drinking. In an Ovidian conceit – indeed, an Ovidian indecency – he imagines being the wine that kisses her lips, trickles down her throat, runs through her veins, and finally 'pass[es] by Pleasure's part'. Ovidian metamorphic mythology has furnished Barnes with images through which to convey his desire for a metamorphosis in his own standing with

---

[11] Quintilian, *Institutiones Oratoriae*, 10.2.4; 10.2.1 (all classical quotations are from Loeb editions).
[12] Barnes, *Parthenophil and Parthenophe* (London, 1593), quoted from Sidney Lee's anthology of *Elizabethan Sonnets*, 2 vols. (London, 1904), vol. I, p. 207.

regard to his lover.[13] Ovidian wit has furnished the sonnet with its tail. But the opening quatrain is formulaically dependent on Ovid and the final couplet crude in comparison with him. 'Weaker talents idealize; figures of capable imagination appropriate for themselves,' says Bloom (*Anxiety*, p. 5): the weak Barnes in no way advances on Ovid, in no way strives to outdo him.

But consider Shakespeare's Sonnet 53:

What is your substance, whereof are you made,
That millions of strange shadows on you tend?
Since every one hath, every one, one shade,
And you, but one, can every shadow lend.
Describe Adonis, and the counterfeit
Is poorly imitated after you.
On Helen's cheek all art of beauty set,
And you in Grecian tires are painted new.
Speak of the spring and foison of the year:
The one doth shadow of your beauty show,
The other as your bounty doth appear;
And you in every blessèd shape we know.

In Barnes the Ovidian mythological figures are fixed points, ideal substances which are shadowed in his own love. In Shakespeare the opposite is the case: the lovely boy is the substance, the mythological figure the shadow. 'Describe Adonis, and the counterfeit / Is poorly imitated after you': where Barnes offers counterfeits, poor imitations of Ovidian originals, Shakespeare makes the lovely boy into the ideal figure of beauty and Adonis into the counterfeit. The third quatrain performs a similar trumping, in this instance of those figures of natural plenty who are so central to Ovid's world: 'Speak of the spring and foison of the year', and one would usually speak of Proserpina and Ceres; but here nature is a shadow of the youth's beauty. The sonnet's strength derives from its appropriation of the term 'imitate'. Where a poet like Giles Fletcher announces on the title-page of his sonnet-sequence *Licia* (1593) that he is writing in 'imitation of the best Latin Poets, and others', Shakespeare claims within his poem that classical figures are imitations of his own

beloved. 'Figure' is an analogous term: *paradigma* is a figure of speech whereby classical figures serve as authorities, but Sonnet 106 goes so far as to make the claim that all praises of past beauties 'are but prophecies / Of this our time, all you prefiguring' (lines 9–10). The ideal figures are but prefigurings of the poet's present love.

When Shakespeare deploys this effect of inverted *paradigma*, he exercises a turn on the concept of metamorphosis. The paradigmatic function of myth is to provide poet and reader with a stock of archetypes. But where it is customary to suggest the force of a present change by comparing it to a traditional mythological metamorphosis that is known to be forceful, Shakespeare makes the myths into the shadow, the present change into the archetype or true substance. In Ovid, extreme emotion precipitates the metamorphosis of a person into an object of nature, whereas in Sonnet 113, extreme emotion precipitates the metamorphosis of the objects of nature into a person:

[Mine eye] no form delivers to the heart
Of bird, of flower, or shape which it doth
    latch.
Of his quick objects hath the mind no part,
Nor his own vision holds what it doth catch;
For if it see the rud'st or gentlest sight,
The most sweet favour or deformèd'st
    creature,
The mountain or the sea, the day or night,
The crow or dove, it shapes them to your
    feature.   (lines 5–12)

---

13 This is a much-used topos which may be traced back to Ronsard's 'Je vouldroy bien richement jaunissant' (*Amours*, 20), a lyric translated closely as sonnet 34 of Thomas Lodge's *Phillis* (1593) and more freely as 'Would I were chaung'd into that golden showre', a poem in *The Phoenix Nest* (1593) attributable to Ralegh. Sidney, who so often detaches himself from the literariness of other sonneteers, mocks the topos in *Astrophil*, 6: 'Some one his song in Jove, and Jove's strange tales, attires, / Broidered with bulls and swans, powdered with golden rain.'

This is Bloomian revision in that Ovid is being read antithetically. The Elizabethan would have used the term 'inversion' rather than 'revision', to judge from the headnote to the ninety-sixth poem of *Hekatompathia*, one of Thomas Watson's few revisionary strokes: 'In this Passion, the Authour in skoffing bitterly at *Venus*, and her sonne *Cupid*, alludeth unto certaine verses in *Ovid*, but inverteth them to an other sense, then Ovid used.' Bloom would call this *Tessera*, the second of his 'Six Revisionary Ratios': '*Tessera*, which is completion and antithesis . . . A poet antithetically "completes" his precursor, by so reading the parent-poem as to retain its terms but to mean them in another sense, as though the precursor had failed to go far enough' (*Anxiety*, p. 14).

Although on a few occasions such as this Watson swerves away from his models, he never approaches the climactic sixth revisionary ratio, '*Apophrades*, or the return of the dead', in which 'the new poem's achievement makes it seem to us, not as though the precursor were writing it, but as though the later poet himself had written the precursor's characteristic work' (*Anxiety*, p. 16). *Apophrades* is at work in the group of sonnets around Sonnets 59 to 64, for there it is as if Shakespeare has written Ovid.

Sonnet 59 opens with Shakespeare's darkest expression of poetic belatedness:

> If there be nothing new, but that which is
> Hath been before, how are our brains beguiled,
> Which, labouring for invention, bear amiss
> The second burden of a former child!
>
> (lines 1–4)

The darkness of this is manifest if we recollect Holofernes' distinction between *imitari*, which is nothing, and 'the jerks of invention' to which the poet should aspire (*Love's Labour's Lost*, 4.2.125–6). Whereas Shakespeare proved his inventiveness in Sonnet 53 by appropriating the idea of imitation, now he laments that the labour for originality is fruitless since nothing is new, what one writes will be already written, and what one imagines to be the child of one's invention will turn out to be the child of one's poetic father. 'Burden' is a key word: together with 'labouring' it establishes an image of writing as giving birth, but at the same time it suggests the burden of the past, the oppressive weight of the wits who have gone before. The notion of eternal repetition on which the sonnet rests carries the melancholy implication that all writing is mere imitation of previous writing. Line eight, 'Since mind at first in character was done', evokes an originary act of writing that can never be recovered. The sense of loss derives from the contrast between that 'at *first*' and the poet's own '*second* burden'.

Sonnet 59 exemplifies its own contention that there is nothing new by means of its own nature as something that is not new. For what is its argument about repetition other than a repetition of Pythagoras' argument in book eleven of *Metamorphoses*? The image of birth as rebirth of something that has been before is itself the second birth of Ovid's 'nascique vocatur / incipere esse aliud, quam quod fuit ante' or, as Arthur Golding has it, 'For that which wee / Doo terme by name of being borne, is for too gin too bee / Another thing than that it was'.[14] Ovid's technique in the *Metamorphoses* is to slide from one story to the next in a process of repetition and variation that embodies the neo-Pythagorean theory of constancy and change. The structure of the Sonnets is the same: 60 picks up from 59.[15] In particular, it picks up on the language of Pythagoras' discourse. As every

---

[14] *Metamorphoses*, 15.255–6. Golding's 1567 translation is quoted from *Shakespeare's Ovid, being Arthur Golding's Translation of the Metamorphoses*, ed. W. H. D. Rouse (London, 1904; reprinted 1961), 4.279–81.

[15] I follow Katherine Duncan-Jones, 'Was the 1609 *Shakespeares Sonnets* Really Unauthorized?', *Review of English Studies*, NS 34 (1983), 151–71, and John Kerrigan, ed., *The Sonnets and A Lover's Complaint* (Harmondsworth, 1986), in ascribing authority to the 1609 order.

educated Elizabethan reader would have recognized,

> Like as the waves make towards the pebbled
>   shore,
> So do our minutes hasten to their end,
> Each changing place with that which goes
>   before;
> In sequent toil all forwards do contend.
>
> (Sonnet 60, 1–4)

is a version of

> But looke
> As every wave dryves other foorth, and that
>   that commes behynd
> Bothe thrusteth and is thrust itself: Even so the
>   tymes by kynd
> Doo fly and follow bothe at once, and
>   evermore renew.   (Golding, 15.200–3)

Here Shakespeare is imitating closely: his 'sequent' derives from Ovid's 'sequuntur' (15.183) and 'in the main of light' in the following line translates 'editus in lucem' (15.221). He pursues a similar *imitatio* with the image of sea encroaching on land and land on sea in Sonnet 64. But he is also revising, for he undertakes an elision that is thoroughly Ovidian but which is never actually explicitly articulated by Ovid. It is in this sense that Shakespeare is, in Erasmus' terms, being most like his paradigm when he is unlike him, or, in Bloom's terms, making it seem as though he has written his precursor's own most characteristic work.

The elision consists of a movement from past to future. Where Sonnet 59 looks back, and ends with the rather half-hearted couplet 'O, sure I am the wits of former days / To subjects worse have given admiring praise', Sonnet 60 frees itself from eternal repetition by claiming that the verse itself will endure. A few sonnets earlier, in 55, Shakespeare had reiterated the great envoi of the *Metamorphoses*: 'Iamque opus exegi, quod nec Iovis ira nec ignis / nec poterit ferrum nec edax abolere vetustas' (15.871–2); 'Nor Mars his sword nor war's quick fire shall burn / The living record

of your memory' (lines 7–8).[16] Now in the couplet of Sonnet 60 this idea of triumphing through writing recurs and offers itself as the overcoming of time's inexorability: 'And yet to times in hope my verse shall stand, / Praising thy worth despite his cruel hand.' In book fifteen of *Metamorphoses*, the envoi stands alone, not as a reply to Pythagoras. It is Shakespeare who makes the connection and thus uses one part of Ovid to unwrite or rewrite another. Shakespeare thus both clears a space for himself, enables himself to say something new, and at the same time remains responsive to his paradigm. In the very act of asserting his own immortality, he asserts Ovid's. There is a kind of mutuality whereby imagining the past and imagining the future are one and the same; Ovid's paradigmatic status proves his immortality and implicitly opens the way for Shakespeare to achieve similar immortality through becoming paradigmatic to eyes not yet created and when rehearsed on tongues to be. As Puttenham put it in his account of *paradigma*, the example of the past gathers probability of like success for the present.

The idea that Ovid has been reborn in sonnets such as 60 effects a curious effacement of the poetic 'I'. The conceit of Shakespeare writing Ovid will not do here. Meres's image of 'the sweete wittie soule of Ovid liv[ing] in mellifluous and hony-tongued Shakespeare' carries the converse implication that it is Ovid who is writing Shakespeare. If it is Ovid who 'lives', Shakespeare has disappeared in the very moment of asserting his own enduring life. Consider the 'I' of Sonnet 64:

> When I have seen the hungry ocean gain
> Advantage on the kingdom of the shore,
> And the firm soil win of the wat'ry main,
> Increasing store with loss and loss with store;
> When I have seen such interchange of state...
>
> (lines 5–9)

---

[16] Being an eclectic rather than a Ciceronian, Shakespeare has in this sonnet combined Ovid's envoi with Horace's 'Exegi monumentum aere perennius' (*Odes*, 3.30.1).

and so on. Who is this 'I'? Is it the speaker of the Sonnets, or is it Ovid's speaker, Pythagoras – or the speaker of the Englished Ovid, Arthur Golding?

> Even so have places oftentymes exchaunged
>   theyr estate.
> For I have seene it sea which was substanciall
>   ground alate,
> Ageine where sea was, I have seene the same
>   become dry lond,   (Golding, 15.287–9)

The 'I' has been transformed into a polyphony of voices. According to one view, this dissolution is a source of anxiety. One might apply to Sonnet 64 the conclusion of Terence Cave's chapter on Renaissance imitation theory in *The Cornucopian Text*: 'it recognizes the extent to which the production of any discourse is conditioned by pre-existing instances of discourse; the writer is always a rewriter, the problem then being to differentiate and authenticate the rewriting ... Rewriting betrays its own anxiety by personifying itself as the product of an author; it imprints on itself – one might even say *forges* – an identity' (Cave, pp. 76–7). But the polyphonic 'I' can equally well be seen as an expansion rather than a dissolution, a product of generosity rather than anxiety. There is, I think, a modesty about Shakespeare's self-effacement which is the counterpart to the arrogance of his inverted *paradigma*. Again, there is a process of repetition and variation in the movement from sonnet to sonnet: 60 overcomes the anxiety of 59, then 64 assuages the potential egotism of 60.

John Kerrigan sees modesty at work in Sonnet 55, and differentiates Shakespeare's claims for immortality from Ovid's. The final word of the *Metamorphoses* is in the egotistic first-person future: 'vivam', 'I shall live.' Golding renders the poem's last line 'My lyfe shall everlastingly bee lengthened still by fame' (Golding, 15.995). 'Strikingly, though,' says Kerrigan, 'Shakespeare promises to preserve the young man in verse, not himself.' Kerrigan notes that this difference has led to the citation of a third possible 'source' for Sonnet 55, an

elegy of Propertius (III.ii) where immortality is bestowed on the person praised, not the poet himself; he is rightly dismissive of this possibility, since Propertius was barely read in the 1590s. 'It seems more likely', Kerrigan concludes, 'that Shakespeare adapted Ovid and Horace in Sonnet 55, and virtually certain that early readers would have understood the lines that way.'[17] I am not so sure that early readers would have understood the lines this way. I think that, like nearly all modern commentators who have thought about Shakespeare and Ovid, Kerrigan has overlooked the fact that any Elizabethan who had been to a grammar school would have been well versed not only in the *Metamorphoses*, but also in Ovid's other works. I would suggest that in Sonnet 55 Shakespeare is again revising Ovid by making Ovid revise himself through the conflation of two different works. Images of the text outliving sword and fire derive from the end of the *Metamorphoses*, but the modesty of '*You* live in this' derives from the end of the *Tristia*:

> Quanta tibi dederim nostris monumenta
>   libellis,
>   o mihi me coniunx carior, ipsa vides.
> detrahat auctori multum fortuna licebit,
>   tu tamen ingenio clara ferere meo;
> dumque legar, mecum pariter tua fama legetur.
>   (v.xiv. 1–5)

[What a monument I have raised to thee in my books, O my wife, dearer to me than myself, thou seest. Though fate may take much from their author, thou at least shall be made illustrious by my powers. As long as I am read, thy fame shall be read along with me.]   (Loeb trans., adapted)

It is from the tender 'tibi' and 'tu' of this passage, I would suggest, that Shakespeare works his immortalization of the beloved, just as it is from the structure of repetition in the

---

17 *The Sonnets and A Lover's Complaint*, p. 241; see also p. 21. For the citation of Propertius, see J. B. Leishman, *Themes and Variations in Shakespeare's Sonnets* (London, 1961), p. 42.

last line of this – 'As long as I am read, thy fame shall be read along with me' – that he creates the couplet of Sonnet 18, 'So long as men can breathe or eyes can see, / So long lives this, and this gives life to thee.'[18] The transformation of Ovid's wife into Shakespeare's fair youth is another suggestive revision: between the antique and the modern pen there is a constancy in love but a change in the object of love.

In such patterns of reiteration and variation, there is a rapid interchange between *verba* and *res*. The language of such sonnets as 18 and 19, 60 and 64, is for ever shifting as it interlocks with and then extricates itself from the words, *verba*, of Ovid. And such shiftings furnish the alert reader with a reminder of the metamorphic substance, *res*, which Ovid and Shakespeare share. And in responding to the *res*, Shakespeare is going beyond the imitative poet like Watson who is stuck with the *verba* of his models. The Pythagoras of book fifteen has a figure which comes to the quintessence of the *res*, the matter, of both the *Metamorphoses* and the Sonnets:

> And even as supple wax with ease receyveth
>   fygures straunge,
> And keepes not ay one shape, ne bydes assured
>   ay from chaunge,
> And yit continueth alwayes wax in substaunce:
>   So I say
> The soule is ay the selfsame thing it was, and
>   yit astray
> It fleeteth intoo sundry shapes.
>   (Golding, 15.188–92)

That the soul, the self, is like wax is an idea which possessed Shakespeare deeply. One thinks of Theseus addressing Hermia,

>   you are but as a form in wax,
> By him imprinted, and within his power
> To leave the figure or disfigure it.
>   (*A Midsummer Night's Dream*, 1.1.49–51)

And one thinks of related images of 'impression' and 'imprint' in the Sonnets (e.g. 112.1; 77.3). It is an idea that brings us to another kind of influence and another kind of anxiety.

I have been arguing that in his frequent references to antique books, and especially in Sonnet 59, Shakespeare reveals his susceptibility to the anxiety of literary influence, but that in most of the Ovidian sonnets, and especially Sonnet 60, he overcomes that anxiety by means of a process of reiteration and variation that corresponds to both Pythagorean metempsychosis and Bloomian 'revision'. But what the Sonnets cannot escape is the anxiety of personal influence. The real melancholy of the sequence comes from the way in which the poet is *impressed*, not by Ovid, not by the 'rival poet', but by the fair youth himself. The sense in which Ovid, and indeed the whole panegyric tradition, begets the Sonnets is far less troubling than that in which the youth himself begets them, in which he is the book that is the poet's burden. Nobody can take the poet's Ovid away from him; even if his library is burnt like Ben Jonson's, he can always buy a replacement copy. But the youth is a costly unique incunabulum:

> Farewell – thou art too dear for my possessing,
> And like enough thou know'st thy estimate.
> The charter of thy worth gives thee releasing;
> My bonds in thee are all determinate.
> For how do I hold thee but by thy granting,
> And for that riches where is my deserving?
> The cause of this fair gift in me is wanting,
> And so my patent back again is swerving.
> Thyself thou gav'st, thy own worth then not
>   knowing,
> Or me to whom thou gav'st it else mistaking;
> So thy great gift, upon misprision growing,

---

[18] It is strange that scholars (e.g. Baldwin, *Literary Genetics*, p. 215; Lever, *Elizabethan Love Sonnet*, p. 201) have derived the first line of Sonnet 19, 'Devouring Time, blunt thou the lion's paws', from *Tristia*, 4.6.5, but not the couplet of Sonnet 18 from *Tristia*, 5.14.5. An earlier poem in the *Tristia* also gives immortality to the poet's wife: 'quantumcumque tamen praeconia nostra valebunt, / carminibus vives tempus in omne meis' [Yet so far as my praise has power, thou shalt live for all time in my song] (1.6.35–6, Loeb trans.).

Comes home again, on better judgement
    making.
Thus have I had thee as a dream doth
    flatter:
In sleep a king, but waking no such
    matter.

(Sonnet 87)

This sonnet is anxious not about books but about the whims of the beloved. Like Hermia's father, the youth has power to mould another person's self; he is able to shape the poet, 'To leave the figure or disfigure it'. Anxiety is wrought by the fear of losing the beloved; the really terrifying thought is that he has only been possessed in a dream. This sonnet con-tains two words that are crucial to Bloom's theory of poetry: 'swerving' and 'misprision'. For Bloom, all poems are misprisions, mis-interpretations, of other poems, and all poets make room for themselves by swerving – executing a *clinamen*, he calls it – away from their precursors. One might say that the effect of misprision is to guarantee the later poet's copyright. But in Sonnet 87 there is a patent rather than a copyright, and the swerve is in a relationship on which writing only has some bearing. In the last resort, the idea that our loves are built on misprision is a much more disturbing one than that our poems are built on it.

THE PLAY OF *SIR THOMAS MORE* AND SOME CONTEMPORARY EVENTS

E. A. J. HONIGMANN

In previous discussions of the play of *Sir Thomas More* much has been said about the opening 'ill May Day' scenes and little about the play's third and final phase, Sir Thomas's fall. In this short paper I want to look at the play's ending and at some associated problems.

First, though, a question. What *kind* of play is it? Scott McMillin, in his important recent study, called it a history play, and, the history play being a 'hold-all' genre, perhaps rightly.[1] I think, however, that a subgenre that became popular in the 1580s and 1590s provides a more useful label – the 'wise man play', which included *Dr Faustus*, *Friar Bacon*, *John of Bordeaux*, *John a Kent* and probably lost plays such as *The Wise Man of Westchester*. These plays celebrated the deeds of a non-aristocratic wise man who rises to be a friend of princes; he solves the prince's problems, plays tricks on others, and in some cases overcomes a rival wise man (Friar Bungay, John a Cumber; Sir Thomas More has a contest in courtesy with a rival scholar, Erasmus). Though Sir Thomas makes no use of magic, his play follows a recognizable model, which could end either as a tragedy, as does *Dr Faustus*, or with a hero still alive or even flourishing (*Friar Bacon*, *John a Kent*). I mention these alternatives because Munday and his fellow-dramatists could have ended the play with Sir Thomas as Lord Chancellor, loved and respected by all.

They chose not to. Why? As A. W. Pollard pointed out, it was a risky decision. 'More is

shown refusing to sign the articles exhibited to him by the King's command, but the contents of the articles are carefully left unexplained . . . blind as these playwrights were to the difficulties in their path they had at least the wit to see what must inevitably happen if they let him argue his case.'[2] Even if the 'articles' that Sir Thomas refused to sign are left unexplained, merely to show him resisting the king on an issue of conscience (a word repeated several times in these last scenes) could only mean one thing, especially as the play links Sir Thomas's refusal with the Bishop of Rochester's. Campion, Babington, and other so-called traitors were executed in the 1580s and 1590s because they remained loyal to 'the old faith', denying Queen Elizabeth's supremacy in matters of conscience and religion. Sir Thomas and the Bishop, though not accused of attempted regicide, were among the very first to resist the Act of Supremacy, were both executed, and were already honoured by Catholics as English martyrs. A sympathetic portrayal of the most illustrious English 'recusant' of the sixteenth century, and of Sir Thomas's courageous acceptance of death, could therefore have been politically even

---

[1] Scott McMillin, *The Elizabethan Theatre and 'The Book of Sir Thomas More'* (Ithaca, New York, and London, 1987).

[2] Alfred W. Pollard, W. W. Greg, E. Maunde Thompson, J. Dover Wilson, and R. W. Chambers, *Shakespeare's Hand In The Play of Sir Thomas More*, Shakespeare Problems II (Cambridge, 1923), p. 3.

more inflammatory than the 'ill May Day' scenes.

Towards the end the play adopts the conventions of tragedy, as in Lady More's dream, modelled on Clarence's dream in *Richard III*.

> Methought 'twas night
> And that the king and queen went on the
> Thames
> In barges to hear music. My lord and I
> Were in a little boat, methought. Lord, lord,
> What strange things live in slumbers. And,
> being near,
> We grappled to the barge that bare the king.
>
> (lines 1292–7)[3]

Tragedy usually demands some sympathy for its hero, yet neither *Dr Faustus* nor any other Elizabethan tragedy of roughly the same date seems to me as unreservedly sympathetic to its hero as our play. Strange, considering that Sir Thomas is cast in the role of a recusant, and his recusancy, as I have said, need not have been dramatized. Nevertheless, after he refuses to sign the King's 'articles' he is repeatedly referred to, or addressed, as 'good Sir Thomas', 'that good man, Sir Thomas', not only by the poor but even by the King's officers, the general attitude being that 'A wiser or more virtuous gentleman / Was never bred in England' (lines 1613–14). The build-up for this response begins *before* he refuses to sign and carries over to the end. 'Good Sir Thomas' resembles 'Good Duke Humphrey' in *The First Part of the Contention* (*2 Henry VI*), except that Sir Thomas's goodness and wisdom receive even more emphasis.

Sir Thomas's wisdom, demonstrated in the opening and middle scenes, unavoidably affects our response when he refuses to sign the 'articles'. Was that wise? or not? The 'worthiest counsellor that tends our state', he had been described as preoccupied with the 'safety and the peace' of the realm, which depended on 'the golden anvil of his brain' (783ff). Appropriately, he took the part of 'Good Counsel' in the play within the play – how, we must therefore ask, could so good

and wise a man be mistaken in opposing his king? Or perhaps we should take one more step, and ask – 'how certain are we that the dramatists wished us to believe that he was mistaken?'

The scenes in which Sir Thomas approaches his end – mildly insisting that he follows his conscience, disregarding all material advantages, beautifully in command of himself – persuade me that the dramatists might not have agreed with those modern critics who describe the conclusion of the Lord Chancellor's career as his 'disgrace'. I prefer to think that the play culminates in Sir Thomas's triumph – his spiritual triumph over all things worldly. The play continues to the end of Sir Thomas's life, even though other 'wise man' plays sometimes stopped with the hero riding high in his worldly affairs, because the dramatists appreciated that Sir Thomas's special gifts reached perfection in his fall – his quiet dignity, his independence of mind, courage, wit, and his impressive classlessness, equally at his ease with earls and artisans. Nothing in his life became him like the leaving it; everything in the play points forward to this necessary end – whether Lincoln's brave death, or Falkner's uncut hair and vow (compare Sir Thomas's concern for his beard and his conscience), or, more troublingly, the play's bold insistence on bad law and miscarriages of justice.

No one can fail to observe the dramatic irony when Sir Thomas preaches obedience to the King as the gospel of good citizenship. He continues in this belief even after the King sends him to the Tower – which, however, need not imply that the king must always be right. The play stops short of stating that the king and the law are in the wrong – that would have been unacceptable in the 1590s – yet it

---

3 *The Book of Sir Thomas More*, ed. W. W. Greg; revised by F. P. Wilson and Arthur Brown, Malone Society Reprints (1911; Oxford, 1961). Quotations from *Sir Thomas More* are from this edition and are modernized by the author.

persists in raising the spectre of this possibility. In the first scene we hear that lawless strangers can compel the Lord Mayor to send law-abiding citizens to prison. Englishmen dare not 'revenge their own wrongs'; they 'must be bridled by law, and forced to bear . . . wrongs' (lines 25, 52–3). In the second scene Justice Suresby, condemned out of his own mouth by Sir Thomas More's witty stratagem, proves the law to be an ass; the Lord Mayor makes certain that we take this point. It is curious, he says, that Justice Suresby 'will fall in that which [he] condemned in other[s]' (line 309). In the third scene we learn that 'supplication made unto the King' (line 333) protected a stranger against wronged citizens. The law fails again when the royal pardon arrives too late to save Lincoln's life: Surrey blames the sheriff, *he* blames the Council's warrant, and Lincoln, poor man, is dead. The law, the law's officers, and the King himself are shown to be fallible, whereas Sir Thomas is invariably good . . . and wise. After so much careful preparation, which establishes that miscarriages of justice can and do occur, we reach the trial of Sir Thomas, and the play's attitude, I think, is summed up by the servant who says 'I have nothing to do with matters above my capacity, but as God judge me, if I might speak my mind, I think there lives not a more harmless gentleman in the universal world' (line 1683). Even if technically treasonous, Sir Thomas remains innocent after all, in the eyes of many bystanders. And this, of course, was the view of Harpsfield, one of the play's principal sources: Sir Thomas 'lived and died . . . most innocently and most honourably'.[4]

I must now brace myself for the reply that the play, as I have interpreted it, would certainly have been censored, and that Tilney, the Master of the Revels, who censored the 'ill May Day' scenes, did not object to Sir Thomas's triumph, as I have called it. There is a misunderstanding here, for which Greg's Malone Society edition may be responsible. Greg claimed that Tilney wrote 'in the margin of the first page a very conditional licence' (*The Book of Sir Thomas More*, p. x). Tilney's phrasing, however, holds out no promise of a licence, conditional or otherwise.

Leave out the insurrection wholly and the cause thereof, and begin with Sir Thomas More at the Mayor's sessions with a report afterwards of his good service done, being sheriff of London, upon a mutiny against the Lombards. Only by a short report and not otherwise, at your own perils. E. Tilney.   (*The Book of Sir Thomas More*, p. 1)

A. W. Pollard, I believe, explained this note correctly. When Tilney began to read the play he thought that the 'ill May Day' scenes might be allowed, with some changes; but when he reached the end of these scenes he 'saw that half measures would be useless, so he went back to the beginning' and wrote in his drastic order to 'leave out the insurrection wholly'.[5] In short, we do not know how Tilney reacted to the end of the play, except for the fact that he did *not* give it his licence. It may be that he refused to read on when he came to the scene of Sir Thomas's 'capital contempt' (line 1249), feeling that the play was politically beyond redemption, or that he finished it and accepted the ending but would not license it for some other reason.

How could Munday and his colleagues hope to get away with such a challenge to the powers that be, in two out of three sections of the play, if my argument holds? Their strategy seems to have been copied from *Dr Faustus*. The 'ill May Day' rioters are condemned, and confess their fault; Sir Thomas is condemned, and executed. Disobedience is punished, and this, it was hoped, would put the play in the clear, politically speaking. Yet I note that Sir Thomas, though very willing to die at the King's behest, refuses to the end to surrender on the point of conscience. In his extraordinary

---

4 Nicholas Harpsfield, *The Life and Death of Sir Thomas Moore*, ed. Elsie V. Hitchcock, Early English Text Society (London, 1932), p. 63.

5 Pollard, *Shakespeare's Hand*, p. 4.

steadfastness he differs from Dr Faustus; and, I have contended, the third and final section is not a happy afterthought but an integral part of the whole. The end transforms Sir Thomas from a mere wise man, a mere Lord Chancellor, into something greater – that seems to be the play's *raison d'être*.

Disobedience is condemned – yet condemned so sparingly that one must wonder at the dramatists' reticence. When Sir Thomas first refuses to subscribe to the King's 'articles' the Earls of Surrey and Shrewsbury comment, quite minimally:

> 'Tis strange that my Lord Chancellor should refuse
> The duty that the law of God bequeaths
> Unto the king.
> SHREWSBURY
>   Come, let us in. No doubt
> His mind will alter, and the bishop's too.
> Error in learned heads hath much to do.
>
> (lines 1276–81)

Later, the two Earls argue with the Bishop of Rochester, and Surrey condemns the Bishop – yet so mildly as to suggest that there is not much to be said on the King's side. He tells the Bishop

> We not misdoubt your wisdom can discern
> What best befits it. Yet in love and zeal
> We could entreat it might be otherwise.
>
> (lines 1388–90)

The Earls are then sent to Sir Thomas at Chelsea.

>   We are sent to you
> From our mild sovereign, once more to demand
> If you'll subscribe unto those articles.
>
> (lines 1539–41)

They warn him that the bishop has been sent to the Tower 'for the like obstinacy' (line 1546); and 'if you now refuse for to subscribe, / A stricter course will follow' (lines 1548–9).

The rhetoric of condemnation being so highly developed elsewhere in the play, and not only in Sir Thomas's speech to the rebels, I feel that the dramatists pull their punches when they state the case against Sir Thomas. The only eloquent pleas to him to submit come from his family, and are based on self-interest. He, in reply, rests his case on 'conscience', a powerful court of appeal in both Catholic and Protestant eyes. And, as everyone agrees, he remains a good Christian, and wise. The final summing-up speech repeats, *very* briefly, the charge that his death was not wise, but a result of error. The play's surprising failure to push home the case against Sir Thomas becomes clear when we compare this laconic speech with its model, the ringing epilogue of *Dr Faustus*:

> Cut is the branch that might have grown full straight,
> And burned is Apollo's laurel bough
> That sometime grew within this learned man.
> Faustus is gone: regard his hellish fall,
> Whose fiendful fortune may exhort the wise
> Only to wonder at unlawful things.
>
> (Epilogue 1–6)[6]

The play of *Sir Thomas More* also presents a 'learned man' drawn to 'unlawful things'. The epilogue speech, however, still depicts Sir Thomas as 'worthy', and glides past his 'error' as swiftly as may be, just acknowledging it and no more.

> A very learned, worthy gentleman
> Seals error with his blood. Come, we'll to court.
> Let's sadly hence to perfect unknown fates,
> Whilst he tends progress to the state of states.
>
> (lines 1983–6)

Faustus is dragged off to hell; Sir Thomas goes to heaven.

Most of those who have tried to date the play have placed its original composition in or close to 1593. By a strange coincidence, Rowland Lockey painted, in the year 1593, the huge

---

6 Christopher Marlowe, *Doctor Faustus*, ed. John D. Jump, The Revels Plays (London, 1962).

1   *Sir Thomas More and His Descendants.* Rowland Lockey, 1593

canvas of 'Sir Thomas More and his descendants' which now hangs in the National Portrait Gallery (illustration 1), and in the same year, or shortly thereafter, two other pictures of Sir Thomas and his family, all three being partly copied from a lost original by Holbein. The date of the National Portrait Gallery picture is fixed by a Latin inscription giving the age of members of the family in the year 1593. This picture may help us with some of the problems of the play, particularly its sympathetic treatment of recusancy.

Hans Holbein the Younger came to England in 1526, with an introduction from Erasmus to More. He painted a famous portrait of More, a large canvas of More and his household, now lost, and he also sketched individual members of More's family. At Basel there survives a pen and ink sketch of Sir Thomas and his household, a preliminary study by Holbein, which

'must have been completed before More's fifty-first birthday in February 1528'.[7] The large canvas which followed belonged to Andreas de Loo in the later sixteenth century, until his death in 1590, when it was sold, almost certainly to More's grandson, Thomas More II. Art historians inform us that More's grandson 'commissioned at least three versions of this precious heirloom – the exact copy now at Nostell Priory [illustration 2], the National Portrait Gallery picture, and a miniature which closely resembles it'.[8] 'The National Portrait Gallery painting was surely conceived by Thomas More II as a pictorial genealogy, demonstrating his family's loyalty

---

[7]   Angela Lewi, *The Thomas More Family Group* (HMSO, 1974), p. 3.

[8]   Lewi, *The More Family*, p. 7.

2 *The Family of Sir Thomas More.* Rowland Lockey, *c.* 1593

to the Catholic faith. As if to emphasise the point they are holding red prayer books, whereas their forebears are reading the classics.'[9] Stanley Morison drew attention to a special feature of the National Portrait Gallery picture: 'across the full width of the picture are a series of seven coats of arms, the first of which carries the significant motto "Christiano Catholico More"'.[10] Some years later, however, the picture was cleaned, and it was shown that parts of it, including the motto, were additions. Yet 'two of the pictures commissioned by Thomas More II from Lockey', said the catalogue of the National Portrait Gallery's quincentenary exhibition, *The King's Good Servant*, 'explicitly emphasise his family's unbroken allegiance to the Catholic faith'[11] – for example, by giving prominence to the madonna lily, associated with the Virgin

Mary, and to the columbine, a flower associated with the dove, hence with the Holy Ghost.[12]

Thomas More II (1531–1606) owned property in Yorkshire and at Lower Leyton in Essex. In 1582 Richard Topcliffe raided More's house in Essex and More, a known recusant, was imprisoned in the Marshalsea until 1586. After his release 'he was allowed to live in peace in the country, apart from his periodic appearances as a recusant before the

[9] Lewi, *The More Family*, p. 8.
[10] Stanley Morison, *The Likeness of Thomas More: An Iconographical Survey* (1963), p. 23.
[11] J. B. Trapp and Hubertus Schulte Herbrüggen, '*The King's Good Servant': Sir Thomas More 1477/8–1535* (National Portrait Gallery, 1977), p. 18.
[12] Lewi, *The More Family*, p. 6.

Justices of the Peace at the Sessions, the Essex Assizes, the Court of the Archdeacon of Essex and the Consistory Court of the Bishop of London'.[13] When Thomas More was apprehended a copy of Harpsfield's *Life* of Sir Thomas More was found. The Harpsfield manuscript in Emmanuel College, Cambridge, is inscribed 'This book was found by Richard Topcliffe in Mr Thomas More['s] study among other books at Greenstreet, Mr Wayfarer's house, where Mr More was apprehended the xiiith of April 1582' (spelling modernized). Harpsfield's then still unprinted life, according to Vittorio Gabrieli,[14] was a major source of the play of *Sir Thomas More*, and Anthony Munday, it is known, assisted Topcliffe in ferreting out and arresting Catholic recusants.

I have suggested that the play of *Sir Thomas More* celebrates its hero's life and acceptance of death – and, by implication, his loyalty to the Catholic church. At the very same time, it seems, Sir Thomas's grandson commissioned canvases that have been similarly explained by art historians. Could the two celebrations of Sir Thomas be connected? Is it a coincidence, also, that the play and the canvases place Sir Thomas so meaningfully in his family? It has been said that 'Holbein's painting of the More Family was the first example in Northern Europe of an intimate group portrait that is both non-religious and non-ceremonial.'[15] Two of the copies painted in the 1590s introduced Sir Thomas's descendants, who must have asked for this arrangement, another step in the celebration of the family. The play, likewise, gives a special prominence to the hero's family and household, more so than any other 'wise man' play, or any other play of the period known to me. One assumes that Rowland Lockey painted under instructions from Sir Thomas's grandson. Is it conceivable that the dramatists also had contact with Sir Thomas's descendants? Anthony Munday, I readily admit, was no friend of English Catho-

lics – yet, as others have suggested, Munday seems to have had one or more collaborators when he first worked on the play, quite distinct from the play-patchers who later tried to salvage it. The plan, or 'plot', for the play is likely to have come from someone less hostile to English Catholics than Munday, even though Munday was later praised as 'our best plotter'. The idea behind the play – a celebration of Sir Thomas's humane wisdom and recusancy – does not suggest Munday, and the dramatic thinking that went into it is far more imaginative than that in Munday's acknowledged work. The plot must have come from someone willing to take political risks, someone drawn to independent-minded men like Sir Thomas, someone with a taste for sardonic humour and practical jokes, someone, also, endowed with considerable theatrical talent. And this person had access not only to Harpsfield's unprinted life of Sir Thomas More, he also consulted Thomas Stapleton's *Tres Thomae* (1588), a second anti-Protestant biography that would not be easy to get hold of in England (it was printed in Douai). If we could identify a dramatist with these unusual characteristics – an admirer of self-made men, daringly independent himself, especially in his religious thinking, interested in forbidden books, one who might wish to celebrate a Catholic martyr knowing that this would rattle a Protestant audience[16] – we would still wish to know why he did not choose to write the play he had plotted. This, and other questions raised in this paper, would

---

[13] Roy Strong, ed., *Catalogue of Tudor and Jacobean Portraits* (National Portrait Gallery, 1969), p. 349.
[14] V. Gabrieli, '*Sir Thomas More*: Sources, Characters, Ideas', *Moreana*, 23 (1986), 19.
[15] Lewi, *The More Family*, p. 16.
[16] Compare Baines's report on Marlowe's 'damnable judgement of religion', 'that if there be any god or any good religion then it is in the papists ... That all Protestants are hypocritical asses' (F. S. Boas, *Christopher Marlowe* (Oxford, 1966), p. 251).

be answered if our dramatist did not live to complete what he had barely begun – if, let us say, he died unexpectedly on 30 May 1593. I do not wish to press the case for any single claimant; on the other hand, I suggest that the dramatic and political thinking that went into *Sir Thomas More* still needs some attention.[17]

17 The Lord St Oswald writes from Nostell Priory of the Nostell portrait of the Thomas More family that 'the canvas and pigment have been authenticated as being contemporary with Holbein. This resulted from sending samples to the University of Arizona in 1982. We believe that Holbein started the painting, which was later finished most probably by Lockey. The portrait in the National Gallery is different in many ways but particularly because, as I recall, it is a composite picture which includes two or perhaps even three generations and therefore must have been done much later than Holbein.'

'NOBODY'S PERFECT': ACTORS' MEMORIES AND SHAKESPEARE'S PLAYS OF THE 1590s

LOIS POTTER

In Act 3, Scene 1 of Sheridan's *The Critic*, Dangle and Sneer are watching the rehearsal of Mr Puff's tragedy about the Spanish Armada, and he excitedly awaits the entrance of his 'principal character', Lord Burleigh: 'I only hope the Lord High Treasurer is perfect – if he is but perfect!' When I first read the play, I did not understand this line. The joke, I thought, lay in the disproportion between the modesty of Puff's tone and the impossibility of his wish. In fact, the real point soon becomes apparent. Lord Burleigh enters, goes through an elaborate series of facial expressions, but says nothing. 'Hush!', Puff warns, 'or you'll put him out.'

SNEER. Put him out! how the plague can that be, if he's not going to say anything?

    (*The Critic* 3.1.15–16, 23–5)[1]

The joke, in other words, is based on the fact that the theatrical meaning of the word 'perfect' is 'word-perfect'. An actor is the sum of his or her lines, and a perfect performance is one in which these lines have been perfectly learned. It is the association of being word-perfect with other kinds of perfection that I want to explore in this article.

It seems, oddly enough, to be a new topic. Actors' lapses of memory are generally regarded in the same category as other technical hitches, like doors that do not close properly and offstage noises in the wrong place. It is an unwritten rule that theatre reviews ignore all but the most spectacular lapses on the opening night of a production. By contrast, you can hardly read any actor's biography or memoirs without coming across anecdotes about 'drying', most of them comic, some of them extremely implausible. This very eagerness to discuss the subject shows how deep-seated is the fear of forgetting, or of the fear that makes one forget. Shakespeare's Sonnet 23 refers to

  an unperfect actor on the stage
 Who with his fear is put besides his part.

    (lines 1–2)

And the phrase 'besides his part', like 'out of his part', indicates the extent to which identity is bound up with memory. When an actor is 'out', he suffers a double loss of identity, both as the character he represents and also as an actor, failing to do the one thing essential to his profession. It is no wonder that young actors, like the dramatist Thomas Otway, have been put off a theatrical career for life by one terrifying experience. Charles Macklin, still playing Shylock at the age of eighty-nine, made a formal apology to his audience for forgetting his lines:

Ladies and Gentlemen: Within these very few hours I have been seized with a terror of mind I never in my life felt before; it has totally destroyed my corporeal as well as mental faculties.[2]

---

[1] *The Dramatic Works of Richard Brinsley Sheridan*, ed. Cecil Price (Oxford, 1973), vol. 2.
[2] William W. Appleton, *Charles Macklin, An Actor's Life* (Cambridge, Mass., 1961), p. 226.

He requested their patience and was lucky enough to get it, for that evening at any rate. Audiences in those days could be vicious: they were made up of people experienced in verbatim learning who were as likely to shout 'Out!' during a performance as twentieth-century sports fans.

Modern theatre audiences tend to be embarrassed rather than angry in a comparable situation, but this fact does not diminish the actor's fear of forgetting. No one who has read Antony Sher's brilliant *Year of the King*, his account of rehearsing *Richard III*, can forget his nightmares and his confession that 'Each time I have to take a prompt it feels like a tiny humiliation.'[3] The fear is so private that at one point he even hesitates to write it in his diary (p. 233); when he dries during a preview, and someone comments on it afterwards, he feels that perhaps bringing the subject out in the open will help to lay the jinx (p. 240). The main source of his difficulty in line-learning is obviously fear, a fear in this case related to a complicated identity crisis (how to be Richard without being Olivier). Once the production opens and his constructed identity has been validated by the critical response, the lines cease to be a problem (p. 249).

This deeply personal fear seems as close as anything can be to a universal trait of actors, but it may have been of particular relevance to actors of the early 1590s, of whom Shakespeare was one. This period was one in which a number of short-lived, unstable dramatic companies were struggling for survival and competing for the favours of audiences and patrons with a constantly changing repertoire. Most recent theatrical histories have shown an awareness of the unusual demands that this situation would have made on the actor, though they differ as to how effectively he would have coped with them. Bernard Beckerman claims that the Elizabethan actor had to 'cultivate a fabulous memory';[4] G. E. Bentley is more pessimistic:

Not only were most companies producing scores of new plays, but in the earlier years of the period, 1590–1610, rarely was a play given consecutive performances; in the later years there were seldom more than three consecutive performances. Under such conditions a letter-perfect rendition must have been unheard of, and prompting a constant necessity.[5]

There has been surprisingly little attempt to investigate the truth of either of these claims. Although the study of memory is an important branch of psychology, I have been unable to find any work devoted to the specific problems of actors. This is because the learning of lines happens both in isolation and communally, as part of the rehearsal process: it is too long-term and complex an event to lend itself to the collection of experimental data. Psychological research has concentrated instead on controllable experiments in the memorizing of nonsense syllables, numbers, and short stories. Most evidence about actors' experiences of memorizing and forgetting is therefore anecdotal and unverifiable. Early in 1988, in an attempt to supplement this kind of information, I sent a questionnaire about memory to members of the English Shakespeare Company, which has for some years been touring with productions of the two history cycles (though with the three Henry VI plays condensed into two). I was particularly interested in this group because the size and nature of the ESC repertory, which also involved a great deal of doubling, seemed to offer the closest available analogy with the problems of the actor in the early 1590s. Fifteen out of

---

3 Antony Sher, *Year of the King, An Actor's Diary and Sketchbook* (London, 1985), p. 207.

4 Bernard Beckerman, *Shakespeare at the Globe 1599–1609* (London, 1962), p. 130.

5 Gerald Eades Bentley, *The Profession of Player in Shakespeare's Time 1590–1642* (Princeton, 1984), p. 82. For the idea that only *some* scenes would have been thoroughly memorized and rehearsed, see Peter Thomson, *Shakespeare's Theatre* (London, Boston, Melbourne, Henley, 1983), pp. 116–17.

twenty-five actors replied, many of them very helpfully. Such a small sample can hardly be statistically significant, but it offers a starting point for further research, and I shall use the answers to the questionnaire at various points in what follows.

One subject on which I was eager to get the company's views was the effect on memory of playing many parts in quick succession. The actors of the ESC agreed that doing several plays in a day had very little effect on their memory except to the extent that, obviously, it was tiring and therefore might affect concentration. One actor claimed that the conditions in which they were working actually made concentration less of a problem than usual. This corroborates the evidence of psychology. Long-term memory does not appear to be finite, though in the short term one thing may crowd out another.[6] According to many twentieth-century actors, the real difficulties with memory occur during a long run; Maggie Smith, for example, refers to 'those awful blank moments when you get "I don't know what act I'm in", or "Have I said that before?"'[7]

Elizabethan actors would, of course, have laboured under difficulties from which their modern counterparts are free, but these may not have been so serious as is sometimes suggested. First, they were not supposed to speak any lines outside those in the official copy of the play approved by the Master of the Revels. In practice, however, this rule must have referred to the content rather than the precise words of the text; unless the Master of the Revels had a phenomenal memory, he could hardly have checked on the latter in detail. Second, they may have worked at a disadvantage in having to learn their parts from 'sides' which gave only their lines and cues.[8] On the other hand, the size of the major roles and the fact that the minor actors doubled so many parts may have given the cast a clearer view of the shape of the play as well as allow-

ing them to do more complete run-throughs. It is even possible that the modern practice of spending most rehearsal time in detailed work on individual scenes, running through the whole play only at a very late stage, actually makes things harder for the actors. Research appears to show that verbatim memorizing is easier if a text is perceived and studied as a whole, not bit by bit.[9] We come back to the subject of fear: the greatest problem for Elizabethan actors was not the difficulty of learning their lines but the circumstances which created the fear of forgetting: the insecurity of their position in relation to their audience and patrons and the competitiveness of their relationship to other acting companies.

Nashe's *Summer's Last Will and Testament* (acted 1592) dramatizes this insecurity and in part exorcizes it by transposing it to the relationships between members of the cast. A clown pretending to be Will Summers, Henry VIII's famous fool, begins the play by pretending to improvise, then pretends to be embarrassed by the sight of his patron and declares that he will now pretend that all his ad libs were part of his part. After speaking the prologue, he announces that by way of vengeance on the author he will remain on stage for the rest of the play and make rude comments, trying to put the other characters out. He knows, he says, that they will not dare to interrupt him, 'for feare of marring of all' (line 93). And he warns the actors,

looke to your cues, my masters; for I intend to play the knaue in cue, and put you besides all your parts,

---

[6] An easily accessible summary of findings on these points is I.M.L. Hunter, *Memory* (Harmondsworth, 1957; revised edn 1964), especially the chapters on 'Short-term Memory' (pp. 56–93) and 'Memorizing' (pp. 94–142).

[7] Ronald Hayman, ed., *Playback 2* (London, 1973), p. 110.

[8] See Beckerman, *Shakespeare at the Globe*, p. 132, and Peter Holland, *The Ornament of Action, Text and Performance in Restoration Comedy* (Cambridge, 1979), p. 65.

[9] Hunter, *Memory*, pp. 114–20.

if you take not the better heede. *Actors*, you Rogues, come away, cleare your throats, blowe your noses, and wype your mouthes ere you enter, that you may take no occasion to spit or to cough, when you are *non plus*. (lines 93–9)[10]

In fact, the actors simply ignore him, like the professionals they are, and give a 'perfect' performance. But we have only the evidence of the printed text, which also shows that Will Summers' apparent anarchy is completely under authorial control: we have no way of knowing whether the performance itself escaped this authority. The clown's startling description of how actors carry on when they have dried up is presumably an exaggeration, but it brings out what I think is a real distinction between the clown who is allowed to step outside his part and the performer who has to be 'perfect' because he has no alternative; if he forgets his lines, he simply looks ridiculous. This distinction is reflected in two kinds of writing: the elaborately patterned and artificial speeches of serious characters would have been relatively easy to learn and relatively difficult to improvise; on the other hand, the parts that are hard to learn – the clowns' passages of prose or doggerel – allowed them to show their skill at improvisation or to give the illusion of it. The juxtaposition of the two styles is social as well as stylistic. It results from the peculiar social status not only of acting but also of memory.

Acting is two things: a demonstration of skill and an imitation of natural behaviour. These are not always compatible. The contrast between apparent spontaneity on the one hand and 'being perfect' on the other is clearly recognized in the classical treatises on rhetoric and the Renaissance works derived from them. Cicero points out early in *De Oratore* that, whereas in all other arts we have most admiration for the practitioner who is 'farthest removed from the understanding and mental capacity of the untrained', the best orator is the one who stays closest to the language and style of an ordinary human being.[11] Although the

various speakers in this dialogue frequently mention the actor Roscius with respect, they are nevertheless concerned to emphasize the difference between him and the orator: 'Who would deny that in his movements and carriage the orator must have the bearing and elegance of Roscius? Yet no one will urge young devotees of eloquence to toil like actors at the study of gesture.'[12] Abraham Fraunce goes still farther in his *Arcadian Rhetorike* (1588): 'The gesture must follow the change and varietie of the voyce, answering thereunto in euerie respect: yet not parasiticallie as stage plaiers vse, but grauelie and decentlie as becommeth men of greater calling.'[13] Fraunce here makes explicit something which is only implicit in Cicero, the *social* difference between actors and other kinds of public speakers such as statesmen and preachers. The latter must be more 'natural'; they must show that what is only learned behaviour in an actor is part of their very nature – as in Castiglione's concept of *sprezzatura*, which is a calculated 'imperfection'. If the orator wishes to emphasize the spontaneity of his speech, hesitation is actually an embellishment, since it can be taken to show that he is thinking on his feet; it may also help him to win his audience over by showing that he feels a proper deference towards them. *De Oratore* suggests that a speaker who begins hesitantly (compare Mark Antony at Caesar's funeral) is more likely to carry his audience with him.[14] Similarly, a preacher wishes to seem inspired and almost literally to pull words out of the air. By contrast, although the actor is pretending to speak his own words,

---

[10] Thomas Nashe, *Summer's Last Will and Testament, The Works of Thomas Nashe*, ed. Ronald B. McKerrow, vol. 3 (London, 1905), p. 236.

[11] Cicero, *De Oratore*, translated by E. W. Sutton and H. Rackham, Loeb edn (London and Cambridge, Mass., 1943), I.iii, p. 11.

[12] Cicero, *De Oratore*, I.lix, p. 183.

[13] Edited by Ethel Seaton, Luttrell Society no. 9 (Oxford, 1950), p. 120.

[14] Cicero, *De Oratore*, II.xlix, pp. 347–9.

the audience knows that he is really reciting them. If he hesitates, he simply makes the audience afraid that he has forgotten his lines. While the deference due to the speaker's audience can still be found in the apologetic tone of the prologue or chorus of a play, the performance itself needed to demonstrate complete professional competence, and, for most spectators, the indispensable sign of competence was being word-perfect.

How would the actors have achieved this? Would classical and Renaissance theories of memory have been any use to them? As is well known by now, the classical art of memory emphasizes the visualization of images in specific places as a principle of order. The concept of order and classification which was associated with the work of Peter Ramus is also part of classical rhetorical theory, since it is based on the obvious fact that (as Quintilian points out) it is easier for both speaker and audience to remember something with a clear structure.[15] This was in any case how the mind was thought to work; Aristotle insisted that 'it is not possible to think without an image', and that one's memory was a memory of images rather than of the things which the images denote.[16] The 'art' of memory consisted, therefore, in making these images as vivid as possible, even to the point of grotesqueness, and in arranging them in an order which would facilitate remembrance.

Recent psychological research bears out the validity of both imaging and ordering as valuable encoding processes, though there is some debate as to whether the grotesque images recommended in the classical theory are any better than conventional ones; the main point seems to be the principle of linkage between concept and image, however it is done.[17] However, both Cicero and Quintilian point out that the technique is primarily useful for the order of ideas rather than verbatim recall.[18] Some actors deliberately make use of visual techniques; several of the ESC actors wrote of the importance of 'pictures' and 'images'. It is also possible to visualize the words on the page. (It may be that complex stanza forms, like the one used in some of the mystery cycles, helped visualization of the lines.) Sometimes a very visual and ordered speech, like Jaques's description of the seven ages of man, sounds as if it had been written for the place-and-image method of learning, but in fact the method would have helped only with the order of the speech; it would not have told the actor what the precise words should be. Actors learn their lines through a combination of encoding techniques: rhythm, visualization (on the page and in terms of stage movement), emotional memory for the feeling of a scene, and, above all, semantic memory for the meaning of the lines.

Early Shakespeare plays, and plays of the 1590s generally, tend to be easier to memorize than later ones, precisely because of the number of such techniques that they use: they are much more obviously rhythmical and patterned, for instance, than the later works; their imagery is striking; they make a good deal of use of rhyme. These qualities also make them less naturalistic than the later plays, to the point where the actors' concern with 'per-

---

[15] Quintilian, *Institutio Oratoria*, translated by H. E. Butler, 4 vols., Loeb edn (London and New York, 1922), vol. 4, pp. 232–4. Frances Yates, *The Art of Memory* (London, 1966), is the best-known study of this subject. It is usefully corrected and supplemented in David Newton-De Molina, 'A Critical Select History of the Classical Arts of Memory and their Interpretation, with Special Reference to English Arts of Memory 1509–1620' (unpublished Ph.D. thesis, University of Cambridge, 1971); I owe this reference to Brian Vickers, *In Defence of Rhetoric* (Oxford, 1988), p. 65.

[16] Aristotle, *De Memoria et Reminiscentia*, in *Aristotle on Memory*, edited and translated by Richard Sorabji (London, 1972), p. 48.

[17] P. E. Morris, 'Strategies for Learning and Recall', in M. M. Gruneberg and P. E. Morris, ed., *Applied Problems in Memory* (London, New York, and San Francisco, 1979), p. 47.

[18] Cicero, *De Oratore*, II.lxxxviii, pp. 470–1 and Quintilian, *Institutio Oratoria*, vol. 4, p. 225.

fection' actually becomes part of their substance. Obviously, it would be disastrous if the audience of a play were aware only that they were watching a feat of memory, but there are times when this awareness can work to the advantage of the actors. Moments when characters are shown trying to remember something, when they recite rather than speaking, or when they speak in a manner which diverts attention from the content to the form of what they are saying – all these exist on the borderline between acting-as-mimesis and acting-as-skill.

For the sake of simplicity, I shall consider some of these devices under the headings of comic, historical, and tragic, and I shall begin with the tragic, because I have comparatively little to say about it. I think this is because – to use a vastly oversimplified generalization – comedy is about showing off one's memory, history is about trying to remember, and tragedy is about being unable to forget. This last view seems implicit in a famous reply often quoted in books of rhetoric: when someone offered to teach Themistocles the art of memory, he replied that he would rather be taught how to forget.[19] Richard II (*Richard II* 3.4.137–8) and Constance (*King John*, 3.4.48–50) are among those who express the same wish. The sense of lyricism in early Shakespeare plays comes largely from the detailed evocation of small-scale effects, whether pictorial (the Queen Mab speech) or verbal (the obsessive punning). While at times this excessive verbal and visual awareness seems purely decorative, in moments of extreme emotion it can be seen as the result of a mental state in which the mind can no longer select, or in which the desire for order and classification is taken to extremes. In what I call the Kennedy Assassination Syndrome, everything in one's immediate surroundings is vitrified by the shock of a traumatic experience, and one has the illusion of total recall of those surroundings every time the subject comes up. Romeo's 'I do remember an apothe-

cary' (5.1.38) is a case of prophetic Kennedy Syndrome: the news of Juliet's death makes him remember not only the apothecary but – in amazing detail – the contents of his shop:

> And in his needy shop a tortoise hung,
> An alligator stuffed, and other skins
> Of ill-shaped fishes; and about his shelves
> A beggarly account of empty boxes,
> Green earthen pots, bladders, and musty
>   seeds,
> Remnants of packthread, and old cakes of
>   roses
> Were thinly scattered to make up a show.
>
> (5.1.43–9)

The relation between memory and imagination, a key philosophical question, is obviously relevant to this speech. Romeo himself later wonders whether he has lost the ability to distinguish between them: 'Said he not so? Or did I dream it so?' (5.3.79). Madness, loss of identity, and disorder of memory go together in tragedy. The reason these plays have relatively little to say about the kind of memory specific to the actor is that tragedies involve a higher proportion of semantic memory than the other plays and thus draw less attention to their status as a learned text. Even their mad speeches can be shown to 'make sense' in the context of the play as a whole. Romeo's inventory of the apothecary's shop, for example, sounds like a random list but it is unified by the idea of the extreme poverty which will make the apothecary willing to break the law by selling poison.

Thus the art of memory *is* relevant to this subject, though in a negative way. A speech obviously lacking the qualities of order and method which were supposed to facilitate recall would not only have been difficult to learn, it would have been recognized as a feat of memory. Such speeches are much commoner in comedies and histories than in tragedies. In comedy, there are several devices by

---

[19] E.g. in Cicero, *De Oratore*, II.lxxiv, pp. 426–7.

which actors draw attention to their memory skills. One is by the speed of their playing: as with a difficult piece of music, the easiest way to make an impression is to show how fast one can do it. Speed of repartee was one of the characteristics for which boy actors were known. More highly drilled than adult actors, they were likely to think of learning lines as a branch of the rote-learning familiar from school. The fact that boys in the adult companies were associated chiefly with women's parts may have contributed to the emphasis on the speed of women's tongues familiar to most readers of Renaissance drama. In the anonymous boys' play, *Jacob and Esau* (first printed in 1568), Mido, the boy servant, comments to Isaac on the argument between him and his wife;

> she hath as quick answers as ever I saw.
> You could not speak anything unto her so thick,
> But she had her answer as ready and as quick.
> *Isaac.* Yea, women's answers are but few times to seek.[20]

There are indications that boys, as women, delivered their repartee at a cracking pace: Rosaline and Catherine are complimented on 'a set of wit well played' (*Love's Labour's Lost*, 5.2.29). Richard of Gloucester refers to his stichomythic exchange with Anne as 'this keen encounter of our wits' from which he wants to move into 'a slower method' (*Richard III*, 1.2.115–16).

Another device is to draw attention to the fact that a passage is difficult to remember. The comic actor is relatively secure from the humiliation of drying up, because he never pretends to be anything other than he is, and his traditional role is to 'mistake the word'. Forgetting, or pretending to forget, the lines in comedy may actually be his opportunity to show his intellectual superiority to the character he is portraying. He can be given lines – like the nonsense speeches in the traditional Vice role – which draw attention to their own artifice and to the difficulty that he must have

had in memorizing them. An obvious case is Biondello's speech about Petruccio coming to the wedding:

Why, Petruccio is coming in a new hat and an old jerkin, a pair of old breeches thrice-turned, a pair of boots that have been candle-cases, one buckled, another laced, an old rusty sword ta'en out of the town armoury with a broken hilt, and chapeless, with two broken points, his horse hipped, with an old mothy saddle and stirrups of no kindred, besides, possessed with the glanders and like to mose in the chine, troubled with the lampass, infected with the fashions, full of windgalls, sped with spavins, rayed with the yellows, past cure of the fives, stark spoiled with the staggers, begnawn with the bots, weighed in the back and shoulder-shotten, near-legged before and with a half-cheeked bit and a headstall of sheep's leather which, being restrained to keep him from stumbling, hath been often burst and now repaired with knots, one girth six times pieced, and a woman's crupper of velour which hath two letters for her name fairly set down in studs, and here and there pieced with pack-thread. (*Taming of the Shrew*, 3.2.43–61)

This speech (written for a boy actor) is a fiendish combination of vivid detail with what seems a total lack of order. The actor would probably learn it by finding his own ordering principle, but he usually conceals this order in performance by delivering it at breakneck speed, like a Gilbert and Sullivan patter song. This, of course, emphasizes its technical difficulty and explains why it often gets applause in production. A further joke occurs when Baptista responds as if he had just heard not a virtuoso performance but an ordinary piece of information, asking the mundane question, 'Who comes with him?'

The absence of order also draws one's attention to the virtuoso element in the jangled reminiscences of Juliet's Nurse and Mistress Quickly, and the unsuccessful attempt at 'method' in Dogberry's 'sixth and lastly they

---

[20] Edited by John Crow, Malone Society Reprints (Oxford, 1956), lines 442–5.

have belied a lady, thirdly they have verified unjust things, and to conclude, they are lying knaves' (*Much Ado About Nothing*, 5.1.210–12). This is also an example of an actor's memory being tested on stage: Don Pedro, parodying Dogberry in his reply, has got to repeat this illogical order correctly. Another clear case of an actor displaying his memory is Touchstone's elaborate set piece on lying in the last act of *As You Like It*. After the clown has gone through the whole sequence, Jaques then asks, 'Can you nominate in order now the degrees of the lie?' (5.4.86). In 1967 the Royal Shakespeare Company's *As You Like It* featured a Touchstone who was also a professional comedian, Roy Kinnear. During his first sequence, in one performance, he either lost track, or pretended to lose track, of 'the degrees of the lie', with the result that Jaques's line had the effect of a challenge from one actor to another and Kinnear's successful repetition of the list got audience applause.

Memory-testing is part of the plot of *Love's Labour's Lost* (a play about broken and forgotten promises). Its last act develops the device which Nashe had used as the framework for *Summer's Last Will and Testament*. The spectators of the masque of Russians and the pageant of the Nine Worthies clearly regard themselves as taking part in a competition: the actors have to remember their lines, the spectators try to 'put them out'. Just as Mote is about to refer to the brightness of the ladies' eyes, he discovers that they are wearing masks and moreover have turned their backs on him. He promptly adapts his lines to the new circumstances:

> A holy parcel of the fairest dames –
> *The ladies turn their backs to him*
> That ever turned their – backs to mortal
> views.   (5.2.159–60)

However, Mote is not allowed to behave like Will Summers. Instead of being pleased at his resourcefulness, Berowne and the others make it clear that they want the boy to stick to his text, however inappropriate; the result is that,

after being 'out' in the sense of inaccurate, he is out in the full sense; he starts repeating lines and finally leaves in confusion. During the show of the Nine Worthies, the other actors display the full range of difficulties with memory. Costard's memory is semantic, but his lack of 'literary competence' makes him deliver his first line as 'I Pompey am, Pompey surnamed the Big' (5.2.545). Sir Nathaniel is an actor put beside his part with fear. Holofernes and Don Armado are the victims of the spectators' deliberate attempt to use interruptions and improvisations to put them 'out of countenance' and thus out of their parts. Holofernes admits defeat, but I am not sure whether he means that he has lost track of his lines as a result of all the interruptions, or simply that he has decided to give up in the face of so much competition. Costard and Armado are the two characters who cannot be put out of their parts, Costard because he was never in it, and Armado because he is never out of it: he has always identified himself with the worthies of the past and can talk in no other style. It is the two would-be intellectuals, the schoolmaster and vicar, who suffer, and their uncertain social status is a counterpart of their uncertainty about coping with stage fright and barracking. The scene effectively indicates the helplessness of actors in their relationship as servants to their social superiors. But it also indicates the superiority of the Lord Chamberlain's men to the amateur actors who in other respects might have looked down on them. The fact that Costard can ad lib whereas Mote cannot illustrates something which might have begun to arouse the envy of the 'straight' actors, the clown's greater freedom in relation to his text.

In the history plays, by contrast, it is not the comic characters who have the most difficulty in remembering. The relation of memory to history is a commonplace of the period – as in Puttenham's account of 'historicall Poesie':

There is nothing in man of all the potential parts of his mind (reason and will except) more noble or more necessary to the actiue life the[n] memory . . . For these regards the Poesie historicall is of all other next the diuine most honorable and worthy.[21]

In oral cultures – and the Elizabethan age was still partly such a culture – repetition and remembering of the past are essential to the identity both of the individual and of the group. The psychologist I.M.L. Hunter describes four ways in which memories can be preserved: through versification of the material to be remembered; through formalized recital by a group; through the association of legends with geographical locations; and through specialized remembrancers who have the responsibility for keeping, and handing on, this tradition.[22] Hunter also cites examples of how memory can be deliberately modified to suit the needs of the present, as when a legend of northern Ghana, originally intended to explain the existence of seven dominant chiefdoms by the fact that the founder of the state had had seven sons, was altered after the number of these chiefdoms was reduced to five: 'When the legend was recorded again, sixty years later, the founder was said to have had five sons, and no mention was made of the two divisions which had now vanished from the political map.'[23]

The mnemonic devices listed by Hunter have obvious counterparts in the plays about English history, whether in the versified genealogies and lists of those slain in battle, the roles of elderly 'remembrancers', or such formalized group recitals as the 'I had an Edward, till a Richard killed him' sequence in *Richard III* (4.4.40ff.). But it is likely that the theatre's depiction of what Puttenham calls 'the lively image of our deare forefathers' was more effective in creating the illusion of a communal recovery of lost history. The difficulty of making purely verbal information either interesting or memorable is illustrated in what happened to Richard of York's claim to the throne (*The First Part of the Contention* (*2 Henry VI*), 2.2.10–52), the most obviously important example of this genre. The actor playing

Warwick is thought to have been responsible for the reported version of this speech in the Bad Quarto of the play.[24] If so, he was not only one of the two persons to whom York addressed his lengthy explanation, he also responded to it with the admiring 'What plain proceedings is more plain than this?' (line 53). Yet the equivalent passage in the Bad Quarto shows that he was unable to remember either the names or the order of Edward III's seven sons. This is hardly surprising, since the speech has little more shape than a clown's nonsense speeches. The same can be said of purely ritualistic announcements like those spoken by heralds and marshals. The actor who played the Lord Marshal in the ESC production of *Richard II* had difficulty learning the lines he speaks in the lists at Coventry, partly because they were not identical for each contestant and partly, as he suggested, because they were not spoken *to* anyone, but simply left in the air. The dramatic function of such lines is equivalent to the trumpet fanfares in the same scene; meaning resides in the form rather than the content of what the actor says.

Another device which these plays share with the oral epic is the amazing accuracy with which characters repeat speeches and messages, as when the messenger sent by Edward IV to France gives him a verbatim report of what the audience has already heard directly from Queen Margaret, Warwick, and the French royal family. People also remember

---

[21] George Puttenham, *The Arte of English Poesie (1589)*, Scolar Press reprint (Menston, 1968), p. 31.

[22] I. M. L. Hunter, 'Memory in Everyday Life', in M. M. Gruneberg and P. E. Morris, eds., *Applied Problems in Memory* (London, New York, and San Francisco, 1979), pp. 1–24.

[23] J. Goody and I. Watt, 'The Consequences of Literacy', in J. Goody, ed., *Literacy in Traditional Societies* (Cambridge, 1968). Cited in Hunter, 'Memory in Everyday Life', pp. 12–14.

[24] Stanley Wells, Gary Taylor, John Jowett, and William Montgomery, *William Shakespeare: A Textual Companion* (Oxford, 1987), p. 175.

lines formerly spoken because they have come true, often in an ironic sense. In *Richard III* characters repeat their own words as they realize that these have turned against them. In the *Henry IV* plays, the relationship is much more complex. Characters constantly hark back to the events of *Richard II* and to the words spoken there. If *Richard II* had been dropped from the repertory these repetitions might have been necessary for the plot. If, on the other hand, the audience had the opportunity to see all three plays staged in close proximity to each other, the test of memory would have affected not only the actors but the audience as well. Henry IV quotes Richard's own words, 'now proved a prophecy' (*2 Henry IV*, 3.1.64). He was not in the scene where they were spoken, but, if we are meant to remember this, we are probably expected to assume that Richard has become a legendary character whose words have passed into folk memory and acquired prophetic force. When Worcester tells Hotspur that Richard II proclaimed Mortimer heir to the throne and Northumberland says twice that he heard the proclamation himself (*1 Henry IV*, 1.3.143–55) we might compare our own recollections of *Richard II*, in which no such thing is staged. Do we assume that it happened between the scenes or that Hotspur's father and uncle are lying as usual?

Uncertainties of this sort are endemic to the *Henry IV* plays, where the fallibility of characters' memories is constantly stressed. By the time he came to write them, Shakespeare was 'the leading dramatist of the capital's leading company',[25] which, unlike its rivals, was a stable and established group. The actors' familiarity with each other and the audience's acquaintance with them may well have facilitated the development of a style of acting which relied on more than simply demonstrating the competence of the actors' memories. As early as *Richard II* one can see the exploitation of mental confusion in the character of York, with his slip of the tongue so

like the ones actors sometimes make: 'Come, sister – cousin, I would say; pray pardon me' (2.2.105). If my theory is correct, the histories from *1 Henry IV* on should also be harder to memorize than the earlier ones, because of their greater naturalism, even randomness. Since the English Shakespeare Company version compresses the three parts of Henry VI's reign into two, and thereby also removes most of the repetitions and patterns which characterize its style, my questionnaire does not throw a great deal of light on this point. There was evidence that some roles in the later histories were found particularly difficult: Falstaff because he speaks prose and because there are *three* tavern scenes in the *Henry IV* plays; Pistol because he speaks nonsense. Michael Pennington, however, suggested tentatively that perhaps Buckingham in *Richard III* was harder for him than Richard II because his lines lacked the 'bright images'.

This point about imagery was clearly much more important for some actors than for others. However, the fact that colourless and nondescript lines are the hardest ones to remember emerged clearly from the replies of the two actors who had had the experience of speaking lines from the wrong play. Both incidents involved confusion between similar and unimportant speeches. John Darrell, who had to say 'Good my lord of Lancaster' in one play and 'My Lord of Gloucester' in another, found himself addressing Richard of Gloucester as 'Good my lord of Lanc-, Leicester – Gloucester' ('all famous cheeses', he pointed out). Andrew Jarvis, whose parts included Sir Piers of Exton and Richard of Gloucester/Richard III, gave an illuminating account of a similar incident:

It was a simple line in *Henry VI, Part 3*: 'Sirrah, leave us to ourselves, we must confer.' When the moment came I couldn't think of it and so said a line from *Richard II* which had immediately sprung to mind: 'Fellow, give place, we must confer.' I'm not

25 Wells *et al.*, *A Textual Companion*, p. 229.

actually on stage in *Richard II* when the line is spoken but am waiting to go on and so hear the line repeatedly (spoken in a Northern accent – my native accent – so perhaps it stuck more because of that).

Interestingly, the line in *Richard II* does not actually go as he remembers it. As Exton, waiting in the wings, he would have heard the keeper say to the groom, 'Fellow, give place. Here is no longer stay' (5.5.95). This example thus appears to corroborate the memorial reconstruction theory of the Bad Quarto of the *Contention*: an actor can hear another character's lines repeatedly without knowing them verbatim. An important factor in memory is motivation, and one does not learn what one does not need to know.

The fallibility of memory is relevant, however, not only to the actors of these plays but to the plays themselves. Except for *King John*, where the characters spend little time on the past, cynically recognizing the fact that a king relies on 'Your strong possession much more than your right' (1.1.40), the characters of the history plays are rival historians, struggling for possession of the 'true' interpretation of the past. The fact that their memories are often linked with specific places may reflect the actual workings of oral tradition; it also supplies identifying patterns for the audience. In his first scene, Hotspur goes through agonies trying to remember the name of Berkeley Castle:

> In Richard's time – what d'ye call the place?
> A plague upon't, it is in Gloucestershire.
> 'Twas where the madcap Duke his uncle kept –
> His uncle York – where I first bowed my knee
> Unto this king of smiles, this Bolingbroke.
> 'Sblood, when you and he came back from
> Ravenspurgh.   (*1 Henry IV* 1.3.240–5)

Hotspur's difficulty is rendered realistically, down to the oath which probably reflects a common type of ad libbing such as the legislation of 1606 was intended to curb. The association of events with places was a classic mnemonic device, but in this case the speaker

is using his recollections of events there in an unsuccessful attempt to remember the name of the place where they happened. Worcester does the same thing when he is accusing the king of broken promises:

> You swore to us,
> And you did swear that oath at Doncaster,
> That you did nothing purpose 'gainst the state,
> Nor claim no further than your new-fall'n right,
> The seat of Gaunt, dukedom of Lancaster.
>   (*1 Henry IV* 5.1.41–5)

Hotspur has already made the same accusation, but he locates the event at Ravenspurgh. The audience themselves hear Bolingbroke swear the same thing to York in *Richard II*, and York is told about the previous oath. Are they also meant to remember an earlier scene? In *The True Tragedy of Richard Duke of York* (*3 Henry VI*) Edward IV, after landing at Ravenspurgh, arrives at the gates of York and finds that the Mayor, having sworn allegiance to King Henry, is unwilling to admit him. He declares, 'I challenge nothing but my dukedom' (4.8.23), to which Richard of Gloucester adds in an aside,

> But when the fox hath once got in his nose,
> He'll soon find means to make the body follow.
>   (4.8.25–6)

The Mayor is persuaded to let the Yorkists enter, and Edward's followers exchange sarcastic comments on his willingness to be persuaded:

> HASTINGS
> The good old man would fain that all were
>   well,
> So 'twere not long of him ...   (4.8.31–2)

All this runs so close to the pattern of the scene at Berkeley Castle, even to the way in which the function of the Mayor of York is taken over by the Duke of York, that it naturally raises doubts as to whose memory is in question here. Is Shakespeare simply replaying the structure of a scene but with a totally different emphasis, making the characters seem less simple-minded on the one hand, and less crafty on the other, than in the earlier play? Or is it the spectators who are being asked to remember the earlier scene and to apply what they have already learned about the way politicians keep their word? In general, the difference between the two groups of 'Henry' plays seems to be that, whereas in the earlier ones characters are shown cynically breaking their word, in the later ones they genuinely 'forget' what they have said. Even Worcester, when he accuses Henry IV of having betrayed his supporters by usurping the throne, only says that he 'Forgot your oath to us at Doncaster' (*1 Henry IV* 5.1.58). Within the plays, forgetfulness can be an evasion of responsibility; an awareness of the fallibility of human memory can also enable the author to avoid taking sides.

However, I see the dramatization of forgetfulness as, above all, a sign of the actors' new status, no longer as expert memorizers depicting an impossible 'perfection' but as imitators of precisely the graceful negligence which was supposed to be the exclusive property of gentlemen. It would seem that having a bad memory could be a kind of good manners: Hamlet apologizes several times for forgetting someone or something, and makes a false start when he is trying to recall Aeneas' tale to Dido. His advice to the players is the counterpart of Cicero's to the orator, and is designed to enable them to look *not* like actors but gentlemen. He even objects to the clowns' ad libbing, because, in this more naturalistic context, it makes the play look not less but more artificial. Somewhere behind this, I suspect, lurks Hamlet's desire to play the clown. Perhaps by now – certainly at some point in the seventeenth century – it was felt that having too good a memory was pedantic. La Rochefoucauld's famous maxim that 'Everyone complains of his memory and no one complains of his judgment' is borne out by Witwoud's 'my Memory is such a Memory' in *The Way of the World*, and by Mirabell's

warning that this is one of those things that every fool tends to say (1.305–9).[26]

The movement towards greater naturalism in Shakespeare's plays is thus part of the upward social mobility of the more successful members of the acting profession. It also reflects his company's growing confidence in its relationship with its audience and thus its increasing willingness to take risks. For instance, there is the case of the stage silence. Where not all the audience could see the actors' faces at any given time, it must have been hard to hold a pause without giving the impression that something was wrong. In *Much Ado About Nothing*, a stage silence, when Claudio is granted Hero's hand in marriage, is followed by Beatrice's 'Speak, Count, 'tis your cue' (2.1.286). A joke about missing a cue defuses anxiety that someone might have missed a cue. The 'O's and 'So's of some of the texts as we have them are generally regarded as actors' interpolations. They may be ways of creating a pause without a silence, an extra beat in a line.

The later plays and what I see as their distrust of 'perfection' are a subject in their own right, but I should like to end by sketching some directions in which such a study might go. *Coriolanus* is clearly a play obsessed with memory in the sense of gratitude; it contains a realistic depiction of a lapse of memory, when Marcius asks mercy for a citizen of Corioles, then fails to remember his name; when he is asked to play the impossible role of a mild-tempered statesman he insists that he cannot do it, and Cominius has to say that the patricians will 'prompt' him (3.2.106). At the climax of the play, his confrontation with the women of Rome, he compares himself to an actor drying up:

> Like a dull actor now
> I have forgot my part, and I am out
> Even to a full disgrace. (5.3.40–2)

---

[26] *The Comedies of William Congreve*, ed. Anthony G. Henderson (Cambridge, 1982).

This follows his attempt to stand 'As if a man were author of himself / And knew no other kin' (lines 36–7), and it precedes the most famous stage silence in Shakespeare, one for which a specific stage direction is given (line 183). The play thus prepares its audience for a moment which will look as if something has gone terribly wrong. As in the moment where Prospero breaks off his masque because he has just remembered something he had forgotten, the apparent breakdown in the production coincides with the hero's recognition that he is not 'Of stronger earth than others': he is not 'perfect' in either sense of the word. It is possible because the theatre is now part of the establishment; instead of trying to be perfect, it can pretend to be imperfect.

THE BOYHOOD OF SHAKESPEARE'S HEROINES

P. H. PARRY

Attempts at reconstructing the earliest performances of Shakespeare's plays are notoriously hit-and-miss affairs: nowhere more so than when we attempt to gauge the impact of male actors playing female roles.[1] We are so used to reading the plays (or, when we see them, to seeing true-sex interpretations of the various character-parts) that we too easily set up our modern experience of the plays as the goal towards which an Elizabethan performance was tending. The present paper invites us to reconsider this presupposition.

I

Samuel Johnson's claim that theatre audiences 'are always in their senses, and know, from the first act to the last, that the stage is only a stage, and that the players are only players' is typical of its period.[2] When they came to discuss the large matter of the relationship between artistic representation and the reality to which such representation alludes, eighteenth-century authors regularly displayed both a lively interest and a great deal of intelligence and good sense. Samuel Richardson, for example, wrote a tactful letter to William Warburton in which he rejected the bishop's proposed Preface to *Clarissa* on the grounds that it punctured the illusion of reality which he wished his novel to maintain. In the small space available to him he manages to do a large amount of justice to a complex matter: he indeed wishes 'that the *Air of Genuiness* had been kept up' in Warburton's

Preface, but hurries on to admit that 'I want not the Letters to be *thought* genuine'; he wishes merely that they 'should not prefatically be owned *not* to be genuine', and this in order to 'avoid hurting that kind of Historical Faith which Fiction itself is generally read with, tho' we know it to be Fiction'.[3] In short, Richardson thinks that a reader needs enough faith to keep the writer's fiction buoyant but not so much that he ever forgets that what he is reading is fictional.

In watching a play too, as eighteenth-century critics well recognized, a similar situation arises and a similarly even-handed response is required. We need to be carried forward in faith, but there is a too great degree of involvement in what we see that robs us of

---

[1] A good deal of work has been done on the Boys' acting companies, but much less on boy actors in the adult theatres. William Robertson Davies, *Shakespeare's Boy Actors* (London, 1939), has some splendidly lurid section headings ('Physical Love-making on the Elizabethan Stage with reference to the Boy Actor') but is uninformative and ill-documented. Michael Jamieson, 'Shakespeare's Celibate Stage', in *Papers Mainly Shakespearian*, ed. G. I. Duthie (Edinburgh and London, 1964), pp. 21–39 (reprinted in *The Seventeenth-Century Stage*, ed. G. E. Bentley (Chicago and London, 1968), pp. 70–93), is much more reliable.

[2] Samuel Johnson, 'Preface to *The Plays of William Shakespeare*' (1765), in *Eighteenth Century Essays on Shakespeare*, ed. David Nichol Smith, second edition (Oxford, 1963), pp. 104–50; p. 119.

[3] Cited in Alan Duguld McKillop, *Samuel Richardson: Printer and Novelist* (Chapel Hill, 1936), pp. 163–4.

an essential distance between spectator and performance: the degree of credence that we give to what is acted out before us is held in proportion by our overarching awareness of the fictiveness of the action. We stay firmly in our seats when Stoppard's Rosencrantz shouts 'Fire!' Henry Fielding, in the chapter in *Tom Jones* entitled 'A Comparison between the World and the Stage', argues of dramatists that 'we might fairly pay a very high Compliment to those, who by their Writings or Actions have been so capable of imitating Life, as to have their Pictures in a Manner confounded with, or mistaken for the Originals'.[4] But that this is not his last word on the matter, and that his 'in a Manner' is no empty formula, is evident from the incident (2.16.5; pp. 852–7) during a performance of *Hamlet* when Partridge, despite stoutly declaring 'I am not afraid of any thing; for I know it is but a Play', nevertheless hopelessly confounds 'Pictures' and 'Originals' and completely fails to understand what is going on. The wiser policy, as Goethe knew, was to cultivate a simultaneous awareness of the requirements of plot and the realities of performance. When, in 1788 in Rome, he saw a production of Goldoni's *La Locandiera* in which men acted the women's parts, he gave classic expression to that bifurcated response which, in varying degrees, is an essential ingredient of all theatrical experience. 'In the particular kind of representation we witnessed', Goethe claimed, 'the idea of imitation ... was called forth vividly'. But, 'on the other hand' (and despite 'skilful playing'), 'only a kind of self-conscious illusion was produced'. The result was for the audience 'a double charm' that stemmed 'from the fact that these people are not women, but play the part of women'.[5]

Elizabethan playwrights were well aware of such basic truths. Thomas Heywood in his *Apology for Actors* (1612) claims that an English spectator (an 'English blood') seeing 'the person of any bold English man presented' on stage responds 'as if the Personator were the man Personated'.[6] But to gloss Heywood's observation as though it meant that one watched (in the words of a modern authority) 'as if the historical personage were actually there' is to promote a serious misunderstanding of his argument.[7] Heywood is as fully alive to realities as were Johnson and Goethe, as he shows when he defends the boy actors against scriptural objection. The basis of this objection was that their dressing up as women leads to a serious confusion of sexual identity, and he defends them by appealing to the obvious fictiveness of the situation in which they perform:

To see our youths attired in the habit of women, who knowes not what their intents be? who cannot distinguish them by their names, assuredly knowing, they are but to represent such a Lady, at such a time appoynted? (c3ᵛ)

So completely accepting of such truths were they that playwrights of the Elizabethan period frequently write their plays in a way which requires us to adopt a double-focus approach towards them – requires us, that is,

---

4 Henry Fielding, *The History of Tom Jones*, ed. Martin Battestin and Fredson Bowers, 2 vols. (Oxford, 1974), vol. 1, Book 7, Chapter 1; p. 324.

5 Goethe's account is reproduced in A. M. Nagler, *A Source Book of Theatrical History* (New York, 1952), pp. 433–4. Jamieson ('Celibate Stage', *Papers*, p. 25) cites this passage but argues that Goethe's familiarity with practical aspects of theatre work has here made him unduly sophisticated and self-analysing.

6 Thomas Heywood, *An Apology for Actors. Containing three briefe Treatises: (1) Their Antiquity (2) Their ancient Dignity (3) The true use of their quality* (London, 1612), B4ʳ.

7 B. L. Joseph, *Elizabethan Acting*, second edition (London, 1964), p. 1. The 'as if' and the 'actually' pull here in opposite directions. Later (p. 108) Joseph argues that the Elizabethan spectator was able 'to imagine a place, a person, an incident as if it were real, while knowing it to be represented', but this is merely a laborious way of saying that the Elizabethan spectator was able to imagine a place, a person, or an incident. The first edition of *Elizabethan Acting* (London, 1951), though very heavily criticized by its reviewers, seems to me much less open to objection than the 1964 revision.

to bear in mind both the character that we think we see before us and the actor that we in fact see. Here, for example, is the moment when Othello demands ocular proof from Iago:

> I think my wife be honest, and think she is not.
> I think that thou art just, and think thou art not.
> I'll have some proof. My name, that was as fresh
> As Dian's visage, is now begrimed and black
> As mine own face.   (3.3.389–93)

Clearly at this point Othello is made to share the white man's assessment of his colour's moral value. There is nothing incredible, of course, in such sharing, for worse things have happened in the history of racial prejudice, and perhaps we are witnessing just one further step down into Othello's self-abasement. But it is surely easier to contemplate showing this added depravity if what you have in your mind as you write (or view) the play are the words spoken by an actor who can wash his grimy blackness off an hour or so after the words are spoken.[8]

Another powerful instance is provided at 4.2.69–70 where, in the Quarto text (1622), Othello addresses Desdemona:

> O thou blacke weede, why art so louely faire?
> Thou smell'st so sweete.   (K4^r)[9]

The Folio reads:

> Oh thou weed:
> Who art so louely faire, and smell'st so sweete
>   (lines 2762–3)

Editors who follow the Folio here sometimes do so because they want to avoid the incongruity of black Othello's using the word 'black' pejoratively.[10] But the contrasts between blackness and fairness that run throughout the play (Othello, called a black devil by Iago, calls Desdemona a fair devil when he resolves to kill her) are much more clearly picked up by the Quarto reading, and perhaps the passage is simply another example

of one where Shakespeare's having written for a white actor is allowed to emerge. With an effectiveness that is here intensely powerful (and sadly lost in the revised text) the showman does not disappear into what he shows us.

II

Such insistence upon a two-fold envisioning of what is shown to us is commonplace throughout Shakespeare's work. One might think for a moment of the famous Prologue of *Henry V*:

> But pardon, gentles all,
> The flat unraisèd spirits that hath dared
> On this unworthy scaffold to bring forth
> So great an object. Can this cock-pit hold
> The vasty fields of France? Or may we cram
> Within this wooden O the very casques
> That did affright the air at Agincourt?
>   (Pro.8–14)

These are not difficult questions: the answer to both is clearly 'No'. The Prologue then proceeds to tell us that our imaginations can make amends for the poverty of what is at the actors'

---

8 Andrew Gurr, *The Shakespearean Stage, 1574–1642* (Cambridge, 1970), pp. 131–2, citing Eldred Jones, 'The physical representation of African characters on the English stage during the 16th and 17th centuries', *Theatre Notebook*, 17 (1962), 17–19; p. 18, argues that negroes were masked rather than blacked-up until Queen Anne appeared in Jonson's *Masque of Blackness* in 1605. The citation is misleading, however. Jones clearly distinguishes between what happened in court masques and the practice of the popular stage, where, he argues, 'paint seems to have been the general device used for blackening the features of these characters [blackamoors]' (p. 19). I take *Othello* 3.3.392–3 as evidence, if any were needed, that Shakespeare's Othello was painted rather than masked.

9 The Quarto reading is preferred in the new Arden *Othello*, ed. M. R. Ridley (London, 1958).

10 Alice Walker, *Textual Problems of the First Folio* (London, 1953), pp. 150–1, claims that 'from the black Othello the words [of the Quarto version] are singularly *mal à propos*'.

disposal, but – if we are really being asked to ignore the stage and its inadequacies – why are they set down so vigorously before us? What the Prologue does here is to move us between two poles, one acceptable and the other not. Entirely acceptable is the claim that we must agree to abide by a representational convention, so that we may indeed:

> Suppose within the girdle of these walls
> Are now confined two mighty monarchies.
>
> (lines 19–20)

But a convention is not an illusion: here we are made aware, at one and the same time, both of what is being represented and of the limitations within which the representation is achieved ('girdle of these walls' / 'confined').[11] Merely rhetorical and not at all acceptable is the command that an audience should:

> Think, when we talk of horses, that you see them,
> Printing their proud hoofs i'th' receiving earth.
>
> (lines 26–7)

But, of course, as the context makes clear, the audience is not really expected to think that it sees horses: playgoers are merely being enjoined, by means of a fitting hyperbole, to use their imaginations. A point worth dwelling on, however, is that the entire emphasis of the Prologue is pitched against the notion that what we imagine cancels out what we see. Both what is represented and the means of representation are equally objects of our awareness.

Gradually (though never quite completely) this double focus has been weakened in the subsequent history of the drama. Indeed Andrew Gurr has argued that the weakening started in Shakespeare's lifetime and in response to his increased sensitivity as a playwright.[12] Whenever it began, however, we can be reasonably certain that by the time the drama had reached the high noon of nineteenth-century naturalism any act of self-reference within a play was seen to weaken its illusionistic impact and lessen its seriousness.

The fight back against naturalism, which has been (in however ambiguous and compromised a fashion) so much a feature of the new drama of the last thirty or so years, has inevitably seen the establishment of this double focus. Indeed something very similar to such double awareness lies at the heart of Bertolt Brecht's recommendations for a revived dramaturgy.

Brecht, as early as 1929, was saying that he wanted a style of acting that would prevent a theatre audience from plunging into 'self-identification with the protagonist's feelings'.[13] Such self-identification could best be prevented, he later claimed (in about 1936), by having the actors in his epic theatre 'refrain from going over wholly into their role, [by] remaining detached from the character they were playing and [thus] clearly inviting criticism of him'.[14] Such detachment and distancing, Brecht was quick to insist, had long been a feature of certain traditional theatres: in a famous essay on 'Alienation Effects in Chinese

---

[11] Joseph, *Elizabethan Acting* (1964), pp. 109–10, has some grotesque comments on the nature of convention. He argues, for example, that when an Elizabethan actor simulated darkness (by moving about on stage carefully, or by carrying a lighted lantern), his performing such bits of stage-business and an audience's responding to them were not matters 'of offering and accepting conventions in place of realistic imitations of reality'. Instead we are asked to believe that 'the audience imagined darkness when an actor came on stage with a lantern, not because this was a convention, but because he held it as if he really needed to see where and with whom he was standing'. Similarly an audience accepted that a piece of canvas-rigging was a castle or the defensive walls of a town 'not as the result of a convention but because the actors imagined it to be really what it represented, and behaved as if it were'. But, misuse words as you will, what Joseph is giving examples of here are conventions.

[12] Gurr, *Shakespearean Stage*, pp. 75–6. I discuss Gurr's argument at greater length below.

[13] Bertolt Brecht, 'Dialog über Schauspielkunst', in *Brecht on Theatre*, ed. John Willett, second edition (New York and London, 1974), p. 28.

[14] Brecht, 'Theatre for Pleasure or Theatre for Instruction', in Willett, *Brecht on Theatre*, p. 71.

Acting' he wrote that 'above all, the Chinese artist never acts as if there were a fourth wall ... [but] expresses his awareness of being watched'. As a result 'the audience can no longer have the illusion of being the unseen spectator at an event which is really taking place'.[15] And Brecht's observations are now commonplace in modern discussion of traditional Chinese theatre. Here, for instance, is what one recent American critic has to say on this matter:

The oriental theatre, like traditional non-realistic theatre in the west, is rich in signs, never masking them beneath an illusion, but instead allowing us the double experience of actor *and* character which has been the theatrical experience since the beginning.[16]

Without claiming that his own brand of alienation would serve the same purposes as those served by Chinese 'alienation effects' Brecht nevertheless believed that modern German theatre had a lot to learn from such traditional theatre practice and acting techniques, and summed up what he thought needed to be done in his most famous theoretical work, 'A Short Organum for the Theatre'.[17] If a Brechtian actor playing Lear were to be told by a critic that 'he didn't act Lear, he was Lear' such a seemingly favourable review would in fact be 'an annihilating blow to him' (par. 48). And here the double-awareness which is the subject of the present paper becomes central: the basic principle of epic acting, Brecht says – citing the example of Charles Laughton's performance as Galileo – is 'that the actor appears on the stage in a double role, as Laughton and as Galileo ... the showman Laughton does not disappear in the Galileo whom he is showing' (par. 49).[18]

Brecht's insistence elsewhere that an actor does not dance but shows us a man dancing can now be understood. A similarly incomplete assimilation of the showman into what he is showing us is commonplace on the Elizabethan stage. There is no suggestion, of course, that Elizabethan playwrights were

modern German dramatists several centuries ahead of their time. Brecht's epic-theatre and the alienation effects which sustained it were ultimately designed to serve political ends, but in order for them to do so he had first to challenge the naturalistic conventions which held sway over so much nineteenth-century western theatre. Shakespeare and his contemporaries were not challenging such conventions: they were simply writing before naturalism had acquired its dominating hold over the European stage.

III

What is sometimes thought to tell against the sort of argument which is here being advanced is the belief that in Shakespeare's lifetime, largely indeed at Shakespeare's prompting, the English theatre (at least at its most sophisticated) was moving towards a much more naturalistic style of representation. Andrew Gurr, for example, cites one Jacobean (it appears to have been John Webster) who said of the actor that 'what we see him personate, we think truely done before us' – which, if we take 'truely' to mean 'really', is as naked an

---

[15] Brecht, 'Alienation Effects in Chinese Acting', in Willett, *Brecht on Theatre*, p. 91.

[16] Leonard C. Pronko, '*Kabuki*: signs, symbols and the hieroglyphic actor', in *Drama and Symbolism*, Themes in Drama, vol. 4, ed. James Redmond (Cambridge, 1982), p. 42.

[17] Brecht, 'A Short Organum for the Theatre' (1948), in Willett, *Brecht on Theatre*, pp. 179–205. The 'Organum' consists of a Prologue and seventy-seven numbered paragraphs. References in the text are to these paragraphs.

[18] Brecht's opinion here seems completely at odds with a remark made by Pirandello that actors 'when they come on stage ... must not be actors any longer, they must be the characters in the play they are acting' (cited in Susan Bassnett-McGuire, *Luigi Pirandello* (London and Basingstoke, 1983), p. 21) But the *structure* of Pirandello's plays enforces a double awareness upon us, and his remark should be taken as a reminder that a 'realistic' acting style is not a sufficient indicator of naturalistic drama.

avowal of crass naturalism as one could hope to find anywhere.[19] Gurr lays a good deal of stress on that word 'personate' and concludes that acting devices not strictly conformable to naturalistic 'personation' were old-fashioned and in decline from about 1600 onwards:

Like explanatory prologues, the explanatory soliloquy or aside to the audience was a relic of the less sophisticated days which developed into a useful and *more naturalistic* convention of thinking aloud.[20]

But this is surely the merest prejudice, and one moreover with a very odd pedigree. In *The Old Drama and the New*, William Archer distinguishes between those soliloquies (he cites Hamlet's) which are 'the externalisation of inward processes' and which pass without his objection, and those (he cites Richard's opening speech from *Richard III*) in which the speaker 'is made to utter things which would not naturally pass through his mind in that form, because it is important that certain information should be conveyed to the audience'. Soliloquies of the former sort do not 'conflict with ordinary possibility': those of the latter 'make a hopeless rift in the illusion of the scene'. As for the aside there is, in Archer's view, nothing to be said in its favour, since 'it is a reflection spoken under circumstances which outrage possibility, forcing us to pretend to believe that the other person or persons on the stage are deaf'.[21] This is a remarkable passage, at once a bull's-eye and an own goal: what is clear, however, is that one either takes Archer's point or leaves it. But if one takes it, one does so at the expense of almost every play written in English prior to the nineteenth century.

I very much doubt whether Shakespeare's soliloquies and asides (too many of the latter the inventions of modern editors who are themselves proceeding along naturalistic lines) ever became simply a way of recording 'thinking aloud' – because the Elizabethan actor, like the Chinese actor of Brecht's essay, 'expresses his awareness of being watched'. When in

Othello, in the middle of a straightforward soliloquy, Iago says:

> Divinity of hell:
> When devils will the blackest sins put on,
> They do suggest at first with heavenly shows,
> As I do now. (2.3.341–4)

the speech is, of course, evidence of Iago's self-aware, self-delighting viciousness, but it is also quite clearly (the 'As I do now' especially) a speech directed out into the audience, and not merely thoughts which we are privileged by convention to overhear.

Webster's comment ('What we see him personate, we thinke truely done before us') is not the substantial obstacle to the present argument that at first it seems to be. Gurr's emphasis upon Webster's use of the word 'personate' is certainly exaggerated, and besides the word 'truely' here means 'truthfully' (rather than 'in fact'). Gurr tells us that the word is first used in the Induction to John Marston's *Antonio and Mellida*, played by the Children of Paul's in 1599 or 1600, and yet *Antonio and Mellida*, perhaps more than any other play of its period, forces a double awareness, of actor and of what is represented, upon us, so as to make it impossible for us in any naive fashion to think truly done before us what we see the actors personate.[22] The Induction begins with the boy players coming on stage:

---

[19] Gurr, *Shakespearean Stage*, p. 62. See also Nagler, *Source Book*, p. 126.

[20] Gurr, *Shakespearean Stage*, p. 76 (my emphasis). Gurr acknowledges his indebtedness to S. L. Bethell's *Shakespeare and the Popular Dramatic Tradition* (London, 1944), pp. 87–9. This acknowledgement is deceptive. There is nothing in the pages cited which supports Gurr's conclusions: Bethell, for example, stresses the element of direct address to the audience that is to be found in the supposedly more naturalistic aside.

[21] William Archer, *The Old Drama and the New* (London, 1923), pp. 39–40.

[22] John Marston, *Antonio and Mellida*, Regents Renaissance Drama Series, ed. G. K. Hunter (London, 1965).

Enter *Galeatzo, Piero, Alberto, Antonio, Forobosco, Balurdo, Matzagente* and *Feliche,* with parts in their hands, having cloaks cast over their apparel

Though in the printed text they are referred to in speech headings by the names of the characters that they will play, it is clear that this is only a printer's convenience: they are simply actors. 'Whom do you personate?' one actor asks another. 'Whom act you?' another asks, and the answer comes back promptly:

ALBERTO   The necessity of the play forceth me to act two parts, Andrugio the distressed Duke of Genoa, and Alberto a Venetian gentleman enamored on the Lady Rossaline.   (lines 21–3)

And a third is asked:

FELICHE   Thou promisest more than I hope any spectator gives faith of performance. – (*To Antonio*) But why look you so dusky, ha?

ANTONIO   I was never worse fitted since the nativity of my actorship; I shall be hiss'd at, on my life now.

FELICHE   Why, what must you play?

ANTONIO   Faith, I know not what, an hermaphrodite, two parts in one; my true person being Antonio son to the Duke of Genoa, though for the love of Mellida, Piero's daughter, I take this feigned presence of an Amazon, calling myself Florizel and I know not what. I a voice to play a lady! I shall ne'er do it.

ALBERTO   O, an Amazon should have such a voice, virago-like. Not play two parts in one? away, away; 'tis common fashion. Nay, if you cannot bear two subtle fronts under one hood, idiot go by, go by, off this world's stage. O time's impurity!

ANTONIO   Ay, but when use hath taught me action to hit the right point of a lady's part, I shall grow ignorant, when I must turn young prince again, how but to truss my hose.

FELICHE   Tush, never put them off; for women wear the breeches still.   (lines 63–80)

It is clear, surely, that here is a play that ostentatiously parades before us its own status as a play. And having reminded its audience (which can hardly have needed any reminder) that it has come to watch schoolboys perform,

the play goes on to issue several camp reminders in speeches that are funny when we remember to see through the (quite minimal) stage illusion. In fact, so overfreighted with awareness of its own artificial status is *Antonio and Mellida* that it is virtually impossible to concentrate attention upon the unfolding of its plot. Double awareness (of performance and of what is performed) is here constantly in danger of collapsing into single awareness, but emphatically not into that single awareness which Gurr associates with the word 'personate'.[23]

Of course plays acted by the Boys' companies, in which all of the players were boys (though some were in their late teens and a few were even older), are perhaps more likely to be self-aware in such matters than were the plays of the adult companies.[24] Quite early on this

---

[23] Professor Gurr repeats his point about the growth of naturalism in his more recent *Playgoing in Shakespeare's London* (Cambridge, 1987), though this time he dates the advent of more naturalistic techniques a good deal earlier than 1600. Of Tarlton he says that: 'He based his act on direct address to the audience and exploited the gap between the player and his play-role *at a time when plays were generally moving towards the more illusionistic mode of the self-controlled play*' (p. 187; my emphasis). But then he complicates matters by allowing (what, as I show below, is most certainly true) that the Boys' companies sponsored 'well before 1605' a form of drama that was in an 'anti-mimetic mode', which favoured 'flaunting the artificiality of stage pretence', and which required that audiences should not become 'spell-bound believers but sceptical judges' (p. 153). The pattern which Gurr seems to have in mind is this: that before about the late 1590s there was a crudely non-naturalistic drama which was succeeded by (a) the sophisticated naturalism of William Shakespeare and those dramatists sensitive enough to be influenced by him and (b) by the sophisticated non-naturalism of the Boys' companies. The trouble is that Shakespeare's 'naturalism' turns out to be so sophisticated that one might just as well classify it as 'sophisticated non-naturalism'.

[24] J. A. Lavin, 'The Elizabethan Theatre and the Inductive Method', *The Elizabethan Theatre: II*, ed. David Galloway (London, 1970), pp. 74–86, warns us (pp. 78–9) against supposing that the Children's companies simply

self-awareness developed into the spirit of high camp in the work of John Lyly. His *Gallathea*, for instance, performed perhaps as early as 1585, shuffles the sexes around madly, but for a comic effect that depends upon our knowing that the actors are schoolboys.[25] Gallathea and Phillida, two girls (living improbably in Lincolnshire) are, unknown to each other, made to dress up as boys in order to escape the wrath of Neptune. Both resent the disguise and Gallathea laments: 'O woulde the gods had made mee as I seeme to be' (2.1.4–5). The joke here is that a boy pretending to be a girl but dressed as a boy asks the gods to turn him into what the audience knows he already is. Later, still disguised, Gallathea and Phillida meet and fall in love, causing Phillida to ask her/himself: 'Art thou no sooner in the habite of a boy, but thou must be enamored of a boy?' (2.5.3–4) – a question which may not be subtle but which certainly plays around with an audience's double awareness. At one point, each still believing the other to be a boy (but beginning to suspect him of being a girl), they agree to an arrangement whereby Phillida refers to Gallathea as his mistress (4.4.15–17). The sexual complications assume awesome proportions, and in the end Venus offers to sort out the mess by changing one of the 'girls' into a boy; but their fathers object on financial and legal grounds so that the transformation (in the circumstances the easiest of all to effect, requiring no more than the dropping of a pair of hose) has to take place off stage.

IV

So far the evidence cited has been taken in the main from plays performed by the Boys' companies: obviously within such companies a frank acknowledgement of the performance status of their productions was probably inevitable, and would certainly have been wise, granted the constraints under which they performed. For a time at least (between 1599 and 1602) Paul's Boys adopted the practice of

not assuming false beards when they impersonated old men.[26] The age discrepancy, even with a beard, would have been obvious, but it is still worth noting that the company did nothing to lessen the discrepancy. Ben Jonson's claim that Salomon Pavy, one of the children of the Chapel Royal, was so good at impersonating old men that the Fates mistakenly called him to an early grave (he was thirteen when he died) is a conceit. Whatever was the case with the Fates, it is impossible to believe that an audience was similarly mistaken: indeed most of the pleasure that came from watching Pavy act must have come from playing off one's awareness of the boy actor's youthfulness against the old age of the characters that he impersonated.

But would a similar consistent, and insisted upon, awareness of performance status be a feature of plays performed by adult companies? There can, clearly, be no straightforward shifting of evidence from one type of company to another. The senior companies were, naturally, well supplied with adult males, so that there would have been little difficulty in impersonating older men, and they seem also to have kept a small number of boy actors in order to play the parts of romantic heroines and to sing and dance.[27] But one wonders whether there were enough boys with unbroken voices to act all of the women's and pages' parts, and it is likely that older men were pressed into service as occasion required.[28] Indeed, if one of Professor

---

consisted of children, and mentions the case of Nathan Field who was twenty-two on the first night of *Epicoene* (1609) and who did not join an adult company until he was almost thirty.

[25] *The Complete Works of John Lyly*, ed. R. Warwick Bond, 3 vols. (Oxford, 1902), vol. 2, pp. 431–72.

[26] Reavley Gair, *The Children of Paul's 1553–1608* (Cambridge, 1982), p. 143.

[27] Gurr, *Shakespearean Stage*, p. 60.

[28] The matter is complicated. G. E. Bentley, *The Profession of Player in Shakespeare's Time, 1590–1642* (Princeton, 1984), argues (p. 113) that 'the boy apprentices were assigned *all* female roles in the plays pro-

Honigmann's conjectures in his recent *Shake-speare: The 'Lost Years'* is correct, Shakespeare himself at the age of twenty-six was playing a woman's part in the second part of *The Seven Deadly Sins* (c. 1590).[29] Even here, then, I doubt whether the illusion that one was really watching a woman on stage was more than fitfully maintained, and Shakespeare (no less than Lyly and Marston) goes out of his way to expose his heroines' maleness.

v

One major contributor to an audience's 'double awareness' throughout a performance (though not, as we have seen, the only one) must have been the practice of having male actors impersonate women. Every English dramatist who wrote for the public stage prior to the Restoration of the monarchy knew, when he imagined a woman in his plays, that she would have to be presented to an audience by a man – and by a man moreover who would be known to be a man throughout the entire length of the performance. This being so, one would expect some at least of the growing band of students of Shakespeare's presentation of womanhood to have given some attention to this matter. But there seems to be among them a curious reluctance to do so. Few of the feminist critics who are working in this area are prepared even to mention the fact that Shakespeare's heroines were acted out by men, and even those who do mention it contrive to minimize its significance.[30] Consider, for instance, Rosalind's last speech in *As You Like It* – her famous epilogue:

And I charge you, O men, for the love you bear to women – as I perceive by your simpering none of you hates them – that between you and the women the play may please. If I were a woman I would kiss as many of you as had beards that pleased me, complexions that liked me, and breaths that I defied not.
(Epi. 13–19)

Clearly the words 'If I were a woman' are spoken not by Rosalind the character but by

the 'actor-as-Rosalind'. It simply will not do to argue, as Catherine Belsey has done, that the 'extra-textual sex of the actor' is here a bit of an irrelevancy.[31] Admittedly when we read the play (the only occasion when the term 'extra-textual' is appropriate, for in performance no play has a text) the sex of the actor is indeed not relevant: Rosalind is straightforwardly a woman, just as she is in the prose romance upon which Shakespeare based *As You Like It*. But when the play was performed in Shakespeare's lifetime I find it hard to believe that the sex of the actor who played Rosalind was something merely clamped on to the part of necessity but so much of an embarrassment to all concerned that it was promptly forgotten about (or 'taken for granted' and thus

---

duced by the troupes of Elizabethan, Jacobean, and Caroline London', but (p. 249) has evidence of one 'boy' actor (John Thompson) playing one woman's part in 1619 (or even, just possibly, 1614) and another in 1631. It must surely be clear that even if Thompson were prepubertal in 1619 he can hardly (barring grievous illness or accident) have been still such in 1631 (and yet Bentley, p. 263, continues to refer to him as a boy actor). J. B. Streett, 'The Durability of Boy Actors', *Notes and Queries*, 218 (1973), 461–5, has, however, provided good reasons for doubting whether two other actors who have become famous in this context (Theophilus Bird and Ezekial Fenn) were playing women's roles when they were twenty-four years old.

29 E. A. J. Honigmann, *Shakespeare: The 'Lost Years'* (Manchester, 1985), p. 59.

30 The honourable exception is Lisa Jardine's essay 'Female Roles and Elizabethan Eroticism' in her *Still Harping on Daughters: Women and Drama in the Age of Shakespeare* (Brighton, 1983), pp. 9–36.

31 Catherine Belsey, 'Disrupting sexual differences: meaning and gender in the comedies', in *Alternative Shakespeares*, ed. John Drakakis (London and New York, 1985), pp. 166–90; p. 181. A little later on, though, when she discusses Rosalind-as-Ganymede, Dr Belsey is prepared to grant 'if we imagine the part played by a male actor ... a certain autonomy to the voice of Ganymede' and concludes that, within severe limits, 'the extra-textual sex of the actor may be seen as significant' (p. 183). Belsey is really interested in only one part of the disguise process (that in which the woman dresses as a man); hence the grudging nature of the admissions just cited.

ignored). If the play depends in any measure upon our forgetting a piece of its foundation mechanism why are we so carefully reminded here of what we are supposed to forget? It is surely altogether more plausible to suppose that the conditions of performance which prevailed at the time were such as to provide the Elizabethan playgoer with an extra layer of pleasure in the performance that is denied to those who go to see the play today. Rosalind (as Ganymede) protests 'I thank God I am not a woman' (3.2.337–8) – a joke which is funny when spoken by a woman pretending to be a man, but funnier still (or at least funny in a different way) when the pretence involved is doubled. And Celia's joking condemnation of Rosalind cannot be properly understood (which here means 'understood improperly') if we forget the boyhood of Shakespeare's heroines:

> You have simply misused our sex in your love-prate. We must have your doublet and hose plucked over your head, and show the world what the bird hath done to her own nest. (4.1.191–4)

This nest has a cock sitting in it; an Elizabethan audience's awareness of the stage-Rosalind's maleness will have allowed it to catch Shakespeare's smutty joke. And if anyone protests that Celia is much too nice a girl to tell such a joke, I can only reply that she is not a nice girl at all.[32]

Much more cautionary, and evidence of how the simplest truths may go entirely unregarded, is an example from Linda Bamber's *Comic Women, Tragic Men* (1982), which, its subtitle lets us know, is 'a study of gender and genre in Shakespeare'.[33] Ms Bamber is, she is at pains to establish, a moderate, sane, and level-headed 'heterosexual feminist'. Yet moderation, sanity, and level-headedness count for nothing in the following observation in which we are told that 'when Viola, Rosalind, and Portia dress up as young boys, we know all along that these are women and not men, and so do they' (p. 41). Portia, of course,

does not dress up as a young boy; that error is merely the unbidden acknowledgement of the truth which is being suppressed. And the claim that Rosalind knows all along that she is a woman is a piece of nonsense which too sharply separates Rosalind-as-character from the actor-as-Rosalind, and does so, moreover, in order simply to discard the latter.

What then are we to make of the Induction to *The Taming of the Shrew*? It seems to fit with gratifying neatness into the present argument. Christopher Sly, a drunken tinker, is thrown out of an ale house and falls asleep in a ditch, from which he is rescued by a huntsman who orders that he be taken home and looked after. He also instructs one of his pages to dress up 'in all suits like a lady' in order to pretend to be Sly's wife:

> I know the boy will well usurp the grace,
> Voice, gait, and action of a gentlewoman.
> (Induction 1.129–30)

Sly awakes, sees his 'wife', responds appropriately, and asks her to take off her clothes: something which no woman on the Elizabethan stage could ever do. In order to divert his mind from such inconvenient thoughts the play proper is performed before him by a troupe of travelling players. I cannot tell whether there was any warrant for doing so in Elizabethan stage practice, but, were I directing the play now in an all-male version, I should certainly want the page to come back on stage as Kate. Though in the Folio text he is

---

[32] Jamieson ('Celibate Stage', *Papers*, pp. 29–32) discusses *As You Like It*, and argues in favour of Rosalind's 'essential femininity'. He concludes that the convention of the 'boy-actress' presents Shakespeare with a 'technical problem which no woman Rosalind would have' – which is doubtless true, but the 'boy-actress' also presents Shakespeare with an opportunity that no woman Rosalind would present. Jamieson's argument that Shakespeare stresses Rosalind's femininity in those passages where she regrets that she is *not* a man seems to me misguided.

[33] Linda Bamber, *Comic Women, Tragic Men* (Stanford, 1982).

not one of the acting troupe, he could certainly join the actors on an *ad hoc* basis, just as Rafe does in *The Knight of the Burning Pestle*.[34] All that would be required would be a simple bit of stage business to cover Sly's final words in the Induction: 'Come, madam wife, sit by my side/And let the world slip. We shall ne'er be younger' (Induction.2.138–9) and the transfer of the words 'My lord, 'tis but begun' (1.1.250) from the page-as-wife to the page-as-Kate. And not even this much would be required in the Quarto version, where the boy who plays the wife exits immediately *prior* to the performance of the play-within-the-play.[35] His promise to return might thus be fulfilled by his reappearance as Kate. But, whether this conjectural reconstruction is accurate or not, the major point is surely clear: a play which, even by Elizabethan standards, uses disguises immoderately has an induction which lays bare the principle of disguising in order to bring to our attention the boyhood of Shakespeare's heroines.

VI

Two beliefs have prompted the present essay: first that theatre proceeds by means of conventions rather than illusions; and secondly that we too often subscribe to a 'Whig' interpretation of theatrical history in which we posit an in-built or pre-planned movement forwards from naivety (assessed negatively) towards sophistication (considered only in its positive aspect). But we should not become the prisoners of the words that we use. Is (to take a commonplace of modern staging) a theatre naive or sophisticated which allows an actor to convert himself from one character to another by means of only the most minimal adjustment of dress? Why should we applaud Elizabethan dramatists – Shakespeare in particular – for striving to move away from naive practices, and at the same time applaud Brecht for inventing a sophisticated dramaturgical theory which allows similar practices to be reintroduced? The point of closest contact between Elizabethan practice and modern theory lies in this matter of double awareness – the double focus which Brecht tried to keep alive in performance by means of half-curtains and mechanical speaking and movement. But a theatre, such as Shakespeare's, in which women are always 'personated' by boys and young men (and black men by white actors) is likely to have such a double focus built into itself. And there are other conventional theatres, too, which insist upon such a focus. A really serious puppet theatre, for instance, requires us to see through the illusion which it creates – a point which Shaw makes in the Preface to his own puppet play, *Shakes versus Shav* (1949), where he warns against the dangers of a too sophisticated illusionism:

I can imagine the puppets simulating living performers so perfectly that the spectators would be completely illuded. The result would be the death of puppetry.[36]

These are wise words. It is the claim of the present essay that in a dramatic performance no Elizabethan spectator was ever 'completely illuded'; that no Elizabethan dramatist expected him to be; and that no Elizabethan play is posited upon the need for, or desirability of, naturalistic illusionism.

---

[34] Francis Beaumont, *The Knight of the Burning Pestle*, ed. Sheldon Zitner, The Revels Plays (Manchester, 1984), Induction 65; 1.212.

[35] *A Pleasant Conceited History called The taming of a Shrew* (London, 1594), 2.54–59, in Geoffrey Bullough, *Narrative and Dramatic Sources of Shakespeare*, vol. 1 (London and New York, 1957), p. 73. It is not clear from the 1595 text whether the boy who dresses up as Sly's wife is a page boy or a boy actor attached to the visiting company; though very little hinges upon which conclusion we reach, in my opinion the boy (as in the Folio text) is a page.

[36] George Bernard Shaw, *Buoyant Billions, Farfetched Fables, & Shakes Versus Shav* (London, 1950), p. 136.

SHAKESPEARE'S 'BRAWL RIDICULOUS'

CHARLES EDELMAN

'A little touch of Harry in the night' makes such a splendid finish to the famous Act 4 prologue of *Henry V* that directors are tempted to cut the following final six lines:

> And so our scene must to the battle fly,
> Where O for pity, we shall much disgrace,
> With four or five most vile and ragged foils,
> Right ill-disposed in brawl ridiculous,
> The name of Agincourt. Yet sit and see,
> Minding true things by what their mock'ries be.
>
> (4.0.48–53)

Apart from the fact that the prologue does indeed lead directly to 'a little touch of Harry', with the Battle of Agincourt to follow some time later, another cause for this omission might be that the director does not wish to call attention to what will in fact *be* a 'brawl ridiculous' – combat scenes on the modern Shakespearian stage are all too often a cause for merriment rather than intense excitement.

What of the Elizabethans themselves? Were they also frequently contemptuous of actors' attempts to represent a great battle on stage, or if they were not, was Shakespeare merely adding some spectacle to please the uncultured masses standing in the yard – 'sit and see' being directed to the more refined patrons in the galleries?

My essay examines the Elizabethan expectations of such episodes as the trial by combat in *King Lear*, the battlefield encounter of Prince Hal and Hotspur, or any other of the seemingly countless Shakespearian sword-fights as they were first witnessed; it also attempts to determine what the dominant style was with which actors met these expectations. When investigating the original productions of Shakespeare's plays, one faces the necessity of reconstructing a theatrical entity without documentary evidence; stage business is always ephemeral, but at least in more recent eras there are prompt-books and reviews to consult. Within the very few eyewitness accounts of Shakespeare's plays in Elizabethan times, however, there is not a single descriptive reference to any of the sword-fights therein.

Generally, scholars point to the well-known comment in Sidney's *Defence of Poesie* (c. 1583) as being the earliest published critical opinion of sword-fighting on the Elizabethan stage: 'while in the meantime two Armies flie in, represented with four swords & bucklers, and then what hard hart will not receive it for a pitched field?'[1] At first glance, it might appear that Sidney is decrying the lack of good, realistic stage sword-fighting, hence giving the impression that the theatrical fights of Elizabethan times were unconvincing. It is important to realize, however, that Sidney is not referring to the staging of sword-fights *per se*, but to the overall theatrical representation of a

---

[1] Sir Philip Sidney, *The Defence of Poesie* 1595; reprinted London, 1928), unpaginated [p. 60]. I am grateful to Dr Alan Brissenden of the University of Adelaide for his many helpful suggestions during the preparation of this essay.

pitched battle, a different, albeit related topic. While Sidney objects to the depiction of a battle with only a few soldiers, he says nothing about how believably the four soldiers, with their 'four swords and bucklers', actually fought.

Jean MacIntyre, in a discussion of Elizabethan stage battles, puts Sidney's comments in perspective:

Sidney, to be sure, may have had in mind shows by the small professional troupes of the 1570's, performing *Horestes* with six actors or *Cambyses* with eight . . . [He] could have seen performances at the Theatre . . . more probably, however, he is thinking of performances in a hall, an inn, or a booth, with a cleared area of platform some ten by twelve feet, which would hardly accommodate even six men safely in rigorous combat.[2]

The initial point to be made is that where battles and the sword-fighting that took place in them are concerned, Sidney, who died in 1586 and saw no Shakespearian combat, was criticizing a convention belonging to a different theatrical tradition, in which there may not have been an attempt at verisimilitude in the fighting. More importantly, he has absolutely nothing to say about how individual combats, be they between supernumeraries playing foot-soldiers or professional actors playing principal characters, were fought.

A famous comment which does relate to Shakespearian combat scenes is found in Jonson's prologue to *Every Man in His Humour*:[3]

> with three rusty swords,
> And help of some few foot-and-half-foot
> words,
> Fight over York, and Lancaster's long jars:
> And in the tiring-house bring wounds, to scars.
> (Prologue, lines 9–12)

This passage does not appear until the Folio version of 1616, giving it more of the status of a satiric gibe at a tetralogy by then about twenty-six years old, rather than a complaint about contemporary theatrical practice.

Furthermore, like Sidney, Jonson is referring to the practice of 'dividing one man into a thousand parts', not to how that one man used his weapons.

Indeed, the action of supernumeraries portraying foot-soldiers is the least interesting, and least important, feature of Shakespeare's battle scenes. From the siege of Orléans in *1 Henry VI* to the war in *Cymbeline*, Shakespeare's armies do much of their fighting off stage, while the visible sword-fighting is undertaken by principal characters; our picture of Talbot, Richard III, Prince Harry, Troilus, and Macbeth, to name but a few, is less than complete until we carefully consider how they conduct themselves when engaging in single combat.

Schlegel, writing in the first decade of the nineteenth century, was one of the first to address himself specifically to the swordplay within Elizabethan stage battles. After first reminding us that the Greeks wanted no part of onstage fighting, he says

It is certainly laughable enough that a handful of awkward warriors in mock armour, by means of two or three swords, with which we clearly see they take especial care not to do the slightest injury to one another, should decide the fate of mighty kingdoms. But the opposite extreme is still much worse. If we in reality succeed in exhibiting the tumult of a great battle, the storming of a fort, and the like, in a manner calculated in any way to deceive the eye, the power of these sensible impressions is so great that they render the spectator incapable of bestowing that attention which a poetical work of art demands, and thus the essential is sacrificed to the accessory.

Nevertheless, he finds himself forced to admire, at least in theory, some stage combat:

With all the disadvantages that I have mentioned, Shakespeare and several Spanish poets have con-

---

[2] Jean MacIntyre, 'Shakespeare and the Battlefield', *Theatre Survey*, 23 (1982), 31–44; p. 33.
[3] Quoted from the New Mermaid edition, ed. Martin Seymour-Smith (London, 1966).

trived to derive such great beauties from the immediate representation of war, that I cannot bring myself to wish they had abstained from it. A theatrical manager of the present day will have a middle course to follow; his art must, in an especial manner, be directed to make what he shows us appear only as separate groups of an immense picture, which cannot be taken in at once by the eye, he must convince the spectators that the main action takes place behind the stage; and for this purpose he has easy means at his command in the nearer or more remote sound of warlike music and the din of arms.[4]

It is evident that Schlegel is discussing Shakespearian production in his own day, and not Shakespeare's, but his comments do strike at the fundamental nature of the problem: in saying that one should, in effect, make it real, but not too real, Schlegel raises the whole subject of what the basic conventions of theatre are, whether or not they change from age to age, and how these conventions might have been applied by Shakespeare's company in scenes of violent physical action.

He comments that we, the spectators, are likely to find the battles in Shakespeare 'laughable', since we see only 'a handful of awkward warriors in mock armour, by means of two or three swords, with which we clearly see they take especial care not to do the slightest injury to one another'. But what of that? Does not the audience 'know' that *everything* it sees on the stage is not 'true', but is it not willing, in Coleridge's phrase, to suspend its disbelief? Assuredly, sword-fights do look bad when we see that the actors are taking care not to hurt one another – just as bad as a love scene when we 'see' that the leading lady does not find the thought of kissing her co-star an attractive proposition. But just as good actors can convince us that the characters they play are in love, so a good Richard III and Richmond should also be able to convince us that they are out to kill one another, with Richmond succeeding in an exciting fashion. The problem is actually one of relative difficulty: for us, as for

the audience of Schlegel's time, the demands which stage combat makes of the actor, with its associated problems of costuming (Schlegel's point about mock armour is a salient one) and wounds, contrive to render it one of the more difficult theatrical effects, particularly for the modern actor who is not necessarily adept at fencing; but 'difficult', as has been shown by some exciting stage combat in today's Shakespearian theatres, does not mean 'impossible.'

Given that the Elizabethan actor, who wore a sword in everyday life, would have been competent, or even, as Tarlton was, a recognized master in the art of fencing, it is unlikely that he would consider the Richard–Richmond fight or any other stage sword-fight as being necessarily forbidding, although anyone who has played a fencing role knows it is both very strenuous and, given the ever-present chance of an accident, mentally exhausting.

Schlegel then concedes, without saying he has ever seen it happen, that it is possible to present a stage fight realistically, but suspects that it would detract from the poetic content of the play, thereby betraying a basic misconception about what dramatic production, particularly Shakespearian dramatic production, is. A Shakespeare play is assuredly 'a poetical work of art', but the poetry is to be found in the totality of all its parts, including its (sometimes violent) stage business. Those who want only the 'poetry', as I understand Schlegel to use the term, are better advised to stay home and read the Sonnets.

It is not surprising that Schlegel felt as he did, considering the style of Shakespearian production in his time. A realistic sword-fight would (and does) look out of place in a declamatory production behind a proscenium arch, probably as preposterous as the fight at the beginning of Mozart's *Don Giovanni* usually

---

[4] A. W. Schlegel, *A Course of Lectures on Dramatic Art and Literature* (1809–11), translated by John Black (London, 1871), pp. 430–1.

appears. Not only Schlegel but later critics bemoan the fact that a good sword-fight is something rarely seen in their day. Writing in the 1920s of Burbage's bouts in a number of roles, T. W. Baldwin imagines they 'were not the creaky-kneed performances of the modern stage, but fencing exhibitions'. Dover Wilson, in his introduction to George Silver's fencing manual of 1599, *Paradoxes of Defence*, also yearns for the spectacular fight: 'to the modern spectator the fencing-match in *Hamlet* seems tame as the ghost scenes slightly ridiculous'.[5] It is important to note the implicit assumption in Wilson's view which is explicit in Baldwin: that the fights were scenes of exciting action in Elizabethan times. It is necessary, then, to ascertain, as much as possible, whether this assumption is warranted.

Baldwin helpfully points us towards T. F. Ordish's history of the London theatres for support of his view. Ordish makes the very cogent point that the Theatre, the Globe, and the other playhouses were all used for fencing prizes and were constructed with this function in mind, this association between the 'play' of drama and the 'play' of sporting combat having its origins deep in the Anglo-Saxon tradition of community displays of martial prowess:

The existence of the playhouse implied a more highly organized celebration of the national plays or games: and the Elizabethan drama grew up amid the ancient and traditional sports and pastimes of the people in an age quick with new ideas and new life. To understand these conditions is to understand why acting-plays written for the old playhouses were so full of action, energy, and varied movement; why military pomp and circumstance so frequently entered into the traffic of the stage; why broadsword, buckler, lance and shield, javelin, rapier, and harquebuse were brought into the dramatist's story . . . the fight between Macbeth and Macduff must have been a magnificent spectacle. It requires some study on our part to realize what such a climax to a sublime play meant to Englishmen in an Elizabethan playhouse.[6]

In his comprehensive study of the development of the Elizabethan playhouse, Glynne Wickham cites ample evidence to support his contention that its association with fencing was particularly strong. He notes that 'feats of activity' were 'frequently coupled with Elizabethan stage plays', and that 'of all "feats of activity" . . . gymnastic, balletic, and pugilistic, none was more popular than fencing'.[7] Of great importance for our purposes are the three documents from the Chamber Accounts which show that from 1588 to 1590 both the Admiral's Men and Lord Strange's Men performed feats of activity as part of their regular operations;[8] although the performances alluded to in the documents were at court, it is most unlikely that both companies would have limited feats of activity to that venue and excluded them from the playhouse.

Wickham's aim is to show that the design of the Elizabethan playhouse owed as much to the pre-existing arenas for trial by combat and combat sport as it did to the innyard. Regarding trial by combat, he cites a 'remarkable building' built in Tuthill Fields for a trial involving one Thomas Paramour, noting that it 'provides a magnificent prototype for the Fortune Theatre if not the circular Swan'.[9]

In discussion of the circular ground plans for

5 T. W. Baldwin, *The Organization and Personnel of the Shakespearean Company* (New York, 1927), p. 252; George Silver, *Paradoxes of Defence* (1599), ed. J. Dover Wilson, Shakespeare Association Facsimiles no. 6 (Oxford, 1933), p. xx.
6 T. F. Ordish, *Early London Theatres* (London, 1889), pp. 48–9.
7 Glynne Wickham, *Early English Stages: 1300–1600*, vol. 2 in two parts (London, 1963–72), vol. 2, part 2, p. 42.
8 Wickham, *Early English Stages*, vol. 2, part 2, pp. 164, 42–4.
9 Wickham, *Early English Stages*, vol. 2, part 1, pp. 163–72. See also John Stow, *The Annales of England: Faithfully collected out of the most authenticall Authors, Records, and other Monuments of Antiquitie, lately corrected, encreased, and continued, from the first inhabitation until the present yeere 1601* (London, 1601), pp. 1132–3.

the Cornish Miracle Cycle and *The Castle of Perseverance*, Wickham agrees with Ordish that there must have been some connection between these 'round' theatres, tournament arenas, and the round theatres used for plays and fencing in Elizabethan times. He terms the first Elizabethan theatres – the Theatre, the Curtain, the Globe –

playhouses in the literal and traditional sense of that word – houses for plays; i.e. for recreation, for 'feats of activity,' for entertainment including stage plays. In building his theatre in Finsbury Fields therefore Burbage was in one sense at least no innovator: for he was simply copying what he had done several times already in respect of recreational activities in Tuthill Fields and in Southwark.[10]

He later notes:

. . . in Elizabethan London the multipurpose game-house proved to be the most useful, profitable, and most sought-after locality for presenting stage plays because it admitted the largest number of spectators and allowed a stage, tiring house, and scenic emblems to be erected and dismantled with that degree of ease which was obligatory for companies of entertainers whose economy was nomadic and not residential.[11]

Wickham provides a wealth of documentary evidence to support this perceived relationship of fencing to the Elizabethan playhouse, and to look at the documents he cites, along with some which he does not, is to have one's impression confirmed that he, and Ordish before him, are correct.

The Register of the Masters of Defence (c. 1565–90), and Documents of Control (reprinted in Chambers' *Elizabethan Stage*) show constant use of the playhouses, and the innyards before the playhouses were erected, for fencing prizes. The documents consistently link fencers with players as persons whose dangerous activities must be limited through licensing, as does Stephen Gosson in his well-known tract *The Schoole of Abuse* (1579), where fencers are attacked in language as virulent, and at nearly as great a length, as are players.[12]

Glimpses of the Elizabethan fencer's life (and death) in the playhouse are tantalizingly few. John Manningham's *Diary* mentions the notorious Turner–Dun incident, in which the professional fencer Dun was killed, perhaps deliberately, by a sword-thrust to the eye, at the Swan on 7 February 1602. There is also a record of Henslowe letting the Rose to fencers in 1598: 'James cranwigge the 4 of november 1598 playd his callenge [sic] in my howsse & I sholde haue hade for my parte xxxx s which the company hath Rd & oweth yt to me.'[13]

Perhaps today's spectator can best picture the association of the Shakespearian theatre with skilful fencing by imagining a modern *Hamlet* performed in a boxing arena, and then having a pugilistic, instead of a fencing, prize-fight end the play. Furthermore, the imagined crowd would be composed largely of the smoking, beer-drinking denizens of this colourful, Runyonesque world.[14] Then let us have a Hamlet and a Laertes who cannot fight believably at all, either because of physique or

---

[10] Wickham, *Early English Stages*, vol. 2, part 1, pp. 164, 168.

[11] Wickham, *Early English Stages*, vol. 2, part 2, p. 4.

[12] Stephen Gosson, *The Schoole of Abuse* (1579), facsimile reprint. The English Experience, vol. 253 (New York, 1972), fos. 28–32; see also E. K. Chambers, *The Elizabethan Stage*, 4 vols. (Oxford, 1923), vol. 4, p. 205.

[13] Robert P. Sorlien, ed., *The Diary of John Manningham of the Middle Temple: 1602–1603* (Hanover, New Hampshire, 1976), pp. 187, 379. J. D. Aylward gives a fascinating account of the possibility of deliberate murder in 'The Creighton Case', *Notes and Queries*, NS 4 (1957), 245–50. The Henslowe reference is from *Documents of the Rose Playhouse*, ed. Carol Chillington Rutter, Revels Plays Companion Library (Manchester, 1984), Document 73, p. 155.

[14] That smoking and beer-drinking at the playhouses was common is well documented. In particular, see Chambers, *Elizabethan Stage*, vol. 2, p. 365, citing a contemporary account by Thomas Platter, and vol. 2, p. 549, where there are several citations. One amusing piece of evidence is afforded by the fact that when the Globe burnt down, a man whose trousers caught fire managed to have the flames extinguished by a bystander's prudent use of a bottle of beer (C. Walter Hodges, *Shakespeare's Theatre* (New York, 1964), p. 101).

simple lack of skill, and imagine the crowd's reaction. Given that the *Hamlet* audience at the Globe was exactly this sort of crowd, sitting or standing in what was not only a theatre but a prize-fight arena, one is led to the conclusion that anything less than a totally verisimilar fight would have been laughed off the stage, or worse. To return to Schlegel's original objection that the crowd 'knows' the actors are trying hard not to hurt one another, the only answer, as indicated previously, is to point to the basic nature of the theatrical event, and to say that an audience, by definition, always accepts a good deal of artifice, with the amount dependent on the style of the play and the common dramatic conventions of the time; the circumstances of Shakespearian production in the Elizabethan age were such that the audience would have wished to see only the most convincing of fights.

A view which in some respects may be described as 'alternative' is presented by Alan C. Dessen.[15] He argues that some sword-fights and other violent action on the Elizabethan stage did call, even in Shakespeare's time, for another 'logic' (i.e. set of conventions) apart from the basic one of theatrical verisimilitude. While Dessen's discussion is presented in a most stimulating and scholarly fashion, it suffers to some degree from a not-always-clear delineation as to what he feels was the case in Shakespeare's time, and what should be the case in our own.[16] His choice of an example to demonstrate that some violent stage business was necessarily symbolic rather than verisimilar is an odd one: 'enter Nessus with an arrow through him', from Thomas Heywood's *The Brazen Age* (*c.* 1613). As any vaudevillian knows, to rig an arrow, making it appear as if it has pierced the actor, and to have the actor stagger on stage, is the simplest of theatrical tricks, and, contrary to Dessen's implication, is not always comic: in the Royal Shakespeare Company's 1977 production of *3 Henry VI*, the director, Terry Hands, decided to follow the reported text's stage direc-

tion, having Clifford enter in exactly this way. To the company's surprise it was anything but funny.[17]

That point aside, Dessen argues persuasively, and I think correctly, that an alternative style of stage swordplay was 'widely available in the English dramatic tradition'. He refers to the elaborate mock battles of royal entertainments, morality plays such as George Wapull's *The Tide Tarrieth No Man* (1576), where Vice takes on a variety of opponents with his wooden dagger, and to similar combats found in plays which are contemporary with Wapull's, such as William Wager's *Enough is as Good as a Feast* (*c.* 1564) and Ulpian Fulwell's *Like Will to Like* (*c.* 1568). These allegorical dramas clearly call for a symbolic representation of sword-fighting where sword-fighting is included in the action.

Dessen then goes on to apply some of these ideas to Shakespeare and his contemporaries, stating his premise concisely:

Can we be confident that a blow in a non-allegorical Elizabethan play would be delivered with the speed, force, and timing of a similar blow in the street outside the theatre? Need a moment of stage violence in the Globe exist as an end in itself, adhering to a logic derived from an equivalent moment in 'real life,' or could it be linked to a symbolic and patterned logic relevant to the world of the play?[18]

As did Schlegel's concerns about fight scenes, Dessen's questions (he admirably refrains from claiming to have any definite answers) raise a fundamental dramaturgical question: is it only the more difficult requirements of staging which call on a 'symbolic,

[15] Alan C. Dessen, *Elizabethan Stage Conventions and their Modern Interpreters* (Cambridge, 1984).
[16] This criticism of Dessen is given by Michael Shapiro in reference to an earlier work. Michael Shapiro, 'Annotated Bibliography of Original Staging in Shakespeare's Plays', *Research Opportunities in Renaissance Drama*, 24 (1981), 23–49; p. 30.
[17] H. D. Swander, 'The Rediscovery of Henry VI', *Shakespeare Quarterly*, 29 (1978), 146–63; p. 151.
[18] Dessen, *Stage Conventions*, pp. 110–11.

patterned, logic?' The very nature of presentation, even in the most naturalistic modern play, will always call for some symbolic logic – i.e., to use Dessen's phrase, doing things differently from what one would do 'in the street outside the theatre' (p. 110). The proscenium-arch box set with all furniture facing front is but one of the numerous examples which could be offered.

One play which probably is contemporary with early Shakespeare and which indeed does, as Dessen observes, call on an 'alternative logic', is the historical drama *Edmond Ironside*, where the author uses a dumb show 'to bring complex events on stage'.[19] Like so many Elizabethan plays, it cannot be dated with any certainty; Irving Ribner suggests 1590, while Eric Sams, though arguing for Shakespeare's authorship of the play, offers 1588. In *Ironside*, which is, as is noted by Ribner, a 'confused and uncertain' piece stylistically very different from Shakespeare,[20] the hero meets Canutus (King Canute) in single combat on the battlefield three times (lines 962, 976, and 985), and the entire battle sequence is narrated by the Chorus, who tells us

> I faine would have you understand the truth
> and see the battailes Acted on the stage
> But that theire length wilbe tedious
> then in dumb shewes I will explaine at large
> theire fightes theire flightes and Edmonds
>   victory. (lines 969–73)

As the Chorus proceeds with his florid explanation, Edmond and Canutus mime the fight. Such 'neo-Senecan dumbshows', as Ribner refers to them,[21] could hardly be assumed to be verisimilar in presentation.

While Dessen is correct, then, in asserting that an alternative style of symbolic swordplay was a part of English dramatic tradition, he fails to observe that, contemporaneously with the allegorical drama, a rich genre of drama calling for verisimilar stage combat also existed. In the heroical romances *Sir Clyomon and Sir Clamydes* (*c.* 1570) and *Common Conditions* (*c.* 1576), the hero engages in some exciting onstage combat, and there is nothing to indicate that the fighting would be 'allegorical' in either of them. Indeed, it is likely that Shakespeare was influenced by these or similar 'heroical romances' in including such an extraordinary amount of sword-fighting in his 'heroical history', as David Riggs calls it, *Henry VI*.[22]

Another play requiring consideration is Richard Edwardes's *Palaemon and Arcyte* (1566), performed before a royal audience in the Hall of Christ Church, Oxford. There is no extant text, but the description by the contemporary witness John Bereblock, written in Latin, recounts the exciting formal combat between the two title roles, which all at Oxford who had read Chaucer's *Knight's Tale* or its source, Boccaccio's *Teseida*, would have keenly anticipated:

> . . . the blast and blare of trumpets is heard. Then in hand to hand combat they fight fiercely. When at the very first the weapons resounded and the shiny blades gleamed, a great shudder seized the spectators. For a time success fell to neither contestant, and, wearied with fighting, they twice stop to rest; at the third onset, when not only the movements of their bodies and the parrying of their swords, but even their wounds and blood are visible to everybody, Palaemon sinks to the ground and lies prostrate before his victorious cousin.[23]

---

19 Dessen, *Stage Conventions*, p. 13.
20 Irving Ribner, *The English History Play in the Age of Shakespeare* (Princeton, 1957), pp. 242–3; Eric Sams, ed., *Shakespeare's Lost Play: Edmund Ironside* (New York, 1985), pp. 9–40; the following quotation is from Eleanor Boswell, ed., *Edmond Ironside*, Malone Society Reprints (London, 1927).
21 Ribner, *English History Play*, p. 243.
22 David Riggs, *Shakespeare's Heroical Histories* (Cambridge, Mass., 1971).
23 W. Y. Durand, '*Palaemon and Arcyte, Progne, Marcus Geminus* and the Theatre in Which They Were Acted, as Described by John Bereblock (1566)', *PMLA*, 20 (1905), 502–28; p. 511. Bereblock's description is mentioned by Dessen in 'The Logic of Elizabethan Stage Violence: Some Alarms and Excursions for Modern Critics, Editors, and Directors', *Renaissance Drama*, NS 9 (1978), 39–69; p. 40.

Although, as Durand notes, part of this account is taken from Livy verbatim, this in itself is not sufficient cause to doubt, as does Dessen, its basic veracity.

Finally, the only *Shakespearian* examples of swordplay Dessen cites in his discussion of 'stage violence' which 'run counter to the verisimilar assumptions of most critics, editors, and directors', are those featuring Joan in *1 Henry VI*, where the supernatural is involved.[24] He also mentions fights in *King Lear* and *Cymbeline* where it may be assumed that a staff or cudgel goes up against a sword, although it is not clear whether or not he feels that victory of the more primitive weapon is indicative of a symbolic mode of staging. If there is such an assumption, it is unwarranted; both George Silver and the Jacobean master Joseph Swetnam give clear advice as to how a staff can defeat a sword,[25] and in the Oregon Shakespearean Festival's production of *Cymbeline* in 1968, for which I directed the combat scenes, an enthusiastic Guiderius and Arviragus, fighting with staffs, were most effective in their defeat of the Romans in the 'Battle of the Narrow Lane'.

Dessen goes on to make many useful points about the thematic significance of some of Shakespeare's sword-fights, and poses some ideas which the modern fight arranger should consider, but as far as the 'original verisimilitude' of the sword-fights in Shakespeare is concerned, he does not cite a single example to dissuade one from the view that they were presented with anything other than the most convincing sort of realism.

---

24 Dessen, *Elizabethan Stage Conventions*, p. 114. His two examples from Heywood do little to advance his argument. The fight in *If You Know Not Me, You Know Nobody* is part of a dumb show which also involves the supernatural. In *A Woman Killed With Kindness*, he objects to having a 'supernumerary maid' realistically stay the hand of Frankford, but unlike Dessen I cannot see where this presents a problem for the 'verisimilar' devotee, although Dessen may be right in saying that the moment could be improved if done in a symbolic way. Dessen also mentions, in passing, the Nurse's intervention in Romeo's attempted suicide, but I, like Alan Brissenden, do not see any real difficulty in staging the 'staying' of a male hand by a female. Thomas Heywood, *If You Know Not Me, You Know Nobody*, ed. Madeleine Doran, Malone Society Reprints, 2 vols. (London, 1934); Heywood, *A Woman Kilde with Kindnesse* (1607), University Microfilms, Early English Books 1475–1640 (Ann Arbor, n.d.), reel 891; Alan Brissenden, '*Romeo and Juliet*, III.iii.108: The Nurse and the Dagger', *Notes and Queries*, NS 28 (1981), 126–7.

25 Silver, *Paradoxes*, pp. 38–44; Joseph Swetnam, *The School of the Noble and Worthy Science of Defence* (1617), University Microfilms, Early English Books 1475–1640 (Ann Arbor, n.d.), reel 1190, pp. 134–48. Swetnam, who ran a fencing academy in Bristol, was also one of the most noted misogynists of the age; his anti-female tract, *The Araignment of Lewde, Idele, Froward, and Unconstant Women*, attracted several responses, including the anonymous play *Swetnam the Woman Hater, Arraigned by Women*, performed at the Red Bull in 1617.

SHAKESPEARE'S HANDWRITING

GILES E. DAWSON

On the controversy over Shakespeare's hand-writing in *Sir Thomas More*, the best arguments supporting Shakespeare are to be found in *Shakespeare and the Play of Sir Thomas More* (Cambridge, 1923), edited by A. W. Pollard. Here, the most persuasive contributions are those of Sir Edward Maunde Thompson, J. Dover Wilson, and R. W. Chambers. A chapter by the last of these in his *Man's Unconquerable Mind* (London, 1939) made a further cogent contribution.

All the best work on the subject up to 1948 is reviewed and expanded by R. C. Bald in his '*Booke of Sir Thomas More* and its Problems' in *Shakespeare Survey 2*. Bald believed that the attribution of the 147 lines of Hand D was correct. Greg a little later concurred in that view.[1] In my own view, Thompson's article in the book cited above, 'The Handwriting of the Three Pages Attributed to Shakespeare Compared with his Signatures', by itself leaves little room for doubt. Yet the steady stream of contrary argument runs on apace, and most of those who count themselves believers are but 90 per cent believers. Had it been otherwise when the 1983 meeting of the Shakespeare Association of America was being planned, the need for a seminar on 'Shakespeare and *Sir Thomas More*' would hardly have been felt.

This lingering scepticism is partly to be laid at Thompson's own door. He has some of the facts but presents his evidence weakly and buries it in irrelevant matter, taking fifty pages to say what could have been more effectively said in a dozen. My primary business is to state succinctly the two valid pieces of evidence that he presents.

The first of Thompson's important observations takes us to a scene near the end of Shakespeare's life. We may suppose that when Shakespeare prepared to subscribe his signature to the third page of his will he was conscious of the solemnity of the occasion. Five of his neighbours stood by to witness this important signature. He started with the words 'By me', and in forming the *m* in 'me' he began with a little flourish, a preliminary up-stroke of the pen. This he repeated on the *W* of 'William'. These strokes were not a form of embellishment that he thought up on the spur of the moment. He had been making them for years, and others, a few others, had been making them for a long time. The earliest I have seen were produced in 1572.

Thompson saw these embellishments, and he made a further important observation – that in making the up-stroke on the *W* Shakespeare began with a down-stroke. This is not readily seen because the up-stroke retraces, or nearly retraces, the down-stroke, and this can be seen only where the retracing is imperfect and leaves what Thompson calls a 'needle-eye'.

The writer of the 147 lines of Hand D made use of these up-strokes. He attached them to initial *i, m, n, r, v,* and *w*, but those on *m* and *w*

---

[1] 'In the present discussion it will be assumed that the three pages [of *More*] are in Shakespeare's autograph' (W. W. Greg, *The Shakespeare First Folio* (Oxford, 1954), p. 99).

signature 3A

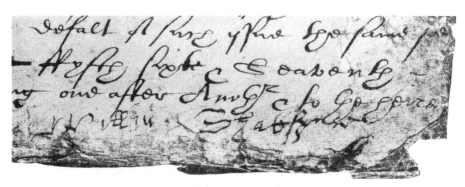

signature 3B

signature 3C

3 Shakespeare's Signatures to the Three Sheets of His Will, 25 March 1616 (Public Record Office, Principal Probate
Registry, Selected Wills, Prob. 1/4). A: Sheet One; B: Sheet Two; C: Sheet Three

4   *Sir Thomas More*, page 3 of the 147 lines in Hand D (Addition IIC, fol. 9; British Library MS Harley 7368)

far exceed the others in number. In the 147 lines 65 words begin with *m*, and on 44 of these the up-stroke may be seen. Of 79 initial *w*s 34 bear the up-stroke. A small number of these up-strokes carry down-strokes. The most conspicuous of these occur in a cluster near the bottom of page 3: on 'needes'[2] (line 130), 'mountanish' and 'inhumanity' (both in line 140), and on 'weele' (line 142).[3] In the word 'needes' (line 130) Thompson observed another 'needle-eye' almost exactly like that on the *W* of 'William'. Yet another one, unnoticed or passed up by Thompson, is on 'weele' (line 142). This is bigger but still very similar to the other two.

Usages such as these up-strokes and down-strokes are of evidentiary value in identifying a writer only if, and only to the degree that, each one can be shown to have been an uncommon practice among the writers of a given time. Thompson was aware of this principle but does not take it as seriously as he ought to do. He believes (pages 77–8) that Shakespeare's use of the up-strokes in his sixth signature constituted 'a habit which he would have acquired in his schooldays' and that the up-strokes were 'a common feature in the copy-books of children at school'. It is true that they appear in some of the copy-books, attached to a *v* or a *w*, but if schoolboys were indeed taught to use them, almost all of them soon forgot their teaching.

In the course of my work on Shakespeare's handwriting I went through a collection of Elizabethan and Jacobean letters and documents, examining those written by 250 writers in order to observe several writing habits. In this exercise I chose letters or groups of letters of more than 200 words. The first time I performed this task I was looking for three usages in the writing. The second time I was looking for others. To these searches I shall refer in the pages following.

Of the up-strokes I can report that I found them in only seven hands, and that in all of the seven the incidence of the up-strokes was light. The biggest number in one hand was nineteen.

Some gave me only one or two. One of the seven put up-strokes only on the initial letter *v*, of which there were five in about 300 words. The first one he formed with a preliminary down-stroke. This is the only down-stroke preliminary to an up-stroke that I have seen, apart from the one in Shakespeare's signature on the final page of his will (3.c) and ten in Hand D.

The second of Thompson's important contributions concerns the letter *a*. In the two words 'add ampler', the third and fourth words in line 101 of Hand D, the initial *a* in each is an ordinary *a* in both the secretary hand and our own of today. In the last word of line 97, 'ar' is made with a strange *a*. In forming this the writer began at the left side and brought the pen round in a clockwise direction until it began its approach to the base-line in a straight course. If we were to erase all of that loop except the straight line, we should have an *a* with what is called a spur. Some writers use the spur only on initial *a*. The reason for this preference is that in a cursive hand it would appear to be difficult to link an immediately preceding letter to a spurred *a*. Most of those in Hand D are initial.

This fad appears to have been started about 1550, and its early practitioners made their spurs a little differently. In the word 'ar' the spur is brought down to, or very close to, the base-line, where the pen's course was reversed for about one millimetre before turning downward to finish the letter with a final minim, leaving the top of the *a* open. The practitioners

---

[2] The last character of this word is not an *s* but a contraction of *es*.

[3] The reproduction of page 3 of the manuscript of *Sir Thomas More* is taken (by permission of the British Library) from the collotype reproduction in E. M. Thompson's monograph, *Shakespeare's Handwriting* (Oxford, 1916). That reproduction is better than the manuscript itself is today. Still, Thompson's reproduction of pages 1 and 2 shows damage that renders them quite illegible in some places and difficult to make out in others. I therefore do not reproduce those pages here.

of 1550 and a few years later made the spur shorter and gave it an angle of about 30 degrees with the base-line (which it never reached) before the pen's reversal and turn downward. This one-millimetre reversal is a curiously persistent feature of the spurred *a*, surviving, though often wanting, until in the early decades of the next century the spur itself fell into disuse. About 1570 the spur had commonly become longer and its angle with the base-line greater. In the 1590s the sharply curved spur, like all of those on page 3 of Hand D, became fairly common.

On that page line 108 ends with the word 'handes'.[4] Here the *h* is linked with the *a* by a bulbous structure. I said, above, that to link a letter with a following spurred *a* appeared to be difficult. But here it is done. The spur itself is the link. On this page 3 every *a* that immediately follows an *h* is linked to it in this way. This linkage was practised by at least one writer as early as 1572. Now in the signature in the Belott–Mountjoy deposition (illustration 5A), the *h* and the *a* are linked in this same way. It may be seen that as the pen came round to complete the rough circle, it just touched the up-stroke,[5] then reversed its direction to form a sharp point, and thence it moved in a nearly straight line to the right to complete the malformed *a* with a final minim.

In line 105 of Hand D, if we look closely at the word 'that' in the middle of the line, we can see that the *h–a* link is exactly like the one we have been examining in the signature in having the sharp point precisely touching the up-stroke, and also the same straight line forming the bottom of the mis-shapen *a*. Again, the word 'harber' near the middle of line 127 exhibits the same sharp point (which here fails by a hair's breadth to close the circle) and the same flat-bottomed *a*. And compare the pointed 'a' (third word in line 119) and the *a* in 'against' (line 109).

In my examination of the hands of many writers I found twelve who linked *h* and *a* with those faddish bulbous spurs, but I found no writer who even once produced that link with the sharp point closing the circle and forming an *a* with a long, flat bottom. I have seen such an *h–a* link only in Shakespeare's signature to the Belott–Mountjoy deposition (illustration 5A) and in Hand D.

Here leaving ground covered by Thompson, I venture into unexplored territory.

One of the best known emendations of the Shakespeare text is that in the Hostess's account of Falstaff's death in *Henry V*, 2.3. Where the Folio text, retained by Rowe, reads 'and a Table of greene fields',[6] Theobald (1733) reads 'and a babled [*sic*] of greene fields'. To this reading he supplies a note: 'The conjectural emendation I have given, is so near the traces of the Letters in the corrupted text, that I have ventured to insert them as the genuine reading.' The precise meaning of these words is obscure, but since Theobald wrote them in justification of his reading I can only suppose them to mean that in the handwriting of Shakespeare's time 'bable' could be seen by a compositor as 'table'. This supposition assumes a knowledge on Theobald's part of the secretary hand. That knowledge must have been rare in 1733, but Theobald had written a brief life of Sir Walter Ralegh,[7] in which he shows evidence of having made use of old records of Ralegh's time. If I construe his note correctly, he has hit the nail on the head.

But how could one of Jaggard's compositors, looking at the word 'babbled' or even

---

4 See note 2.
5 Thompson errs in saying that the point does not touch the upstroke, but leaves 'a minute space'. The error suggests that at the age of eighty-three his eyesight was not acute and he lacked adequate optical assistance. But elsewhere he sees existing minute spaces.
6 The capital *T* is not to be understood as meaning that Shakespeare so wrote it. There is good evidence that he seldom used capital letters for any purpose. The compositor who set this part of *Henry V* in the Folio was much given to using capital initials for nouns, and we can assume that he was responsible for this one.
7 Lewis Theobald, *Memoirs of Sir Walter Raleigh* (London, 1719).

'babled', think that he was seeing 'table'? This would be understandable only if we could accept three propositions: (1) that the writer of the copy-text spelt the word 'babld', (2) that he so wrote it as to make the initial *b* look like a *t*, and (3) that his *d* looked like an *e*.

If Theobald did conceive of the spelling 'babld' he was shrewd indeed. A careful look at the 147 lines of Hand D will show that of twelve past participles in it eleven are similarly elided, to give us 'sufferd', 'vsd', 'quelld', and so on. This practice is not to be seen as an eccentricity on the writer's part. It was a well-established convention of dramatists and perhaps other poets to indicate when the *-ed* is to be pronounced as a syllable, and when not. These lines from the F *Hamlet* will illustrate the usage:

> Of Life, of Crowne, and Queene at once
>   dispatcht;
> Cut off euen in the Blossomes of my Sinne,
> Vnhouzzled, dissapointed, vnnaneld
>
> (TLN 760–2)

In F, the compositors usually inserted an apostrophe where the *e* was elided, but occasionally in F and commonly in Q texts they set it as they saw it.

That a *b* could be misread as a *t* will be clear from a comparison of the *b* in 'rebells' (line 109) and 'rebell' (119) with the *t* in 'them' (111), 'the' (116), and 'their' (120). The other way round, 'teares' (108) could easily be read as 'beares'.

To demonstrate the likelihood of mistaking a *d* for an *e* I need first to point out that in the secretary hand the commoner of the two usual forms of *e* is shaped in just the same way as the commonest of several kinds of *d* – with the important exception that the *d* properly made is much bigger or taller than the *e*. But the writer of Hand D (who always uses the commoner *e* and the commonest *d*) often fails to make this important distinction. A look at 'handes' at the end of line 108, and a comparison of that *d* with the final *e* in 'peace' (the

last word in line 109) is a good example of an *e* taller than a *d*. Quite a few *e*s on this page will be found to be bigger than some *d*s. And Maunde Thompson gives us unwittingly a fine demonstration. When he was transcribing the 147 lines for his 1916 monograph, *Shakespeare's Handwriting*, and came, in line 82, upon 'how ordere should be quelld', apparently ignoring the context, he read it, 'how orderd should be quelld'.

We have found in Hand D such carelessness in the forming of certain letters as explains how Jaggard's compositor might reasonably be expected to see 'babld' and read it as 'table'. But if Elizabethan writers in general were much given to carelessness in distinguishing between the letters *b* and *t* and the letters *d* and *e*, then we can learn little more from the 147 lines alone. That, however, is not the case. No such general carelessness is to be found. A friend of mine who is much experienced in the secretary hand tells me that the transcribers of that hand frequently fall into the *d/e* error. That may well be true, but if it is, it must be due to gross carelessness of the readers, not of the writers. My exhaustive testing leads me to the conclusion that the writing-masters, well aware of the danger, made a special point of warning their pupils against it. In each hand that I dealt with, I cannot say that I examined every *d* and every *e*. But in each, I looked at enough of them to enable me to determine whether or not the *d*s and the *e*s were so formed that their relative size was the only feature that distinguished them. This condition I seldom found, and where I did find it I almost always discovered that the writer took sufficient pains with the relative sizes to avoid confusion. I found only one writer who depended only on relative size, and who through negligence occasionally produced difficulty. And he was less careless than the writer of Hand D.

I also found no writer whose *b*s and *t*s could easily be mistaken one for the other.

We now know that Theobald's emendation

was sound, and that the compositor who saw 'babld' and mistook it for 'table' was not much to blame for his error. If it can also be shown that his copy-text was Shakespeare's autograph we shall know more. Greg says that it was so,[8] but today's breed of textual experts, standing on Greg's shoulders, taking second and third looks at the evidence, now pretty well agree that although the author's autograph underlay the F text of *Henry V*, there was some contamination of it from the Q text. One of the experts, Professor Richard Knowles, writes to me as follows:

I think that the two most likely possibilities to explain the mixture in FI are: (1) Jaggard's compositors set from foul papers but consulted the recently published Pavier quarto from time to time, thereby picking up Q readings; or (2) the foul papers were such a mess that Jaggard paid someone to make a transcript of them, and that scribe consulted the Pavier Q2 and picked up some of its readings.

He could not have picked up the words 'and a babld of green fields'; they are not in the quarto text, in which the account of Falstaff's death is shortened. If Knowles's second possibility is the correct one it was the scribe who misread 'babld' as 'table', and the compositor followed his copy accurately.

The copy text used by the compositor, or the scribe, led that person to mistake the word 'babld' for 'table'. That copy-text was Shakespeare's autograph. Shakespeare wrote 'babld' in such a way that the initial *b* looked like a *t*, and the final *d* looked like an *e*. The man who wrote Hand D was given to such carelessness in writing the letters *b* and *d* that they looked, respectively, like *t* and *e*. Shakespeare wrote Hand D. This is not proof, but it is evidence. Of that more is to follow.

The letter *k*, as it appears in four of the Shakespeare signatures, in Hand D, and as formed by secretary writers in general, deserves a close look. In signatures 5A and 3A, its shape cannot be seen. In 5B it bears the form of a *b* closely resembling a number of specimens of that letter on page 3 of Hand D and not much different from the way most writers of the secretary hand form the letter. The *k* in signature 5C under magnification appears also to be a *b*, but with a very small lower loop. In signature 3B it again appears to be a *b*, but with a horizontal line through it. Not one of those letters that we know to be intended as *k* is a *k*, even a carelessly written *k*. Not one, seen out of context, could be recognized as a *k*.

As a test, to find out how other writers of the secretary hand were shaping the *k*, I looked at every *k* in 40 substantial specimens of the hands. What I discovered was a surprising unanimity as to what the *k* ought to look like. The distinguishing badge of a *k* is the small circle on the right side of the shaft. In every hand that little circle was present. That is not to say that every *k* had the loop; sometimes haste caused the circle to be bungled. But every writer formed the required circle in other attempts. Shakespeare evidently made no such attempt in those four signatures.

In the 147 lines of Hand D the writer used the letter 34 times. Of these, 5 cannot be seen clearly in detail; 11 are normal (but twice the loop is blind); 10 are abnormal but would be recognizable out of context; 2 are perfect *b*s like that in signature 5B; 2 are perfect *l*s, but looped and therefore unlike that in signature 3C.

In order that my judgement may be exemplified, a list of the *k*s on page 3 of the 147 lines here follows: 'king' (line 98) normal; 'king' (102) normal but blind; 'lyke' (109) abnormal but recognizable; 'make' and 'kneele' (both 111) both normal; 'make' (112) normal; 'kill' (120) normal; 'lyke' (122) abnormal but recognizable; 'king' (122) normal; 'breaking' (132) abnormal but recognizable; 'knyves' (134) abnormal but recognizable; 'lyke' (twice 135) each a perfect *l*; 'thinck' (138) abnormal but recognizable; 'kinge' (145) abnormal but

---

[8] 'All things considered, there seems to be no doubt that it was from foul papers and not from a prompt-book that F was printed' (Greg, *Shakespeare First Folio*, p. 287).

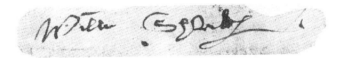

signature 5A

signature 5B

signature 5C

5   Shakespeare's Signatures to Three Legal Documents, 1612–13. A: Belott-Mountjoy Deposition, 11 May 1612 (Public
Record Office, Court of Requests, Documents of Shakespearian Interest, Req. 4/1); B: Blackfriars Gate-House
Conveyance, 10 March 1613 (Guildhall Library); C: Blackfriars Gate-House Mortgage Deed, 11 March 1613
(British Library, MS Egerton 1787)

recognizable; 'seek' (147) normal. Unfortunately the two that look like *b*s are on page 2 and therefore not here reproduced.

In the secretary hand the *k* is a letter rather more complex than most, keeping company with the *h*, the *p*, and the *s*. Writers of the secretary hand gave various shapes to each of these three letters, yet of the *k* they knew only one general shape. Shakespeare was in this respect an eccentric making no effort to conform to the common usage of his day. In the signatures of his that have survived and can be seen clearly no two specimens of the *k* are made in the same way. In the 29 specimens of the *k* in Hand D that can be seen clearly I find much variety. Eleven of the 29 are of the conventional shape; but 18 are not, and several bear the shapes of quite other letters. Two look precisely like the *k* in signature 5B, bearing the shape of the letter *b* that is found commonly in Hand D. Two look like *l*s, but not the *l* of signature 3C, for it is not looped and these two are.

I take the comparison of the *k* as we find it in the signatures and as we find it in the 147 lines to provide strong evidence that one and the same hand wrote the signatures and Hand D.

My last piece of evidence is of linguistic kind. Had the Hostess said, 'and he babld' instead of 'a babld' the scribe could hardly have seen it as 'he table' and would have taken a close look and got it right. The 'a' = 'he' is obviously dialectal, probably cockney. Farmer, in his *Dialect Dictionary*, records the dialectal form in Yorkshire and in a number of southern and western counties, including Worcestershire but not Warwickshire and not London. But his failure to find a word in this county or that proves nothing, and I suppose Shakespeare knew that his London audiences would be comfortable with 'a'.

In the 147 lines 'a' = 'he' is to be found three times: in line 42 Doll, a member of the rabble, says, 'Letts heare him a keepes a plentyfull shrevaltry, and a made my Brother Arthur watchin Seriant Safes yeoman lets heare shreeve moore.' In line 141 'all' (the rabble)

say, 'fayth a saies trewe lets do as we may be doon by'.

In Spevack's *Harvard Concordance to Shakespeare* the dialectal 'a' is listed 190 times in sixteen of the plays. All classes of people use it. In *Much Ado* the Second Watch does, and so do Beatrice and Benedick. In *The Merchant* we hear it from Launcelot Gobbo, but also from the Prince of Morocco. Hamlet uses it a dozen times, and both he and Horatio speak of the late King as 'a'.

In order to find out how many other dramatists were using the dialectal 'a' I went first to Charles Crawford's concordances to Kyd, Marlowe, and Jonson (the last unpublished).

Next, I went with great care through the twenty-four plays listed below in chronological order. In my choice of these plays I was influenced by my determination to use only old-spelling texts and also (I must admit) by my desire to use, as far as possible, texts that I could lay my hands on at home: *Jacob and Esau, Gammer Gurton's Needle, Juli and Julian, Cambises, Damon and Pithias* (Edwards), *Love of David and Fair Bethsaba, Spanish Tragedy, Friar Bacon and Friar Bungay, Knack to Know a Knave, Knack to Know an Honest Man, Edmond Ironside, Sir Thomas More* (all hands except D), *Death of Robert Earl of Huntingdon, Englishmen for my Money, Fair Maid of the Exchange, Woman Killed with Kindness,* 1 *Honest Whore, Parasitaster,* 2 *Honest Whore, The Whore of Babylon, Hog hath Lost his Pearl, Albumazar, Hengest King of Kent, Dick of Devonshire.*

Crawford records 5 occurrences of the dialectal 'a' in two of Marlowe's plays and 4 in one of Jonson's, none in Kyd's. In the twenty-four plays listed above I find it spoken 4 times by one character in *A Knack to Know a Knave,* once in *Sir Thomas More* (apart from Hand D), and 4 times in *Hog hath Lost his Pearl*. These add up to 18 occurrences in five plays and no occurrences in forty-two plays (15 of Jonson's, 4 of Marlowe's and 23 in my list). In one play in nine the dialectal 'a' is to be found. Both Shakespeare and Hand D practise it.

Marlowe's plays, Jonson's plays, and the twenty-four in my list were probably written by 24 playwrights. The dialectal 'a' was employed by 5 playwrights. One writer in 8 was using it. Both Shakespeare and Hand D were using it.

There is another way of comparing these playwrights. The dialectal 'a' occurs 197 times in Shakespeare's plays – an average of 12 times in each of the sixteen. In Hand D's 147 lines the 'a' occurs 3 times. If Hand D had written a whole play of 3250 lines (the average length of Shakespeare's), by extrapolation we can assume that it would contain 22 occurrences of the 'a'. Shakespeare and Hand D employ the 'a' freely. All of the other dramatists known to use it at all employ it sparingly.

A brief summary of the kinds of evidence here put forward may be helpful.

(1)　The up-strokes on the *m* and the *W* of Shakespeare's sixth signature, also found on *m* and *w* in Hand D, have not elsewhere been found on both of these letters. The preliminary down-stroke found on the *W* of 'William', and found also on an initial *w* in Hand D, has been seen elsewhere only on a *v* in a 1572 document.

(2)　The bulbous link of the *h* and the *a* in the second signature are uncommon. The deformed *a* with a long point and a flat bottom occurs in a signature and in Hand D and has been seen nowhere else.

(3)　The confusing *b* and *t*, on the one hand, and *d* and *e* on the other, which caused the misreading of 'babld' as 'table' in the F text of *Henry V*, are to be found in Hand D, but are extremely rare elsewhere in secretary hands.

(4)　The *k* in all of Shakespeare's four legible signatures is always but variously malformed and unrecognizable. So are nearly half the *k*s in Hand D, some closely duplicating that in signature 5B. Writers in general appear to be unanimous in forming the *k* correctly.

(5)　The dialectal 'a' = 'he' is used (always sparingly) by 5 playwrights among 42. It appears much more numerously in Shakespeare's plays and in Hand D.

What then is the mathematical probability that two skilled dramatists, writing simultaneously about the year 1600, would be engaging in all of those unusual practices, some highly unusual? Is it not instead evident that the same hand wrote the six signatures and the basic text of *Henry V* and the 147 lines of Hand D?

SHAKESPEARE PERFORMANCES IN ENGLAND, 1987–8

STANLEY WELLS

The establishment by two actors – Kenneth Branagh and David Parfitt – of the Renaissance Theatre Company offering productions directed by other actors seemed designed to consolidate a shift in the balance of power marked by the English Shakespeare Company's earlier union of the talents of the director Michael Bogdanov and the actor Michael Pennington. And both companies toured during the current year, challenging the theatrical dominance of Stratford and London. The Bogdanov/Pennington completion of the history cycle played mostly overseas, whereas Branagh's group opened its three-play season in the heart of England, in the studio of the Birmingham Repertory Theatre, and travelled in the provinces before its London season at the Phoenix Theatre. The predominantly young company had only fifteen members, one of whom turned up in five different roles in *Hamlet* (for the record, Barnardo, Lucianus, First Player, Sailor, and English Ambassador). Settings were simple, though not undecorative, and sometimes made ingenious use of limited resources. Though the directors, new to their roles, disclaimed the attempt to project 'concepts' of the plays, these were not emptily neutral productions; each represented a coherent attempt to rethink the play for a modern audience.

Geraldine McEwan, exploiting the affinity between the stylization of *As You Like It* and Victorian melodrama, set the play in the late nineteenth century, and, as in productions of this play during that period, ran the forest scenes together. Acting styles acknowledged the conventional aspects of Shakespeare's characterization: Oliver, strongly played by Richard Clifford, wore a riding costume and carried a horsewhip in the opening scene; there was no attempt at a psychological interpretation of the reasons for his mid-play change of heart, but he convinced us of its reality, taking Aliena/Celia confidentially by the arm and telling his story very much for her benefit. There was a touch of melodrama too in the bowler-hatted minions who attended on Duke Frederick, grim authority figures establishing in the court a sinisterness that was dispelled by an enchanting fall of leaves accompanied by a glow of russet-tinted lighting as we moved to the forest. The play's lyrical qualities were admirably realized, with Shaun Prendergast as a touchingly serious Silvius and Richard Easton, carrying binoculars, mellow rather than bitter as Jaques. It was characteristic of the gentle humanity of this production that William, wistfully sad and deeply devoted to Audrey, evoked an audible sigh of only slightly amused sympathy from the audience on his heart-broken departure. James Larkin made a boyish, cheerful Orlando, and Tam Hoskyns a charmingly down-to-earth Rosalind, who looked, in disguise, like a little Dutch boy. The most poetic notes of the role (which occur in its prose passages) were not sounded, but the playfulness of her relationship with Orlando

6 *As You Like It*. Renaissance Theatre Company at the Phoenix Theatre and on tour, 1988. Touchstone (Kenneth Branagh, left), Corin (Jimmy Yuill), and Audrey (Dearbhla Molloy) sing 'It was a lover and his lass' in Act 5 Scene 3

deepened to become disturbingly touching in the mock marriage.

If star quality was lacking in the Rosalind, it abounded in Kenneth Branagh's ebulliently vulgar and cockney bookie of a Touchstone, with hair sleeked back and in Archie Rice costume – a broad bow tie and red-and-orange check suit – and rolling around on his heels with self-conscious enjoyment of his own waggishness. He appropriated 'It was a lover and his lass' to himself, singing it with hand-clapping gusto to Corin's banjo accompaniment, and cleared the hurdle of his set piece on the degrees of the lie with yards to spare, bowled along by the energy of his

self-satisfaction. The production ended charmingly with Hymen – a corn-covered fertility figure – wheeled in on a beflowered cart and Rosalind looking sweet in white. Corn dollies were handed out as all the cast sang the wedding song, and there were streamers for the final dance.

Two productions of *Much Ado About Nothing* adopted very different attitudes towards the play and its characters. Judi Dench's, for the Renaissance Theatre Company, emphasized human values, encouraging her actors to play their roles from the characters' own point of view and letting comedy arise naturally from the situations in

7   *Much Ado About Nothing*. Renaissance Theatre Company at the Phoenix Theatre and on tour, 1988. The dance (Act 2 Scene 1), showing the basic setting. From left to right, Antonio (Edward Jewkesbury), Hero (Tam Hoskyns), Ursula (Dearbhla Molloy), Margaret (Sophie Thompson), Borachio (Jay Villiers), Leonato (Richard Easton), and Don John (Shaun Prendergast)

which they found themselves. At Stratford-upon-Avon, Di Trevis's (in the main house) seemed, on the other hand, to be encouraging in its audience a critical view of the characters and their actions, and achieved much of its comedy at the expense of their credibility. The difference was apparent in the settings and at the play's opening. Judi Dench's production had as its basic setting a white Italian Renaissance facade garnished with four bay-trees. The initial harmony of Leonato's household was established in a wordless opening as Hero and he emerged from a central door and settled down to a jigsaw; other characters went about their business. A pale gold light created a sense of sunshine and warmth; this was a place where people could live companionably

together without speaking a word. Stratford's setting was grander and more impersonal; tall, broad marble pillars and shallow steps leading up to a white central aperture suggested an expensive hotel rather than a comfortable home. As the play opened the stage was set out with loungers, a wrought-iron table and chairs, and an oddly phallic object somewhere between a folded beach umbrella and a space rocket. Leonato and his family were lying around self-indulgently in the sunshine. Judi Dench's costumes (designed by Jenny Tiramani) were Regency in style; Di Trevis's (designed by Mark Thompson), especially elaborate for the women, placed the action in fashionable society of the 1950s or 1960s. A programme note by Barbara Everett described the world of the play as one 'whose criteria are convention and fashion'; certainly the production suggested a highly affluent society whose leisureliness was implicitly criticized by the sudden and violent irruption upon the scene of the returning army: off-stage noises made it clear that Don Pedro arrived in a helicopter which hovered just out of sight as a wounded soldier was lowered on a stretcher. This made a local point very forcibly, but the text draws no attention to the contrast between those who have jobs to do and those who do not.

An emphasis on convention is most appropriate to the Hero–Claudio plot, and at Stratford there was a touch of shallowness in Julia Ford's pretty, pert Hero. Both productions played Claudio as an essentially likeable but callowly inexperienced youth. We can sympathize with this character only if we can patronize him, seeing him as a young man who is so much the victim of his own emotions that they sway him irresistibly against the dictates of reason. At Stratford, particularly, Ralph Fiennes' suffering seemed intense enough to enable us to forgive the failure of trust – and of intelligence – on which it is based; in the last scene he drew us to Claudio as he knelt and kissed Leonato's hand on 'Your over-kindness doth wring tears from me.'

The contrasting performances of Dogberry in these two productions afforded an object lesson in the necessity for an actor of this role to project the impression of a personality that will account for and give rise to the verbal errors on which the comedy depends. In the Renaissance Company production he was played with inadequate conviction by an actor who seemed content to leave everything to his appearance: he simply spoke his lines and left us to find them funny or not as we might. At Stratford David Waller achieved a triumph of character-acting by playing Dogberry entirely from his own point of view as a man with a sublime capacity to say the opposite of what he means. He beamed with self-satisfaction as

he promised to bestow all his tediousness on Leonato; he made a marvellous prose aria of self-righteousness out of 'Dost thou not suspect my place?'; and he smirked with pleasure as Don Pedro declared 'This learned constable is too cunning to be understood', nudging Jeffrey Segal's charmingly subservient Verges into recognition of the compliment. David Waller's performance did not eschew the addition of comic business – there was an ingenious bit of by-play by which he managed to drink Verges's glass of wine as well as his own, and he made a series of failed attempts to shake Leonato's hand, crowned at last with success on his final exit. But the role could bear these elaborations because the character had been so credibly established.

Many of the differences in approach between the two productions were focused on the performances of Beatrice and Benedick. As often, it was impossible finally to distinguish between the directors' and the performers' contributions to the ways in which the characters were portrayed. At Stratford there seemed a deliberate intention to emphasize their folly and to present their relationship as absurdly unlikely. Beatrice was exceptionally tall, Benedick short and costumed to accentuate his puniness. Both performers used a drawling, affected mode of delivery. Maggie Steed deployed an attractive stage presence, a loping, slightly uncoordinated mien, and a warm smile, but conveyed sentiment more easily than wit. A lighter touch was needed for 'There was a star danced...', and we were given little sense of the character's past. In the Renaissance production Samantha Bond (like Judi Dench before her) suggested an inwardness of pain in Beatrice's recollection of how Benedick had let her down in the past, and treated 'What fire is in mine ears?' as the revelation of newly acquired self-knowledge; Maggie Steed made little of the former moment, and her director made the second ludicrous by causing her to come forward with

8 *Much Ado About Nothing*. Royal Shakespeare Company at the Royal Shakespeare Theatre, 1988. Verges (Jeffrey Segal, left) and Dogberry (David Waller)

her skirts dripping wet as the result of concealing herself in what appeared to be an ornamental pond.

This kind of directorial silliness particularly afflicted Stratford's Benedick (Clive Merrison). Both the character and the actor tried too hard to be funny from the start. There was no dignity or charm in this posturing, affected character who spoke almost throughout with exaggerated emphasis, as if in doubt of the audience's capacity to understand what he had to say. His preposterous self-esteem when he is made to think that Beatrice is in love with him reduced him to the folly of a Malvolio; there was no tenderness, nothing to give substance to Beatrice's belief that he might really love her. He adopted a burlesque tone even as he asked the Friar to marry him to Beatrice. This was a far cry from Kenneth Branagh's funny

but wholly credible interpretation, where 'This can be no trick' was seriously spoken, as if he were shaken to hear something that he already half knew, and after this there was a touch of Hamlet in his capacity to learn about himself by assuming new *personae*. The declaration of love at the end of the church scene, ponderous and improbable at Stratford, was here played with touching simplicity, both characters dropping their defences, and Benedick's 'Not for the wide world' was the wounded reaction of a man asked to betray one set of values for another that he also prizes. So the conflict within the play between love and friendship became more than usually prominent; Benedick's challenge was forced out of him, and the final reconciliation with Claudio – 'Come, come, we are friends' – had a tenderness marking the outcome of a strand of the play's action that is easily ignored. This was creative acting and direction.

The Renaissance production ended, as it had begun, with an emphasis on the value of human relationships; in its wit, tenderness, and grace it embodied the qualities for which Shakespearian comedy has traditionally been valued. Stratford's attitude was epitomized in the vulgarities of a final dance in which all the characters joined and in an end to the curtain call in which Benedick aimed a playful kick at Beatrice's behind. The rhythmical hand-clapping with which the audience acclaimed it was, for me, a sign of failure, not success.

A director new to Stratford but already successful elsewhere is Nicholas Hytner, whose production of *Measure for Measure* concluded the 1987 Stratford season. He directed the play as an entirely secular drama of politics and sex. Shakespeare sets it in a fictional Vienna whose brothels and prisons are closely related to those of Elizabethan London; Mark Thompson's designs translated this into modern terms. Courtiers wore formal dress with Ruritanian knee-breeches; the ducal court, in keeping with the play's concern with the fallibilities of human law and of those who administer it, transmuted easily into a court of law. The two vast, gilded bases of pillars dominating the stage in the opening scene could revolve to show prison cells; part of the forestage sank to become a public lavatory, the haunt of drug-peddlers and rent boys, one of whom descended with a respectably dressed gentleman identifiable in the following scene as a court official. The Duke's elegantly gilded table could disappear to be replaced by a cheap desk, and a lift could deliver rows of chairs for the unruly spectators of Master Froth's trial.

The production style called for psychologically credible acting, but this the company only fitfully provided. Phil Daniels was a reptilian Pompey, as sly as they come, gleefully pulling the wool over his judge's eyes, but Master Froth was too little of a simpleton, and Mistress Overdone hopelessly genteel –

though it was a nice touch to make her so much at home in the prison that she went automatically through the admission routines without being asked. David Howey reminded us that the role of the Provost is one of those that, insignificant on the page, can come to warm, compassionate life in the theatre.

Too many of the major roles were played by actors who failed to realize their full complexity. Sean Baker's lean, taut, close-cropped Angelo, clipped of speech, almost puppet-like in movement, was seen too much from Isabella's point of view as 'an arch villain' rather than as one who is initially conscious of his 'strong and swelling evil' and ultimately so penitent as to 'crave death more willingly than mercy'. When Isabella threatened to expose him, his response 'Who will believe thee, Isabel?' was taken as a cue for a violent assault as he cast her to the ground and straddled her in a near-rape. The effect was both melodramatic and moralistic. Angelo, as a character who is taken over by forces within himself of which he had not been previously aware, resembles Macbeth; and Sean Baker as Angelo, like Jonathan Pryce in the previous season's *Macbeth*, seemed more concerned to expound the character's villainy than to relive his tormented fall from grace. Josette Simon's willowy, elegant Isabella, touchingly vulnerable, was no more than sweetly reasonable in her pleading with Angelo; the passion that pulses within her lines, that can make her imagine herself wearing 'Th'impression of keen whips . . . as rubies' and stripping herself 'to death as to a bed / That long I have been sick for', was softened and sweetened into a generalized sense of grievance; so the tension that should build up between her and Angelo was dissipated and drained away.

The Duke in *Measure for Measure* has been seen sometimes as a surrogate playwright manipulating the plot, at other times as a symbolic embodiment of abstract values, and has even been portrayed as a crucifix-bearing Christ figure. Roger Allam signalled the deci-

9 *Measure for Measure*. Royal Shakespeare Company at the Royal Shakespeare Theatre, 1987. Isabella (Josette Simon) kneels before the Duke (Roger Allam) to ask for Angelo's pardon in Act 5 Scene 1. Escalus (Mark Dignam, far left) and Lucio (Alex Jennings, far right) look on

sion to play him entirely for human values even before a word was spoken as, dishevelled like a man who has suffered through a sleepless night, he stared into space, ignoring papers that courtiers thrust before him, then signing them with a shaking hand. This was the kind of interpretative acting (and direction) that requires interpretation by the audience, too; in seeking to suggest a psychological motivation for the lines it went beyond the meaning of the lines themselves.

Similarly, the Friar-Duke's *consolatio* to Claudio, 'Be absolute for death', became not a studied set-piece but an anguished attempt to work something out for himself. And this Duke, so far from knowing the plot in advance, was clearly improvising energetically as he devised the bed trick and acquiesced in the substitution of Ragozine's head for Claudio's. His duologue with Alex Jennings's immaculately timed but over-studied Lucio became a comic highspot in which he experienced such a shock to his sense of identity from Lucio's slanders that he genuinely required the reassurance that Escalus later, unconsciously, provides. In the last scene, too, he was still nervously unsure of himself, a prey to unexpected emotions, so deeply moved by Isabella's plea for Angelo that we could believe in his love for her and feel for him when she showed no sign of response. Director and actor had worked together to make this fine and subtle interpretation of the Duke the most original feature of a consistently interesting production.

Some of the more radical reinterpretations

of Shakespeare's and other classical plays in recent years have been given by the touring Cheek-by-Jowl Company, directed by Declan Donnellan. I saw their *Macbeth* at the Donmar Warehouse in London, where it was played with great economy of means in a black-lined space with the audience on three sides of the playing area. Actors remained within sight when not involved in the action. Very few physical properties were used; the actors rendered them unnecessary by their skilful use of mime, helped by dark costumes and by lighting which concentrated attention on faces and hands. The simplicity of staging encouraged a rapid pace; scenes sometimes overlapped, and changes of location were signalled by sudden shifts of lighting. Tension was raised at certain moments by unmusical scratchings on a couple of violins. There were some symbolical devices – Duncan, for example, was blind (as in Trevor Nunn's Other Place production of 1977, with which there were other resemblances) – and both Malcolm and he shouted *Mea culpa!* at moments of crisis. But overall the director aimed at immediacy of communication on a psychological level, and to this end suggested modern resonances from time to time – crassly so in the Porter scene, often approached with evident embarrassment by modern directors. Here the Porter was a woman, and her speeches were almost entirely rewritten with much obscenity and a number of wholly modern topical allusions. It is, of course, difficult to bring the Porter's faded topicalities to life in modern terms, but it seems to me better to sacrifice his satirical function than to disrupt the dramatic framework with violently jarring updatings.

Elsewhere, too, there were textual changes, but these appeared to be actors' unconscious substitutions resulting from the desire for intelligibility rather than deliberate rewritings. Similarly, and more commendably, contemporary intonations and heavily inflected speaking often conveyed meaning with striking immediacy.

At a number of points actors suggested psychological disturbance as a way of motivating their lines, especially at moments that have become theatrical cruxes. Thus Timothy Walker's Malcolm, who frequently stammered, fell into a fit at the arguably underwritten moment of his reaction to his father's murder, standing immobile and retching; he ended the play seeming both mad and vicious, as if to suggest that he had been infected by the evil around him. The underlying tensions in the scene of Lady Macduff's murder were cleverly exploited; we saw her son playing violent games as if he was suffering mental disturbance as a result of the war around him, and his mother (Anne White) was tense to breaking point. There was a brave though perhaps misguided attempt to bring psychological reality to the English scene. Macduff (played by Des McAleer) tried to strangle Malcolm on 'fit to govern? / No, not to live', so distressed was he at Malcolm's self-condemnation; they were joking together at Ross's entrance, and the difficult episode of Ross's breaking of his dreadful news was skilfully handled by causing Ross (Liam Halligan) to break down before delivering his message; our attention was focused on Ross's suffering; Macduff at first stood quiet and motionless, and, though his emotional tension became apparent as he absorbed the news, he remained stoic by comparison with Ross.

The Macbeths, too, were emotionally volatile. Macbeth (Keith Bartlett) was a tough guy with a plebeian Scottish accent, and a silly, pretty, upwardly mobile wife (Leslee Udwin) who mimed making herself up before a mirror as she prepared for her husband's arrival. As she taunted him with accusations of cowardice his tensions erupted into violence, and he threw her to the ground. In the episode with the murderers he broke down as he declared that Banquo was his enemy – 'So is he *mine*' – and embraced the villains as comrades once he had won their loyalty. There was another emotional collapse as he hinted to Lady

Macbeth of his plan to kill Banquo and Fleance, and he was lying on top of her as he spoke 'Come, seeling night...' At the banquet he belched coarsely before toasting the absent Banquo. Lady Macbeth kept up her appearance of silliness for most of the scene, as if she were quite indifferent to Macbeth's horror, but she too broke down and screamed before the guests departed; there was a long silence before 'It will have blood...', and they were both emotionally drained during the scene's coda.

For the sleep-walking scene Lady Macbeth was allowed a lighted candle which threw shadows onto the back wall as she mimed undressing. Macbeth suggested no depth of feeling in 'I have lived long enough', but seemed rather to be acting out an absence of imagination even at the expense of verbal resonance. He showed emotion on hearing of his wife's death, but was bitter and contemptuous in 'Life's but a walking shadow' and remained hard and unyielding until his death. Keith Bartlett thus exemplified a modern trend in what was essentially a moralistic interpretation, emphasizing Macbeth's brutality at the expense of his troubled conscience. The effect is oddly similar to that of the explicitly moralizing interpolations of Davenant and Garrick, though it is achieved by acting against the implications of parts of the text rather than by textual adaptation. Jonathan Pryce's absurdist interpretation in Adrian Noble's 1987 production permitted more complexity, though that too was essentially judgemental. But there was no shortage of theatrical excitement in a production that gave evidence of much fresh thought about the text and its relationship to our times.

Related production methods characterized Deborah Warner's *King John* at The Other Place. In the previous Stratford production, John Barton had treated the text with the freedom of a Colley Cibber. Deborah Warner offered a full text played in minimalist style. We sat on three sides of the auditorium, and the action occupied most of the floor space. On the fourth side, facing the main entrance, was an upper level liberally garnished with the ladders that are this director's trademark – I counted twenty-six of them during one of the play's less gripping episodes. As in the Cheek-by-Jowl *Macbeth*, changes of location were economically conveyed by sudden shifts of lighting, and the pace was vigorous. Costumes suggested a mixture of periods and styles, sometimes contributing to characterization. Several members of the English nobility wore old army greatcoats. King John was a little man, and his coat, unlike the others, reached down to his feet, giving him a sawn-off appearance. The effect was a touch metatheatrical, as if we were involved in the process of turning the play's happenings into drama, not watching a naturalistic imitation of them.

This was appropriate to so highly self-conscious a play, and its director dealt skilfully with many of its problems of tone. She caught the sardonic comedy of the wrangling between the English and French leaders over Angiers, pointing it by causing Robert Demeger's sharply etched Hubert to munch a baguette as he mimed his reactions to the battle that we heard but did not see. The disparity between notional and actual royal behaviour was sharply (if extra-textually) epitomized by causing the English and French royal parties to be engaged in a vulgar brawl on Pandolf's entrance, so that his 'Hail, you anointed deputies of God' had a deeply satirical force. Constance's potentially absurd insistence on expressing her sorrow by sitting on the 'huge firm earth' became a powerful gesture of protest in Susan Engel's eloquent performance as she implacably blocked the way of the procession celebrating the marriage alliance that she bitterly resents. Nicholas Woodeson's shortness of stature helped him to realize the ignominious aspects of the role of King John, making him a character desperately, humiliatingly in search of a dignity denied him by nature as he shouldered his sword of state, still

10   *King John*. Royal Shakespeare Company at The Other Place, 1988. As Hubert (Robert Demeger, left) stands to one side, the Bastard (David Morrissey, right) tells King John (Nicholas Woodeson) 'But if you be afeard to hear the worst . . .' (4.2.135)

packed in its travelling-case, almost as big as himself. His obsession with the appurtenances of kingship was nicely objectified by the crown chained to his money belt. This crown, indeed, became a highly significant property, as important to John as an umbrella to a City business man, and equally in danger of getting mislaid or lost. Woodeson is an actor of comic detachment, adept at conveying the ironic complexities of the role. Pathos does not come easily to him, so the role did not deepen with his reactions to news of his mother's death, but he stilled the house in the internal tension of one of the play's best stretches of dramatic writing, that in which John slowly nerves himself into manipulating Hubert to agree to dispose of Arthur, and he was fine, too, in the mounting hysteria and self-delusion of the

episode with Hubert in which he claims not to have intended Arthur's death. It was a nice piece of business to make Hubert, on his exit, crumple the warrant and cast it angrily to the ground, after which John furtively picked it up and pocketed it.

Prince Arthur is the play's emotional centre, and much of his own emotion must be conveyed through highly rhetorical verse. In Shakespeare's company he would have been played by a well trained apprentice. The Victorians (with whom the play was much more popular than it has been during this century) got round the problem by casting an actress. This apparently is no longer acceptable, and the difficulty of finding a boy actor who can do justice to the verse must be one of the principal obstacles to modern performance. Lyndon Davies looked touchingly frail and suggested visually an affectionate relationship with Hubert, but limped uninvolvingly through the lines.

This reflected a central uncertainty in the production. *King John* is one of the few Shakespeare plays composed entirely in verse. The language is highly wrought; most of the characters' feelings are given full verbal expression. The verse benefits, then, from a certain distancing in the speaker, a coolness of delivery which makes the language do the work rather than overloading it with the intensity of personal emotion. Antony Brown's deliberately bland, casuistical Pandolf caught this tone admirably; so did Ralph Fiennes's Dauphin. And Susan Engel as Constance was adept at containing emotion within the bounds of a verse structure. But elsewhere too much of the speaking was over-emphatic, so that we as well as the characters were, as the Bastard says, 'bethumped with words'. The Bastard himself was given a larger than life performance by David Morrissey. He burst into the play, terrorizing his brother; he was familiarly hearty with Eleanor; he came across throughout as an engagingly uninhibited, extravagant character, lively, satirical, and irredeemably coarse. In its own terms it was brilliant, but it denied the character's talents as an ironist, an intelligent observer, one who sees himself rather as a mediator than a participant, a character who, from the dramatist's point of view, occupies a position between that of the audience and the actor. In this performance he was too close to a National Front yobbo, at one point draped in a national flag and at another, late in the play, heralded by a snatch of 'Colonel Bogey' played on a trumpet. His role, first as ironic commentator, then as apologist for England, was scuppered.

The season has been marked by an unusual number of productions of Shakespeare's late plays. Sir Peter Hall directed *Cymbeline*, *The Winter's Tale*, and *The Tempest* for his final productions as Director of the National

Theatre, transforming the Cottesloe into an approximation of the Blackfriars. A platform stage thrust forward into the audience, like that in Stratford's Swan but with a protruding tongue that permitted entrances and exits along the central aisle. Above the stage in all three productions hung a great golden circular representation of the Copernican heavens which, like the painted canopy of the Elizabethan public theatres, could form a reference point for the play's many allusions to the celestial powers. It was mirrored by a circle set into the stage whose surface could vary to suit the needs of the scene. At the back was a pale blue wall with movable panels which could reveal a central double door. Costumes were Caroline throughout. In *Cymbeline* the rear doors were framed within a stone archway, as if to hint at the play's historical setting and to match the Welsh landscape of its central scenes.

Bill Alexander's Royal Shakespeare Company production of *Cymbeline* at The Other Place (and later at The Pit) made a virtue of a less splendid setting. Shakespeare's representation of events in this play depends on inset narrations to such a degree that the ways in which stories can be told, and the effect they can have on their listeners, become a prominent thematic concern. Exploiting the intimacy of the studio theatre, Alexander established a story-telling mode from the start, with actors addressing expository passages to individual members of the audience, sometimes sitting companionably beside them. Rather as in Deborah Warner's *King John*, there was a calculated air of improvization in the style of staging, admirably suited to the romantic implausibilities of the action. Both directors laid out the complicated narrative with exemplary clarity, Peter Hall very notably in the difficult, highly compressed battle scenes, and though both acknowledged the play's stylization, they also allowed full expression to its portrayal of human emotion.

Some characters in this play demand a

11 *Cymbeline*. Royal Shakespeare Company at The Other Place, 1987. Innogen (Harriet Walter) agrees to look after Giacomo's (Donald Sumpter) trunk in Act 1 Scene 6

largely two-dimensional presentation. The Queen is Shakespeare's most melodramatic villainess; for Peter Hall, Eileen Atkins played her incisively as a wide-eyed mock-innocent who might well have lured Cymbeline into marrying her; in Stratford Julie Legrand was a professional charmer with piled-up hair and a pillar-box-red slit of a mouth who fastidiously tested her poisons on tame rats which could be heard squealing in the medicine chest in which she carried them. At the National, Ken Stott's foolish but menacing Cloten avoided carica-ture, whereas at Stratford Bruce Alexander overplayed the character's buffoonery and oafishness at the expense of his sinister side; he was the only performer who hectored the audience. Giacomo permits more complexity; at the National, Tim Pigott-Smith, a sexual sophisticate manifestly contemptuous of Peter

Woodward's initially Puritan Posthumus, was visibly disturbed by the sleeping Innogen's beauty as he kissed her breast and slipped off her wrist the bracelet that would support his claim to have seduced her. At Stratford, too, Donald Sumpter, suave and understated, rivetted attention as he turned down the sheet on Innogen's bed and undid the buttons on her night-dress, with difficulty restraining himself as he approached her navel. There was nothing stylized about Geraldine James's (London) Innogen, stately and gracious of presence, warm in affection and touching in grief, womanly rather than saintly. The horror of the episode in which, waking beside the headless body of Cloten dressed in Posthumus's clothes, she mistakes him for her husband was enhanced by the naturalism of the corpse's severed and bloody veins, and by the abandon-

12   *Cymbeline*. The National Theatre, 1988. Posthumus (Peter Woodward) in Act 5 Scene 1: 'less without and more within'

ment with which, embracing it, she transferred the blood on to her own face. Harriet Walter (Stratford) looking like a pre-Raphaelite heroine, with her auburn tresses, was a slighter, frailer figure, but no less spirited in her encounter with the living Cloten. For her, his corpse was shrouded in a bloody hood; she bespread her own cheeks with his blood, and tremulously set the hood aside to confirm that the corpse was truly headless.

Peter Hall's production faltered in its more overtly symbolical effects. A bright light shone on Posthumus from the heavens as he stripped to the waist, bound round his brow the bloody cloth that stood as evidence of Innogen's supposed death, and smeared himself with earth. The vision in which members of his family address him in archaic verse appeared awkwardly from the aperture of Belarius' cave, below stage level, and its lines were chanted in a deliberately mechanical style that had the effect of parody, betraying a mistrust in its incantatory power which, it has to be admitted, has been shared by academic critics. The circle of the heavens split and tilted with a crash for the entrance of Jupiter on his golden eagle, then rose and closed again; we were made over-conscious of the mechanics of the staging. The RSC's studio production inevitably treated these episodes more simply; the vision was simply two white-robed figures, Jupiter an amplified voice with background noises and flashes of lightning.

The play's long last scene is an intensely ambivalent sequence of action, instructively different in impact in the two productions. Its improbabilities can seem merely ridiculous, a series of increasingly implausible manipulations of plot. Bill Alexander encouraged laughter, especially by the dazed bewilderment with which David Bradley's Cymbeline reacted as one improbability exceeded another: there was laughter, for instance, on his 'Does the world go round?' (5.6.233), on Guiderius' 'A most uncivil one' (line 294), on Cymbeline's 'Did you e'er meet?' (line 380) and even

on his 'Nobly doomed!' (line 422), spoken with head nodding to Posthumus on his forgiveness of Giacomo. Tony Church's Cymbeline was entirely different: a sympathetic, compassionate figure seeking to understand the multiple denouements not simply as plot but as experiences that are profoundly important to the people who undergo them. Whereas Bradley was constantly tottering to the edges of the action as if to escape from it, Church stood firmly at the centre of the scene, and the audience responded as he did; the only signs of amusement I noted were a slight titter on Cornelius' 'I left out one thing which the Queen confessed' (line 245), along with gently sympathetic laughter on Guiderius' recognition of Fidele and his account of Cloten's death. At the end of the action, Cymbeline stood as the centre of joy and forgiveness.

Peter Hall unfolded the scene with a masterly control over the audience's reactions, which, however, had its limitations. It could be argued that the wonders of the events should arouse a delight in which there is a place for the laughter that Bill Alexander encouraged, that the fullest realization of the scene's complexities would have us both laughing and crying simultaneously. But certainly Peter Hall's steady-paced, sober unfolding of the action allowed us to experience all its serious emotions with exceptional richness.

In the court scenes of Peter Hall's *The Winter's Tale*, the back wall took on a neo-Palladian appearance. Initially, two large statues of female figures stood to either side of the stage, and a male statue appeared when the central doors opened. For Bohemia, the zodiacal circle of the heavens was matched by a circle of greensward on the stage itself. The setting established a context in which time, the seasons, art, nature, and the supernatural had especial significance: all are important in the play – but though this play, even more than *Cymbeline*, is concerned with abstract issues symbolically presented, and though its language, too, is exceptionally intricate, its plot is

13   *The Winter's Tale*. The National Theatre, 1988. 'Apollo's angry ...' (3.2.145). Leontes (Tim Pigott-Smith) stands
in the foreground, as Hermione (Sally Dexter) rises from her chair

no less occupied with human passions. A television programme filmed during rehearsals of
the three plays showed that Peter Hall had
been especially concerned with treatment of
their language; in this play particularly, I was
struck by the actors' full comprehension of
every nuance of meaning, along with their
sensitive attention to the poetic and musical
qualities of their lines. But occasionally (as also
in *Cymbeline*) the effects of Sir Peter's coaching
were over-apparent in pauses at line-endings
held a fraction too long, unnaturally interrup-
ting the sense.

The Mozartian attention to detail illumined
the play's depths as well as its surface, helping

the actors to realize characters in their full
complexity. In the first half the emphasis fell
inevitably on Leontes and Hermione. Sally
Dexter, high-breasted and ripely pregnant,
warm in affection for both her husband and his
friend, established in Hermione a vivacious
womanliness that developed into a more with-
drawn, queenly dignity as she was afflicted
with Leontes' accusations of adultery. For her
trial she stood, statue-like, on a central
rostrum, speaking her defence directly to us
and to Leontes, who faced her. She looked up
to the heavens as she spoke of the 'powers
divine' that 'behold our human actions', but
there was nothing superhuman about the

controlled clarity of her appeal; she was close to breaking point, and her death-like collapse on Leontes' rejection of the oracle came as the natural human reaction to the stress she had undergone.

Tim Pigott-Smith's Leontes likewise represented a radical rethinking of the role, full of original touches. The *tremor cordis* that afflicts him along with the twinges of his jealousy was a physical symptom, recurring later in the action at moments of especial stress. He was youthfully handsome, eloquent of gesture, full of charm, but the self-regarding nature of his jealous obsession projected itself in adolescently self-pitying vocal inflections (at the end of the 'nothing' speech, for instance), and he was naively dependent on the advice and approval of others. 'I *will* seem friendly, as thou hast advised me', to Camillo, had a comically helpless quality; and his 'Have I done well?' after he has sent Cleomenes and Dion to the oracle also aroused sympathetic laughter. His blasphemous denial of the oracle was quietly spoken, but as consciousness of guilt rose in him his physical symptoms reappeared, he prostrated himself to implore Apollo's pardon, wept as Paulina reported Hermione's supposed death, and curled sobbing in a foetal position as Paulina rebuked him. Finally he laid his head in her lap as she begged forgiveness for her forthrightness. Pigott-Smith's Leontes was a highly intelligent, immaculately executed performance, lacking only the last ounce of passion to convince us of the depths of Leontes' bitterness and anguish.

The placing of an interval at the climax of Leontes' suffering made the first half of the play seem virtually self-contained, and it was slow to regain momentum. Time, with emblematic appurtenances, declaimed his Chorus to a ticking musical accompaniment, and there were distractingly clumsy rearrangements of the zodiacal circle and segments of the stage mechanism. The pastoral scenes were played before the panelled wall;

Sir Peter's rethinking of the sheep-shearing feast drew out its darker elements. There was a wolfish menace in Ken Stott's overloud Autolycus, contemptuous of those he fooled; an elaborate, ferocious dance of half-naked, phallus-bedecked satyrs brought before a scared Florizel and Perdita an image of the wilder forces of nature and sexuality, and Polixenes' angry disowning of Florizel visibly paralleled Leontes' rejection of the baby Perdita. Though Shirley Henderson made a charmingly natural Perdita, her Florizel lacked the vocal magic to create a sense of the time-conquering power of his love for her.

The play's magic began to reassert itself with the return to Leontes' court. He was now a chastened penitent, spiritually ready for the revelations that Eileen Atkins's watchful Paulina had in store for him. Attendants carrying candelabra lined the stage as the 'statue' was wheeled forward from the central aperture within a net-curtained booth, and, astonishingly, with its back to us. This was surely a mistake. Admittedly, it enabled us to focus on Leontes' reactions, but we, as well as he, need to marvel at Hermione's appearance; and we should hold our breaths along with the actress, expecting against expectation that the impossible will happen, the stone will become flesh, art will be transformed into nature. Leontes broke down as he saw her; slowly she turned, put aside the curtains, and moved forward unsmiling. This was no easy happy ending. Shakespeare has her address only the gods and Perdita, not Leontes; there was a world of unspoken emotion between husband and wife as, left alone together, they tentatively, sombrely, joined hands again.

For Peter Hall's *Tempest*, played with no interval, the stage circle was covered with sand. The central doors could open to reveal Prospero's cell, a book-lined sanctum suggesting that someone on the island had talents as a handyman. Nicholas Hytner's Stratford-upon-Avon production used an initially neutral setting, allowing full play to the text's symbolic resonances. His acting level was an off-white, heavily raked wooden circle with a curved ramp leading up to it. Behind it a semi-circular green-blue backcloth could become transparent, creating beautiful effects as drapes slowly rose and descended behind it, or as the shadows of departing characters were cast on to it. Both directors wisely orchestrated the sounds of the opening scenes of shipwreck so that all the words could make their proper impact. Hytner created spectacular visual effects as St Elmo's fire crackled around the sides of the stage and great blue curtains descended to represent the sails of the ship; Hall played it in a thunder-filled half-light.

Peter Hall declared an unromantic view of the play by casting Michael Bryant as a portly Prospero whose authority was not based on natural dignity but had to be constantly reasserted by displays of violent anger. Rage swelled up chokingly within him as, telling Miranda of her infancy, he paced up and down at the memory of Antonio's treachery, reliving rather than recollecting his emotion, which spilled over into unprovoked irritation with Miranda. Though this gave impetus to speeches that can easily seem undramatic, it sacrificed that sense of a past and a present held in suspension, of 'foul play' that was 'blessedly' alleviated 'by providence divine', which gives Prospero's lines much of their poetic power. Prospero was angry, too, with Steven Mackintosh's high-voiced, asexual Ariel, for whose entries from on high the circle of the heavens cracked apart. And both Prospero and Miranda paced in fury around Tony Haygarth's Caliban, a burly Pan figure with fanged teeth and little horns on his head who emerged from a trap, streaked with blood and excrement, naked but for a great wooden block belted and padlocked over his genitals. As usual in modern productions, it was not easy to believe in the actuality of Caliban's evil; he was a brow-beaten figure, sympathetic in his suffering and in his longing for freedom,

expressed in a gently swaying dance. Prospero's control of him seemed so absolute that we were more aware of the comedy than of the menace in his scenes with Tim Pigott-Smith's bemused, clown-like Trinculo and John Bluthal's more robustly comic Stefano.

This unromantic Prospero was matched by strong elements of grotesquerie in the effects of his supernatural soliciting. Ariel had a posse of attendant spirits, garbed, like him, in flesh-coloured body stockings, but faceless, like figures from a Henry Moore drawing. Appearing as a 'nymph o'th'sea' Ariel donned a half-mask, long fair hair, and plastic female breasts. His songs, mimed to a prerecorded countertenor voice, were eerily set by Harrison Birtwistle, and when he flew in as a harpy, this time in an auburn wig and with great black-feathered wings, he had a look-alike on each side of him. Even the masque seemed designed to have little aesthetic appeal, as if to undercut Prospero's account of its splendours.

In the past, angry Prosperos have sometimes made the episode in which Ariel recommends forgiveness the turning-point of the role, suggesting it is only at this moment, and as a result of a profound internal struggle, that Prospero decides not to exact vengeance; but Michael Bryant, for all his crossness, seemed already to have decided to let his 'nobler reason' predominate over his 'fury'. He reserved his climax for 'Ye elves of hills...', in which he seemed appalled at the memory of the uses to which he had put his power, pausing in horror before confessing that he had raised the dead from their graves. Now he was unsure of himself, waiting anxiously to hear whether the 'heavenly music' for which he called would really sound, and immensely relieved when it did. As he broke his staff and knelt, the heavenly circle tilted, as if to mark some great change; his embrace of Ariel on 'I shall miss thee' suggested more affection than he had displayed for his daughter, but otherwise there was little sign of mellowness; responding to

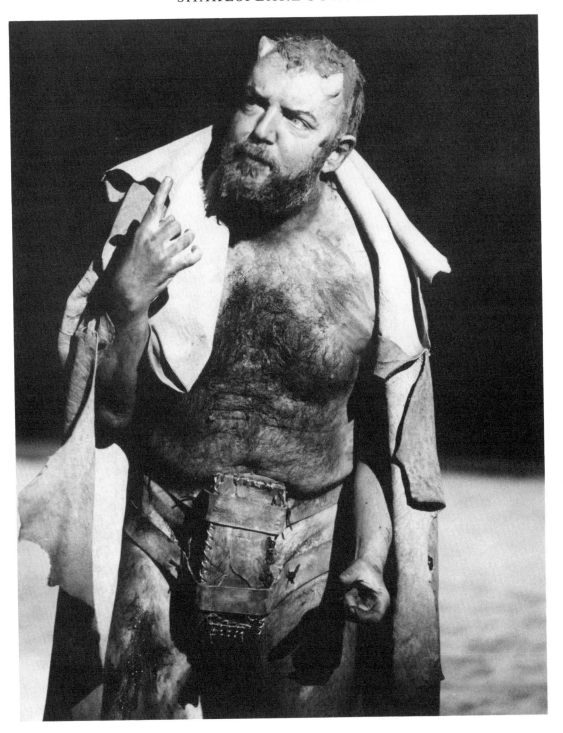

14   *The Tempest*. National Theatre, 1988. Caliban (Tony Haygarth)

Miranda's naive wonder at the 'brave new world' she sees around her, he spoke ' 'Tis new to thee' as a rebuke to Antonio and Sebastian. The epilogue was quietly spoken, still in character; his plea for our approval was humble and heartfelt; the urgency with which he sought our applause paralleled that with which he had begged for 'heavenly music' and embarrassed us into delaying to grant his request; when at last we did, he sighed again with relief, and advanced upon us as the lights faded.

At Stratford, John Wood's Prospero projected a far more likeable image of the role. This gaunt figure with an amiable, self-amused grin, loping around in baggy trousers obviously unpressed since he left Milan, conveyed a basic naivety and innocence which easily explained his usurpation. Whereas Michael Bryant had been still angry as he recalled his brother's treachery, John Wood was still deeply distressed. His first-act narration compelled attention through the excitement and emotion with which Prospero relived his past in pain. His voice was remarkable, resonant over a great range, like a clarinet, and used with highly calculated variations of tone and pace. At times the actor seemed to be almost singing, yet he was capable too of sudden, deflationary spontaneities. He was petulant when Ferdinand did not quickly obey him, touchingly concerned for his daughter's happiness, comically pleased with the extent of his power. This Prospero never seemed likely to exact vengeance, nor did we quite believe his claim to 'have bedimmed / The noontide sun, called forth the mutinous winds, / And 'twixt the green sea and the azured vault / Set roaring war'. He was very much the family man, unqualified in his forgiveness of Antonio: voicing it, he embraced and kissed him. Antonio remained implacably stern.

Duncan Bell's Ariel was a mature young man naked to the waist, with silvered hair and skin darkened to a greyish-blue colour that toned into the backcloth, not particularly tricksy in spite of a tendency to abseil down the sides of the proscenium arch. His entry from above as a harpy, face and body initially covered by his great wings, was an impressive moment; even more striking was his final exit, disappearing over the rim of the stage in a flash of both time and light at exactly the moment that Prospero snapped his staff. John Kane's Caliban was even more sympathetic than Tony Haygarth's. There was nothing specially monstrous or fish-like about this largely naked, robust male body, its skin mottled over with dark blotches and partially encrusted with sand, and the actor made the most of the role's opportunities for lyricism.

Perhaps the most remarkable achievement of this production was Desmond Barrit's highly original Trinculo. Like Dogberry, this role can fall flat if it is not played by an actor with the talents of a natural comedian; Barrit was both funny and credible from his first entry, a fat, epicene Harlequin dressed in pale green and pink satin and speaking plaintively in 'a monstrous little voice', like Bottom. With his plastered lock of black hair, his painted lips and rouged cheeks, he looked like a caricature of an emasculated Oscar Wilde, and he exploited the suggestion of sexual ambivalence that his appearance created, suspecting prurience in the audience's laughter as he declared his intention to creep under Caliban's gaberdine, and bridling defensively as he said 'There is no *other* shelter hereabout.'

As often, the masque was imperfectly realized. John Wood in a lecture said he was treating it as Prospero's dream, which no doubt explains why he was lying prone on the stage as it took place, but the interpretation did not easily communicate itself. The words of the black, singing goddesses were largely lost, and there was more than a touch of kitsch in the vision of 'sunburnt sicklemen' that appeared behind a gauze in a harvest field full of wheat and poppies lit by late-summer sunshine.

Though the two *Tempest*s were not as

15 *The Tempest*. Royal Shakespeare Company at the Royal Shakespeare Theatre, 1988. Act 3 Scene 2: Caliban (John Kane), Ariel (Duncan Bell), Stefano (Clive Morrison), and Trinculo (Desmond Barrit)

instructively different as the two *Cymbelines*, they pointed to ways in which the text is open to a variety of conscious interpretations and also to ways in which the individual personalities and talents of different actors can interact with the text to fresh effect. Peter Hall's emphasis – modern but not new – on the uglier aspects of Prospero's exercise of power was a useful corrective to sentimentalism; it produced a consistent and theatrically gripping interpretation at the expense of some of the qualities for which the play has traditionally been valued, such as harmony and charm. Nicholas Hytner, not attempting to direct our responses to any particular symbolic interpretation of the play's obviously symbolical action, gave full rein to its fantasy and its comedy while presenting the story as an intensely human action. And if any overall trend could be discerned in the year's productions, it was, perhaps, an attempt to explore and realize the emotional reality of individual characters rather than to conceptualize the plays in which they appear.

PROFESSIONAL SHAKESPEARE PRODUCTIONS IN THE BRITISH ISLES, JANUARY–DECEMBER 1987

compiled by

N. RATHBONE

The list includes some amateur productions and adaptations. Information is taken from programmes, supplemented by reviews, held in the Birmingham Shakespeare Library. Details have been verified wherever possible, but the nature of the material prevents corroboration in every case.

ALL'S WELL THAT ENDS WELL

Leicester Haymarket Studio Company, Leicester and tour: 18 Feb. 1987–
Director: Helena Kaut-Howson
Designer: Bunny Christie
Helena: Kate O'Connell
The action was set among the international jet set, and interpreted as a duel between Helena and Paroles to win Bertram.

Leeds Playhouse, Leeds: 4–27 June 1987
Director: John Harrison
Designer: Fran Thompson
Helena: Jenny Funnell
Set in the Napoleonic wars, and interpreted as domestic comedy, with Helena and Bertram equally serious.

ANTONY AND CLEOPATRA

The National Theatre at the Olivier, London: 9 April 1987–
Director: Peter Hall
Designer: Alison Chitty
Music: Dominic Muldowney

Antony: Anthony Hopkins
Cleopatra: Judi Dench
Octavius: Tim Pigott-Smith
See *Shakespeare Survey 41*, pp. 176–8.

Contact Theatre, Manchester: 20 May–13 June 1987
Director: Brigid Larmour
Designer: Nettie Edwards
Antony: Wyllie Longmore
Cleopatra: Clare Dow

AS YOU LIKE IT

Wolsey Theatre, Ipswich: 4–21 Feb. 1987
Director: Antony Tuckey
Designer: David Knapman
Rosalind: Mary Lincoln
Modern dress production.

Belgrade Theatre, Coventry: 30 April–16 May 1987
Director: Jack Lynn
Designer: Trudy Marklew
Rosalind: Anne Kavanagh
Touchstone: Lionel Blair
Set among cowboys in the American West.

York Theatre Royal: 29 Sept.–17 Oct. 1987, and tour of Yorkshire
Director: Gabriel Gawin
Designer: Martin George
Music: G. P. Gawin and Alan Coveney
Rosalind: Gina Landor
A cut version, performed with a cast of seven.

The Horseshoe Theatre Company, Basingstoke: 12–28 Nov. 1987
Director: Ian Mullins
Designer: Neil Bray
Rosalind: Belinda Chapman

COMEDY OF ERRORS

The RSC NatWest tour (with *Hamlet*): 14 Oct. 1987–
Director: Nick Hamm
Designer: Kit Surrey
Music: Colin Sell
Antipholus of Syracuse: Richard O'Callaghan
Antipholus of Ephesus: Michael Mueller

CORIOLANUS

No professional productions recorded

CYMBELINE

The RSC at The Other Place, Stratford: 4 Nov. 1987–
Director: Bill Alexander
Music: Ilona Sekacz
Imogen: Harriet Walter
Cymbeline: David Bradley
Iachimo: Donald Sumpter
See pages 139–42 of this volume.

HAMLET

Hamlet: The Tragedy of a Fat Man
T for A Company, Finborough Fringe Theatre, London: 28 Jan.–14 Feb. 1987
Director: Stephen Hope-Wynne
Hamlet: Steve Western
A seventeen-stone actor played Hamlet in an otherwise straightforward, but severely cut, production.

The Man in the Moon Studio, London: 3–28 Feb. 1987
Director: Alasdair Middleton
Designer: No information
Hamlet: Phelim McDermott
Early twentieth century. A heavily cut version; the 'mousetrap' play was projected on film.

Latchmere Theatre, Battersea, London: 21 April 1987–
Directors: Chris Fisher, Mark Freeland
Designer: Kristina Stephenson
Hamlet: Simon Kunz
A modern set, with video monitors and film clips of Vietnam. Stoppard's *Rosencrantz and Guildenstern are Dead* followed this production.

The Royal Dramatic Theatre, Stockholm, at the National Theatre at the Lyttelton, London: 10–18 June 1987
Director: Ingmar Bergman
Designer: Göran Wassberg
Translator: Britt Hallqvist
Hamlet: Peter Stormare
Modern dress. A violent, explicitly sexual production, with considerable cuts and transpositions.

Moscow Studio Theatre of the South West USSR at the Assembly Rooms, Edinburgh: 16–22 Aug. 1987; Tron Theatre, Glasgow (Soviet première 6 Dec. 1984)
Director: Valery Belyakovich
Designers: G. and T. Tatarinova
Translator: Boris Pasternak
Hamlet: Victor Avilov
Set on a dark stage, with the actors illumined by spotlights, using voice-over for the Ghost.

Hamletmachine, by Heiner Muller, adapted in English by Robert Wilson. New York University, by arrangement with the Herrick Theatre Foundation, at the Almeida Theatre, London, and European tour: 4 Oct.–14 Nov. 1987
Director: Robert Wilson
Designer: Robert Wilson
Translator: Carl Weber
A free adaptation of Muller's meditation on *Hamlet* and the betrayals of recent German history.

The RSC NatWest tour (with *The Comedy of Errors*): 12 Oct. 1987–

Director: Roger Michell
Designer: Alexander Byrne
Music: Jeremy Sams
Hamlet: Philip Franks

HENRY IV PART 1

Northumberland Theatre Company, touring the north of England: 7 Sept.–17 Oct. 1987
Director: Ronan Paterson
Designer: Antony Waterman
Henry IV: Sidney Kean
Hal: Kevin McGowan
Falstaff: Carl Davies
Costumes from no set period, intended to convey the timelessness of political power struggle.

English Shakespeare Company: see *The Wars of the Roses*

HENRY IV PART 2

English Shakespeare Company: see *The Wars of the Roses*

HENRY V

Theatre Clwyd, Mold (in repertory with *Edward III*): 10–25 July 1987; Arts Theatre, Cambridge: 27 July–1 Aug. 1987
Director: Christopher Selbie
Designer: Sean Cavanagh
Music: Donald Fraser
Henry V: Colin Hurley
The production developed the contrast between stark war and the comic elements, using a black set and costumes for the soldiers and camouflage for Pistol and his associates.

English Shakespeare Company: see *The Wars of the Roses*

HENRY VI

English Shakespeare Company: see *The Wars of the Roses*

JULIUS CAESAR

The New Vic at Bristol Old Vic, Bristol: 19 Feb.–14 March and tour: 16 March–11 April 1987
Director: Roger Rees
Designer: Fotini Dimon
Music: Peter Salem
Caesar: Dhirendra
Brutus: Leo Wringer
Antony: David Yip

Birmingham Repertory Theatre, Birmingham: 2–21 March 1987
Director: Derek Nicholls
Designer: Ian MacNeil
Music: Steve Owens
Caesar: John Forbes-Robertson
Antony: Peter Birch
Brutus: Sam Dale
A traditional production, with some First World War overtones.

The RSC at the Main House, Stratford: 8 April 1987–
Director: Terry Hands
Designer: Farrah
Music: Guy Woolfenden
Caesar: David Waller
Antony: Nicholas Farrell
Brutus: Roger Allam
See *Shakespeare Survey 41*, pp. 171–4.

KING JOHN

Bridge Lane, London: Dec. 1987
Director: David Massarella
Designer: No information
King John: Karl James
The Bastard: John Purcell
Updated to the present, with self-made men pitted against entrenched conservatives.

KING LEAR

National Theatre at the Olivier, London: 11 Dec. 1986–11 Nov. 1987
Director: David Hare

Designer: Hayden Griffin
Music: Nick Bicat
Lear: Anthony Hopkins
See *Shakespeare Survey 41*, pp. 174–6.

Compass Theatre Company, London, tour: 5
Feb.–18 April 1987
Director: Don Taylor
Designer: Chris Dyer
Music: Derek Bourgeoise
King Lear: Anthony Quayle
Goneril: Kate O'Mara
Gloucester: Tony Britton
Regan: Isla Blair
A basic set of four moveable megaliths, and
costumes ranging from Elizabethan to punk.
Excellent reviews.

King Lear, adapted by Nahum Tate
National Theatre at the Lyttelton, London:
6 Nov. 1987
Director: Robert Clare
Lear: John Bluthal
A stage reading.

Lear's Daughters, by Elaine Feinstein
Women's Theatre Group, tour: 12 Sept.–5
Dec. 1987
Director: Gwenda Hughes
Designer: Jane Linz-Roberts
Regan: Adjou Andoh
Cordelia: Polly Irvin
Fool: Hazel Maycock
Goneril: Sandra Yaw
Nurse: Janys Chambers
An adaptation of *King Lear* concerned with
women, power, and manipulation.

LOVE'S LABOUR'S LOST

No professional productions recorded

MACBETH

Compass Theatre, the New Ensemble, Sheffield (with *The Tempest*), tour: 9 Feb.–June
1987
Director: Neil Sissons

Designer: None
Macbeth: Nick Chadwin
Lady Macbeth: Jilly Bond
A cast of six, with a white sheet and some
branches as minimal props, costumed in black
and white.

The RSC at the Tyne Theatre, Newcastle: Feb.
1987; at the Barbican, London: 26 March
1987–
Director: Adrian Noble
Designer: Bob Crowley
Macbeth: Jonathan Pryce
Lady Macbeth: Sinead Cusack
Transfer from Stratford. See *Shakespeare
Survey 41*, pp. 170–1.

The National Theatre at the Cottesloe,
London: 14 April 1987
Directors: Peter Gill and John Burgess
Designers: Alison Chitty, Ashley Martin
Davis
A workshop production of work in progress
by twenty-five black actors.

Boulevard Theatre, London: 6–30 May 1987
A heavily cut adaptation, staged with only
five actors.

The Berlin Play Actors at Holland Park Open
Air Theatre, London: 14 Aug. 1987
Director: Rik Maverik
Dancers and a chorus of three performed 'an
eerie fable of majestical/maniacal fantasy'.

The Kunju Macbeth, The Shanghai Kunju
Company at the Leith Theatre, Edinburgh,
and tour: 25 Aug.–14 Nov. 1987
Director: Li Jia Yao
Artistic director: Huang Zuolin; Kunju direc-
tor: Sheng Chuan Jian
Adaptor: Zheng Shifeng
Macbeth: Ji Zhenghua
Lady Macbeth: Zhang Jingxian
A free adaptation in Chinese.

Cheek by Jowl, tour: Theatre Royal, York:
3–19 Sept.; Donmar Warehouse, London: 11
Nov.–5 Dec. 1987

Director: Declan Donnellan
Designer: Nick Ormerod
Macbeth: Keith Bartlett
Lady Macbeth: Leslee Udwin
See pages 135–7 of this volume.

The Ninagawa Company, Tokyo, at the National Theatre at the Lyttelton, London: 17–22 Sept. 1987– (First performance, the Nisei Theatre, Tokyo, 4 Feb. 1980)
Director: Yukio Ninagawa
Designer: Kappa Senoh
Music: Masato Kahi
Macbeth: Masane Tsukayama
Lady Macbeth: Komaki Kurihara
Seen at the Edinburgh Festival, 1985.

The Royal Theatre, Northampton: 17 Sept.–10 Oct. 1987
Director: Michael Napier Brown
Designer: Ray Lett
Macbeth: Michael Irving
Lady Macbeth: Liz Crowther

Theatre Clwyd, Mold: 2–31 Oct. 1987 and Welsh tour
Director: Christopher Selbie
Designer: Terry Brown
Macbeth: Mark Buffery
Lady Macbeth: Eunice Roberts
At the end of this production, the witches reconvened in place of Malcolm's coronation.

St George's Theatre, London, workshop and performance. Performance: 20 Oct. 1987–
Director: Adrian Brown
Macbeth: Hayward Morse
Lady Macbeth: Jill Connick

Half Moon Theatre, London: 7 Oct.–7 Nov. 1987
Director: Chris Bond
Designer: Ellen Cairns
Adapted by Chris Bond
Macbeth: Ron Donachie
Lady Macbeth: Noreen Kershaw
The action of this production was controlled by the witches.

Bristol Old Vic, the Theatre Royal, Bristol: 5 Nov.–5 Dec. 1987
Director: Andy Hinds
Designer: Sally Crabb
Macbeth: Malcolm Storry
Lady Macbeth: Derbhla Molly
Set in a ruined building.

MEASURE FOR MEASURE

The Pocket Theatre, Cumbria, at the Brewery Arts Centre, Kendal, and tour: 13 Jan.–7 Feb. 1987
Director: Laurence Boswell
Designer: Anne Curry
Angelo: Paul Mooney
Isabella: Sara Mair Thomas
Set in the Victorian period.

The Young Vic at The Cut, London: 7 May–6 June 1987
Director: David Thacker
Designer: Ruari Murchison
Angelo: Corin Redgrave
Isabella: Saskia Reeves
Set in the world of modern big business, staged in the round on a black glass platform.

The RSC at the Main House, Stratford: 5 Nov. 1987–
Director: Nicholas Hytner
Designer: Mark Thompson
Music: Jeremy Sams
Angelo: Sean Baker
Isabella: Josetta Simon
See pages 134–5 of this volume.

The Argonaut Theatre Company, Portlands Playhouse, London: 10 March–4 April 1987
Producer: John Grew
Director: Diana West
Designer (costumes): Celia Dodge
Angelo: Keith Myers
Isabella: Helen Masters

THE MERCHANT OF VENICE

The RSC NatWest tour (with *Much Ado About Nothing*): Oct. 1986–Feb. 1987

Director: Roger Michell
Designer: Di Seymour
Music: Jeremy Sams
Shylock: Nigel Terry
Antonio: Paul Webster
Portia: Fiona Shaw
A Dickensian set, based on a wall of office drawers and cubby holes.

The Royal Exchange, Manchester: 2 April–16 May 1987
Director: Braham Murray
Designer: Di Seymour
Music: Chris Monks
Shylock: Espen Skjønberg
Antonio: Malcolm Rennie
Portia: Harriet Walter
The production was set in the world of twentieth-century business. Skjønberg's restrained, dignified Shylock received excellent reviews.

The RSC at the Main House, Stratford: 23 April 1987–
Director: Bill Alexander
Designer: Kit Surrey
Music: Guy Woolfenden
Shylock: Antony Sher
Antonio: John Carlisle
Portia: Deborah Findlay
See *Shakespeare Survey 41*, pp. 162–5.

New Triad Theatre Company, Bridge Lane, London: 29 Sept.–   ; British and Continental tour: 15 Oct. 1987–
Director: John Strehlow
Designer: John Strehlow
Shylock: Kenneth Michaels
Antonio: David Bowen
Portia: Debbie Radcliffe

The Royal Lyceum, Edinburgh: 30 Oct.–21 Nov.; Inverness: 24–8 Nov. 1987
Director: Ian Wooldridge
Designer: Colin MacNeil
Shylock: Andrew Dallmyer
Antonio: Billy Riddock

Portia: Elizabeth Millbank
A sombre, rather static production.

St George's, London: 10 Nov. 1987–
Director: George Murcell
Shylock: Colin Starkey
Antonio: Edward Halsted
Portia: Alaine Hickmott

THE MERRY WIVES OF WINDSOR

The RSC at the Barbican, London: 28 Jan. 1987–
Directors: Bill Alexander, Roger Michell
Designer: William Dudley
Music: Jeremy Sams
Falstaff: Peter Jeffrey
A revival of the 1985 production, which was reviewed in *Shakespeare Survey 39*, pp. 197–9.

The Wolsey Theatre, Ipswich: 11 Nov.–5 Dec. 1987
Director: Antony Tuckey
Designer: David Knapman
Falstaff: Kenneth Gilbert

A MIDSUMMER NIGHT'S DREAM

The Haymarket, Basingstoke: 29 Jan.–14 Feb. 1987
Director: Ian Mullins
Designer: Stephen Howell
Music: John Goodrun
Oberon/Theseus: Tom Knight
Titania/Hippolyta: Beverly Adams
Edwardian period.

The RSC at the Tyne Theatre, Newcastle: 2–7 March 1987; at the Barbican, London: 13 Aug. 1987–
Director: Bill Alexander
Music: Jeremy Sams
Titania/Hippolyta: Janet McTeer
Oberon/Theseus: Gerard Murphy
First staged at Stratford, with designs by William Dudley, which were considerably altered for the London production. See *Shakespeare Survey 40*, pp. 173–4, for a review of the Stratford production.

Derby Playhouse, Derby: 12 March–4 April 1987
Director: Christopher Homer
Designer: Belinda Ackermann
Music: Chris Jordan
Oberon/Theseus: Will Knightley
Titania/Hippolyta: Denise Wong
Costumes mixed modern and traditional dress. The fairies were presented as streetwise minders, in dark glasses, and doubled as the artisans. Titania/Hippolyta was played by a black actress.

The Coliseum, Oldham: 16 May–6 June 1987
Director: John Retallack
Designer: Phil Swift
Oberon/Theseus: Jack Ellis
Titania/Hippolyta: Aletta Lawson
Bottom: Steve Halliwell
The trees in the wood were represented by hammocks in a very physical production.

Redroofs Theatre Company at the Novello Theatre, Sunninghill: 26 May–13 June 1987
Director: Chris Grimmwood
Designer: Marc Allridge
Oberon: David MacArthur
Titania: Rosanna Dane
Bottom: Kenneth McClellan

Nottingham Playhouse, Nottingham: 4–27 June 1987
Director: Andrew Hay
Designer: Robert Jones
Oberon/Theseus: Allister Bain
Titania/Hippolyta: Noreen Kershaw
Bottom: Roger Rowland
A modern-dress production, the fairies doubling as the artisans. Reviews praised the set, which showed an enormous, moving moon.

Kent Repertory Company, Hever Castle Theatre: 17 June–8 Aug. 1987
Director/Designer: Richard Palmer
Music: Mick Gahagan
Oberon/Theseus: Jeremy Browne
Titania/Hippolyta: Diana Kent
Bottom: Christopher Birch

The fairies were in green and white, according to the Elizabethan tradition; the artisans' costumes were Edwardian.

Regent's Park, London: 17 June–12 Sept. 1987
Director: Caroline Smith
Designer: Simon Higlett
Oberon: Paul Shelley
Titania: Lynn Farleigh
Bottom: Ian Talbot
The fairies were presented as earth spirits, in Elizabethan costume.

The Duke's Playhouse, Lancaster, promenade production in Williamson Park: 24 June–18 July 1987
Director: Jonathan Petherbridge, assisted by Gabriel Gawin
Designer: Alice Purcell
Costumes: Pip Nash
Music: Andy Whitfield
Oberon: Leader Hawkins
Titania: Linda Dobell
Bottom: Ian Blower
Edwardian costumes. Excellent reviews.

Chichester Festival Theatre Studio, Chichester: 5–16 Sept. 1987
Director: Alison Sutcliffe
Designer: Paul Farnsworth
Music: Corin Buckeridge
Oberon/Theseus: Geoff Owen
Titania/Hippolyta: Carolyn Backhouse
Bottom: John Peters

The Thorndike Theatre, Leatherhead: 27 Oct.–14 Nov. 1987
Director: Roger Clissold
Designer: Tim Shortall
Oberon/Theseus: Robin Sachs
Titania/Hippolyta: Amanda Boxer
Bottom: Derek Crewe

The Bottom of the Garden and Other Twisted Tales by Nola Rae
Birmingham International Season of Mimes and Clowns: 18 Jan.–5 Feb. 1987 and tour
A mime based on *A Midsummer Night's Dream*.

MUCH ADO ABOUT NOTHING

The RSC NatWest tour (with *The Merchant of Venice*): Oct. 1986–Feb. 1987
Director: Ron Daniels
Designer: Di Seymour
Music: Jeremy Sams
Benedick: Nigel Terry
Beatrice: Fiona Shaw

The Century Theatre, Keswick, on tour: 4 Feb.–28 March 1987
Director: Paul Gibson
Designer: Kate Robertson
Music: Andy Brown
Benedick: Robert Woolley
Beatrice: Carol Noakes
Set in Italy at the end of the First World War.

The Sherman Theatre, Cardiff: 4–21 March 1987
Director: Gareth Armstrong
Designer: Peter Mumford
Benedick: Richard Heffer
Beatrice: Holly Wilson
Set in Vatican City in the 1980s, with a *Saturday Night Fever* dance finale.

The Everyman, Cheltenham, tour of Gloucestershire: 8 Sept.–10 Oct. 1987; Cheltenham Everyman: 29 Sept.–10 Oct. 1987
Director: Phyllida Lloyd
Designer: Chris Crosswell
Benedick: Geoffrey Church
Beatrice: Rosie Rowell

The Argonaut Theatre Company, Portlands Playhouse, London: 21 Oct.–22 Nov. 1987
Producer: John Greco
Director: Diane West
Designer (Costumes): Celia Dodge
Benedick: Simon Bridge
Beatrice: Philippa Williams
Set in the Edwardian period.

Tavistock Repertory Company at the Tower Theatre, Islington, London: 14–21 Nov. 1987
Director: Celia Reynolds

Designer: Malcolm Wynder
Benedick: David Pickard
Beatrice: Sue Styles

OTHELLO

TAG at the Crawfurd Theatre, Glasgow, and Scottish tour: 13 Aug.–3 Oct. 1987
Director: Ian Brown
Designer: Stewart Laing
Othello: Brian Bovell
Iago: Laurie Ventry
Desdemona: Rachel Ogilvy
Set somewhere in the Middle East, with the soldiers in khaki. An adaptation of *Othello*.

Crummles Theatre Company, The Arts Theatre, Great Newport Street, London: 24 Nov.–19 Dec. 1987
Director: Joseph Marcell
Designer: Fay Armitage
Music: Tunde Jegede
Othello: Joseph Marcell
Iago: Doug Fisher
Desdemona: Alyson Spiro
Advertised as the first professional black-directed production staged in Britain. Set in the Edwardian period.

PERICLES

No professional productions recorded

RICHARD II

The RSC at the Tyne Theatre, Newcastle: 9–14 Feb. and the Barbican, London: 30 April 1987–
Director: Barry Kyle
Designer: William Dudley
Richard: Jeremy Irons
Bolingbroke: Michael Kitchen
Transferred from Stratford. See *Shakespeare Survey* 40, pp. 180–1, for a review of the Stratford production.

Ludlow Castle: 20 June–4 July 1987
Director: Paul Marcus

Designer: Bruno Santini
Richard: John Duttine
Bolingbroke: Brian Deacon
The set used a large clock and scaffolding, and costumes were based on track suits.

English Shakespeare Company: see *The Wars of the Roses*

RICHARD III

English Shakespeare Company: see *The Wars of the Roses*

ROMEO AND JULIET

The Brunton Theatre, Musselburgh: 29 Jan.–7 Feb. 1987
Director: Mervyn Willis
Designer: Nick Sargent
Music: Jeffrey Taylor
Romeo: Matthew Wandsworth
Juliet: Elizabeth McGrath
Nurse: John Mitchell
The part of the Nurse was played by a man, in the tradition of the pantomime dame.

Compass Theatre Company, The New Ensemble, Sheffield, tour of Britain and Germany (with *The Tempest*): Oct. 1987–12 March 1988
Director: Neil Sissons
Designer: Jenny Neville
Romeo: David Westbrook
Juliet: Helen Schlesinger

The Young Vic at The Cut, London: 23 Oct.–21 Nov. 1987; British and German tour
Directors: David Thacker and Jeremy Bell
Designer: Fran Thompson
Romeo: Richard Haw
Juliet: Sarah-Jane Fenton
A modern dress production, on a bare stage set in Mafia-infested Verona, and reminiscent of *West Side Story*.

The RSC at the Tyne Theatre, Newcastle: Feb. 1987; at the Barbican, London: 9 April 1987–
Director: Michael Bogdanov

Designer: Chris Dyer
Music: Hiroshi Sato
Romeo: Sean Bean
Juliet: Niamh Cusack
Transferred from Stratford. See *Shakespeare Survey 40*, pp. 178–80, for a review of the Stratford production.

THE TAMING OF THE SHREW

KISS ME KATE, music and lyrics by Cole Porter, book by Sam and Bella Spewack
The RSC at the Main House, Stratford, and tour: 30 Jan. 1987–   ; at the Old Vic, London: 4 May–
Director: Adrian Noble
Designer: William Dudley
Kate: Nichola McAuliffe
Petruchio: Paul Jones

The Everyman Theatre, Liverpool: 5 Feb.–14 March 1987
Director: Glen Walford
Designer: Rodney Ford
Music: Paddy Cunneen
Katherine: Eithne Hannigan
Petruchio: Bob Harris
An Arab setting, more or less in period, with Petruchio as a French legionnaire.

Mussoline: Kate's Part in his Downfall, an adaptation by Kathleen McCreery
Avon Touring Company: 31 July–12 Dec. 1987
Director: Steve Woodward
Designer: Alison Mills
Cast: Kevin Dyer, Shiv Grewal, Corrine Harris and Ava Hunt, with puppets
Set in fascist Italy. Petruchio represented Mussolini, Kate Liberty.

The British Actors' Theatre Company, British tour: 20 Oct.–19 Dec. 1987, and the Jewish Festival, Jordan
Play Manager: Peter Woodward
Katherine: Kate O'Mara
Petruchio: Tim Woodward
A traditional presentation. The actors devel-

oped the production with the assistance of the Play Manager; there was no director or designer.

Red Bull Theatre Company, Boston, Lincs., tour: Sept.–Nov. 1987
Director: David Kershaw
Designer: Bernard G. Maplethorpe
Katherine: Jo Mossman-Ellis
Petruchio: Andrew Sheldon

The RSC at the Main House, Stratford: 3 Sept. 1987–
Director: Jonathan Miller
Designer: Stefanos Lazaridis
Music: Stephen Oliver
Katherine: Fiona Shaw
Petruchio: Brian Cox
See *Shakespeare Survey 41*, pp. 168–70.

THE TEMPEST

Compass Theatre Company, The New Ensemble, Sheffield, tour of Britain (with *Macbeth*): 16 Feb.–June 1987; followed by a tour of Britain and Germany, with *Romeo and Juliet*: Oct. 1987–March 1988
Director: Neil Sissons
Designer: Jenny Neville
Prospero: Richard Heap
Caliban: Nick Chadwin
Produced with a cast of six, doubling, using a large sheet and a pile of logs as an all-purpose set.

The Gateway Theatre, Chester: 5–28 Nov. 1987
Director: Phil Partridge
Designers: Juliet Watkins
Music: Tony Britten
Prospero: Alan Meadows
Caliban: Andrew Tansey

The Movingstage Marionette Company, the Puppet Theatre Barge, London: 18 Nov.–18 Dec. 1987
Director/Designers: Juliet and Grenville Middleton

Music: Rory Allam
Prospero: Kenneth Griffith
Caliban: Roger Lloyd-Pack
Cut to one-and-a-half hours. A glass Ariel puppet was used.

La Tempestada, an adaptation of *The Tempest*. La Cubana, Barcelona, at Sadler's Wells, as part of the London International Festival of Theatre: 13 July 1987
Details of director, designer, and cast were not given in the programme. The audience was disconcertingly exposed to real tempest effects, and the production was cancelled after the first night.

The Swan Theatre, Worcester: 12–28 March 1987
Director: John Ginman
Designer: Anthony Ward
Prospero: Leon Tanner
Caliban: Chris MacDonnell
Set in Prospero's cell, a white room with an enormous wardrobe, doors, fireplace, and bureau. The island landscapes were outlined on the white background in pastel shades.

Moving Parts Theatre Company, Norwich, tour of London and East Anglia: 10 July–2 Aug. 1987
Director: Jonathan Meth
Designer: Felix Gofer
Prospero: Richard Ashton

The New Victoria Theatre, Newcastle under Lyme: 21 Oct.–21 Nov. 1987
Director: Alec Bell
Designer: Eve Stewart
Music: Steve Edwards
Prospero: Dave Miller
Set in a never-never land, emphasized by using costumes from various periods.

TIMON OF ATHENS

R.A.T. Theatre, Hereford Cathedral, and tour: 7 May 1987–
Director: Peter Sykes and Beth Ashton

Designer: Sarah Roberts
Timon: Peter Sykes
Set in Japan.

TITUS ANDRONICUS

The RSC at the Swan Theatre, Stratford: 28 April 1987–
Director: Deborah Warner
Designer: Isabella Bywater
Titus: Brian Cox
Tamora: Estelle Kohler
See *Shakespeare Survey 41*, pp. 178–81.

TROILUS AND CRESSIDA

The Berliner Ensemble, King's Theatre, Edinburgh: 17–19 Aug. 1987 (first performance Berlin, 15 June 1985)
Directors: Manfred Wekwerth, Joachim Tenschert
Designers: Manfred Grund and Klaus Noack
German translation: Manfred Wekwerth
Music: Rainer Böhm
Troilus: Martin Seifert
Cressida: Corinne Harfouch
Set on a bare stage, divided by a white sheet which functioned as backcloth, tents, or bedsheets as required.

The National Youth Theatre at Christchurch, Spitalfields, London: 21 Sept.–2 Oct. 1987
Director: Matthew Francis
Designer: Martin Sutherland
Music: Mia Soteriou
Troilus: Jon Wood
Cressida: Lucy Robinson
The Trojans were presented as Arab guerillas, the Greeks as Levantines and US Marines.

TWELFTH NIGHT

Cheek by Jowl, the Donmar Warehouse, London: 14 Jan. 1987–
Director: Declan Donnellan
Designer: Nick Ormerod
Music: Joanna MacGregor
Viola: Patricia Kerrigan

Malvolio: Hugh Ross
Continuing the run of the 1986 touring production.

The Crucible, Sheffield: 6–28 Feb. 1987
Directors: Steven Pimlott, Martin Duncan
Designer: Tom Cairns
Music: Jeremy Sams
Viola: Janet Dibley
Malvolio: David Ross
The sets were deliberately surreal, and scenes were frequently overlapped or intercut. Reviewers drew parallels with Fellini and Monty Python.

The South West Theatre Consortium, Orchard Theatre, Barnstaple, and Plymouth Theatre Royal, tour of Devon: 11 Feb.–4 April 1987
Director: Nigel Bryant
Designer: Anne Curry
Music: John Kirkpatrick
Viola: Rebecca Harbord
Malvolio: John Surman

Vanessa Ford Productions, tour: 22 Sept. 1987–
Director: Ron Pember
Designer: David Collis
Viola: Susan Bovell
Malvolio: John Barron

The Argonaut Theatre Company, Portlands Playhouse, London: 23 Nov.–21 Dec. 1987
Director: Dee Hart
Producer: John Greco
Designer: Dee Hart
Music: Roy Daniels
Viola: Pauline Cadell
Malvolio: Alistair Finlay

Acter Shakespeare Company (America), The Young Vic Studio, London: 24 Nov.–5 Dec. 1987
A workshop production performed by five actors on a bare stage. Acter toured the USA with this production in 1984 with a different cast.

The RSC at the Main House, Stratford: 2 July 1987–
Director: Bill Alexander
Designer: Kit Surrey
Viola: Harriet Walter
Malvolio: Antony Sher
See *Shakespeare Survey 41*, pp. 165–8.

The Renaissance Theatre Company, Riverside Studios, Richmond: 28 Nov. 1987–16 Jan. 1988
Director: Kenneth Branagh
Designer: Bunny Christie
Music: Pat Doyle and Paul McCartney
Viola: Frances Barber
Malvolio: Richard Briers

TWO GENTLEMEN OF VERONA

Theatre Set Up, tour: 11 June–5 Sept. 1987
Director/Designer: Wendy Macphee
Valentine: Anderson Knight
Proteus: Tony Portacio
An open-air production, in Elizabethan costume.

Regent's Park Open Air Theatre, London: 4 Aug.–9 Sept. 1987
Director: Ian Talbot
Designer: Simon Higlett
Music: Stephen Deutsch
Valentine: Peter Doran
Proteus: Tom Mannion
Set in the 1900s.

TWO NOBLE KINSMEN

The RSC at the People's Theatre, Newcastle: March 1987 and the Mermaid, London: 20 May 1987–
Director: Barry Kyle
Designer: Bob Crowley
Palamon: Gerard Murphy
Arcite: Hugh Quarshie
Transferred from Stratford
See *Shakespeare Survey 40*, pp. 175–7, for a review of the Stratford production.

THE WINTER'S TALE

The RSC at the Tyne Theatre, Newcastle: 9–14 March 1987; at the Barbican, London: 8 Oct. 1987–20 Feb. 1988
Director: Terry Hands
Designer: Gerard Howland
Music: Nigel Hess
Leontes: Paul Shelley (Barbican), Jeremy Irons (Newcastle)
Hermione: Penny Downie
Transferred from Stratford
See *Shakespeare Survey 40*, pp. 177–8, for a review of the Stratford production.

The Watermill Theatre, Bagnor: 23 June–25 July 1987
Director: Ceri Sherlock
Designer: Simon Banham
Leontes/Young Shepherd: Christopher Villiers
Hermione/Mopsa: Kate Lock
A promenade production. The Bohemia scenes were staged out of doors, the Sicilia scenes on a grey and black stage set.

The Northcott Theatre, Exeter: 10–28 Nov. 1987
Director: George Roman
Designer: Sean Cavanagh
Leontes: Christopher Northey
Hermione: Nina Holloway
Reviewers noted the magnificent backcloth painted with tapestry beasts. Leontes' court were dressed in black, and the bear remained offstage.

The Crucible, Sheffield: 6–28 Nov. 1987
Director: Stephen Pimlott
Designer: Tom Cairns
Leontes: Jim Broadbent
Hermione: Helen Cooper
An allegorical production in modern dress with symbolic demons and imps.

THE WARS OF THE ROSES

The English Shakespeare Company. This

cycle comprises *Richard II*, *Henry IV pt 1*, *Henry IV pt 2*, *Henry V*, *Henry VI: House of Lancaster*, *Henry VI: House of York*, and *Richard III*, Bath Theatre Royal, and tour: 8 Dec. 1987–
Director: Michael Bogdanov
Designer: Chris Dyer
Music: Terry Mortimer
For details of individual productions see below.
For a review of Parts One and Two of *Henry IV* and *Henry V*, see *Shakespeare Survey 41*, pp. 159–62.

RICHARD II

The English Shakespeare Company, *The Wars of the Roses*, Bath Theatre Royal, and tour: 8 Dec. 1987–
Richard: Michael Pennington
Bolingbroke: John Castle

HENRY IV PT 1 AND 2

English Shakespeare Company, continuation of the 1986 tour: Jan. 1987–
Hal: Michael Pennington
Falstaff: John Woodvine
Henry IV: Patrick O'Connell
From December 1987 this production toured as part of the *Wars of the Roses* cycle, with Barry Stanton as Falstaff and John Castle as Henry IV.

KING HENRY V

The English Shakespeare Company, continuation of the 1986 tour: Jan. 1987–
Prince Hal: Michael Pennington
Falstaff: John Woodvine
Henry IV: Patrick O'Connell
From December 1987 this production toured as part of the *Wars of the Roses* cycle, with Barry Stanton as Falstaff and John Castle as Henry IV.

HENRY VI: HOUSE OF LANCASTER
(adapted from *Henry VI* pts 1 and 2)

The English Shakespeare Company, *The Wars of the Roses*, Bath Theatre Royal, and tour: 14 Dec. 1987–
Richard Plantagenet, later Duke of York: John Castle
Edmund Mortimer: Michael Pennington
Henry VI: Paul Brennen
Joan of Arc: Mary Rutherford

HENRY VI: HOUSE OF YORK
(adapted from *Henry VI* pts 2 and 3)

The English Shakespeare Company, *The Wars of the Roses*, Bath Theatre Royal, and tour, 15 Dec. 1987–
Richard Plantagenet, Duke of York: John Castle
Richard, later Duke of Gloucester: Andrew Jarvis
Edward, later Edward IV: Philip Bowen
Henry VI: Paul Brennen
Queen Margaret: June Watson

RICHARD III

The English Shakespeare Company, *The Wars of the Roses*, Bath Theatre Royal, and tour: 16 Dec. 1987–
Richard III: Andrew Jarvis
Queen Margaret: June Watson
Lady Anne: Mary Rutherford
Duke of Buckingham: Michael Pennington

SHAKESPEARE APOCRYPHA
EDWARD III

Theatre Clwyd, Mold: 26 June–25 July 1987 (in rep. with *Henry V*); at the Arts Theatre, Cambridge: 27 July–1 Aug. 1987
Director: Toby Robertson
Designer: Sean Cavanagh
Music: Donald Fraser
Acting text: Richard Proudfoot, Toby Robertson, Jeremy Brooks
Edward III: Ian McCulloch
The Black Prince: Colin Hurley
The first professional production since the 1590s.

A YORKSHIRE TRAGEDY

The National Theatre Studio at the Cottesloe, London: 27 Jan. 1987 (one night only)
Director: Stephen Unwin
Designers: Ashley Martin Davis, Alison Chitty
The Hero: Stephen Petcher
The Wife: Mary Jo Randle

Miscellaneous

EXIT BURBAGE by Peter Whitbread; one-man show
Leeds Playhouse: 18 March 1987
Tour of East Anglia.

MORE LIGHT by Snoo Wilson
The Bush, London: 11 Feb. 1987–
Shakespeare: Lizzy McInnery
Directors: Simon Stokes, Snoo Wilson
Designer: Robin Don
A fantasy on Queen Elizabeth's relations with the Vatican in 1600, with Shakespeare portrayed as a woman.

BLACK STAR by David Pownell
The Octagon, Bolton: 11 March–4 April 1987
Director: John Adams
Designer: Nick Bearwish
Ira Aldridge: Joseph Marcell
Based on the life of the black Shakespeare actor Ira Aldridge.

PLUMP JACK by Gordon Getty; world première San Francisco: 13 March 1985; at the Royal Festival Hall, London: 10 July 1987 (European première)

A cantata for several voices and full orchestra in four scenes based on *Henry IV* pts 1 and 2. Act I only.

WILL AID

Sadler's Wells Theatre, London: 12 April 1987
Directors: Ned Sherrin, David Kernan
Designer: Michael Annals
A medley from Shakespeare, including John Poole's *Hamlet Travestie*, 1810.

A VISION OF OPHELIA/LADY MACBETH

Aki Isoda at the Shakespeare Globe Theatre, London: 27–8 July; also at Robinson College, Cambridge
Director: Aki Isoda
Translator: Youshi Odajima
Designer: Shizuo Tohyama
Performed by: Aki Isoda
One-woman plays based on Shakespeare, using traditional kabuki technique. First seen in Japan.

SHAKESPEARE'S WOMEN

Meril Brook; one-woman show. The Questors Studio Theatre, London: 5 Sept. 1987
Excerpts from Shakespeare.

ACTING SHAKESPEARE; excerpts from Shakespeare

Ian McKellen; one-man show
Tour continued from 1986.

THE YEAR'S CONTRIBUTIONS TO
SHAKESPEARE STUDIES

1. CRITICAL STUDIES
reviewed by R. S. WHITE

As a consequence of the reawakened interest in history as a mode of entrance into literary interpretation, *Survey* reviewers are beginning to have friendly demarcation disputes about what is 'Criticism' and what is 'Life and Times'. More and more commentators are coming to fashion criticism out of a close contextualization of Shakespeare's works. Having looked last year at new historicism as a movement, I want this time to examine more directly one of its underpinning concepts, ideology, a subject which was one of the themes at the Twenty-Third International Shakespeare Conference in 1988.

For those who are willing to jump in at the deep end, *Shakespeare Reproduced: The Text in History and Ideology*, edited by Jean E. Howard and Marion F. O'Connor (New York and London: Methuen, 1987), is the place to start. In their helpful Introduction, the editors explain how an ideological historicism differs from traditional 'historical background' studies:

One is interested not just in 'what the Elizabethans thought and did' as reflected in their literature, but in the *uses* of ideas and practices in producing a particular social order and subjects to work within it and in enabling, as well, points of *resistance* to dominant ideologies. (p. 8)

The first two chapters by Walter Cohen and Don E. Wayne respectively trace the development of ideological criticism. As a consequence of the 'categorizing' mode, Cohen and Wayne risk creating a new structure of hegemonies even while their prime intention may be to break down the whole notion of hegemony itself. There is a tendency in both articles at least to imply that if one is not a Marxist or feminist then one cannot claim to be looking at underlying ideologies. Fortunately, essays in the book do not allow this tendency to harden. Marion O'Connor's study of the 1912 'Shakespeare's England' exhibition at Earl's Court ('Theatre of the Empire: "Shakespeare's England"', pp. 68–98) exposes with solid documentation the imperial intention behind the event. Colonialism is also the subject of Thomas Cartelli's essay on the ways in which *The Tempest* has been used as a pretext for brutality. Amongst the rest of the essays, I should single out one written from a feminist point of view, Karen Newman's splendid essay on *Othello*, which concludes with a statement which is central to the book as a whole:

We need to read Shakespeare in ways which produce resistant readings, ways which contest the hegemonic forces the plays at the same time affirm. Our critical task is not merely to describe the formal parameters of a play, nor is it to make claims about

Shakespeare's politics, conservative or subversive, but to reveal the discursive and dramatic evidence for such representations, and their counterparts in criticism, as representations. (p. 158)

The search for ideologies, then, is not confined or even primarily restricted to Shakespeare, but it applies to the whole range of activities generated by Shakespeare. The essays are not uniform in quality, but most have the virtues of being diverse in subjects and generous with references.

All but one of the essays in *Shakespeare Reproduced: The Text in History and Ideology* emanate from the USA. The British equivalent this year is *The Shakespeare Myth*, edited by Graham Holderness (Manchester: Manchester University Press, 1988), where the tone and presentation are very different. The volume has the embattled and sometimes embittered air of a document from the front line in a war against Thatcher's Britain, and references are generally not to the industry of Shakespearian scholarship but to works in cultural, communications, and interdisciplinary studies. The regret running through the book concerns the ways in which Shakespeare has been conscripted to speak for the ideology of an upper-middle class elite, and has been accommodated into the needs of a ruling cultural establishment. The symbol for the struggle is the new Globe Theatre, projected for Southwark on the South Bank of the Thames at the expense of the working class population that will have to leave the area when it becomes a focus for Bardolatrous tourism. Derek Longhurst shows that Shakespeare still lives in English popular culture, but usually in identification with anti-populist sentiments or as a figure of fun. The real villains are seen to be critics who have allowed to go unchallenged the whole takeover bid. Simon Shepherd in an interesting essay argues that sexuality is at issue as well as political ideologies, and he finds that in Shakespearian usages a covert, homoerotic impulse in the plays is distanced and detonated by the critical

process ('Shakespeare's private drawer: Shakespeare and homosexuality', pp. 96–110). All the time, as both David Margolies and David Hornbrook make clear, Shakespeare *could* be presented both in teaching and performance as a more progressive influence, but the feeling is that much of the battle has been lost. Christopher J. McCullough sees even the examples of directors who are trying to be radical and contemporary as turning back into reactionary, universalist assumptions. It is a bleak message. Sandwiched between such essays are interviews with haplessly cheerful figures from the world of current cultural authority who inadvertently reveal the supposedly ideologically suspect attitudes which the book is opposing. This procedure seems unfair to the cooperative participants.

One manifest result of the new concentration on underlying ideologies is that critics who had until now proclaimed the political neutrality of literary criticism are finding the confidence to declare public allegiances to moral and political causes through Shakespeare. René Girard, not known for his outspoken statements on international policy, published an extraordinarily direct and powerful attack on nuclear strategy in his 'Hamlet's Dull Revenge' in 1986:[1]

Should our enormous critical literature on *Hamlet* fall some day into the hands of people otherwise ignorant of our mores, they could not fail to conclude that our academic tribe must have been a savage breed indeed. After four centuries of controversies, Hamlet's temporary reluctance to commit murder still looks so outlandish to us that more and more books are being written in an unsuccessful effort to solve that mystery. The only way to account for this curious body of literature is to suppose that, back in the twentieth century no more was needed than some ghost to ask for it, and the average professor of literature would massacre his entire household without batting an eyelash . . .

[1] *Literary Theory / Renaissance Texts*, ed. Patricia Parker and David Quint (Baltimore and London: Johns Hopkins University Press, 1986), pp. 280–302.

Let us imagine a contemporary Hamlet with his finger on a nuclear button. After forty years of procrastination he has not yet found the courage to push that button. The critics around him are becoming impatient. The psychiatrists have volunteered their services and come up with the usual answer. Hamlet is a sick man. (pp. 299, 300)

Both Alexander Leggatt and James L. Calderwood in books reviewed below make comparably explicit statements about our failure to learn from the past and from Shakespeare in the conduct of international power relations, and again neither is known for his political incursions in the past – not that either, however, would claim to be a new historicist.

In these examples, we may feel that ideology exists in the critic rather than in the text, a fact which at first sight appears to play into the hands of those who assert that we should remain 'impartial' and simply speak of what is manifestly in the text. Terence Hawkes in an article in *Shakespeare Survey* argues to the contrary that we can never be impartial even if we want to, and that *all* criticism is by definition an act of ideological construction: 'the plays have no essential meanings, only uses'.[2] Hawkes presents this case largely through 'uses' of Wittgenstein and Empson on one side, Leavis and Wilson Knight on the other, all writing in 1929–30. The article attacks the smug insularity of a particular English (Cambridge) tradition of criticism, and hails continentalism and philosophy. The introduction of a writer favoured by new literary theorists is presented with the hushed portentousness of announcing a new messiah:

In the same year, in the French colony of Algeria, the wife of the local rabbi gave birth to a son. He was to be called Jacques, and his family name was Derrida. (p. 32)

Nothing is made of this and we seem expected to take the second coming for granted. In the same volume of the *Survey*, Günter Walch implicitly argues that multiple ideologies can exist in a play itself, although critics can choose to highlight one aspect. He argues that the idealizing of the Chorus in *Henry V* is exposed as 'official ideology' at odds with the rest of the play's action.[3] The patriotic appeals are 'an illusion effectively used as an instrument of power' (p. 68). Robert S. Miola, while not directly speaking of 'ideology', shows by examining the history of 'source study' in the case of *Julius Caesar* that even such an apparently neutral activity depends on initial assumptions embedded in the various metaphors lying behind the language of 'sources' (background, imitation, assimilation, etc.).[4] He does not mention the more recent term 'intertextuality' which has the advantage of allowing us to focus on the 'literariness' of source-study, avoiding the metaphors of streams, Darwinian progress, racial integration, and the rest.

Last year I praised the courage of Martin Orkin in publishing from South Africa 'Othello and the "plain face" of Racism',[5] and in the earlier volume of *Shakespeare Survey* can be found his 'Cruelty, *King Lear*, and the South African Land Act 1913'.[6] In 1987 Orkin produced a book which contains both essays and others, *Shakespeare Against Apartheid* (AD. Donker: Craighall, 1987). 'Hamlet and the Security of the South African State' examines the methods of government used in Claudius's court. The emphasis is on state secrecy, spying, factionalism and the protection of privileged, vested interests by dubious stratagems including state-sanctioned assassination. Polonius is a key figure who emerges not as malicious – privately quite decent, in fact – but as dangerous in his ignorant, unthinking

---

[2] 'Take me to your Leda', *Shakespeare Survey* 40 (1988), 21–32; p. 31.

[3] 'Henry V as Working-House of Ideology', *Shakespeare Survey* 40 (1988), 63–8; p. 68.

[4] 'Shakespeare and his Sources: Observations on the Critical History of *Julius Caesar*', *Shakespeare Survey* 40 (1988), 69–76.

[5] *Shakespeare Survey* 41 (1989), p. 210. Orkin's article was published in *Shakespeare Quarterly*, 38 (1987), 166–88.

[6] *Shakespeare Survey* 40 (1988), 135–44.

obedience to a corrupt regime. The argument makes sense of the detail in the play, and Orkin additionally suggests sinister parallels with the working of state power in modern South Africa. In the essay mentioned above on *King Lear*, by concentrating upon connections between property interests and the use of arbitrary power and injustice in the play, Orkin returns us again to the contemporary situation in South Africa. In a brief, concluding chapter, 'Towards a People's Shakespeare', he defends the use of the Shakespearian text to expose contemporary injustices. Shakespeare has already, Orkin argues, been appropriated in teaching and criticism to 'help *apartheid*' in presentations of the plays that tacitly support ideologies of selfish individualism and encourage in the young 'submission to prevailing relationships of domination and subordination' as a reflex response to all situations that threaten the status quo (p. 182). He suggests it is time that Shakespeare be used just as actively to strengthen progressive ideologies. Secondly, he says, black South Africans themselves find pertinent messages in Shakespeare, and their own drama, poetry, and culture exhibit these understandings. Thirdly, there is a consistent argument running through the book which links the specific historical conditions of Elizabethan and Jacobean England and those prevailing in South Africa today. Orkin could well have added that there is plenty of evidence that Elizabethan writers knew full well that they were presenting politically purposive and educative works, full of coded anti-authoritarianism designed to slip under the censor's attention. Writers like Spenser, Sidney, and Shakespeare were not primarily trying to 'delight' audiences with harmless observations on 'the human condition' as a distraction from contemporary political problems and cultural injustices. Orkin's is a strong, committed statement written from a context in which the significance of choosing an ideologically motivated criticism is immediately apparent.

Larry S. Champion in '"Answere to this

Perillous Time": Ideological Ambivalence in *The Raigne of King Edward III* and the English Chronicle Play', in *English Studies*, 69 (1988), pp. 117–29, while not necessarily claiming Shakespearian authorship for *Edward III*, places it alongside Shakespeare's chronicle plays. He argues that they all hold the potential for anti-authoritarian readings. By showing episodes that 'undercut a grandly patriotic reading of the play' (p. 125), Champion suggests it is unwise to assume 'an audience basically sympathetic to the monarchy and its policies and prompt to respond communally and patriotically' (p. 119). He prefers to read the chronicle plays as depicting 'a struggle between aristocratic houses and the monarchic state, between military and civilian interests, as a conflict regarding matters of succession and inheritance – a view of history, in a word, founded on ideological confrontation' (p. 127).

Yet another perspective on the significance of embedded ideology comes in an article which I found vivaciously illuminating, Manfred Pfister's 'Comic Subversion: A Bakhtinian View of the Comic in Shakespeare'.[7] Ostensibly a vehicle for affecting the accommodation into Shakespearian criticism of the theories of Bakhtin (whose books have percolated slowly to the west), Pfister's essay shifts the theoretical balance dramatically from comedy as social corrective (and therefore conservative in function) to comedy that is subversive and revolutionary in its 'levelling', and Leveller, ideological outlook. Pfister is allusive rather than comprehensive, encompassing Hamlet's subversive humour, the function of Jack Cade, and occasional references to the comedies, but he opens up seams for further mining in some of his generalizations:

Generally, one could say that carnivalesque levelling in the histories and tragedies is incidental, and in the comedies structural. (p. 39)

---

7 *Deutsche Shakespeare-Gesellschaft West Jahrbuch 1987*, ed. Werner Habicht (Bochum: Verlag Ferdinand Kamp, 1987), 27–43.

If anybody could lay claim to being the 'leader' of the new historicists and the ideological demystifiers, it would probably be Stephen Greenblatt. It may be unfair to judge by just one slim book, *Shakespearian Negotiations: The Circulation of Social Energy in Renaissance England* (Oxford: Clarendon Press, 1988), although it must be said that Greenblatt, like some other new critics, is a great recycler of his articles, revising them in Wordsworthian fashion. 'Invisible Bullets' should be pretty visible by now, having been republished four times. In other words it is not *so* unfair to take these five essays as representative, for they seem to be ones that Greenblatt values. 'The Circulation of Social Energy' sets out a kind of manifesto which can be paraphrased as saying that all art is the product of collective exchange mediated by the individual artist, that its production is motivated by ideologies, and that when it exists it is something that can be 'negotiated and exchanged' – that is, interpreted and used with ideological ends. The theatre, Greenblatt argues, is a cultural practice which is particularly useful for an analysis of the various stages of negotiation involved. His characteristic strategy is to begin with some little-known and anecdotal report of an incident in Elizabethan England, examine its implicit ideological attitude or usage, and obliquely work towards a Shakespearian text. 'Shakespeare and the Exorcists', for example, begins with a story of exorcisms performed between 1585 and 1586, and then examines Samuel Harsnett's attempts to expose the fraudulence of the practice when he compared exorcisms with stage plays to the disparagement of both. After proposing that an ideology of power lies behind Harsnett's practice, Greenblatt locates it in *King Lear*. 'Martial Law in the Land of Cockaigne' begins with a specific incident of alleged child murder in 1552, contemplates the nature of 'the staging of anxiety' as a strategy for reinforcing authority, and works around to the use of 'managed insecurity' in *The Tempest*. 'Fiction and Friction' opens with Montaigne in September 1580 hearing a story about a rumoured transvestite marriage in a small French town, and – with very amusing results – applies Elizabethan learning on the sexual organs to the 'erotically charged sparring' (p. 89) in *Twelfth Night*. Each essay is entertaining to read and makes genuinely important points about the nature of power and authority, but the general obliquity of approach lessens the impact.

Margaret Loftus Ranald's *Shakespeare and His Social Context: Essays in Osmotic Knowledge and Literary Interpretation* (New York: AMS Press, 1987) would appear in its title to announce an important and brand-new approach to the subject. 'Osmotic knowledge' is defined as the kind of 'common knowledge' that Elizabethans would certainly have had, though we need footnotes – for example, matrimonial law and expected norms of 'wifely behaviour'. The execution, however, is not so revolutionary as the title suggests. The close examination of how marriage laws are significant for our interpretation of *Much Ado* and *All's Well* does pay dividends, but the very fact that *Measure for Measure* is not examined indicates that the author is in reality transferring knowledge which is commonplace for one play to others, rather than doing anything radically new. In the section on 'The Way of Wifely Behaviour', it tends to be assumed that conduct books summed up common knowledge rather than (in the recent parlance) being ideological inscriptions. Furthermore, as the writer emphasizes, her central focus is on texts, and in some sections (such as that on 'trouser roles') there is precious little 'osmotic knowledge' to act as a context. We get traditional, text-based readings of the comedies and chronicle plays. Ranald does willingly accept the description of feminist, and the very choice of her subjects shows a concern with ideology, but not in a rigorously presented way. This is not to say the book is without merits, but rather that it does not live up to its claims to be giving us a new methodology. It reads more like old literary criticism spiced with occasional old historicism.

Of course, ideological readings are meeting constant resistance from those who claim that we can write without any underlying ideology and that 'we should give our support to a scientific study of the complex factors in human development ... based on evidence that compelled the assent of all rational people'.[8] This hope is expressed in the conclusion to Richard Levin's 'Feminist Thematics and Shakespearian Tragedy'. Despite its neutral title and the courteous but often patronizing tone reminiscent of a stern teacher admonishing a bright but wayward student, this article is fundamentally a savage and sweeping attack on feminist criticism, provoked by the rapid and successful rise of this new movement. In its turn it will certainly provoke many detailed responses, and all that is possible here are a few preliminary rejoinders to what I see as a misguided argument. By studiously excluding the central arguments of some of the most important theoretical works (Dusinberre, Belsey, and others) and concentrating on some text-based feminist essays, Levin extrapolates that feminism is axiomatically a 'thematic' approach, differing from other such approaches simply in its subject of concentration, which he reduces to patriarchy. There is some fundamental problem of outlook here, since the writer is so locked into a thematic approach himself that it is hard to see how he would admit any approach which he cannot describe as just a new theme. Jews and Christians differ, presumably, only on the 'theme' of Christ; communists and capitalists are exactly the same but they have different ideas on the 'theme' of politics. The attack could have been launched against any genuinely thematic study for its suppression of evidence which does not fit the chosen focus, for its selectivity and its exclusions. But Levin has singled out feminism for this special treatment, as if, although on the one hand a harmless old theme study, yet somehow it is more pernicious than others. By careful selection and exclusion in his own practice, he

proves 'logically' that patriarchy is rarely if ever an issue in the plays, that male murder is simply an unusual aberration rather than the consequence, rigorously carried through, of tendencies existing in the particular men whom Shakespeare depicts in each play. In an extraordinary move, Levin *seems* to congratulate Othello for his truthfulness when he says 'She's like a liar gone to burning hell: / 'Twas I that kill'd her', while reprimanding Desdemona for her final lie and her 'crucial evasion' in lying also about the handkerchief. When we find positions like this adopted in serious scholarly work, it becomes obvious just why feminism is needed as a possible way of breaking down entrenched, unexamined, and complacent attitudes. More informed and properly critical viewpoints can be found in Ann Thompson's '"The Warrant of Womanhood": Shakespeare and feminist criticism' in *The Shakespeare Myth*, pp. 74–88 (see above, pp. 74–88) – ironically enough the only essay by a woman in that book – and in Carol Thomas Neely's 'Constructing the Subject: Feminist Practice and the New Renaissance Discourses' in *English Literary Renaissance*, 18 (1988), pp. 5–18.

Nor do the new historicists have it all their own way in insisting on some theoretical understanding of ideologies. The dominant mode probably still remains at present what Alexander Leggatt calls the 'practical' approach in his book, *Shakespeare's Political Drama: The History Plays and the Roman Plays* (London and New York: Routledge, 1988). For those who know Leggatt's earlier work on romantic comedy and citizen comedy, the approach will be familiar: play-by-play analysis of the chronicle plays (including *Henry VIII* but not *King John*) and Roman plays (but not *Titus Andronicus*), looking for themes and drawing upon imagery and structural devices to build up a reading. Initially paying tribute to Tillyard (he 'will not go away'), Leggatt dis-

---

8 *PMLA*, 103 (1988), 125–38; p. 136.

tances himself from the 'myth' of world-order, and on the crunch issue of *Coriolanus* he shows himself to be on the people's side, pointing out that they speak 'neither in monosyllables nor in Mummerset but in the thoughtful, sophisticated, sometimes difficult prose of Shakespeare's late period' (p. 196). While he claims not to be imposing any 'myth' of his own on the plays, unsympathetic readers will claim that there is in fact an underlying myth being propagated of the critic as a moderate chap, temperately steering between extremes, and thus implicitly underwriting the normativeness of an order-based, Tillyardian myth of critical neutrality. A saturation in new ideological approaches of course ends up making one examine very closely the buried assumptions beneath critical statements, and this is surely a justifiable and healthy form of scepticism with which to approach critics.

Since we are on to history plays, I might mention here a book which has nothing to do with ideologies, except insofar as it exemplifies some. Frances A. Shirley, the editor of the latest casebook in the Garland series, *'King John' and 'Henry VIII': Critical Essays* (New York and London: Garland Publishing, 1988) would surely have been delighted if Leggatt's book had come out in time for consideration, since it would have bumped up the amount to choose from, at least on the second play. All that can be said about the criticism of these two plays, on the evidence of this volume, is that it is woefully thin both in quantity to choose from and in quality. It is a remarkable editorial feat that over 380 pages are filled. The essay by Robert Smallwood on *King John* is excellent, but as it is the Introduction to his New Penguin edition it is hardly inaccessible. If the series could have waited a year, it might have included A. R. Braunmuller's *'King John and Historiography'*,[9] a detailed essay written with new historicists' preoccupations in mind, regarding ostensible 'history' and drama as sharing the same status as fact (i.e. each equally fictional and ideologically motivated). It

would be interesting to see a new kind of casebook based on thorough scrutiny of underlying ideologies amongst critics, or on the historical evolution of particular ideological positions (such as the use of history, Marxist attitudes, the rise of feminist criticism). Such a development could give a whole new lease of life to the rather jaded genre. And now, having cleverly worked my way around to casebooks in the most unlikely context, I should mention that we are up to volume six of the voluminous *Shakespearean Criticism*, Gale's answer to Garland.[10] The three plays dealt with are *Antony and Cleopatra*, *Richard II*, and *The Two Gentlemen of Verona*. I have been able to test out this series in compiling critical bibliographies and found it useful for the task, at least in saving many trips to the library. Despite its size, however, it is far from thorough (though this is asking too much), it is oriented towards criticism from the USA, and the choice of British critics is restricted and old-fashioned.

FREUDIANS

One of my recent predecessors as reviewer of critical studies for the *Survey* felt as though she would be drowned by the flood of books written on Shakespeare from a Freudian point of view.[11] I still seem to be afloat, but the deluge is as strong as ever. It seems a particularly durable school of criticism that produces several books each year, even at a time when (I understand) the world of psychiatry itself is moving away from Freud. It may be fated to end up as one of those models which

---

9 *ELH*, 55 (1988), 309–32.
10 Edited by Mark W. Scott, *Shakespearean Criticism: Excerpts from the Criticism of William Shakespeare's Plays and Poetry, from the First Published Approaches to Current Evaluations*, vol. 6 (Detroit: Gale Research Company, 1987).
11 Harriett Hawkins, 'The Year's Contributions to Shakespeare Studies', *Shakespeare Survey* 35 (1982), pp. 160–1.

are useful for analysing literature but not 'real' people.

Ruth Nevo in *Shakespeare's Other Language* (New York and London: Methuen, 1987) pursues a post-Freudian, mainly Lacanian approach to the four last plays. The psychoanalytic model used here is one that sees both text and reader as having an unconscious level and a conscious, both being in a state of constant interaction. As in a dream, the narrative, often apparently absurd, is given meaning and made interpretable by the presence of a 'textual unconscious', acting for example in *Pericles* as 'an archaic energy at work like Hamlet's old mole' (p. 44). What happens to Pericles are not random and improbable acts of fortune but something more systematically developed at the level of primal fantasy. Haunted by the fear of incest, Pericles oscillates between listlessness and energy, between the maternal sea and the paternal sin, while seeking a wife and family of his own. 'Desire and dread' provide the pendulum for the psychodrama, a pattern owing its literary provenance to romance conventions of separation and return. In *Cymbeline* 'the fastidious Iachimo and the unspeakable Cloten' (p. 74) are proxy suitors for Posthumus. He in turn is inhibited in desire, a result, Nevo argues, of Shakespeare's own 'deeply repressed desire for his daughter' (p. 94) and related to the death of his mother which significantly occurred in the same year as the birth of a daughter to his own favourite daughter. *The Winter's Tale*, also seen as 'theatre of reverie', is unified at the level of its 'unconscious' by a theme of usurpation. The part of Mamillius is central to this pattern. As Leontes thinks himself usurped by Polonius, so Mamillius thinks himself usurped by his unborn sister:

A momentary maternal rejection, a provocation to sibling jealousy, a child's game effort to master fear with a story – this utterly ordinary little nursery scene has effectively reminded us of the griefs and losses that haunt the minds of children like the very

sprites and goblins in Mamillius' tale; and it throws a melancholy light upon Leontes' breakdown.

(p. 113)

The fact that the chapter on *The Tempest* does not, at least to my mind, say as many new things as those on the other plays leads me into an interesting line of speculation. For it seems that in dealing with this play in particular, criticism has inadvertently already assimilated practices which come very close to Freudian and Lacanian ideas. It is not unusual for critics to examine Ariel and Caliban as proxies for part of Prospero's unconscious, to find fantasies that lie between sleep and waking (a constant image in the play), childhood and adulthood (Miranda), all regarded as an interaction between overt (conscious) and covert (unconscious) states present in the text. Does *The Tempest* lend itself most easily of all the plays to a psychoanalytic reading – so easily that it seems 'natural'? There is no obvious reason why this should be so. Or is it that in this play psychoanalytic criticism and more orthodox approaches accidentally meet? Because it could be argued that it is not possible to analyse the unconscious (analysis is a conscious process), we find that many psychoanalytical models depend heavily on metaphor – even 'the unconscious' must be a metaphor. Nevo, for example, uses analogies with trees, crystals, eclipses of the sun, soldering, and many others. Literary criticism has, sometimes notoriously, relied just as heavily on metaphors to describe the 'inner nature' or 'deep centre' (both metaphors themselves) of a text. Seen from this point of view, it is not inconceivable that psychoanalytical approaches are no farther or nearer the 'object of enquiry' than any branch of literary study. What must, however, find some place in our judgement is the intelligence and sensitivity of the individual critic, and here Nevo scores highly.

A reading of Marjorie Garber's *Shakespeare's Ghost Writers: Literature as Uncanny Causality* (New York and London: Methuen, 1987) is pleasurable enough, as is a detective story to devotees of that genre. The analogy is apt, since some detective work is required to ascertain exactly what the book is about. To recall any substantial point after reading it is as difficult as seeing ghosts by daylight. One straightforward strand leads us to contemplate the dramatic significance of Shakespeare's ghosts in plays like *Richard III, Julius Caesar, Macbeth,* and *Hamlet.* Simultaneously, however, other themes are pursued – the 'uncanny' ways in which postmodernist writers 'are *themselves* haunted by Shakespeare', and how Shakespearian tragedy has eerily 'dominated our present discourses, whether in literature, history, psychoanalysis, philosophy, or politics' (p. xiii). Shakespeare not only gives us ghosts, he *is* a ghost. However, the main ghost in the book turns out to be Freud's, for not only do his ideas of association and transference govern much of the book's methodology, but also the most satisfactory sections show clearly and convincingly the ways in which his own thought was, both consciously and unconsciously, influenced by Shakespeare. Here, maybe, we come close to an explanation for the tribe of Freudian Shakespearians – it was Shakespeare who invented Freud! Intersecting these dominant concerns are different themes again, for example the evidence of 'time's deformed hand' at work in Shakespeare's distortion of historical sources in *Richard III* (a fairly straightforward, not particularly original chapter) and the Medusa's head of 'gender undecidability and anxiety about gender identification and gender roles' in *Macbeth* (and Macbeth). Entertaining as the essays are, the feeling is inescapable that Garber has taken on too much in terms of theoretical frameworks while building upon actual material that is too slight. The best bits are those which find sources in Shakespeare for Freud's own ideas and practice, and I would have welcomed a book that gave a thorough and systematic account of this one subject alone.

Robert N. Watson's *Shakespeare and the Hazards of Ambition* (Cambridge, Massachusetts and London: Harvard University Press, 1984) found its way to this reviewer three years after publication, but it deserves notice even at this late stage. Watson's understanding of ambition is borrowed from Freudian psychology, although he is fairly faithful to his word in not imposing ideas on the text but arguing rather that similar conclusions emerge independently from Shakespeare and Freud (more evidence that Shakespeare created Freud?). Ambition is seen as an attempt to transform the self away from a primally authentic identity inherited from parents. It is thus regarded as a rebellion against the father figure in particular, inviting retribution, at least on grounds of a violation of laws of kind. Even if retribution does not come, the ambitious person may be left in limbo, unable to return to the prior self and living in borrowed or unauthentic robes. The result can be schizophrenia and/or suicide. Watson makes a good case for the operation of this pattern in the History plays, where inheritance and patrimony are directly relevant. He needs to change the terms somewhat for *Macbeth* and *Coriolanus*, where there are conspicuously no fathers. The final chapter on *The Winter's Tale* is interesting in its own right, but here in particular the whole issue of ambition simply does not seem relevant, even with some bending of definitions supplied by the author.

Stanley Cavell is more than a Freudian, but he probably would not object to being placed in this company. His *Disowning Knowledge in Six Plays of Shakespeare* (Cambridge and New York: Cambridge University Press, 1987) is a collection of older essays with some additions. It is not difficult to see why Cavell became something of a cult figure after the publication of his essay on *King Lear*, reprinted here with a postscript. As a professional philosopher he is spared the Shakespearian's burden of textual and technical minutiae that can easily bog down an argument; and he is at the same time an unusually passionate philosopher (with an interest in Freudian psychology), rooting himself in the 'presentness' of drama as an epistemology (see especially pp. 102–5) and revelling in the emotional mélange which is the element in which most of us live. Although he is not unaware of the arguments that confine dramatic characters to a specific linguistic context, he is not afraid to argue from personal experience and from feelings. The result can sometimes be strong and refreshing, especially in the centrepiece essay on *Lear*, 'The Avoidance of Love'. At other times it can be myopic. (I am thinking of the largely Freudian reading of *Coriolanus*, which centres on multiple implications of eating.) Comparing the earlier essays with the later, a regrettable conclusion is that Cavell is becoming more occluded and opaque in his prose as time goes on, a Jamesian hazard facing the precocious who wish to remain precocious. The philosophical heart of the book lies in its insistence that Shakespearian tragedy is created out of the radical 'scepticism' of the male protagonists – their rage to 'know' the world and their fellow beings through concepts of possession, since they are blind to less material modes of knowledge. The jealousy of Othello and Leontes shows the destructiveness of such scepticism, though each case is different:

Like Othello, Leontes obeys the structures of skepticism expressed as a form of insane jealousy; but whereas Othello's skeptical astonishment, or nightmare, is represented as a horror of feminine sexuality, Leontes' state is represented as the torturing sense that his children are not his.   (p. 15)

GENERAL SUBJECTS

After publishing a series of books on particular plays and groups of plays, James L. Calderwood now ranges over the whole field in *Shakespeare and the Denial of Death* (Amherst: University of Massachusetts Press, 1987). As the patron saint of metadrama, he initially surprises us by offering a book based on a theme, in this case the different ways in which Shakespeare's characters try to avoid their inevitable confrontation with death. He reserves metadramatic discussion until late in the piece. As a consequence he ends up largely abdicating his strongest ground, and it is not until he directly confronts this fact in a late chapter on *King Lear* appropriately entitled 'Abdication and Authority' that he retrieves his own authority. The earlier parts of the book are entertainingly written and contain insights into ways in which awareness of death is sublimated by Shakespeare's characters into other areas such as sex, patriarchy, disguise, feeding, and sacrifice in their futile attempts to achieve immortality, but there is the air of a dissertation thesis, without a strong, individual pressure behind the rather bitty presentation. The accounts of the comedies are distinctly thin, and there is some unaccountable repetition in different sections on *Hamlet*. However, the sections on *Lear* (partially reprinted) and the final part, 'Immortality and art', show Calderwood returning triumphantly to metadrama. His distinction between 'reporting' and 'showing' in *Lear* ('saying' the worst is never a closure but preludes the 'showing' of even worse scenarios) is convincingly built up and results particularly in some fine criticism of the 'Dover Cliff' scene ('a metadramatic lightning rod' [p. 162] tempting us, as Gloucester is tempted, to escape from an ordeal only to return us relentlessly to the terrible 'showing').

Graham Bradshaw's *Shakespeare's Scepticism* (Brighton: Harvester Press, 1987) examines dilemmas of judgement – the often conflicting ways in which characters judge each other and we judge them. Taking his cue from Troilus' 'What's aught, but as 'tis valued?' and Hamlet's 'There's nothing either good or bad, but thinking makes it so', Bradshaw discovers in Shakespeare's plays two ways of applying the maxims. One is in the spirit of dogmatic or terminal scepticism, a form of 'materialistic nihilism of a Thersites, Iago or Edmund'. The other is 'a *radical* scepticism, which turns on itself – weighing the human need to affirm values against the inherently problematic nature of all acts of valuing' (p. 39). The latter is the perspective adopted in this book, as the author analyses how differing and even contradictory readings may emerge from *Hamlet*, *Troilus and Cressida*, *Measure for Measure*, and *Macbeth*. In the last of these plays, for example, Bradshaw shows how our evaluation of Macbeth can radically shift from the orthodox view if we throw into the debate a consideration of the contrasts between the marital unit of Macbeth and his wife on the one hand and Macduff and his family on the other. Such a comparison is not at all to the disfavour of the Macbeths. The book is a useful complement to Cavell's, for whereas Cavell's interest lies in philosophical scepticism, Bradshaw's approach is consistently through the dramatic texts. They both stress the importance of process, but in very different ways. Bradshaw is also more attuned to verbal shifts and metaphorical density in the poetry. Indeed, so florid is his own style that he seems to be trying to emulate Shakespeare's purple passages. The real forerunners of the approach are Rabkin, Rossiter (who both emphasize radical ambivalence) and the much-quoted Nietzsche. It is a stimulating and energetic book but, it has to be said, an uneven one. Intriguing and important questions are raised through close scrutiny of texts, but more often than not the solutions offered are simplistic and conventional. Too much of a truly problematical nature is revealed in *Hamlet* and *Measure for Measure* to be neatly packed away by reference to (respectively) the putative *Ur-Hamlet* and the tired distinction between justice and mercy. In the account of 'stylistic registers' in *1 Henry IV* no amount of display of musical analogy and Elizabethan metrics can disguise an undergraduatish cleverness to the argument. I do not understand the decision to give all quotations in Folio spelling when so little in the analysis depends on this kind of detail.

A Kind of Wild Justice: Revenge in Shakespeare's Comedies by Linda Anderson (Newark: University of Delaware Press, 1987) has the merit of drawing attention to neglected aspects of the comedies and revenge drama alike. All too often we assume revenge is a subject appropriate to tragedy, forgetting that it can equally motivate a comedy. There are two plays which fully justify the approach – *The Merchant of Venice* and *The Merry Wives of Windsor*. On the latter Anderson is excellent, and on the former, efficient. She does not, however, convince me either that there is an identifiable shift in Shakespeare's use of comic revenge (from farce to correctiveness), or that it is very helpful to analyse other plays in detail (she includes the problem comedies) from this point of view. It seems too strong to claim that *The Shrew* 'maintains an atmosphere of comic vengefulness' (p. 33), and a misuse of the word to say that 'threats of serious revenge open *The Comedy of Errors* and *A Midsummer Night's Dream*' (p. 24). It is surely the law rather than revenge that threatens Egeus and Hermia respectively. Anderson's analysis, while having its value, shares in common with other books on such single motifs an obsessive, tunnel vision, an undiscriminating need to find revenge everywhere. A general failure to distinguish between revenge and the operation of poetic justice makes such excesses only too possible.

It is hard to put one's finger on precisely what is the organizing principle behind Lachlan Mackinnon's *Shakespeare the Aesthete: An Exploration of Literary Theory* (London: Macmillan, 1988). The book started as a study of the problem plays but spread out to include *Macbeth* and *The Winter's Tale*. There is not a lot of observable 'Theory'. Rather than trying to define the rather nebulous connection which Mackinnon finds between the plays, I simply quote a not-untypical section which indicates something of an approach, which is, at least in its detailed exposition of text, illuminating:

Through Helena and Parolles we experience an atomised society whose decayed social and moral orders breed an aggressive individualism. If the play seems to be being treated partly as a socio-economic fable, this is because its emphasis on money and the replacement of vows by contracts does not suggest historical parallels. (p. 29)

Whilst on the subject of *All's Well*, mention can be made of Susan Snyder's article, '*All's Well That Ends Well* and Shakespeare's Helens: Text and Subtext, Subject and Object' in *English Literary Renaissance*, 18 (1988), pp. 66–77. Snyder sees the naming of the 'Helens' in *All's Well* and *A Midsummer Night's Dream* as not accidental but calculated, ironically reversing expectations of a pursued object by showing us in each case a woman pursuing a man with active desire.

Shakespeare's Soliloquies by Wolfgang Clemen (London: Methuen, 1987) is a translation from a text already well known in its German edition. No doubt it will prove a godsend to students asked to discuss the function of soliloquies in a certain play, since Clemen has systematically combed through each play and assembled his own answers in good examination fashion. I find something dull about the procedure of raising conventional questions and then answering them in orderly fashion, though the educational world being what it is I cannot deny that such projects have their place. Another book which suffers from the tendency to raise unchallenging questions is *Human Conflict in Shakespeare* by S. C. Boorman (London and New York: Routledge, 1987). 'Conflict' is introduced through a series of presumed Elizabethan dichotomies such as soul/body, immortal/mortal; and the one overarching priority is Reason/Unreason, which overlaps considerably with our old, familiar order/disorder. What is constricting about this is not so much an innate conservative tendency that we might expect (acknowledgement is made of the fact that reason can be as inhuman as unreason in its application), but a glossing over of the rela-

tivity of such terms when applied to the Elizabethans and especially to Shakespeare. What is reason to one is unreason to another, and this goes for characters and readers alike. To the author(s) of *Respublica* a rational state involves an absence of monarchy, while to the author of *The Life and Death of Jack Straw* reason means the suppression of rebellion against monarchy. (Boorman draws on both plays.) In Boorman's book, such problems are blandly negotiated by an appeal to the imputed imperatives of 'human nature', which magically dictate what is reasonable in any given situation. Despite my doubts about the whole enterprise, I should not like to deter anybody from reading it, since it is eloquently written and the section on *King Lear*, especially, is moving.

Another book which I must not deter readers from trying is Marina Tarlinskaja's *Shakespeare's Verse: Iambic Pentameter and the Poet's Idiosyncrasies* (American University Studies, series 4, vol. 41 [New York: Peter Lang, 1987]), although it leaves me completely out of my depth. I shall try to summarize it, so far as I am able. Tarlinskaja belongs to the Russian school of verse study, a formalist, linguistic–statistical method of analysing metre and rhythm. Her main aim is to identify with mathematical precision 'the correlation between actual stresses and the metrical law in English verse'. She has published another book, *English Verse: Theory and History* (The Hague: Mouton, 1976), in which she studied these aspects of verse with enormously wide reference, and one of the impressive aspects of the present book is that, although focusing on Shakespeare, it gives us constant and detailed comparisons and analogies with virtually every poet of consequence in English (and some in Russian) from the sixteenth to nineteenth centuries. 'Analysis of rhythmical figures in Shakespeare's verse', writes Tarlinskaja, helps 'to locate the place of his verse style within his own epoch and within the whole English poetic tradition, and to trace a rhythmical evolution within Shakespeare's canon' (p. 336). One might quibble that the chronology is far from settled at the moment, and there may just be some circular reasoning in tracing such evolution, but I cannot really judge the allowable margin for error in the statistics. The 'subtleties of stresses interacting with the metrical scheme' are inspected for their normative and for their distinctive, idiosyncratic qualities, both across plays and within each single play. Questions are raised about how rhythm denotes character, and another line of enquiry shows that Shakespeare's rhythms are more rigid and strict at the beginning of a play, more free and loose at the end. Such conclusions offer tantalizing insights into Shakespeare's creativity, but whether they are soundly based or not is a matter for specialists to judge.

Charles H. Frey's *Experiencing Shakespeare: Essays on Text, Classroom and Performance* (Columbia: University of Missouri Press, 1988) is a fairly heterogeneous 'collection of free-standing essays on Shakespeare' (p. vii), most of which have been published previously in journal form. (Does anybody write *new* books any more?) In general they are marked by a 'teacherly' concern with conveying the message that students should try to see plays as wholes, to incorporate the visual as well as verbal elements, not exaggerate the degree of satire in romantic plays, and all the time try to generate an 'experience' of each play that will include the conceptual and temporal dimensions. Another strand running through the book is a plea that critics should absorb the methodologies of feminism, particularly in noticing the ways in which patriarchal domination is presented. Some feminists may feel these pleas, while well-intentioned, are not comprehensive enough. In a book whose intended destination is the classroom, it is significant that the most interesting essay is on 'Teaching Shakespeare in America'. There is a discussion of this essay (first published in 1984) by Ruth Freifrau von Ledebur in *Deutsche Shakespeare-Gesellschaft West Jahrbuch 1987*.[12]

Another book which will inevitably find its way into schools, if not universities, is John Wilders's *New Prefaces to Shakespeare* (Oxford: Basil Blackwell, 1988). A reprinting of Wilders's brief and lucid introductions to plays produced for television by the BBC, it claims only the modest task of drawing to the attention of general readers the skill behind Shakespeare's dramatic construction examined in each of his plays by turn. It should find some new friends for Shakespeare outside academe.

Of the articles on general matters, I should single out Stephen Orgel's 'The Authentic Shakespeare'[13] as particularly challenging. With a host of elegant examples, Orgel puzzles away at the phenomenon of readers, actors, audiences, editors, and artists all claiming to recover the 'authentic' Shakespeare, and each version, of course, being different from the others. In all cases, Orgel argues, they are reaching beyond 'the text' (which does not exist 'authentically' anyway) towards something that the text is presumed to represent. The diversity of realizations and performances is explained largely by the different historical and aesthetic contexts in which the recipients are working.

Richard Horwich in '"I Sing But After You": Shakespeare's Internal Parody'[14] argues that parodies which break out of the dramatic frame 'can realign our sympathies among the characters and readjust the degree of credibility we are willing to grant them' (p. 238). I have published an article on 'Functions of Poems and Songs in Elizabethan Romance and Romantic Comedy',[15] based on the conviction that former criticism in this area has not concentrated on the (Brechtian) possibilities

---

[12] 'Teaching Shakespeare in America: Anregungen für den Shakespeare-Unterricht', *Deutsche Shakespeare-Gesellschaft Jahrbuch 1987*, 124–33.

[13] 'The Authentic Shakespeare', *Representations*, 21 (1988), 1–27.

[14] *Studies in English Literature 1500–1900*, 28 (1988), 219–40.

[15] *English Studies*, 68 (1987), 392–405.

offered by poems and songs as insights into the dramatic moments where they occur.

HAMLET

Barbara Everett has been hard at work on *Hamlet*. In the *London Review of Books* (31 March 1988, pp. 6–9) we find her simply titled 'Growing'. Beginning with the common perception that early on in the play Hamlet is 'young' and that in the Gravedigger scene he is announced as having suddenly attained the age of thirty, Everett argues that at each stage his role is appropriate to his age. At first as a student he is 'a political subversive' with the 'political vulnerability attending the out-of-power "young" in Shakespeare's England' (p. 7). Later in the play 'Young Hamlet grows up and grows dead in the same instant' (p. 8). When, for the first time, he sheds the role of son and identifies with his father ('This is I, Hamlet the Dane') he is marked in mythical fashion for death. It is difficult to convey through paraphrase the subtlety of this essay, since its strength lies in many local perceptions. A particularly interesting comparison is made between the 'rites of passage' encountered by Hamlet and those undergone by Pip in *Great Expectations*. (By coincidence, the parallel is developed more systematically if less critically by Stanley Friedman in 'Echoes of *Hamlet* in *Great Expectations*' in *Hamlet Studies*, 9 [1987], pp. 86–9.) Everett has contributed another study of *Hamlet* which is more specifically textual, concerning itself with 'Principles of Emendation', although her starting points are, in each case, matters of literary understanding.[16] Sledded Polacks will never again be bewildered Poles cowering on their sleds. The article gives hope to those readers who see textual critics as sometimes antithetical to literary commentators.

There are several book-length studies of *Hamlet* this year. Ion Omesco's *Hamlet ou Le Tentation du Possible* (Paris: Presses Universitaires de France, 1987) is a pyrotechnic display of prose and sporadic insight from a well-known French actor and writer. Designed to demonstrate the chameleon-like qualities of *Hamlet*, this 'essai sur l'ambiguïté' displays many chameleon qualities in its own right. A whole range of aspects of the play is dealt with, from Elizabethan politics and theology, through the psychology of adolescence (à la Everett), folly and melancholy, the Oedipus complex, and ultimately such images as 'L'ange-poète et le démon' and 'un héros fin de siècle'. There is quite a lot of bardolatry that might embarrass our more sceptical Anglo-American colleagues, but the verve and sprightliness of the style are infectious:

> Autour de lui, et comme sortie de son sperme, la pièce: un rituel, un drame de famille, une tragédie de la réflexion, un hymne à la Providence, un bréviare du nihilisme, un éspace symbolique, une pièce naïve jouée par les pensionnaires de Charenton. Mais ce n'est qu'apparence. (p. 255)

The Scottish representative is much more sober. Arthur McGee in *The Elizabethan Hamlet* (New Haven and London: Yale University Press, 1987) seeks to deprive us of many interpretations based on the cherished assumption that the hero is sympathetic. McGee draws on a great deal of contemporary material in an attempt to retrieve Elizabethan modes of thinking about religious issues, and his conclusions are surprising to say the least. He detects a fervent Protestant point of view in the play (and its contemporary audiences) and a strong anti-Catholic bias. Hamlet is Catholic – his link with Wittenberg would have invoked not Luther but Faustus – and the Ghost, condemned to purgatory, is Catholic and, in Elizabethan eyes, entirely satanic. Hamlet, in committing himself to the Ghost's command to revenge, becomes the devil's vice and jester. Soliloquies show him advancing

---

16 'New Readings in *Hamlet* (and Some Principles of Emendation)', *Review of English Studies*, NS 39 (1988), 177–98.

steadily towards despair and hell, and evil increasingly possesses him. Throughout, McGee insists, an Elizabethan audience would have identified far less than we do with such a Hamlet. At first the sheer quantity of supporting evidence taken from plays and documentary works of the time has an inbuilt persuasiveness. But small doubts swell into larger ones. Why is Claudius a murderer and self-evidently a villain if the real target of the audience's hatred is Hamlet? Would it not have been much easier for Shakespeare to have absolved the king of all guilt, making him the victim of a young hothead papist? When we inspect the evidence more closely we find more cause for doubt. Too often quotation ignores context, and there is an easy but fallible assumption that written statements which come in ideologically motivated texts are representative of pervasive attitudes in Elizabethan England, and in some sense 'true'. Ideas of revenge, ghosts, and the devil must have been much more evocative and ambiguous to an age when many people could hardly have been completely Protestantized simply by state decrees away from their folk heritage. To say so much is not necessarily to impose modern concepts or to deny historical specificity; or rather it is no more anachronistic than applying the Cromwellian Presbyterianism of McGee. On the other hand, there is something quite refreshing about seeing such a radically different – and unsettling – case put with conviction.

After reading Everett and McGee, one sees John Halverson's 'Hamlet: Ethos and Transcendence'[17] as a collage of both, drawing independent conclusions. He sees Hamlet's age as significant, though he (rightly or wrongly) takes it to be thirty throughout and therefore a sign of prevailing maturity over the rest of the characters. He draws also on the connection between Wittenberg and Faust to discover not diabolism but high intellectual achievement in Hamlet. He is not Everett's undergraduate but an advanced scholar. All this adds up to a different reading which sees Hamlet throughout the play as 'a modern man in an archaic society' (p. 45), well-travelled and intellectually and morally superior to the Denmark which he visits, a place of 'drab and simple provincialism' and 'a political [sic] primitive state where private vengeance and mob action are normal channels of justice'. He is the rational man plunged into an irrational society, and when he acts brutally, he does so out of self-defence. Strangely enough, I find myself able to be convinced by all three accounts, even though they contradict each other. Yet another solution to similar problems is offered by Cherrell Guilfoyle in 'A Kind of Vengeance: Images of Classical and of Divine Revenge in Hamlet': the play gives a strong 'intimation of Vindicta mihi as the proper alternative to revenge on earth – the reason why man's vengeance should be held back until it is rendered insignificant in the light of God's doom'.[18]

A whole book on the Revenge tradition is Peter Mercer's 'Hamlet' and the Acting of Revenge (London: Macmillan, 1987). Mercer follows the time-honoured procedure of tracing revenge from Thyestes through The Spanish Tragedy and The Revenger's Tragedy to its final destination, Hamlet. The particular 'new angle' here lies in Mercer's belief that the Elizabethan tragedies draw not on a single tradition but on both 'the dramatic mode of revenge tragedy and the rhetorical mode of satire and complaint' (p. 3). These two modes are at least potentially incompatible, and Mercer's argument is that in Hamlet Shakespeare directly faces the contradiction between his hero's satiric role and his fate as a revenger. Like most critics, Mercer concludes that Hamlet can be exonerated from the charge of personal guilt normally associated with the revenger's role. No doubt this is correct, but there is a sense in which critics have to say this

---

[17] Anglia, 106 (1988), 44–73.
[18] Parergon, 5 (1987), 127–34; p. 134.

for their own peace of mind. Returning to the sardonic brand of meta-criticism exemplified in Girard's paragraph quoted above, we can say that a critic who chooses to write a book on revenge (because it is there) realizes it is a somewhat pagan activity and absolves himself by letting Hamlet off the hook.

At this moment it is probably diplomatic to quote the sage words of the editor of *Hamlet Studies*:

Perhaps it is important for each reader to believe that there is (for him/her) one interpretation that is the correct one, while admitting the validity of multiple interpretations of the text. Whereas such multiplicity can, and ought to, exist, it can be argued that for any particular reader a single interpretation should seem more valid than all the others.[19]

After all, as the writer points out, a cloud may be 'almost in shape of a camel', or a weasel, or a whale, depending on the observer's inclination. The philosophy seems as appropriate for interpreting life as a play, and indeed much of the commentary on *Hamlet* might convince an innocent bystander that critics are reflecting upon life itself. While not going so far as Tom Stoppard in fleshing out the existences of incidental characters, some commentators do find it interesting to centralize such figures. Ghanshiam Sharma chooses Horatio, concluding that he is used first as 'a reliable commentator, so as to guide the audience's response',[20] and secondly as an ideal Stoic figure against whom Hamlet is to be judged. Rudiger Imhof makes as much out of a figure who has even less to say. Not content with the argument that Fortinbras is simply another foil for Hamlet, Imhof inspects the cameo role and its implications. Unfortunately, the critic seems to give away his whole argument in his conclusion. After noting that 'Fortinbras simply does not have a just cause' for succession to the throne, and that even at the end he is a character in whom passion and reason are at variance, he fails to consider the possibility that in *Hamlet* Shakespeare is putting kingship on trial as a cause of corruption in men, an argument for

which there is plenty of evidence but which does not yet seem to have been put. Instead, Imhof lamely concludes that 'Shakespeare simply needed a new king at the close of events.'[21] In a later volume of *Hamlet Studies*[22] we have two articles on the play's use of classical or continental models, Geoffrey Aggeler's 'Hamlet and the Stoic Sage' (pp. 21–33) and Barbara A. Johnson's 'The Fabric of the Universe Rent: *Hamlet* as an Inversion of *The Courtier*' (pp. 34–52). Alison G. Hayton's '"The King my father?" Paternity in *Hamlet*' in the same volume (pp. 53–64) does not invoke Freud as one might expect, but instead looks at concepts of legitimacy and illegitimacy. Martin W. Walsh (pp. 65–77) contemplates the skull of Yorick ('examining the prop *as prop*', p. 65) and has some words to say about Death as the fool in Renaissance pictures. Which leads to the thing itself in Michael Cohen's '"To What base uses we may return": Class and Mortality in *Hamlet* (5.1)' (pp. 78–85). This journal continues to evidence the apparent inexhaustibility of the play.

Graham Holderness has few axes to grind in *Hamlet* (Milton Keynes and Philadelphia: Open University Press, 1987), and his approach is openly pedagogical and pluralist. The short book is as much a guide to and demystification of various approaches as an approach in itself. First, the myths of Shakespeare's presumed perfection are challenged and replaced with the image of a man of his times who was in particular a player-actor using to the full the resources of the Elizabethan stage. Three chapters then examine the potential of the text(s) of *Hamlet* from different points of view which incorporate psychological readings, metadrama, a little new histori-

19 *Hamlet Studies*, 8 (1986), p. 6.
20 Ghanshiam Sharma, 'The Function of Horatio in *Hamlet*', *Hamlet Studies*, 8 (1986), 30–9; p. 35.
21 Rudiger Imhof, 'Fortinbras Ante Porta: The Role and Significance of Fortinbras in *Hamlet*', *Hamlet Studies*, 8 (1986), 8–29.
22 *Hamlet Studies*, 9 (1987).

cism, Brechtianism, and feminism. All the time we are persuaded that the text itself is allowed to dictate the direction of discussion rather than it being stretched upon a procrustean bed of theory. If this book is used as intended, by a student working systematically through it and considering each discussion point in turn, then it will be useful. But as a book (rather than a teaching programme) it suffers from its own pluralism which prevents it from having the impact of a fresh and distinctive statement. The organization, following consideration of a scene with a wider 'Discussion' seems both narrowly chronological and fussy, holding back a reader's forward momentum (which is probably exactly the intention).

In *Shakespeare Quarterly* John Hunt's 'The Catastrophic Body in *Hamlet*'[23] contributes to a little sub-genre of 'post-structural body criticism' that I have observed developing over the last couple of years. It is not so much a return to Spurgeon (though it starts with noting recurrent imagery) as a linguistic study (parts of the body function as 'metonymic or synechdocal equivalents for actions and states of body'), and ends up with a moral lesson about the character (in this case Hamlet) coming to live with corporeal reality. As with many things in Shakespearian criticism, there is a suspicion that the idea reveals something of the critic's fears, his sense that the more theoretical the critical stance, the more there must be corporeal compensation somewhere. A more specialized example of the sub-genre comes in 'The imagery of skin disease and sealing', a chapter in Maurice Charney's *Hamlet's Fictions* (New York and London: Routledge, Chapman and Hall, 1988), which contains essays, some revised from previous articles, on topics such as 'Ophelia and other madwomen in Elizabethan plays' and '*Hamlet* as comedy'.

OTHER PLAYS

William F. Martin's brief and intensely written book, *The Indissoluble Knot: 'King Lear' as*

Ironic Drama (Lanham, New York, London: University Press of America, 1987) is an attempt to define the play's 'composite' form. While *Lear* displays elements of various dramatic modes – classical tragedy, comedy, morality, miracle, mystery – it also creates a new, distinctive category which Martin names Ironic Drama. He points to the constant presence of an ironic attitude, a perception of incongruities which produces not perplexity or discord but a tolerance of life's complexities. We may sympathize with the suffering of Lear and Gloucester while simultaneously recognizing that their own ignorant, trivial, and essentially comic actions have precipitated the disasters. Like the evil characters, their pompous assertions of self-sufficiency incapacitate them from adopting the Fool's ironic perspective, and also from feeling the humanitarian bonds (Cordelia, Kent) which work by deflating self-aggrandizement. In its design of ironic drama, Martin interestingly makes *King Lear* prototypical of the romances. It would have been important if he had developed this idea beyond one sentence (p. 73). The approach has the merit of explaining how a writer of tragedy could also compose comedies of love, the common factor being a Shakespearian quality of ironic distancing from even the most passionate moments, whether happy or sad. The book has some faults. There is repetition, and the chapter identifying characters in morality fashion as representative of the seven deadly sins seems like a pet theory, and fairly strained. But overall the book stimulates thought. An article on *King Lear* of great interest is Yang Zhouhan's 'King Lear Metamorphosed'.[24] Partly conceived as a comparison between two Chinese translations of the play, it is much wider in scope than this, showing the fiendish problems of reproducing in another language the many meanings of 'nothing', and more teasingly implying the whole shift of sympa-

---

[23] *Shakespeare Quarterly*, 39 (1988), 27–44.
[24] *Comparative Literature*, 39 (1987), 356–62.

thies which must occur when the play is received into a culture where, according to the Confucian ethical code, 'Filial obedience is as absolute as paternal authority' (p. 358).

Judging from the three titles which have appeared in the Harvester New Critical Introductions to Shakespeare, it promises to be a strong series, but not for quite the reasons envisaged by the General Editor. Graham Bradshaw at least implies a hope that the series will exemplify 'contemporary approaches' while also, more traditionally, dealing with stage history and sources. In fact, none of the books so far published has been based on an identifiable new literary theory, and each has dealt perfunctorily with theatre and sources. What we get, however, are three discrete and interesting works from sound critics who are given enough space to develop arguments. Jane Adamson's account of *Troilus and Cressida* (Brighton: Harvester Press, 1987) is the most comprehensive in its coverage of the text. Adamson combines sharp observation of dramatic moments with an overall conception of the play. She values the contradictions and 'at-oddedness' in the action without trying to smooth out the bumps or turn them into 'problems'. 'The juxtapositions work not to cancel one thing with another but to make us question everything, see it from several angles at once' (p. 43). The book is written in a functional style which can rise to powerful moments when required. After Adamson's carefully indignant rebuttal of unsympathetic accounts of Cressida, this character should no longer be reduced to a knowing 'daughter of the game', for the game is not of her making. (On the other hand, Adamson lets Troilus off far too lightly.) While the firmly held concept of drama as existing in dialogue and relationships is of course a healthy corrective to the many abstract, thematic studies, it does tend to restrict the range of considerations in dealing with this particular play. If only the eyes could be lifted at times to take in Shakespeare's treatment of myth, the presence of a new form

of meta-history which contemplates history in the making, and the Brechtian possibilities raised by the 'at-oddedness' which Adamson memorably defines. Whilst on this play, we can note C. C. Barfoot's article, '*Troilus and Cressida*: "Praise us as we are tasted"',[25] which returns us to the common theme of 'value', this time in terms of trade and commerce reflected in puns and imagery.

The emphases on dramatic context, characterization, and 'ambivalences' of point of view also mark Harriett Hawkins' *Measure for Measure* (Brighton: Harvester Press, 1987). It is cause for thanks that Hawkins has at last had room to expand her missionary-like work on this play which has been pursued over many years. What exhilarates one about her account is the strenuous assertion of clear, demystifying *logic*. She has the ability to shame those critics who deal with themes and 'problems', making them seem woolly-headed in contrast with her own sharp concentration upon who does what, when, and why. The play is seen as a 'tragi-comic treatment of erring humanity' (p. 124), infused with a compassion and charity that encourage us to view

with sympathy and understanding, the least sympathetic of human beings ... It is the critical (and directorial) dialectic, not the Shakespearian dialectic, that prohibits certain sympathetic (or hostile) responses to the individual characters. (pp. 124–5)

The play's greatness, Hawkins argues, lies not in its capacity to make us puzzle over abstract issues but to provoke speculation and passionate responses centred on moral conflicts facing the characters.

The third book in the series, Wilbur Sanders' *The Winter's Tale* (Brighton: Harvester Press, 1987) tends to avoid conceptual arguments and questions altogether, in favour of a delicately monitored concentration on the tone of particular moments and encounters between characters. Many of these tones are captured with sensitivity, and Sanders is

---

[25] *Shakespeare Quarterly*, 39 (1988), 45–57.

especially moving when he speaks of loss and grief. But there is something quaintly reminiscent of an older Cambridge, *Scrutiny* style, and the references to Leavis, James Smith and their ilk do not contradict this impression.

Articles and essays on aspects of single plays are a vast army ever advancing, drawing on an apparently endless number of recruits. Some appear in collections of essays on various subjects and some in journals. *Shakespeare in India*, edited by S. Nagarajan and S. Viswanath (New Delhi: Oxford University Press, 1987), collects papers read at the University of Hyderabad in 1984 in the first of a series of annual seminars. Two papers at least will be of use to future researchers. Anjana Desai has compared five adaptations of *Coriolanus* (by Dennis, Tate, Piachaud, Brecht and Osborne) with the Shakespearian text (pp. 53–78). The piece concentrates on the theatrical changes, and others will want to explore and expand the briefly illuminating comments on the ways in which the play has been used to present political points of view at crucial moments of history. Sudhakar Marathe's 'Eliot and Shakespeare: A New Perspective' (pp. 79–97) is 'new' in its concentration not on what Eliot can tell us about Shakespeare but on the ways in which Eliot's language echoes Shakespeare's. It will be of interest especially to reader-response critics. There is also a gem of an essay from Molly Mahood – one of the best of the year – on 'Minimal Characters in *King Lear*' (pp. 18–34). Using the audacious method of examining the roles and ethical stances of characters who have only a few words or lines to speak (almost invariably 'good' people), she manages to light up many aspects of the larger conflicts in the play. The Shakespeare that emerges is one who hearkened back to the feudal values of community solidarity, standing against Machiavellian individualism. Her comments on the bravery of Cornwall's servant are unforgettable.

'Fanned and Winnowed Opinions': Shakesperean Essays Presented to Harold Jenkins, edited by John W. Mahon and Thomas A. Pendleton (London: Methuen, 1987), is an offering richly deserved by its distinguished recipient. Professor Jenkins's equally distinguished cohort in general editorship of the Arden Shakespeare series, Harold Brooks, opens the collection with an urbane consideration of the generic problems of *Troilus and Cressida*, and suitably enough there are contributions from other Arden editors: Brian Gibbons (on the conscious fictiveness in *As You Like It*), Arthur Humphreys (on the movement from 'antithesis to synthesis' observed in Shakespeare's unfolding use of history throughout his writing career), E. A. J. Honigmann ('Sir John Oldcastle: Shakespeare's Martyr'), Kenneth Palmer (on the protean rhetoric of Iago), and Kenneth Muir ('Shakespeare and Massinger: Resemblances and Contrasts'). The new General Editor of the Arden, Richard Proudfoot, offers a brief, historically based essay suggesting analogues for Gertrude as an exemplar of woman's frailty and discussing her possible complicity in the murder of old Hamlet, at least in the eyes of the young Hamlet. Non-Arden editors seem like gatecrashers at the party, but they end up stealing the show with the liveliest essays. The two most searching are Ruth Nevo's reading of *All's Well*, a development of her Freudian readings reviewed above, and Sandra Clark's '"Wives may be merry and yet honest too": Women and Wit in *The Merry Wives of Windsor* and Some Other Plays'. Antony Hammond presents an interesting argument about the 'plural text' through the reader's apprehensions of contradictory patterns in *Henry V*. John W. Mahon is entertaining on the significances of meals ('conviviality and conflict'), while Thomas A. Pendleton offers us the kind of firm statement that can help other scholars:

There is no earlier play that utilizes the device of the disguised duke as it is utilized in common by *The Phoenix*, *The Malcontent*, and *Measure for Measure*.

(p. 81)

Alistair Fowler displays the structural and numerological approach (with schematic results, for better or worse) that is associated with his name in an analysis of scene-balancing in *Hamlet*. George Walton Williams sifts evidence like a prosecuting lawyer to conclude that there was political skulduggery ('a little shuffling') behind Claudius' succession to the throne.

On the other side of the Atlantic, *The Huntington Library Quarterly* honours one of its luminaries with a number dedicated to Hallett Smith (volume 50, number 3, 1987). Since Smith's interests encompassed the whole Elizabethan range, we find essays dealing with Holinshed, Nashe, Spenser, and, from the later period, 'Lycidas'. But Shakespearian essays predominate. Smith himself traces the ways in which Shakespeare learned from his own practice in the 'giant step' he took from the chronicle *Henry V* to the complex, tragic depiction of Brutus. Roland Mushat Frye examines the equally giant step taken by Macbeth in Act I from an apparently decent, conscientious man to a king-killer, while Arthur Humphreys finds 'Two Readings of Life' (one harsh and audacious, the other generous and romantic) by comparing *The Jew of Malta* and *The Merchant of Venice*. I find both plays fairly harsh. R. A. Foakes attempts to explain the demise of *Hamlet* in the early 1960s and the rise of *King Lear* in critics' estimation by an impressionistic reading of mid-twentieth century British history. Judging from the section above, it can no longer be said that *Hamlet* is in eclipse.

Cherrell Guilfoyle, mentioned above in the section on *Hamlet*, has also contributed two short source studies of *King Lear*[26] and *Othello*[27] respectively, in which she argues convincingly for an Arthurian background to the former and a connection with the Charlemagne Romances (revived in Shakespeare's day by Spenser) in the latter. The links between Shakespeare and medieval romance are sorely in need of thorough study. Still on

source studies, Robert P. Merrix suggests that the Ovidian allusion in Richard II's 'Down, down I come like glist'ring Phaethon' (3.3.177) is an indication that Richard 'has assumed a false identity – the God-protected and thus impotent king'.[28] Maurice Hunt argues in 'Compelling Art in *Titus Andronicus*'[29] that quotations from and allusions to earlier writers, especially Ovid, belong to the characters and express their attitudes to situations rather than necessarily implying an authorial point of view.

Many critics have considered the importance of money and economic motives in *The Merchant of Venice*, but few have considered doing so for *Measure for Measure*. Nigel Smith argues[30] that in the latter monetary imagery is used insistently enough to place the play at a time when 'money was emerging as an autonomous force from the notion that it should be controlled by a moral law':

The co-existence of money as metaphor with a presentation of the real power of money and wealth makes the play difficult and resistant to a clear comprehension of the patterns of thought in the language. (p. 228)

Christopher Roark, beginning with the role of Lavatch, whose comments significantly mirror situations in which Helena finds herself, moves towards an interpretation of *All's Well That Ends Well* that emphasizes the metaphor of pregnancy in multiple forms.[31] Just as contradictory elements create questionable closures in this play, the tragedies are seen

---

26 'The Way to Dover: Arthurian Imagery in *King Lear*', *Comparative Drama*, 21 (1987), 214–28.

27 'Othello, Otuel, and the English Charlemagne Romances', *Review of English Studies*, NS 38 (1987), 50–5.

28 'The Phaeton Allusion in *Richard II*: The Search for Identity', *English Literary Renaissance*, 17 (1987), 277–87.

29 *Studies in English Literature: 1500–1900*, 28 (1988), 197–218.

30 'The Two Economies of *Measure for Measure*', *English*, 36 (1987), 197–232.

31 'Lavatch and Service in *All's Well That Ends Well*', *Studies in English Literature*, 28 (1988), 241–58.

to be born out of its increasingly realistic vision.

Kathryn L. Lynch returns to an old preoccupation with hands in *Macbeth*, and she traces the emblematic and traditional significances of hands through medieval thought.[32]

A. P. Riemer's 'Deception in *The Winter's Tale*'[33] is an examination not only of the thematic use of deception but also the deceptions practised by the dramatist upon his audience. Riemer seeks to return the play from the literary and poetic fields to the theatrical. Helmut Castrop ponders the generic problems of the play in 'Romanze, Tragikomödie und Satyrspiel in *The Winter's Tale*',[34] and in the same volume of *Deutsche Shakespeare-Gesellschaft West Jahrbuch*, Brian Gibbons reassesses *Cymbeline* from the point of view of its historical content.[35] Genre seems inadvertently to be the theme of this volume, since we also have Wolfgang Weiss's '*Measure for Measure* – Eine satirische Komödie?'.[36]

David Ward in '"Now I will believe that there are unicorns": *The Tempest* and its Theatre'[37] examines the ways in which the audience is implicated in making certain decisions – whether 'it will accept or refuse the initial dramatic premisses' (p. 98), whether it will see the action as a trial, a judgement, or an initiation into self-understanding. On a deeper level, we are involved in a debate based on 'a calculated ambivalence about the ethics of power, of artistry' (p. 100). It all starts from the discrepancies between Gonzalo's, Antonio's, and Sebastian's reports of the island and the wetness or dryness of their garments. The play as a whole, Ward argues, tests

a series of perspectives upon reality, in which the nature of truth and the nature of falsehood are questioned, strained, altered, tested in the theatre's alchemical crucible.   (p. 109)

SONNETS AND POEMS

Shakespeare set his greatest practical joke in just two lines of the Sonnets: 'Your name from hence immortal life shall have' (Sonnet 81); and 'flesh stays no farther reason, / But, rising at thy name, doth point out thee / As his triumphant prize' (Sonnet 151). Having stressed the importance of two 'names' in particular, why could he not have told us who they were, saving us all the bother? It might be better, however, that he kept his secret, since the questions of the identities of the young man, the dark lady, and the rival poet have led to one of the most entertaining genres in Shakespearian criticism. Such books always begin by sweeping away all older theories as so much rubbish in the way and then advance a new one, only to see it in time swept away by the next sailor lured onto the rocks. K. D. Sethna is well aware of the dangers, and of Auden's dismissal of such an attempt as that of a 'fool', but he none the less chooses to pursue the matter in *'Two Loves and a Worthier Pen': The Enigmas of Shakespeare's Sonnets: An Identification Through a New Approach* (New Delhi: Arnold-Heinemann, 1984; it has just reached the *Survey*). Like the best representatives of this genre, Sethna's book reads as an excellent detective story. The 'New Approach' is through the method of 'internal chronology', scouring the Sonnets for clues about when they were written and how old each protagonist was at each stage, then matching up the findings to any available external facts. I should not spoil the plot by revealing the ending, but our readers deserve some notice. The Sonnets are dated later than usual (1598–

---

32 '"What Hands Are Here?" The Hand as Generative Symbol in *Macbeth*', *Review of English Studies*, NS 39 (1988), 29–38.

33 'Deception in *The Winter's Tale*', *Sydney Studies in English*, 13 (1987–8), 21–38.

34 *Deutsche Shakespeare-Gesellschaft West Jahrbuch 1987* (see note 7 above), 57–77.

35 'Fabled *Cymbeline*', *Deutsche Shakespeare-Gesellschaft West Jahrbuch 1987*, 78–99

36 *Deutsche Shakespeare-Gesellschaft West Jahrbuch 1987*, 44–56.

37 *English*, 36 (1987), 95–110.

1607); the friend is (not unconventionally) William Herbert; and there were not one but three rival poets; two 'minor competitors', Francis Davison and Samuel Daniel, and one 'major' one, Ben Jonson. For the dark lady, Sethna inspects Shakespeare's puns and concludes that she was a swarthy Italian woman with a double-barrelled name, Anastasia-Guglielma. He cannot actually find anybody of that name, which is all the better because it starts off a no doubt even more fascinating hunt. The whole enterprise is closely reasoned, absorbing to read, and, like all the rest, 'not proven'. I prefer Oscar Wilde's foray into the field, conjuring up a beautiful boy-actor, master-mistress of Shakespeare's passion, since it claims to be nothing but fiction. Or failing that, the charming scenario created by Barbara Everett of an Anne Hathaway who, not realizing that the 'creative and haunted solitude' of the Sonnets would ensure them oblivion in contemporary readers' estimation, packed off with her brother to a publishing house in London 'the bundle of fair-copied, brilliant, confused poems which her obstinate husband wouldn't publish and which she in any case remembered, rightly or wrongly, as being addressed to herself and therefore arguably her own'.[38]

Speculation is not for David K. Weiser. At the outset of *Mind in Character: Shakespeare's Speaker in the Sonnets* (Columbia: University of Missouri Press, 1987) he solemnly claims to speak of the text, the whole text and nothing but the text. He scornfully rejects 'theory' of any kind:

I do not intend another prologomena for future studies of the reader in the text and/or the text in the reader. I simply have written what I think the sonnets are about, what they say and how they say it. (p. vii)

Nothing is ever as simple as this when there are dedicated ideology-hunters around. The trouble with such fine and ingenuous statements is that even when a writer does not intend a theoretical study, there is always and inevitably a theory behind what the book says, and by refusing directly to disclose or justify it the writer in fact lays himself open to the charge of *dis*ingenuousness. The unstated but pervasive theory behind Weiser's book is that literature exists neither for readers nor writers but for critics, who can exercise their ingenuity in creating patterns and formal classification. He divides the Sonnets first into four major modes: the impersonal, where an anonymous speaker addresses an unspecified audience; the self-effacing, where 'I' is excluded in favour of 'you' or 'thou'; soliloquy, a vehicle for introspection; and dialogue, where the other is a co-partner in discourse. The classification has a conceptual neatness that lifts it into the realms of 'theory' whether the writer intends it or not. When we find each of these categories subdivided into three or four sub-groups, we realize that the underlying theory is a version of formalism, and we suspect the author is more interested in his *schemata* than in the expressiveness of the 'texts'. Certainly, there is ample close criticism of some sonnets, but the intention is to substantiate the classificatory system and also (often ingeniously) to find internal linkages within a poem. However, the tonal shifts within and between sonnets – intimacy, hortation, haughtiness, ruefulness, anger, and so on – are lost. John C. Coldewey presents the clever suggestion that in Sonnet 73 we have what the Quarto gave us, bare, ruined 'quiers' (the printer's term for a stitched gathering of papers as part of the binding process).[39] This reading can make sense of the specificity of the yellow leaves or none or few, and produces an overall meaning which is an ageing poet's self-reflexive comment on 'the frailty of the poetic endeavour' (p. 7), but it would have been more safely advanced as a pun rather than as an exclusive

---

[38] 'Mrs Shakespeare', *London Review of Books*, 18 December 1986, 7–10.

[39] "'Bare rn'wd quiers": Sonnet 73 and Poetry, Dying', *Philological Quarterly*, 67 (1988), 1–9.

interpretation. The idea is valuable and should not be lost.

R. Rawdon Wilson sees the self-reflexive quality of narrative in *The Rape of Lucrece* as anticipating the functions of inset narrative in the plays.[40] There is something interesting in this idea, but the way the article is written tends to obscure it. In particular, the unusual word 'focalize' is given too much work to do. Much clearer is an article by Barbara Hardy dealing with almost the same idea in the context of a play, 'Aspects of Narration in *King Lear*'.[41]

Finally, John Klause in '*Venus and Adonis*: Can We Forgive Them?', *Studies in Philology*, 85 (1988), pp. 353–77, works from the aspect of the poem which used to be condemned as an artistic flaw but is now seen as its great strength – the 'pluralistic' and ambivalent range of attitudes it elicits. Klause examines what lies beneath such responses, arguing that the poem's irony becomes a plea for judgemental charity, enforcing upon the reader a willingness to forgive faults and even wickedness. It is, in the phrase borrowed from R. G. Hunter, a comedy of forgiveness, which sums up precisely the spirit in which this reviewer hopes to be read. If we shadows have offended...

[40] 'Shakespearean Narrative: *The Rape of Lucrece* Reconsidered', *Studies in English Literature*, 28 (1988), 39–59.
[41] *Deutsche Shakespeare-Gesellschaft West Jahrbuch 1987* (see note 6 above), 100–8.

2. SHAKESPEARE'S LIFE, TIMES, AND STAGE
reviewed by RICHARD DUTTON

Lives, like texts, may be read many ways. Peter Levi's *The Life and Times of William Shakespeare* is the reading of a distinguished poet and Oxford Professor of Poetry, immersed in and thrilled by the range of Shakespeare's verse, but less conversant with the scholarship of Elizabethan history, particularly theatrical history, and essentially out of sympathy with the modern 'reductionist' strain of academic Shakespearian biography, pre-eminently represented by S. Schoenbaum's *Compact Documentary Life*.[1] The temperamental difference between the two 'readings' is best indicated by their reactions to 'The Phoenix and Turtle'. Schoenbaum originally overlooked the poem altogether, but grudgingly describes it in the revised edition as 'a much discussed curiosity ... [which] shows Shakespeare in the unfamiliar role of nonce poet' (pp. 327–8). For Levi, it 'is the most breathtaking of all his poems, and I have heard old critics, devoted to poetry of many kinds all their lives, agree on it as the greatest poem in the English language' (p. 214). Shakespeare the writer of supreme verse, rather than Shakespeare the practical man of theatre, is Levi's hero, and there is nothing inherently wrong with that – odd though it may sound to late twentieth-century ears. The problem is that Levi has chosen to write a 'Life and Times', in which appreciations of the works emerge from attempts at a comprehensive contextual biography, and the resulting mix is often oil-and-water. The issue is at its most disturbing when Levi's appreciations, based on an acute ear and refined sensibility, begin to dictate to questions of fact or conjecture: '*The Two Noble Kinsmen* ... has overawed a number of scholars, but Shakespeare did not write it' (p. 64); 'sonnet 145 [with its possible pun on Anne Hathaway's name] does fit very neatly between its neighbours in the collection. The suggestion that it is meant to do so

[1] Peter Levi, *The Life and Times of William Shakespeare* (London, 1988); S. Schoenbaum, *William Shakespeare: A Compact Documentary Life*, revised edition (New York and Oxford: Oxford University Press, 1987).

was made by Andrew Gurr in *Essays in Criticism* in 1971 and must stand until it is demolished, which it has not yet been. I find it almost too tasteless to credit, but not quite' (p. 40). This mixture of patrician judgement and uneasy deference to scholarship is typical of the book as a whole. A little more *attention* to the scholarship of Gurr and others would certainly not have been amiss throughout the text. We are told that 'threepence, then sixpence, was the minimum entry fee [to the public theatres] and it was up to a shilling by the end of the reign' (p. 46), while Drayton rather than Daniel is credited with the *First Four Books of the Civil Wars* (p. 181 – a confusion with the *Mortimeriados*?).[2] We are told that 'Shakespeare was now working for the Chamberlain' (p. 135), an odd summation of the facts of dramatic patronage, while Sir Henry Herbert's comment on relicensing *The Winter's Tale* 'though the allowed book was missing' elicits: 'This confirms that the precise text of the play as permitted was supposed to be the text printed, though in fact it might have perished or been altered in revivals' (p. 311). This thoroughly confuses the processes of 'allowance' for performance (signified by the Master of the Revels's licence at the end of a scribal master-copy of the text) with 'allowance' for print. Such confusions are compounded by a variety of mistakes that really ought to have disappeared at proof stage (e.g. Master of the Rolls several times for Master of the Revels; Northwick for Northwich; numerous mislineations; 'half of [*All's Well That Ends Well*] is in prose and of that half about eighteen per cent is in rhyme', p. 239).

There must be fundamental doubts about whether Levi was well advised to take on a book of this scope, rather than sticking to an appreciation of Shakespeare's verse. These doubts are at their most acute in respect of the 'discovery' associated with the book, but portentously rushed into print by the publishers earlier in the year in *A Private Commission: New Verses by Shakespeare*, a twenty-eight page

booklet, and heavily leaked to *The Independent* newspaper on 22 April 1988 (no. 478, p. 17). The verses are for a masque called *The Entertainment of the Dowager Countess of Derby*, given in 1607, and would clearly be uniquely significant as the only piece of drama known to have been privately commissioned from Shakespeare. Unfortunately, the W.Sh. or W.Sk. of the signature (possibly tampered with by John Payne Collier, and all the more suspect for that) almost certainly belongs to Sir William Skipwith (died 1610) rather than to Shakespeare.[3] The manuscript was neither as unknown nor as unregarded as Professor Levi apparently assumed. The 'discovery' appears in *The Life and Times of William Shakespeare* as the first of eleven appendices, all of less usefulness than proper annotation and an efficient index would have been.

A *cause célèbre* from an earlier, hardly less controversial 'reading' of Shakespeare's life, has resurfaced. Roger Prior has revived A. L. Rowse's suggestion that the 'Dark Lady' of the Sonnets was Emilia Lanier (née Bassano). Stanley Wells seriously undermined Rowse's case by pointing out that a phrase in a manuscript which the latter had read as 'very brown in youth' actually said 'very brave in youth'.[4] As Schoenbaum laconically put it, 'It is useful for a Dark Lady to be demonstrably dark' (p. 170); Levi remains open-minded if sympathetic to the identification: 'If coherence and coincidence of detail could make a proof, Rowse's case would be proved' (p. 106). What Prior has done (building on the researches of

---

2 The admission charges are way out of line, for example, with Andrew Gurr's findings in *The Shakespearean Stage*, revised edition (Cambridge, 1980), pp. 197–8, but are not substantiated.

3 See, for example, the comments of James Knowles and I. A. Shapiro, quoted in *The Guardian*, 27 April 1988, p. 2.

4 Rowse first made the suggestion in his *Shakespeare the Man* (London, 1973), pp. 106ff. Wells pointed out the misreading in *The Times Literary Supplement*, 11 May 1973, p. 528.

Anselm Bassano and Peter Goodwin – the former no relation of the lady, though the latter is ironically descended from her uncle) is to expand the range of coherence and coincidence, and to establish an association with darkness that Rowse's manuscript failed to give.[5] The Bassano family crest is a silkworm moth proper; the upper half of the shield depicts three silkworm moths, the lower half a mulberry tree. The associations are with the Italian silk trade, which strongly suggests that they were Jewish. Moreover, the Italian for mulberry tree is 'moro', which also means 'Moor' or 'negro', or as an adjective, 'black'. Heraldically (and Shakespeare's own coat of arms, with its spear, reflects the punning on identities the Elizabethans indulged in) Emilia was a Moor and 'black', whatever her personal colouring. And what of the mulberry tree that, legend has it, Shakespeare himself planted at New Place? It is an intriguingly rich set of possibilities. Emilia Lanier features in her own right in one of *English Literary Renaissance*'s invaluable bibliographies, Elizabeth H. Hageman's 'Recent Studies in Women Writers of the English Seventeenth Century'.[6] That appears in a second special 'Women in the Renaissance' issue of the journal, several items in which will be of interest to Shakespearians: I single out two of these in another context, below, regretfully omitting for reasons of space those strictly beyond the scope of this review.[7]

The *Dictionary of Literary Biography* represents biography of a less speculative kind than we have considered thus far. With volumes 58 (Jacobean and Caroline Dramatists) and 62 (Elizabethan Dramatists) it brings together biographical outlines of all of the major, and many of the minor, playwrights of the Shakespearian period.[8] The dividing line between the two volumes is inevitably rather arbitrary, and they are meant to be companion pieces; Shakespeare, Jonson, Chapman, Dekker and Thomas Heywood are among the Elizabethans, while Middleton, Webster and Marston are among the Jacobeans and Carolines. Given the inclusion of someone like Sir John Denham, on the strength of one play, and of entries on individual anonymous plays, like *Arden of Faversham, Mucedorus,* and *A Yorkshire Tragedy,* some of the omissions are surprising: nothing on George Gascoigne, John Heywood (though Nicholas Udall is here from the earlier generation), Robert Wilson, Thomas Nashe, Henry Chettle, Robert Armin, Thomas Drue, or William Heminges, for example, though it is possible that some of these will appear in subsequent (non-dramatic) volumes in the series, and total comprehensiveness may be beyond even this massive series. Perhaps a more serious issue is the level of address of the entries that are included, which are uniformly sound and scholarly, though rather mixed in their pitch. Each entry is preceded by dates of birth and death (for some Jacobeans and Carolines this includes details of immediate family, education, marriage, and place of birth and death); a chronological list of all dramatic works, with place and date of first performance, if known; a chronological list of early editions of all works (dramatic and non-dramatic) with details of printers and booksellers where known; details of principal modern editions. The main biographical essay is followed by details of bibliographies, biographies, a listing (necessarily quite select in some cases) of other criticism and scholarship,

---

[5] 'More (Moor? Moro?) light on the Dark Lady', *Financial Times*, 10 October 1987, Weekend Section, p. xvii.

[6] *English Literary Renaissance*, 18 (1988), 138–67.

[7] Especially of interest will be: Gabrielle Bernhard Jackson, 'Topical Ideology: Witches, Amazons, and Shakespeare's Joan of Arc', pp. 40–65; Susan Snyder, *'All's Well That Ends Well* and Shakespeare's Helens: Text and Subtext, Subject and Object', pp. 66–77; Suzanne Gossett, '"Man-maid, begone!": Women in Masques', pp. 96–113.

[8] *The Dictionary of Literary Biography*, volume 58 (Jacobean and Caroline Dramatists) and volume 62 (Elizabethan Dramatists), both edited by Fredson Bowers (Detroit: Gale Research Company, 1987).

and the whereabouts of surviving manu-scripts. Besides these, the text is very liberally broken up with photographic reproductions of title-pages and other prefatory matter of early editions, illustrations from masques and other texts, portraits, and a wide range of manu-scripts (including, for example, the whole of the fragment from a lost play dubbed *The Duke of Florence* and tentatively ascribed to Webster, put up for auction in 1986). The quality of reproduction of the manuscripts would preclude the most intensive study, and one could quibble with details (John F. Andrews's Shakespeare entry, for example, implies that all public performances of his plays between 1594 and late 1599 were at The Theatre, when many argue that the Chamber-lain's Men used The Curtain 1597–99), but all of this is extremely useful reference material for scholars and graduate students. By com-parison, the biographical essays themselves, though well written and accurate in their detail, seem rather anodyne. They are con-tinuous narratives, surveying the life, offering brief descriptions of the dramatic works and key points of interest, and saying something in general terms about their modern reception: they seem on the whole to be addressed to undergraduates and general readers. To take an (admittedly extreme) example, I have recently been interested in Lodowick Carlell's *Osmond, the Great Turk.* Is the 1657 text we have the play to which Sir John Astley refused a licence in 1622, but was overruled by the Lord Chamberlain? If so, why does the title-page ascribe it to 'the Queenes Majesty's Ser-vants' when Astley explicitly dealt with the King's Men? Why, in any case, is Osmond described as 'the Great Turk' when he is not the Emperor but the 'Noble Servant' of the sub-title? None of this is touched on in Karen Woods's otherwise unexceptionable discuss-ion of Carlell. A more familiar example: Andrews mentions the discrepancy between the quarto Epistle's description of *Troilus and Cressida* as a comedy and its placement in the

First Folio between the histories and the trage-dies; there are also reproductions of the variant introductory pages to the 1609 Quarto. So all the conundrums about the play – its generic indeterminacy, whether it was ever staged, and if so where – are on display, but hardly discussed. The essays do not seek to grapple with 'facts and problems': at best they acknowledge their existence, not even opting to refer us to more detailed discussions. To some this will seem an opportunity missed, particularly in respect of the lesser dramatists, who so rarely receive full-scale treatment of any kind. Nevertheless, there is much of sub-stance in these handsomely presented volumes (including helpful appendices to the Eliza-bethan Dramatists volume on 'The Theater in Shakespeare's Time' by Andrew Gurr, 'The Publication of English Renaissance Plays' by Fredson Bowers, and an annotated bibliog-raphy of 'Sources for the Study of Tudor and Stuart Drama' by Albert H. Tricomi) which will warrant their place in all reference li-braries.

The Lord Chamberlain at odds with Astley over *Osmond, the Great Turk* was William Herbert, third Earl of Pembroke, a central figure in Michael G. Brennan's *Literary Patron-age in the English Renaissance: The Pembroke Family.*[9] This surveys the literary patronage of the first four Earls of Pembroke (and, to an extent, of the Sidneys, to whom they were related by the marriage of Mary Sidney, Philip and Robert's sister, to the second earl), placing it within the context of their political careers. It centres very much on 'the Leicester-Sidney-Essex-Prince Henry chain of political descent' (p. 132), to which the third earl was seen as a worthy successor, though it does not claim that such ideological considerations dominated the practice of patronage to the exclusion of other factors. Indeed, although Brennan acknowledges that literary and political

---

[9] London and New York: Routledge, 1988.

patronage might sometimes go hand in hand (pp. 155–6), he has no clearly formulated view of the relationship between the two, or of the status of literature as an adjunct of power: his history is very much revisionist, rather than cultural materialist. At the same time (partly a consequence of covering a century in two hundred pages) he is resolutely unspeculative. For example, Thomas Scot's *Vox Populi* pamphlets are mentioned in connection with the anti-Spanish feeling of the early 1620s (p. 170), and again as sources for Middleton's *A Game at Chess*, in which famous scandal 'Pembroke may ... have been influential behind the scenes' (p. 175), but Brennan makes nothing of the DNB claim that in 1622 Scot was employed as Pembroke's chaplain – potentially a more tangible linking of literary/political patronage than emerges here. Similarly, though he refers to the third earl's role in helping his kinsman, Sir Henry Herbert, to buy the Mastership of the Revels from Astley, he does not examine its occurrence in the context of a struggle by Pembroke (almost certainly with Buckingham) to maintain the Lord Chamberlain's traditional claims to patronage over that post. The Shakespearian connections with the Herberts (including the dedication of the First Folio) are touched upon in the same unspeculative way: the possibility of William as the 'W.H.' of the Sonnets is left open, the reference to Shakespeare as present at Wilton for a performance of *As You Like It* in December 1603 dismissed as a Victorian fabrication. Overall, the book is useful and clearly written, but not as challenging as it might be.

Astley, Herbert, and the two Pembrokes who were Lord Chamberlain continuously from 1615–1641 are among the principals whose activities surface from time to time in the *Jacobean and Caroline Revels Accounts, 1603–1642*, now scrupulously edited by W. R. Streitberger in another of his significant contributions to our understanding of the Revels Office and its functionaries.[10] The accounts themselves – the Declared Accounts from the Audit and Pipe Offices and the auditors' copies of the Revels Office Books – will mainly be of use to specialists, but there is much here that anyone interested in the drama of the period will find extremely helpful, including Professor Streitberger's Introduction, which gives the most lucid brief account of the Revels Office, its organization and activities, currently available. In the course of this (pp. xi–xiii) he authoritatively clears up the confusion about the transition of the Mastership from Tyllney to Buc: 'neither Buc's signature nor his name appears on any document in any capacity until after Tyllney's death in 1610', though he did receive some retrospective payments for unspecified activities and certainly was the first person connected with the Revels Office (from 1606) to license plays for the press. (It would not have been amiss here to refute yet again the still widely propagated fallacy that Buc was Tyllney's nephew.) Streitberger's summaries of Revels activities at the head of each set of declared accounts are also meticulously clear, being most precise about dates wherever possible in a way that any scholar who consults this book will be grateful for; an appendix of biographical notes is similarly punctilious about dating births, deaths, knighthoods, peerages, court offices and commissions – information not always readily accessible in standard reference books but crucial for a clear understanding of court responsibilities and favour. This is an exemplary piece of scholarship, alongside which I should mention T. H. Howard-Hill's painstaking account of Buc's censorship of Fletcher and Massinger's *Sir John Van Olden Barnavelt*, one of the few plays of

---

[10] *Collections Volume XIII: Jacobean and Caroline Revels Accounts, 1603–1642*, ed. W. R. Streitberger (Oxford: The Malone Society, 1986). Streitberger's *Edmond Tyllney, Master of the Revels and Censor of Plays: A Descriptive Index to His Diplomatic Manual on Europe* (New York, 1986) was mentioned here last year.

the period to survive in manuscript which shows the attentions of a Master of the Revels.[11] As Howard-Hill shows, Buc was uniquely qualified to comment on this play (unusual in itself in its open depiction of recent and very sensitive events), because he knew the principals concerned from his own diplomatic activities in the Low Countries and this is reflected in his detailed attentions to the manuscript. These special circumstances make it difficult to know whether Buc's treatment of his play-book was typical of the censorship to which the Masters of the Revels subjected other plays, but this study is consonant with other recent works on the topic (by, among others, Philip Finkelpearl, Annabel Patterson, Janet Clare, Streitberger, and Howard-Hill himself) which suggest that the censorship was less repressive, less bent on proscribing all discussion of current affairs, than received opinion suggests.

Two other primary 'texts' upon which our understanding of the Shakespearian stage is based, the De Witt/Van Buchell drawing of the Swan Theatre and Henslowe's *Diary*, have received fresh attention. Johan Gerritsen has re-examined the probable relationship between what de Witt may originally have drawn and what van Buchell is likely to have made of it, with results which – while properly tentative – must be very disturbing for anyone using the Swan drawing as serious testimony about the Elizabethan stage.[12] The evidence he adduces suggests that de Witt is unlikely to have sent to van Buchell the drawings he actually made in London; he is more likely to have sent a considered reworking of his own original, made perhaps several years later (with heaven knows what emendations, especially given his stated interest in the building because it reminded him of a Roman amphitheatre). Moreover, Gerritsen demonstrates that van Buchell probably scaled up what de Witt sent him on octavo paper to his own quarto sheets, a process that might well have entailed significant distortion, even if

van Buchell had been a good draughtsman which (contrary to earlier generalized impressions) Gerritsen shows him not to have been: he had a distinct tendency in other architectural sketches to be weak on perspective and to include items that he could not have seen from his chosen perspective but knew or supposed to be there. This is a glass in which we see even more darkly than we formerly supposed.

Henslowe's so-called *Diary* has never been the most perspicuous of documents, even when ably edited, but it is an indispensable mine of information on all aspects of the Elizabethan theatre industry. Neil Carson will thus have answered many prayers in providing *A Companion to Henslowe's 'Diary'*.[13] The central element of this is a functional abstract of the diary's theatrical entries, rendered in tabular form, providing: a chronological list of all the plays mentioned there; performance calendars for the years 1592–7 (keyed numerically to the play list, and showing the takings in daily and weekly totals); details of literary expenses (i.e. payments to authors) and production expenses season by season from 1596/7 to 1602/3, presented on facing pages revealing relative outgoings in these two areas; the consolidated weekly accounts from 1592 to 1603; summaries of all the above. This is all keyed to the original folio pages, and so will be equally helpful to users of the Greg (1904), Foakes-Rickert (1961), and Scolar facsimile (1977) editions. Hardly less useful than all this will be Carson's very substantial introduction in which he reviews the information for what it may tell us of the management of the various

---

11 'Buc and the Censorship of *Sir John Van Olden Barnavelt* in 1619', *Review of English Studies*, NS 39 (1988), 39–63.

12 Johan Gerritsen, 'De Witt, Van Buchell, The Swan and The Globe', originally published in *Essays in Honour of Kristian Smidt*, ed. Peter Bilton *et al.* (Oslo: University of Oslo Press, 1986), pp. 29–46. Reviewed here from an offprint, reprinted with corrections and an extra plate, copyright the author, 1988.

13 Cambridge: Cambridge University Press, 1988.

companies with which Henslowe was associated in this period, professional relationships between actors, playwrights, and entrepreneurs like Henslowe, and the ways in which plays were commissioned, written, rehearsed, and brought into the repertoire. The Henslowe who (I think convincingly) emerges here is not a barely literate, disorganized usurer, as the Victorians sometimes conceived him to be, but a relatively compassionate and efficient businessman who succeeded in an industry he knew very well.

The Revels Accounts and Henslowe's *Diary* remind us of the daily economic realities of Renaissance theatre, both in its close association with the court and as an example of capitalist enterprise. Two new books concentrate on a very different dimension of its existence, on its anthropological origins outside the established social structures and containments of its day. In *Creating Elizabethan Tragedy: The Theater of Marlowe and Kyd* the late C. L. Barber combines a complex sense of the historical moment of Elizabethan drama with Freudian models of behaviour to investigate how 'the new institution, the Elizabethan public theater, could free itself from traditional ways of framing human experience, institutionalised by church and state, and make its vital, historical contribution to a new understanding of human possibility' (p. 31).[14] The words are those of Richard P. Wheeler, in an illuminating introduction which not only describes how he pieced the book together from Barber's successive redraftings over nearly twenty years (editing is a wholly inadequate term for what he has done) but also 'places' Barber's achievement, particularly in relation to subsequent New Historicist criticism, with which it has clear affinities if also important differences. The main substance of the book is three sustained essays on *Tamburlaine*, *Dr Faustus*, and *The Spanish Tragedy*, each a text which translates religious instincts ('worship') into secular obsessions in ways pregnant with possibilities for the generation

of Elizabethan/Jacobean dramatists to follow. The book is perhaps too late (too much anticipated in print) to be as influential for the study of tragedy as *Shakespeare's Festive Comedy* was for that of comedy, but it is no less cogent a work, particularly suggestive in the ways it refuses to reduce 'religious' and 'revenge' drama to simplistic categories.

Steven Mullaney is a full-blooded New Historicist (or, as he prefers, cultural materialist, pp. x–xi). His *The Place of the Stage: License, Play, and Power in Renaissance England* examines the siting of the main Elizabethan playhouses in the 'Liberties', just outside the jurisdiction of the City of London, not simply as an expedient ploy, but in relation to the traditional status of those necessary but unloved No Man's Lands, the sanctioned sites of leper hospitals, mad-houses, places of execution and formal exile, and semi-sanctioned sites of brothels, which paradoxically confirmed the authority of those who had no legal control over them: 'The playhouses were a scandal: that is to say, they made apparent a tradition of cultural license that had always reigned in the Liberties, but whose subversive potential had remained latent, to an extent mystified or obscured by the ceremonial needs and pretensions of the community. If the margins had not for centuries said what they did, Elizabethan drama would not have been able to shape the audacious method it did.'[15] Readers familiar with the writings of Stephen Greenblatt, Louis Montrose, and others will know to expect (and either relish or abhor) a slow circularity of argument, an ingenious accumulation of *exempla*-by-analogy, an insistence that the central concerns of this drama are as familiar and modern as the circumstances of its creation are alien and archaic.

---

[14] Edited with an introduction by Richard P. Wheeler (Chicago and London: University of Chicago Press, 1988).

[15] Chicago and London: University of Chicago Press, 1988; the quotation is on p. 47.

The model of the argument is already some-what formulaic, but Mullaney's insights are fresh and frequently illuminating, not least when he applies his general thesis to specific Shakespearian texts – the *Henry IV* plays, *Measure for Measure, Macbeth, Pericles*. Shake-speare provides the examples here (one from each of the four main genres) not because he was in some sense the 'best' dramatist of the period but because he was 'one of the few playwrights whose career encompassed both the height and the decline of popular theater in Elizabethan and Jacobean England' (p. x).

The influence of the 'cult-historicists' (Carol Thomas Neely's helpful, though possibly ironic, conflation of new historicists and cul-tural materialists) is widely apparent, even in the writings of those who do not unequi-vocally share their views. Neely herself con-siders the relationship between feminist prac-tice and these forms of discourse about the Renaissance, looking for ways that 'Shake-speare might be demystified, decentered, de-naturalized, and genuinely historicized; the Renaissance might be not merely reproduced, but reengendered'.[16] Two writers offer reveal-ing accounts of the rhetorical self-fashioning of female royalty at the courts which Shakespeare served: Mary Thomas Crane explores Eliza-beth's own use of a 'symbolic system, that of political counsel' (pointedly distinct from Pet-rarchan, pastoral, and courtly idioms applied to her by male courtier/politicians) 'in order to show how she asserted and protected her authoritative involvement in the making of public policy', while Sara Jayne Steen looks at the letters of Arbella Stuart (who *might* have been queen), which show 'a verbally talented woman giv[ing] rhetorical shape to a self she thought would be more acceptable to a mis-ogynistic king and his court than her un-reformed one ever could be'.[17] When self-presentation may be seen to affect history, the presentation of history itself becomes critically important, a case argued by both A. R. Braun-muller and (in two companion-piece essays)

by Larry S. Champion.[18] Braunmuller quar-rels with the traditional categorization of Elizabethan historical texts into 'naive' chron-icle history (such as Holinshed), dramatic his-tories, and 'sophisticated/politic' history (Camden, Bacon), insisting that the 'essen-tially fictive or recreative is present in all three, and all three operated under similar cultural constraints and threats of censorship or worse' (p. 327). Champion addresses two plays often associated with Shakespeare (by some more strongly than others), *Edward III* and *Edmund Ironside*, though his argument is not about authorship but more generally about the English chronicle history play and the view of human affairs it presents. In the former essay he encapsulates his case: 'Embodying their own internal dialectic, these plays begin to view history as a process of change, as self-determined, as a struggle between aristocratic houses and the monarchic state, between mili-tary and civilian interests, as a conflict regarding matters of succession and inheri-tance – a view of history, in a word, founded in ideological confrontation' (p. 127). Alden T. Vaughan inclines to the 'cult-historicist' con-viction that history is properly what we con-struct today, not what we recover from the past, in his review of the association of Caliban with the American Indians, which he demon-strates to be a fairly recent development though now virtually a truism: '*The Tempest*

16 *English Literary Renaissance*, 18 (1988), 5–18; p. 18.
17 Mary Thomas Crane, '"Video et Taceo": Elizabeth I and the Rhetoric of Counsel', *Studies in English Literature 1500–1900*, 28 (1988), 1–15; pp. 1–2; Sara Jayne Steen, 'Fashioning an Acceptable Self: Arbella Stuart', *English Literary Renaissance*, 18 (1988), 78–95; p. 95.
18 A. R. Braunmuller, '*King John* and Historiography', *ELH*, 55 (1988), 309–32; Larry S. Champion, '"Answere to this Perillous Time": Ideological Ambi-valence in The Raigne of King Edward III and the English Chronicle History Plays', *English Studies*, 69 (1988), 117–29, and '"By Usurpation Thine, By Conquest Mine": Perspective and Politics in *Edmund Ironside*', *Studies in Philology*, 85 (1988), 211–24.

and Caliban retain their American identities, possibly because they represent Shakespeare's vision of the New World and its natives but – more probably and more significantly – because they reflect recurrent themes in American, indeed world, history.'[19] Nothing, finally, could be less 'cult-historicist' than Marc L. Schwarz's report of discovering that the lawyer, Sir Edward Coke, quoted from John of Gaunt's 'This scept'red isle' speech in an address to the Grand Jury at Norwich in 1606 – though one wonders what someone of that persuasion might make of the information.[20] Intriguing in itself as an early example of an establishment appropriation of Shakespeare, it takes on added significance when linked to the fact that Coke was one of the prosecutors in the 1601 Essex trials. Schwarz points out that Coke then referred to 'the story of Henry IV being set forth in a play' (p. 56) in attacking Sir Gelly Meyrick; he assumes that the play performed on the eve of the rebellion was Shakespeare's *Richard II*. This is a common assumption (though cautioned against, notably, by Schoenbaum). The fact that Coke was demonstrably able to quote from that play five years later perhaps tips the scale a little further towards the presumption of Shakespeare's being the play involved. Even so, a leading jurist found one passage in the play, at least, anything but subversive.

The dating of the start of Shakespeare's career is an issue that has rumbled through the four years I have been doing this review. Sidney Thomas, who has figured here in this regard in each of the last two years, has now attempted a reconciliatory overview of the subject.[21] He reviews the evidence for the 'early-start' theory, mainly as advanced by E. A. J. Honigmann, in *Shakespeare's Impact on His Contemporaries* (London, 1982) and *Shakespeare: The 'Lost Years'* (Manchester, 1985), against the 'later-starters', represented by E. K. Chambers and Schoenbaum. He points to a number of apparent weaknesses in Honig-

mann's case, finding Chambers on balance more convincing, but concedes that subjective judgements about style and substance will inevitably weigh heavily in the absence of hard evidence, hoping for temperate debate on a subject which will not go away. Eric Sams, well known for giving short shrift to subjective judgements when he considers there to be evidence hard enough to contradict them, has now turned his guns on a subject at the heart of the Thomas/Honigmann debate, the relationship between *The Troublesome Reign of King John* (1591 Quarto, usually described as anonymous) and *The Life and Death of King John* in the Shakespeare First Folio.[22] His scholarly villains here are Honigmann and Robert Smallwood, as editors respectively of the Arden and New Penguin *King John*s, both of whom complicate matters in his view by constructing unnecessary (and mutually contradictive) arguments about the influence of one text upon the other – arguments about what Sams would regard as plagiarism had either substantiated his case. But: 'Nobody plagiarized Shakespeare; Shakespeare plagiarized nobody. All the *Hamlet*, *Henry V*, *Henry VI*, *Lear*, *Shrew*, and other variant texts, just like the two *King John* plays, represent his own plays at different stages of development' (p. 44). This will not convince everybody, any more than some of Sams's earlier pieces have, but it demands attention as one of the bluntest expositions of what has rapidly emerged as a new orthodoxy: Shakespeare as purposeful reviser of his own plays. The idea that the different texts we have of some of his plays reflect *ad hoc* adaptations within the playhouse,

---

[19] 'Shakespeare's Indians: The Americanization of Caliban', *Shakespeare Quarterly*, 39 (1988), 137–53; p. 153.
[20] 'Sir Edward Coke and "This Scept'red Isle": A Case of Borrowing', *Notes and Queries*, NS 35 (1988), 54–7.
[21] 'On the Dating of Shakespeare's Early Plays', *Shakespeare Quarterly*, 39 (1988), 187–94.
[22] 'The Troublesome Wrangle Over *King John*', *Notes and Queries*, NS 35 (1988), 41–4.

or for specific purposes (court or private performances, for touring outside London) is hardly new. But the debate over the texts of *King Lear* has rapidly installed in people's minds a Shakespeare who repeatedly and deliberately revised his own texts, which is something rather different. Apart from Sams, see pieces by William C. Carroll and Paul Werstine (editorial rather than biographical/background in emphasis) that both work off this premise.[23]

Andrew Gurr puts a stimulating new perspective on a key mid-point in Shakespeare's career, the move to The Globe.[24] This is often projected as a natural development, a new quality of playhouse fit for Shakespeare at his peak. Gurr sees it as a crisis measure, with the blocking of the Blackfriars venture and the failure to renew The Theatre's lease, suggesting that Burbages and the Lord Chamberlain's Men were both squeezed for money – hence the apparent sale of the scripts of *Richard III*, *Richard II*, *1 Henry IV*, and *Love's Labour's Lost* at this juncture and some skimping on the new playhouse (illegal reuse of The Theatre's main timbers, thatched roofing) when it was built. He then goes on to consider the financial illogicality of running two playhouses in tandem once the Blackfriars became available (and the even greater illogicality of rebuilding what might be seen as a redundant Globe in 1613), suggesting it reflects the success of the system of actors sharing in their theatres' management. Whether by design or good fortune, the dual theatres may have protected the King's Men from attacks by the apprentices, such as that on Beeston's Cockpit in 1617, which Gurr insists was not random violence but a sign of resentment against the popular repertoire of the Red Bull being taken out of their price range in the private theatre. Graham F. Barlow has been reconsidering the nature of the Phoenix Theatre that Beeston erected on the ashes of the Cockpit, arguing that it is wrong to discount the evidence of Wenceslas Hollar's *View of West London* (1657)

which, among other things, would seem to render impossible John Orrell's suggestion that the drawings of an Inigo Jones theatre among the Jones/Webb papers at Worcester College, Oxford represent what was built in Drury Lane.[25]

Three articles in *The Theatrical Space*, volume 9 of Themes in Drama, relate specifically to Elizabethan playhouses and their relationship with the audiences they served. Jonathan Haynes considers 'the question of how the space of the theater is related to the space of real life in social-historical terms' (p. 59), approaching the Elizabethan self-consciousness about the theatrical medium (particularly as evinced in numerous inductions) in relation to a self-confidence about the strength of dramatic illusion, to a sense of competition with the audiences themselves (there were two performances going on at once, especially in the private theatres), and to an increased subject-realism in the satiric citizen comedies of the early 1600s. Sharon Tyler approaches the Chorus in *Henry V* as a possible response to Sidney's neoclassical objections to the absurdities of romantic theatre in *The Defence of Poesy* (first published in 1595). And Adrian Weiss argues that Marston's *Antonio* plays did not exploit Paul's Boys in a parodic manner (aping the adult actors) but firmly and deliberately located them within the confines of their own playhouse, its locale and traditions, to facilitate a serious exploration of the revenge genre – an

---

23 William C. Carroll, 'New Plays vs. Old Readings: *The Division of the Kingdoms* and Folio Deletions in *King Lear*', *Studies in Philology*, 85 (1988), 225–44; Paul Werstine, 'The Textual Mystery of *Hamlet*', *Shakespeare Quarterly*, 39 (1986), 1–26.

24 'Money or Audiences: The Impact of Shakespeare's Globe', *Theatre Notebook*, 42 (1988), 3–14.

25 'Wenceslas Hollar and Christopher Beeston's Phoenix Theatre in Drury Lane', *Theatre Research International*, 13 (1988), 30–44. Orrell first advanced his case in *Shakespeare Survey 35*, reprinted in his *The Theatres of Inigo Jones and John Webb* (Cambridge, 1985).

argument with important general applications to the question of the 'little eyases' and possibly also of boys playing women's roles in the public theatres.[26] John Wasson properly reminds us (at this time of another north/south divide) that these sophisticated London theatres were not the only sites for drama in early seventeenth-century England.[27] Drawing in part on the Records of Early English Drama series, he has been tracing the activities of touring companies in the north of England, particularly those associated with Clifford households. They clearly operated on terms that passed away in the London area thirty or forty years before, still patronized by aristocrats like the Earl of Derby, not royalty, possibly never having heard of the Master of the Revels.

It is frequently difficult to draw lines between general influences upon an author, traditions within which he worked, analogues of which he may or may not have been aware, and sources upon which he consciously drew. The following items may all be said to fit one or other of these categories, if (in the case of the first) the nature of language itself may be described as a tradition or an influence. *A Reader in the Language of Shakespearean Drama*, edited by Vivian Salmon and Edwina Burness, brings together thirty-three previously-published essays (all self-contained, not extracted from larger works) in a hefty tome.[28] They cover a wide variety of linguistic topics – grammar (syntax and inflection), vocabulary (including lexical innovation), special colloquial usages, metrics, rhetoric, punctuation, and so on; of the topics one might expect to be represented, only phonetics and stylistics are, to my unskilled eye, conspicuous by their absence. Yet this is distinctly a 'reader' rather than an overview of Shakespeare's language; the essays (photographically reproduced, so that we have a fountain of fonts, a babel of typefaces) are aimed at a varied readership. Some will recognize pieces of a general introductory nature by Randolph Quirk and Brian

Vickers from *A New Companion to Shakespeare Studies*;[29] other essays have valuably been mined from very specialist journals; some are interested in language as a study in itself, others for the light it throws on Shakespeare's artistry. It is very useful to have all this brought together, though I suspect it is a volume that will be dipped into rather than read cover-to-cover.

Shakespeare must have learned a good deal about the possibilities inherent in language from his compulsory attendance at church. Dorothy M. Meade's *The Medieval Church in England* stops before the Reformation and Shakespeare's own time, but is a clearly written account of the institution still intact while his grandparents were growing up and often glimpsed in his English histories, many of whose ceremonies, terms, and traditions were still alive in Shakespeare's own day.[30] A student of Shakespeare could do worse than spend an afternoon finding out about the church year, why priests were called 'Sir', who the real Sir John Oldcastle was, and what happened to him. Helen Peters picks up on a specific item of scripture (1 Corinthians 2), Augustine's writing on dreams, and a Donne sermon dealing with the primacy of sight among the senses to reflect on Bottom's inability to express his 'dream', concluding that

---

[26] *The Theatrical Space*, Themes in Drama, volume 9, ed. James Redmond (Cambridge: Cambridge University Press, 1987): Jonathan Haynes, 'The Elizabethan audience on stage', pp. 59–68; Sharon Tyler, 'Minding true things: the Chorus, the audience, and *Henry V*', pp. 69–80; Adrian Weiss, 'A pill to purge parody: Marston's manipulation of the Paul's environment in the *Antonio* plays', pp. 81–98.

[27] 'Elizabethan and Jacobean Touring Companies', *Theatre Notebook*, 42 (1988), 51–7.

[28] Amsterdam Studies in the Theory and History of Linguistic Science, Series 3: Studies in the History of Language Science (Amsterdam and Philadelphia: John Benjamins Publishing Company, 1987).

[29] Edited by Kenneth Muir and S. Schoenbaum (Cambridge, 1971).

[30] Worthing, Sussex: Churchman Publishing, 1988.

he does remember what has happened to him even though he cannot find the words.[31] In the same play, John W. Velz (to my mind convincingly) posits a passage in Arthur Brooke's *Romeus and Juliet* as a suggestive background to the discussion of Snug's representation of the lion in 'Pyramus and Thisbe': this further advances the already strong case for *A Midsummer Night's Dream* and *Romeo and Juliet* as 'companion plays'.[32]

A Midsummer Night's Dream is often central to discussions of a more contentious 'influence' upon Shakespeare's drama, the folk and carnival festivities of his day. François Laroque's *Shakespeare et la fête* is carefully subtitled *Essai d'archéologie du spectacle dans l'Angleterre élisabéthaine* and described by its author as 'résolument empirique dans son approche d'un domaine encore mal exploré' [resolutely empirical in its approach to a field still ill-explored] (p. 301).[33] That is, what M. Laroque aims to do is to provide a dispassionate (archaeological) account of Elizabethan festive culture and some of the ways that it manifests itself in Shakespeare's plays, rather than to invest the issue with larger political and anthropological dynamics in the manner of Bakhtin, Northrop Frye, C. L. Barber, Peter Stallybrass, and others. It may be culturally disingenuous to pretend that empiricism is not itself ideologically located, but his is a very thorough survey of festive customs and of festive motifs within the drama, and is likely to fuel the wider contentions. Plutarch's *Life of Antony*, the basis for *Antony and Cleopatra*, is one of the most striking of Shakespeare's sources, being a psychologically acute and narratively assured work in its own right – something often not true of the materials from which he forged his plays. G. B. R. Pelling has produced an edition of the *Life* (in the original Greek) with an eye to Shakespearians as potential readers; he acknowledges (p. 37) that Shakespeare's having worked from North's translation (itself based on Amyot's French) did affect some details, but argues that

'borrowings of material, emphasis and characterisation' remain faithful to Plutarch, and so traces the significant borrowings and adaptations through his extensive commentary in ways that illuminate both the original and what Shakespeare made of it.[34] A more pervasive classical influence upon Shakespeare was the poetry of Ovid (particularly, though not exclusively, in Arthur Golding's translation). This has long been acknowledged, though doubts about the seriousness and substance of Ovid as a writer have often muted the point. *Ovid Renewed* is a collection of essays dedicated to demonstrating the inherent quality of Ovid's writing by tracing its remarkable impact on art and literature from the middle ages to T. S. Eliot – often in the face of critical disapproval.[35] Indeed, as David Hopkins points out, an author like Dryden could vividly appropriate Ovid to his verse while formally expressing disapproval in his criticism.[36] Shakespeare is invoked in several contexts, but two essays here are particularly relevant: Laurence Lerner focuses on the epyllion, pointing to the ways in which Marlowe, Shakespeare and the others borrowed from Ovid not only their stories but also his capacity to mix an amused scepticism about their content with a sheer enjoyment of them.[37] A. D. Nuttall ingeniously explores the

---

[31] 'Bottom: Making Sense of Sense and Scripture', *Notes and Queries*, NS 35 (1988), 45–7.

[32] 'Arthur Brooke and the Lion Among Ladies in *A Midsummer Night's Dream*', *Notes and Queries*, NS 35 (1988), 47–9.

[33] Paris: Presses Universitaires de France, 1988.

[34] *Plutarch: Life of Antony*, ed. G. B. R. Pelling, Cambridge Greek and Latin Classics (Cambridge: Cambridge University Press, 1988).

[35] *Ovid Renewed: Ovidian Influences on Literature and Art from the Middle Ages to the twentieth century*, ed. Charles Martindale (Cambridge: Cambridge University Press, 1988).

[36] 'Dryden and Ovid's "Wit Out of Season"', *Ovid Renewed*, pp. 167–90.

[37] 'Ovid and the Elizabethans', *Ovid Renewed*, pp. 121–35.

relationship (one of analogy rather than source) between Ovid's telling of the Narcissus myth and Richard II's self-examination with the aid of a mirror.[38] The process of overreading illuminates both texts, raising a number of intriguing questions about psychological insight, self-knowledge, interiority, and the capacity of literature before the novel to handle such matters.

Mannerism as a style and tragicomedy as a genre are both traditions with which Shakespeare is frequently associated, often simultaneously. John Greenwood's *Shifting Perspectives and the Stylish Style: Mannerism in Shakespeare and His Jacobean Contemporaries* is a lively and informed account of Shakespeare's Jacobean phase in the context of artistic, architectural, and literary fashions in and around the court of King James.[39] He has not entirely overcome the usual problems: 'mannerism' as a critical term has no clearly defined limits, being a descriptive label for one phase (hardly even a movement) in late Renaissance art, many of whose characteristics overlap with what some would call 'baroque'; moreover, as a term relating to the visual arts, it has no direct application to the literary and performed arts (at least, not to theatre until it adopted illusionistic staging): it has to be applied metaphorically or by analogy, usually in connection with self-conscious artifice, a knowingness about the trickery of perspective, sudden shifts of points of view. These are Greenwood's central concerns: 'Much of Shakespeare's Jacobean canon ... can be distinguished from its Elizabethan counterpart by the degree to which the playwright seems concerned with the illusory nature of his art: the meditation is more deliberate and sustained in the Jacobean canon ... As speeches become more frequently and more explicitly self-reflexive, the playwright appears to be exploring both the limits of his own craft and the impact that it has on its audience' (pp. 40–1). It is all a matter of degree, of emphasis, and may or may not have grown out of Shakespeare's

first-hand knowledge of Italian painting and sculpture (Giulio Romano is much invoked, though the riddles are not resolved), or Inigo Jones's stagecraft, or the use of indoor theatres, or the influence of rivals like Marston or Beaumont and Fletcher. It is all very familiar territory, though explored with good sense and a proper appreciation of the limitations of 'our associative method' (p. 186), which pays off in some illuminating readings and comparisons of Shakespeare with, besides those mentioned, Jonson, Webster, and the author of *The Revenger's Tragedy*. Nancy Klein Maguire has assembled a collection of essays, *Renaissance Tragicomedy: Explorations in Genre and Politics*, the core of which derive from MLA sessions in 1983.[40] Such is the current interest in this particular field that some of the contributions here already feel a little dated, though none is without interest. Barbara A. Mowat, for example, is sensibly and fruitfully tentative about employing Guarinian definitions of tragicomedy to Shakespeare's 'problem plays', where subsequent critics have made sweeping claims in this area, linking them with the supposed politics of those plays.[41] It is a striking feature of this essentially pre-New Historicist collection that the essays on English Renaissance tragicomedy are markedly less political in their emphasis (even when they appear in the 'Political Context' section) than those on Spanish and French tragicomedy, though this is not true of the essays by Lois Potter and Nancy Klein Maguire herself, who tackle periods – respectively the Civil War/Commonwealth and the Restoration – strictly outside most people's definition of the Renais-

---

38 'Ovid's Narcissus and Shakespeare's Richard II: the Reflected Self', *Ovid Renewed*, pp. 137–50.
39 Toronto, Buffalo, and London: University of Toronto Press, 1988.
40 AMS Studies in the Renaissance, number 20 (New York: AMS Press, 1987).
41 'Shakespearean Tragicomedy', *Renaissance Tragicomedy*, pp. 80–96.

sance, though with retrospective implications for Shakespeare and his contemporaries.[42] Potter's incisive essay argues for a developing identification of one strand of tragicomedy with royalism in the 1640s and 50s; much traditional criticism (J. F. Danby on Beaumont and Fletcher, for example) has *assumed* that identification from the first appearance of Guarinian tragicomedy in England at the beginning of the century. This volume as a whole should reopen a number of questions on the generic and political status of tragicomedy and of Shakespeare's plays in relation to them.

Robert N. Watson's *Ben Jonson's Parodic Strategy: Literary Imperialism in the Comedies* and George E. Rowe's *Distinguishing Jonson: Imitation, Rivalry, and the Direction of a Dramatic Career* both focus on Jonson's determination to forge his own identity, to assert his own voice, in a medium dominated by Shakespeare's example (most notoriously in the tragicomedies with their 'Tales, Tempests, and such like drolleries').[43] Watson (whom Shakespearians will know from *Shakespeare and the Hazards of Ambition*, 1984) returns to ambition in an altered form. He approaches Jonson's comedies (the omission of the tragedies from the argument is never explained) as 'acts of theatrical imperialism ... He systematically subsumes the more conventional plays of his competitors, forcing them to work for his exaltation ... Those rival plays become colonies within Jonson's empire, their native languages and value systems redefined as merely quaint by incorporation into the imperial scheme' (p. 1). It is a lively and provocative conceit, energetically reiterated and advanced at the beginning of each chapter, though the bulk of those chapters is given over to a reading of the dramatic strategies Jonson explores within his plays rather than to the ways in which he might be seen as appropriating the generic models of his competitors. Rowe rather more systematically examines the ways in which Jonson sought to define himself by distinguishing himself from the opposition,

from his classical forebears, from poets like Beaumont, Donne, and Daniel (not, perhaps surprisingly, dealing with Jonson's contrast of himself with Daniel as a masque-writer), from mis-readers like the Earl of Northampton, but pre-eminently from rival dramatists, of whom Shakespeare is inevitably the prime example. *Bartholomew Fair* is invariably the touchstone of Jonson criticism, especially as regards his position in relation to Shakespeare. Watson signals his stance by calling his chapter on the play 'The Theater of Forgiveness and the Forgiveness of Theater', rather overstating the case in claiming that the 'critical consensus' sees the play as representing 'a radical departure for Jonson in its sheer generosity' (p. 139). Rowe, in seeing the play as the culmination of Jonson's uneasy coming to terms with Shakespeare, argues for something much more sceptical, 'a drama that is a *reductio ad absurdum* of Shakespearean romance. And if that comedy seems more genial and good-humored than some of his earlier works, its geniality is function not of acceptance but of disillusionment' (p. 157).

Jonson's reactions to Shakespeare lead us into other areas of the after-life. James Ogden demonstrates that the 'heath' in *King Lear* – so much part of the Lear mythology, aspects of which (*Wuthering Heights*, *The Return of the Native*) he outlines – has no basis in the Shakespearian text, but is a feature of Nahum Tate's Restoration adaptation (probably derived from the veritable 'blasted heath' in *Macbeth*), canonized by Rowe and subsequent editors.[44]

---

[42] Cf. Walter Cohen, 'The Politics of Golden Age Spanish Tragicomedy', pp. 155–76; Perry Gethner, 'Affairs of State and French Tragicomedy in the Seventeenth Century', pp. 177–95; Lois Potter, '"True Tragicomedies" of the Civil War and Commonwealth', pp. 196–217; Nancy Klein Maguire, 'The "Whole Truth" of Restoration Tragicomedy', pp. 218–39.

[43] Cambridge, Mass., and London: Harvard University Press, 1987; Lincoln, Nebraska, and London: University of Nebraska Press, 1988.

[44] 'Lear's Blasted Heath', *Durham University Journal*, 81 (1987), 19–22 (four illustrations).

Irena Cholj has looked again at two related prompt-books in the Folger Shakespeare Library, one of John Wilson's *Belphegor* and one relating to Charles Gildon's 1700 adaptation of *Measure for Measure*, arguing that they are both of London origin rather than from Dublin, as had been suggested, the latter helpful in reconstructing personnel and features of the production.[45] Paul H. D. Kaplan begins some intriguing sleuthing by considering an unusual painting by Francesco Capella (*c.* 1760) of a black man giving a geography lesson to a white lady; he convincingly relates this to *Othello* – the Moor 'bewitching' Desdemona with tales of his outlandish exploits. This is possibly the earliest image we have of Othello (Kaplan relates it to others *c.* 1760–90); he is unmistakably a Blackamoor rather than a Moor.[46] If those eighteenth-century images of the play strike us as alien, what should we have made of the 1866–7 American production revived for consideration by Daniel J. Watermeier and Ron Engle, in which Othello was played by the German star, Bogumil Dawison, speaking German, Iago was played by the notable American actor, Edwin Booth, speaking English, while Maria Methua-Scheller played Desdemona, speaking German to Othello and English to Iago? Apparently audiences loved it.[47]

Jill L. Levenson's *Romeo and Juliet* is the first volume I have seen in the new Shakespeare in Performance series, edited by J. R. Mulryne – a competitor of sorts, on Shakespearian texts, for both Macmillan's Text and Performance series and Bristol Classical Press's Plays in Performance series, welcomed here last year.[48] Unlike most of the former, this volume does offer a brief historical survey of the play prior to the twentieth century (concentrating particularly on Garrick and Charlotte Cushman) before devoting 80 of its 130 pages to three 'modern' productions (those by John Gielgud, 1935; Peter Brook, 1947; and Franco Zeffirelli, 1960, adapted for film 1968), and it has chosen to exclude the accessible television productions (though this is apparently Levenson's own choice, not series policy). Unlike the latter, it does not provide a text of the play, but analyses the broad features of each production rather than attempting to describe moment-by-moment items. I was slightly disappointed by the coverage of the 'Elizabethan' *Romeo and Juliet*, where there is surely something to be made of Kempe's playing the Nurse's 'man', Peter (whether or not the part was originally devised for him), but the description of later productions, well chosen for their contrasts, is lively, balanced, well researched and informative. If other volumes maintain this standard, these will be strong competitors in what is becoming a crowded market. Those who subsequently research the history of *Romeo and Juliet* production will be able to turn to *Players of Shakespeare 2: Further Essays in Shakespearean Performance by Players with the Royal Shakespeare Company*, edited by Russell Jackson and Robert Smallwood, the follow-up to a similar 1985 volume edited by Philip Brockbank.[49] This contains accounts of their roles by Roger Allam, Mercutio in a 1983 touring and 1984 Other Place production, and by Niamh Cusack, Juliet in the 1986 Stratford/ 1987 Barbican production. All of the thirteen essays are illuminating, once more pointing to possible fruitful links between performance and critical analysis, as the previous volume did. Antony Sher's account of his Fool in the 1982 Stratford/1983 London production of *King Lear* stands out, only partly because it is so fully illustrated with photographs and his own sketches and painting, while Kenneth Branagh's comments on his 1984 Stratford/ 1985 Barbican *Henry V* are particularly reveal-

---

[45] 'London Prompt Books for *Belphegor* and *Measure for Measure*', *Theatre Notebook*, 42 (1988), 57–62.

[46] 'The Earliest Images of Othello', *Shakespeare Quarterly*, 39 (1988), 171–86.

[47] 'The Dawison-Booth Polyglot *Othello*', *Theatre Research International* 13 (1988), 48–56.

[48] Manchester: Manchester University Press, 1987.

[49] Cambridge: Cambridge University Press, 1988.

ing in view of his subsequent involvement with the Renaissance Theatre Company. It is really invidious to single out essays for particular comment, though the David Suchet model (blow-by-blow of his 1985 Stratford/1986 Barbican Iago) is perhaps more to be recommended than Edward Petherbridge's rather abstract reflections on Armado (1984), and all the more illuminating alongside Ben Kingsley's emotionally-charged account of his Othello in the same production. Such multiple perspectives on the same production are perhaps, in the long run, most revealing of all: Fiona Shaw and Juliet Stevenson collaborated on their essay as, respectively, Celia and Rosalind in the 1985 Stratford/1986 Barbican *As You Like It*, while Alan Rickman has also written about his Jaques in the same production: and between the two essays we see a long way into the craft that produced the finished product. Liisa Hakola's *In One Person Many People: The Image of the King in Three RSC Productions of William Shakespeare's 'King Richard II'* has been a long labour of love, composed over twenty years, with multiple journeys from Finland to Stratford.[50] The result is somewhat uneven – we get discussion of the history of the RSC, of poetic imagery and poetic drama, and background details on various actors and directors, which are only marginally relevant to the thesis as a whole – but the nub of the book, detailed discussions of the John Barton 1973/74, Terry Hands

1980/81 and Barry Kyle 1986/87 *Richard II*s, and comparative accounts of their central roles, directorial methods, and the image they presented of the king, is solidly researched and well-informed, and justifies her labours.

I conclude with what I confidently take to be a first for these pages, a piece by a Professor of Mechanics in the *International Journal of Mechanical Sciences*.[51] Professor W. Johnson set out to throw some professional light on the phrase 'an enginer hoist with his own petard', so colloquially familiar though the military device to which it refers is fairly obscure. In the course of this he encountered many puzzles, including the fact that the spelling and meaning of his own profession ('enginer') has changed down the ages, that the passage in question is not in the First Folio text of *Hamlet*, indeed that '*Hamlet* is, or was, not one clear item but an indefinite thing which is in parts of uncertain authenticity' (p. 597). In short, he discovered Shakespearian scholarship, and his struggle to come to terms with it makes fascinating reading. It perhaps ought to be *required* reading in all universities, where 'hard' and 'soft' disciplines rub shoulders with each other, not always amicably, and really know nothing of each other's concerns.

---

50 Helsinki: Suomalainen Tiedeakatemia, 1988.
51 'An Enginer Hoist With His Own Petard', *International Journal of Mechanical Sciences*, 29 (1987), 587–600.

3. EDITIONS AND TEXTUAL STUDIES
reviewed by MacDonald P. Jackson

Far from transcending farce, as critics have claimed, *The Comedy of Errors* 'uses farce to achieve ends that are proper to farce – surprise, suspense, laughter'; in this play characters 'do not so much relate as collide with one another'.[1] Patrick Swinden's no-nonsense account remains true to one's experience of the play in performance: the hectic pace of the

complicated plot ensures that its puppets have about as much psychological and emotional reality as Keystone Cops. It seemed wholly apt that in the BBC TV production Egeon's long opening tale of woe – in which a delightfully

---

1 Patrick Swinden, *An Introduction to Shakespeare's Comedies* (London: Macmillan, 1973), pp. 28 and 25.

improbable series of coincidences and mishaps serves to set up the situation for the delightfully improbable confusions that follow – was comically mimed by a troupe of street-theatre harlequins, and drew histrionic sniffles and tears from the listening Ephesians.

T. S. Dorsch, editor of the New Cambridge *Comedy of Errors*, takes the more common view that 'we must ... feel deeply for Egeon as he tells his woeful story' (p. 14).[2] He sees the play as 'a finely-balanced mixture of pathos and suspense, illusion and delusion, love turned bitter and love that is sweet, farce and fun' (p. 12), and briefly expands this description in the kind of old-fashioned character analysis that worries away at the differences in the dispositions of Dromio of Ephesus and his Syracusan twin. It is true, of course, that the play incorporates Adriana's jealousy, the wooing of her sister Luciana by Antipholus of Syracuse, and the hurt perplexity of Egeon in the closing scene before the joyous family reunion. But have even these elements ever aroused much feeling in an audience? Dorsch's 'Stage History' is too perfunctory to provide an answer. A more detailed account of some key productions might have conveyed a stronger sense of the range of theatrical possibilities. 'One would suppose that no producer in his senses would put on the stage two pairs of actors who could not be told apart', he writes (p. 12). But James Cellan-Jones, who directed the BBC TV version, not only had each set of twins played by a single actor – the split screen making possible even the final confrontation – but judged that Shakespeare had himself arranged the comings and goings so as to allow the Antipholuses and the Dromios to be doubled, so long as two other actors 'dressed the same and facing upstage' were brought on for the last three minutes when the whole cast assembles.[3] The dialogue always enables an audience to sort out who is who. A 1987 Auckland production by the Tantrum Theatre Company made entertaining use of the doubling technique, the concluding

exchanges between twins being in each case performed by one actor who ostentatiously shifted his position and direction of address while changing the colour of his reversible cap.

Dorsch has no interest in newer forms of criticism, exemplified by Ruth Nevo's likening of *The Comedy of Errors* to 'a schizophrenic nightmare' in which 'identities are lost, split, engulfed, hallucinated, imploded' as apparently solid citizens suffer acute forms of 'ontological uncertainty' and in which an incident in 5.1 becomes 'a deliciously comic forerunner of a Lacanian *stade du miroir*'.[4] Of the twenty-nine items on his 'Reading List' (p. 115) only one postdates 1970.[5]

Dorsch's discussion of the date of composition of *The Comedy of Errors* stresses its affinities with *The Taming of the Shrew* and finds the evidence converging on the period 'between April 1591, when the English expeditions went to France and an allusion to the Armada could still have awakened proud memories in an English audience, and June 1592 when the plague, never far away, again became a serious menace to the people of London' (p. 6). The play's main source is Plautus' *Menaechmi*, supplemented by his *Amphitruo*; besides examining these relationships, Dorsch lays more stress than usual on the influence of the Bible and devotes an appendix to relevant sections from the Epistle of St Paul to the Ephesians. But the strongest part of his introduction is that which considers the likely means of staging the comedy at

---

[2] The three editions reviewed here were all published by Cambridge University Press, 1988. Passages and words in them are located by each edition's own line-numbering.

[3] See the edition in the BBC TV Shakespeare series, *The Comedy of Errors* (London: BBC, 1984), p. 26.

[4] *Comic Transformations in Shakespeare* (London and New York: Methuen, 1980), pp. 22, 34.

[5] The list has a curious bias towards critics whose names begin with one of the first five letters of the alphabet: twenty-three of the entries are for names beginning A–E.

Gray's Inn on the night of 28 December 1594, when it was given its earliest recorded performance. Dorsch outlines and evaluates three hypotheses, one of which is his own response to a visit to the Inn and envisages use of three arched doors in the carved oak screen that extends across the west end of the Great Hall.

Confusions and inconsistencies in characters' names within the stage directions and speech prefixes of the First Folio text of *The Comedy of Errors* have led twentieth-century editors to suppose that Shakespeare's foul papers must have served as printer's copy. Dorsch shares this belief. His examination of the evidence is necessarily a good deal less thorough than Paul Werstine's in an article that assesses the contribution of the Folio compositors to the ambiguity and variety of nomenclature, and concludes that once compositorial variability has been taken into account and the inconsistencies are viewed in the light of 'the standards achieved in playbooks actually used to guide Renaissance performances', then 'the possibility that Folio *Errors* could have been set from such a playbook' cannot be eliminated.[6] More generally, Werstine claims that W. W. Greg's attempt to distinguish between texts based on foul papers and texts based on prompt books was vitiated by his mistaken assumption that Renaissance prompt books exhibited 'a regularity in the identification of characters in stage directions and speech prefixes that was not achieved until the edited texts published in the late nineteenth and twentieth centuries' (p. 244). William B. Long has sounded the same warning: 'Greg and others assume that playhouse personnel customarily worked through a play making certain kinds of regularizations, clarifications, and additions to a playwright's manuscript. Extant playbooks contradict such assumptions.'[7] The issue raised here is of the utmost importance for editors of Shakespeare. But in order fully to persuade us that Greg's notions about Renaissance prompt books were anachronistic, Long needs more carefully to discri-

minate between surviving 'playbooks', which represent various phases in the theatrical evolution of the plays, and to explain precisely what is wrong with Greg's cautious remarks on Renaissance dramatic manuscripts in, say, *The Shakespeare First Folio*.

As far as *The Comedy of Errors* is concerned, the King's Men would surely have considered their official prompt book, which presumably contained the Revels Office licence, too precious to be submitted to the hazards of the printing house. Since, in Gary Taylor's words, the Folio text shows 'much evidence of authorial practice, but no evidence of theatrical use, and little concern for theatrical convenience',[8] Dorsch's acceptance of the orthodox view that the play was set from foul papers is perfectly reasonable.

Dorsch's edition clears up the confusions in the Folio's names but adds a couple of gross misprints at 1.2.91 and 2.1.11, where speech prefixes for Antipholus of Syracuse and Luciana are set in lower case and incorporated into the dialogue. Sense is restored to the text by a sprinkling of traditional emendations. Dorsch seems to me mistaken in refusing to emend at 1.1.38, 1.1.54, 1.2.102, 2.2.181, 2.2.185, and 5.1.406. In the last of these instances 'nativity' must have been accidentally repeated from the end of line 404: 'festivity' or 'felicity' is clearly required, though Dorsch does not even comment on 'nativity' or record the conjectural emendations in his collation notes. At 1.2.102 Dorsch, following F, allows Antipholus of Syracuse to end his catalogue of the jugglers, sorcerers, witches, cheaters, and mountebanks rumoured to

---

6 '"Foul Papers" and "Prompt-Books": Printer's Copy for Shakespeare's *Comedy of Errors*', *Studies in Bibliography*, 41 (1988), 232–46; p. 245.

7 '"A bed / for woodstock": A Warning for the Unwary', *Medieval and Renaissance Drama in England*, 2 (1985), 91–118; p. 92.

8 Stanley Wells and Gary Taylor, with John Jowett and William Montgomery, *William Shakespeare: A Textual Companion* (Oxford: Clarendon Press, 1987), p. 266.

inhabit Ephesus with the line 'And many such-like liberties of sin' and glosses the last three words as 'licensed transgressors'. In his introduction he bases a critical point on the theological tonings of the phrase 'liberties of sin' (p. 13). But although by 'liberty' Shakespeare often enough denotes 'licentiousness', it is hard to see how 'liberties' could mean 'transgressors' rather than 'transgressions', and Hanmer's 'libertines' provides a much more satisfactory summation of the list of villainous types. At 2.2.180–1 Dorsch follows F in reading:

> This is the fairy land. O spite of spites,
> We talk with goblins, owls, and sprites.

On line 181 he comments: 'Need we be worried by a line which is metrically short? It is effective. Various suggestions have been made to regularise the line, but none has authority.' The last phrase merely fudges the issue: *of course* no conjectural emendation has 'authority', which for this play can derive only from the First Folio itself. The sole pertinent question is whether any emended version of the line is more likely than any other version of the line, including F's, to represent what Shakespeare intended. What is especially 'effective' about a couplet that rhymes a tetrameter with a pentameter? Are there other such couplets in the play? Whether or not a case can be made for filling the metrical gap (and R. A. Foakes's proposal that 'goblins' should be followed by 'urchins' is easily the best), 'owls', for all the folklore about screech-owls, are obviously out of place in a line dealing with spirits in human form, such as 'elves' or 'ouphes' (Theobald's suggestion).[9]

Critically F. H. Mares's *Much Ado About Nothing* is a more satisfying edition. His long 'Stage History', concentrating on productions in London and Stratford-upon-Avon, traces continuities and variations in the tradition of presenting the play in the theatre. 'Always the main interest has been in Beatrice and Benedick, not Hero and Claudio, with the humours

of Dogberry in second place' (p. 28), but Beatrices have ranged from the self-possessed and golden-hearted to the vindictive and maladroit. Mares is helpful in picking out those details of production that affect the balance of sympathies and make for a particular interpretation of the script. He adds an interesting couple of pages on his involvement with a 1987 production by the State Theatre Company of South Australia.

'The chroniclers of the theatre, like editors who see the text systematically deconstructed in the collation, are less likely to be disturbed than traditional literary critics by philosophers who insist on the ineluctable fluidity of texts and the impossibility of arriving at fixed or even especially privileged readings. For them this is a matter of plain common experience, though it may not have been elegantly theorised' (p. 30). Mares's own account, well informed about recent approaches to *Much Ado About Nothing* and about developments in modern criticism and theory, is an intelligent attempt to define the limits within which interpretative ingenuity can most profitably operate. Relevant factors include Shakespeare's treatment of his sources, late sixteenth-century social attitudes, and 'the relation of parts within the work itself, or between the particular work and the rest of Shakespeare's *oeuvre*' (p. 31). My own sense of Claudio's role in the play is closer to that of the Arden editor, A. R. Humphreys, as Mares quotes him (p. 34), than to Mares's own, but I suspect that little further progress will be made

---

[9] The word occurs twice in *The Merry Wives of Windsor*: 4.4.49 (in association with 'urchins' and 'fairies') and 5.5.56. Dorsch misquotes Foakes's plausible suggestion in his Arden edition of *Errors* (London: Methuen, 1962) that 'the compositor saw *olues* in MS., an initial *e* looking like *o* . . . and made sense of it by transposing letters'. The difficulties in Adriana's speech at 2.1.101–13 are more complex. A solution eludes Dorsch, as it has eluded other editors. His adoption of Theobald's 'But' for F 'By' in line 111 seems to me to make the passage less, rather than more, meaningful.

in this kind of debate without a radical rethinking of the subtle interaction between plot and character in Shakespearian drama and the relative extent to which the one or the other is felt to govern behaviour at any given point. The problems of *Much Ado About Nothing* arise, as E. K. Chambers saw long ago, from the near incompatibility of its tragicomic melodrama and the more earthbound comedy surrounding Benedick and Beatrice, Dogberry and Verges. 'The triumph of comedy in *Much Ado About Nothing* means . . . that the things which happen between Claudio and Hero have to stand the test of a much closer comparison with the standard of reality than they were designed to bear.'[10] It is not so much that Beatrice and Benedick 'demonstrate in action a genuineness and strength of feeling that shows up the superficiality of the other characters', as Mares puts it (p. 6), as that the two sets of lovers exist in different dramatic planes.

There can be little doubt that the 1600 Quarto of *Much Ado About Nothing* was set from foul papers and that the Folio text was set from a copy of Q that had been lightly annotated with reference to the prompt book, from which a few of F's alterations to stage directions probably derive. The main authority for *Much Ado About Nothing* is thus a quarto printed from Shakespeare's untidy pre-production draft. 'What the text offers . . . is a becoming, a process, not a finished product' (p. 148). Mares is not always persuasive in his handling of Q's inevitable confusions. I think that he is quite wrong, for instance, in rejecting the usual redisposition of speech prefixes at 3.3.142–3, 4.2.56–60, 5.3.2 and 22–3, and 5.4.54. 4.2 is a scene between the constables Dogberry and Verges, the Watch, Conrade and Borachio, and the Sexton as Town Clerk. In Q the Sexton, after ordering that the accused be bound and taken to Leonato, makes his exit, and the dialogue proceeds as follows:

Constable Come, let them be opiniond.
Couley Let them be in the hands of Coxcombe.

Kemp Gods my life, wheres the Sexton? let him write down the Princes officer Coxcombe: come, bind them, thou naughty varlet.

(Q, G4ᵛ, lines 13–17)

'Kemp' here as elsewhere in the scene is Dogberry, the role evidently having been written for Will Kemp. It is equally clear that Shakespeare must have wanted Richard Cowley to play Verges. 'Constable' might be either Dogberry or Verges: both, but especially Dogberry, are given to such malapropisms as 'opinioned' (for 'pinioned'). The scope for a compositor's misinterpreting Shakespeare's intentions would have been increased by use in the foul papers of the abbreviation 'Con', which might stand for 'Constable' (Dogberry or Verges) or 'Conrade', or be misread as 'Cou'. The best solution to Q's muddle combines the suggestions of various editors:

DOGBERRY Come, let them be opinioned.
VERGES Let them be, in the hands –
CONRAD Off, coxcomb!
DOGBERRY God's my life, where's the Sexton? Let him write down the Prince's officer coxcomb. Come, bind them. Thou naughty varlet![11]

Mares reads:

VERGES Come, let them be opinioned.
CONRADE Let them be in the hands of coxcomb.
DOGBERRY God's my life . . .

He admits that the proposal to give Conrade the interjection 'Off, coxcomb!' is 'certainly

---

[10] I quote Chambers from the Penguin edition of *Shakespeare: A Survey* (Harmondsworth: Penguin Books, 1964), p. 106. The essays in that volume originally appeared from 1904 to 1908 as introductions to the Red Letter Shakespeare.

[11] This is the solution adopted in the Oxford *Complete Works*, *Much Ado*, 4.2.65–70, and in A. R. Humphreys's Arden edition (London, 1981), except that Humphreys omitted the comma after Verges's 'Let them be'. For 'in the hands' Warburton substituted 'in hand', Capell 'in bands'. 'Of' is, of course, a common Elizabethan spelling of 'off'.

attractive', but finds a 'difficulty' in the impossibility of choosing 'on any objective grounds' among 'the number of alternative proposals for the left-over beginning of the line'. He claims that 'if the line is taken as an aside by Conrade to Borachio, which is overheard by Dogberry, it makes good sense and requires no tinkering' (p. 147). An aside that is plainly audible to a character for whom it is not intended seems highly unlikely, and the line Mares gives to Conrade is not only improbably lame but unidiomatic: one would expect 'a coxcomb' or 'coxcombs'. And instead of being incapacitated by the variety of suggestions for dividing the line, should not an editor boldly choose the best? If the graphic similarity of 'Cou' and 'Con' could lead a compositor to attribute to 'Couley' (Verges) a line intended for Conrade, as Mares notes, it could just as easily have led him to attribute to Couley alone a line intended to be divided between them.

Mares's rejection of Pope's emendation at 3.2.22 and Capell's at 5.1.15–18 also seems to me mistaken, and his retention, wherever possible, of Q's punctuation, incongruous in a modern-spelling edition, leaves him with unnecessarily weak readings at 3.2.84, 3.2.91–2, 3.5.26, and elsewhere. My other complaint about this useful edition is that Mares does not mark any of the dozens of asides or adequately indicate to whom speeches or parts of speeches are addressed. There is a trivial error, 'hath' for 'have', at 1.1.64. As the cover promises, 'There is a full commentary which includes annotation of the many sexual jokes in the play that have been obscured by the complexity of Elizabethan language.' But Hilda Hulme's notion that 'pubic hair' is relevant to Hero's use of the word 'thatched' at 2.1.70 might better have been forgotten, and sometimes, as at 1.1.23, a supposed 'sexual innuendo' works against the passage's real wit: it is obvious, to take another instance, that when Beatrice says of Benedick at 2.1.107 'I would he had boarded me' she intends 'boarded' to mean 'tackled' or 'challenged' but has unconsciously, as it were, used a word susceptible of a sexual interpretation, but Mares's suggestion that Beatrice also puns on 'bawd' merely ruins the joke.

Marvin Spevack's New Cambridge *Julius Caesar* is another edition in which the record of the play's history in the theatre is full and illuminating. His solidly documented discussion of the play itself – under the subheadings 'The Frame', 'Structure', 'Theme', and 'Persons and Politics' – makes some interesting use of concordance-derived data about repeated words and linguistic devices and how these contribute to a fundamental opposition between 'the rational and the irrational' (p. 25). Spevack's manner is not exactly winsome – he proceeds by a dogged piling up of detail – but he does offer the reader plenty to think about.

'As with many other concerns, less may in the long run be more' (p. 7), he writes in connection with the multiplicity of suggested sources for *Julius Caesar*, and he might more consistently have heeded his own maxim. His sections on the date, sources, and text of the play are marred by loose phrasing and the kind of dithering that results from inability to evaluate the evidence and distinguish between the relevant and the irrelevant. Like a medieval schoolman, Spevack sets against one another the views of various 'authorities' without any searching examination of the bases for those views. In discussing the date of composition, for example, he devotes a paragraph to Alfred Hart's studies of Shakespeare's vocabulary, which cast no light on the problem, but ignores the highly pertinent work of Eliot Slater on word-links within the canon,[12] and mentions metrical analyses that are 'inconclusive or noncommittal', while neglecting

---

[12] Slater's work is briefly analysed by M. W. A. Smith, 'Word-Links and Shakespearian Authorship and Chronology', *Notes and Queries*, 35 (1988), 57–9. He concludes that, modestly applied, Slater's technique 'is a useful addition to the Shakespearian scholar's armoury for attacking some problems of chronology' (p. 59).

genuinely useful studies by Langworthy, Wentersdorf, Oras, and others.[13] However, despite pointlessly quibbling that three scholars use different terms ('quotation', 'echo', and 'paraphrase') for one of Ben Jonson's two references to *Julius Caesar* in his own *Every Man Out of His Humour*, Spevack eventually recognizes that in view of the several apparent allusions to Shakespeare's play from 1599 onwards it was probably first produced in that year.[14] The 'Textual Analysis' on pages 148–53 is a dreadful muddle: anyone who wants to know what the issues are would do well to avoid it and turn instead to John Jowett's lucid and precise exposition in the Oxford *Textual Companion*.

Julius Caesar was well printed in the First Folio, and Spevack's is an accurate text. I cannot believe in F's 'laughter' at 1.2.72; 4.3.114, which Spevack cites in support of his gloss 'subject or matter for laughter', is not really comparable: 'Hath Cassius lived/To be but mirth and laughter to his Brutus' is idiomatic and Shakespearian, but 'Were I a common laughter' is not – the indefinite article makes all the difference. Spevack resists a few other emendations that strike me as desirable: for example, the omission of 'a' at 2.1.67, 'put' for 'path' at 2.1.83, 'Of' for 'And' at 2.2.81, 'unstrung' for the highly unsatisfactory 'in strength' (on which there is no comment) at 3.1.173, 'unlucky' for 'unluckily' at 3.3.2, 'meinies' for 'means' at 4.1.44, 'charge' for 'change' at 4.2.7, and 'ensigns' for 'ensign' at 5.1.79. Spevack's 'ancestors' at 1.3.81 is a sensible innovation.

The collation notes are cluttered with worthless variants from derivative folios and quartos. Why, in an edition for non-specialist playgoers and readers, bother to record, for example, that F2 reads 'hurried' for F1's 'hurtled' at 2.2.22 ('The noise of battle hurtled in the air'), or that an undated quarto of the late seventeenth or early eighteenth century reads 'augures' where F1's 'What say the augurers?' is so patently correct (2.2.37), or that

when Cassius soliloquizes 'Well, Brutus, thou art noble' at 1.2.297, F2 ludicrously mispunctuates 'art: Noble'? Spevack's commentary is less stimulating, his glosses less sharp than Arthur Humphreys's.[15] One critic, Spevack tells us, detects in Antony's line 'This was the most unkindest cut of all' (3.2.174) 'the possibility of an "oblique" reference to a detail from Plutarch ... which Shakespeare omits: that in the assassination of Caesar "Brutus himself gave him one wound about his privities"'. This news will no doubt be welcomed by some over-excitable director, but has it anything at all to do with Shakespeare's play? On the credit side, a thirty-page appendix reprints excerpts from North's Plutarch, and, appropriately in a modern-spelling edition, the spelling of this source material has been judiciously modernized.

Dorsch, Mares, and Spevack might all have benefited from a careful reading of Gary Taylor's '"Praestat difficilior lectio": *All's Well that Ends Well* and *Richard III*', a lively and clear-headed discussion of that aspect of an editor's labour 'which requires the exercise of critical sensitivity and the application of aesthetic principle'.[16] Taylor's aim is to illustrate and enunciate some criteria for deciding whether or not to accept a standard emendation of a reading that is suspect but not indisputably nonsensical. He draws a distinction between passages in a 'style of poetic indefinition' which 'while creating difficulties for rational exegesis, is aurally effective' and passages 'which are impossible for listeners to follow, however cleverly editors may supply them with contorted grammatical justifications' (p. 36); only the latter are likely to need emendation. Pointing out that error,

[13] These are described or listed in the Oxford *Textual Companion*, pp. 106–7; 141–4.

[14] Thomas Platter witnessed a performance of a tragedy about *Julius Caesar* on 21 September 1599.

[15] In his Oxford edition (1984), noticed in *Shakespeare Survey 38* (1985), pp. 250–1.

[16] *Renaissance Studies*, 2 (1988), 27–46; p. 27.

whatever the mode of textual transmission, is apt to produce 'unusual readings' by producing nonsense, or at least deficient sense, and that printing errors in particular – such as those made in typesetting and distribution – may accidentally result in non-words or unusual words 'in a way which is relatively rare in scribal transmission', he proposes that editors of Shakespeare might more appropriately act on the principle *insolitior lectio apta potior* ('the more unusual of two apt readings should be preferred') than on the principle *praestat difficilior lectio*, which is applicable chiefly to the handling of classical texts, and which 'as popularly (mis)understood, creates an unjustified editorial bias towards obscurity, particularly obscurity of syntax and construction – a bias which, for modern editors, is strongly (though irrationally and anachronistically) reinforced by the ethos of difficulty in modern literature' (p. 41).

I am not sure that even Taylor's new formulation of an old principle or his suggestions about the limits of its applicability sufficiently allow for the power of sheer mechanical accident to create readings that are attractive to modern critics because they are so boldly metaphorical. The germ of Malcolm Lowry's amusing epigram, 'Strange Type', was one such creative misprint; the poem begins, 'I wrote: in the dark cavern of our birth / The printer had it tavern, which seems better'. Lowry's preference for the erroneous 'tavern' – and his willingness to admit it into a new composition of his own – was based on its greater shock value as an image: typographical accident can create metaphor in which the gap between tenor and vehicle is excitingly and challengingly large, necessitating a larger leap by the reader's imagination. But the more unusual figure was perhaps 'less apt' to the original context. Ultimately, editors will always, as Taylor recognizes, be reliant on their sense of what is 'apt' to the context and characteristic of Shakespeare's use of language.

Most of the articles published during the period covered by this review have been concerned with similarly broad issues. Marga Munkelt's 'Disambiguation and Conjecture: Modes of Editorial Decision in Shakespeare's Early Plays' looks at a selection of 'ambiguous readings in substantive texts' and how they have been represented in derivative texts, early and modern.[17] The standard of discussion is set with her first example. In *Romeo and Juliet*, 2.1.189–90, Juliet says in the good Q2 (1599), 'And all my fortunes at thy foote ile lay, / And follow thee my L. throughout the world' (D4ʳ). Q2's 'L.' is 'disambiguated' in the First Folio and in Q1 (1597) as 'lord', which all modern editors read. Munkelt complains that 'a second possible expansion offered by intermediate quartos is completely ignored' (p. 53). Q4 printed 'Loue', which was taken over into some early editions by Pope, Theobald, and Warburton. 'The decision of modern editors in favor of the "better" text . . . renders [*sic*] a less emotional and more conventional note to Juliet's words . . . this is a love scene in which the woman appears more mature than the man. Juliet is superior to Romeo in her decisive faculties and demonstrates her independence from social conventions in proposing to him. Why should she not call him *love*?' (p. 53). Quite apart from the fact that the hierarchical term 'lord' is better suited than 'love' to Juliet's avowal that she will surrender all her fortunes to her future husband, the plain fact is that 'L.' is a standard Elizabethan abbreviation for 'lord', but is never used in a Shakespearian play as an abbreviation for 'love'. To suppose that Q2's 'L.' stands for 'love' is like supposing that in a reference to the work of 'Dr Marga Munkelt', 'Dr' stands for 'dear'. Besides, although Munkelt talks vaguely of Q2's being 'based . . . on the "bad" Quarto [Q1]', responsible recent scholars agree that Q1's influence on Q2 did not extend to the portion of the play in which this speech of Juliet's occurs; the

---

[17] *Analytical and Enumerative Bibliography*, NS I (1987), 52–74; p. 52.

reported Q1 thus affords independent testimony that 'lord' was the word spoken in the Elizabethan theatre. Q4, on the other hand, has no authority whatsoever. Not all the cases considered by Munkelt are so utterly unproblematic as this one, but her article does make much ado about next to nothing.

The same author also examines 'Stage Directions as Part of the Text' in the early quarto and First Folio versions of some Shakespeare plays.[18] 'The purpose is mainly one of demonstrating the interdependence of spoken and nonspoken material by interpreting the stage directions within their dramatic contexts and of calling attention to the heterogeneous nature of the material not as a disqualifying factor but as a possible reflection of various points of view in literary and theatrical interpretations. Irregularities, inconsistencies, and other seeming "deficiencies" are not necessarily the result of errors and misunderstandings in the process of transcription and printing but can serve as a key to the author's intentions' (p. 253). Though not primarily concerned with textual criticism, Munkelt concludes that 'editors should observe two caveats – not to expand or correct unnecessarily and not to blend their material. Each text may have its own perspective' (p. 268). The word 'unnecessarily' begs the question, and not to draw on both the 1594 Quarto and the Folio for stage directions of Titus Andronicus, for example, would be to shy away from any attempt to produce a 'critical edition', as Greg, Bowers, and others have understood the term.[19]

'The first requirement of an old-spelling edition is that it be critically edited', as Bowers says, differentiating such an edition from 'an exact reprint in a diplomatic, or documentary, manner'.[20] His 'Readability and Regularization in Old-Spelling Texts of Shakespeare' is a marvellously lucid and thorough enquiry into the kinds and degrees of regularization and normalization that are allowable or desirable in the interests of making an old-spelling edition more readable than the copy-text itself. Bowers retains an enviable capacity for ordering a formidable mass of diverse detail. His suggestions, which are 'far from prescriptive' (p. 202), relate to such features as stage-directions, speech prefixes, act and scene divisions, use of italic for proper names, spacing of contractions, the treatment of u-v, i-j, and long s, and lineation. The discussion is illustrated with a wealth of examples, mainly from Henry VIII and The Two Noble Kinsmen. Bowers's characteristically lengthy footnotes add to the value of the article, which all old-spelling editors will need to consult, and from which modern-spelling editors can also learn.

Manfred Draudt also professes an interest in matters of general principle. He begins 'The Rationale of Current Bibliographical Methods: Printing House Studies, Computer-Aided Compositor Studies, and the Use of Statistical Methods' with references to Copernicus, Galileo, Kepler, Newton, the psychologist R. D. Laing, and such expositors of the new physics as Gary Zukav, Herbert Pietschmann, and Fritjof Capra, and goes on to invoke Heisenberg's uncertainty principle.[21]

---

[18] Shakespeare Studies 19 (1987), 253–72.

[19] For a discussion of stage directions in Titus Andronicus see chapter 4, 'The Editor and the Theatre: Act One of Titus Andronicus' in Stanley Wells's Re-Editing Shakespeare for the Modern Reader (Oxford: Clarendon Press, 1984), pp. 79–113.

[20] Huntington Library Quarterly, 50 (1987), 199–227; p. 199. One long-awaited old-spelling edition of a Renaissance dramatist has been received for review, The Plays of George Chapman: The Tragedies with 'Sir Gyles Goosecappe': A Critical Edition, general editor Allan Holaday, assisted by G. Blakemore Evans and Thomas L. Berger (Cambridge: D. S. Brewer, 1987). This serves as a companion volume to the old-spelling edition of The Comedies published in 1970. Spot checks indicate a high standard of accuracy and thoughtful attention to the kinds of detail discussed by Bowers. There is a full apparatus, on the lines of the Cambridge Dekker, Beaumont and Fletcher, and Marlowe. Of particular interest is John Hazel Smith's decision to provide a parallel-text edition of Bussy D'Ambois, with Q1 and Q2 on facing pages.

[21] Shakespeare Survey 40 (1988), 145–53.

But his article is in essence an unconvincing attack on Paul Werstine's admirable work on William White's 1598 Quarto of *Love's Labour's Lost*. Werstine effectively demolished Draudt's case for supposing that a single compositor set the first three or four gatherings of Q from printed copy (a bad quarto) and the rest of the play mainly from manuscript.[22] Werstine, who also methodically exposed some weaknesses in George R. Price's earlier bibliographical study of the Quarto of *Love's Labour's Lost*, showed that Q was almost certainly set by at least two compositors, with a third man probably taking responsibility for one page, and that, regardless of the correctness of his attempt to determine the compositorial stints, a comparison of the spelling pattern of *Love's Labour's Lost* with the spelling patterns in other books printed in White's shop between 1598 and 1600 pointed to the Q compositors' having worked from printed copy throughout. Werstine's was a model of meticulous bibliographical investigation, accurate in its compilation of a vast amount of data and modest in its inferences from the evidence; indeed his concluding paragraph speaks only of the 'possibility' that Q was set from an earlier print, although the article establishes a definite probability. Draudt's accusation that Werstine 'treats possibilities as probabilities, and probabilities as if they were facts' (p. 150) is patently unjust.

Draudt wishes to 'question some developments in the analysis of Shakespeare's texts, where measurement and quantification recently appear to be used excessively and at the expense of other aspects' (p. 145) and criticizes Werstine for his reliance 'on large quantities of data and statistics' and alleged adherence to 'the fallacious dogma that figures *per se* are objective . . . and are therefore best suited for finding the truth' (p. 149). In fact, Draudt and Werstine reached different conclusions over *Love's Labour's Lost* not because Werstine had any superstitious regard for statistics or neglected Draudt's mysterious

'other aspects' of bibliographical enquiry or because the interpretation of spelling tests is always 'highly subjective' (p. 151), but because Werstine built a case on evidence that would sustain it whereas Draudt did not. In analytical bibliography 'large quantities of data', intelligently assessed, are almost always better than small quantities of data and a bit of naive speculation. Although Draudt adopts a tone suggestive of commendable scholarly caution, his 'Rationale of Current Bibliographical Methods' is vitiated by illogicalities, misunderstandings, and irrelevancies.[23]

The new Oxford edition of Shakespeare's

---

[22] Paul Werstine, 'The Editorial Usefulness of Printing House and Compositor Studies' with an 'Afterword', in *Play-Texts in Old Spelling: Papers from the Glendon Conference*, ed. G. B. Shand with Raymond C. Shady (New York: AMS Press, 1984), pp. 35–42 and 42–64 (the first part of the article had originally appeared in *Analytical and Enumerative Bibliography*, 2 (1978)); Manfred Draudt, 'Printer's Copy for the Quarto of *Love's Labour's Lost* (1598)', *The Library*, 3 (1981), 119–31. Draudt's footnote 3 on p. 146 of 'Rationale' gives full references to other relevant articles, including Price's. There is a judicious evaluation of Draudt's 'Printer's Copy' in the Oxford *Textual Companion*, pp. 270–1.

[23] The second paragraph on p. 147, citing George Walton Williams's comment on an article by Stanley Wells, is irrelevant to Draudt's subject; Wells's concern was with the haphazard preparation of an exemplar of the *Love's Labour's Lost* Quarto to serve as copy for the First Folio. On p. 151 Draudt writes: 'Whereas in his study of the stop-press corrections Werstine concluded that "the extant press corrections divide neatly into two groups, for correction in sheets A and C is much lighter than in sheets D and E", three years later he minimizes the distinction: "the difference does not seem great enough" (p. 53)'. Draudt muddles two separate matters. It remains true that, as Werstine claimed in 1979, extant copies of the Quarto of *Love's Labour's Lost* yield considerably fewer stop-press corrections in sheets A and C than in sheets D and E. On p. 53 of 'Editorial Usefulness' Werstine is addressing a different matter: he shows conclusively that differences between the Quarto's sheets A–B and sheets D–E in the quantity and nature of their errors are 'not enough to support Draudt's theory that quires D and E were set from copy different from that used for quires A and B'.

complete works was reviewed last year. 'The most original, and also the most controversial, feature of this edition is its acceptance of the hypothesis that Shakespeare revised some of his plays, that revision sometimes calls for both omission and addition, and that a revised, theatrical version, even if it is short-ened, has more authority than a longer, unre-vised version that is closer to Shakespeare's original conception'; so asserts one of the general editors, Stanley Wells, in his published lecture *Shakespeare and Revision*,[24] a careful and readable exposition of the new 'revisionism' and its assumptions 'that a play-wright's prime allegiance is to the theatre, that he is consequently one of a team, because he cannot achieve performance, or even finally shape his script into a performable document, without the collaboration of his performers, and that therefore a script on which the dramatist has worked along with performers with whom he is closely involved provides better evidence of his intentions as a drama-tist, as well as of the dramatic event itself, than a script before it has been put into rehearsal' (p. 13). In 'Revising Shakespeare', the same theme is taken up by Wells's co-editor, Gary Taylor,[25] who sees as part of the same conti-nuum those duplications which, in Shake-spearian good quartos, show the playwright changing his mind 'in the very act of making it up' (p. 287) and the more substantial vari-ation between Quarto and Folio texts of such plays as *Othello*, *Troilus and Cressida*, *Hamlet*, *King Lear*, and *2 Henry IV*, or between the different surviving versions of certain sonnets. Taylor's tone is more polemical than Wells's: 'The hypothesis that Shakespeare, like every other author, revised his work, depends fundamentally upon the sheer weight of his-torical and bibliographical evidence for vari-ation in the canon as a whole — variation which cannot be convincingly explained in any other way' (p. 303). The implications of the revision theory for critical interpretation of two-text plays are sensitively explored by John Kerrigan in a fine chapter added to the

new edition of *English Drama to 1710* in the Sphere History of Literature series.[26]

The *cause célèbre* for the revision hypothesis has been *King Lear*. William C. Carroll is unhappy about certain arguments that have been advanced by those believing in two *King Lear*s; in particular he denies that the Folio's deletion of the mock trial in 3.6 and its changes to the role of Edgar contribute to any supposed theatrical superiority over the Quarto.[27] Carroll makes some telling objections to the terms in which 'the *interpretive* privileging of the Folio text over the Quarto text' has been conducted (p. 227). He is prepared to concede that Shakespeare did revise *King Lear*, but asks us to admit 'that some of the deletions in F are not improvements' (p. 244). I doubt whether contributors to *The Division of the Kingdoms* would disagree with him. Although they were anxious to find artistic reasons for F's cuts, their 'privileging' of F stemmed primarily from a belief that, whatever the gains or losses, it was the text which better represented Shake-speare's 'final intentions' for his play.

At one point Carroll expresses a preference for a couple of Q's verbal variants. F has Edgar say, 'The Gods are iust, and of our pleasant vices / Make instruments to plague vs' (F 3131–2; 5.3.161–2). Q reads 'vertues' rather than 'vices', and 'scourge' rather than 'plague'. Carroll claims that 'the paradox that we suffer

[24] Delivered 3 December 1987 as the Hilda Hulme Mem-orial Lecture, and published by the University of London, 1988; the quotation is from p. 3.

[25] *Text: Transactions of the Society for Textual Scholarship*, 3 (1987), 285–304. In the same volume, Fredson Bowers's 'Mixed Texts and Multiple Authority', pp. 63–90, includes Shakespearian examples.

[26] 'Shakespeare as Reviser', in *English Drama to 1710*, ed. Christopher Ricks (London: Sphere Books, 1987), pp. 255–75.

[27] 'New Plays vs. Old Readings: *The Division of the Kingdoms* and Folio Deletions in *King Lear*', *Studies in Philology*, 85 (1988), 225–44. Also worth recording is John L. Murphy, 'Sheep-Like Goats and Goat-Like Sheep: Did Shakespeare Divide *Lear*'s Kingdom?', a review essay on *Division of the Kingdoms*, *Papers of the Bibliographical Society of America*, 81 (1987), 53–63.

forms of our goodness – is truer to the tragic experience in *Lear* than the far more moralistic and finally untrue, or at least incomplete, maxim about our vices' (p. 238). This may well be so, but Edgar knows less than the play knows, and Q's 'vertues' is hardly compatible with his glib assertion that 'The Gods are iust'. *Just*, to punish us for our virtues? Would Edgar think that?

Hamlet seems to be replacing *King Lear* as focus for studies of Shakespeare as reviser.[28] Paul Werstine doubts that it is possible to distinguish between the several sources of variation between Quarto and Folio *Hamlet* – 'authorial changes of mind ... scribal transcription, unauthorized playhouse cuts or additions, printing-house errors', and so on.[29] Rather than trying to determine the origins of the variants, he prefers to 'examine what we have – namely, the early printed texts themselves – with a view to assessing the extent to which the two may be compatible or incompatible with each other' (p. 2). His essay, in which textual, literary, and dramatic criticism meet, offers an acute analysis of some differences between Q and F in their representation of the relationships between Laertes, Claudius, and Hamlet. Werstine 'tentatively suggests that much of the enduring mystery that is *Hamlet*/Hamlet has been produced through the editorial construction of *Hamlet* as the combination of the second-quarto (Q2) and Folio (F) versions' (p. 2). Yet he concludes: 'While, like other revisionists, I have been intent upon asserting continuities within each of the early printed texts and discontinuities between them, there are no grounds for privileging the alleged integrity of each of Q2 and F to the host of aesthetic forms that critics have produced from their reading of the combined Q2/F text' (p. 23). In the final section of his article, which invokes Foucault on the futility of 'the search for origins', Werstine leaves me. At one point he writes: 'While the historicity of the variants discussed in this paper is evident from the printed documents themselves, just as the historicity of the playwright Shakespeare is well

documented, there is no document to link the variants to the playwright. As purely aesthetic patterns the variations discussed in this paper can have no claim to historicity; they do not exist beyond this paper. To claim that such patterns must originate with Shakespeare is to abolish the distinction between history and aesthetics' (p. 24). Werstine's notion of what is 'historical' strikes me as strangely circumscribed. Granted that we will be dealing not in certainties but in degrees of probability, may we not try to deduce from time's material relics the past events that created them? In my view, Werstine has given us additional grounds for thinking that F preserves Shakespearian revisions to the *Hamlet* behind Q, it remains a reasonable ambition to discriminate between F variants for which Shakespeare was responsible or which he approved and the unauthoritative F variants of other agents, and the preparation of a critical edition that accepts only the F changes putatively sanctioned by the playwright is still a worthwhile goal.

Also concerned with *Hamlet* and with the meeting ground between textual and literary criticism is Barbara Everett, who proposes some new readings while seeking to evolve principles of emendation.[30] As she says, 'scholarly minutiae can be governed by large critical preconceptions. The reverse is true too: the meaning of *Hamlet* is located in an epithet or stage direction' (p. 183). Of her many suggestions, I like best 'articled design' (for Q

---

28 The 1988 meeting of the Shakespeare Association of America in Boston, 31 March–2 April, included a seminar entitled 'Three *Hamlets* vs. Three *Hamlets*' chaired by Thomas Clayton of the University of Minnesota; the title alludes to Q1, Q2, and F, and the recent editions of Jenkins (Arden), Edwards (Cambridge), and Hibbard (Oxford). Revision was a major theme, and much attention was paid to Q1 as a theatrically viable script of interest in its own right.

29 'The Textual Mystery of *Hamlet*', *Shakespeare Quarterly*, 39 (1988), 1–26; p. 2.

30 'New Readings in *Hamlet* (and Some Principles of Emendation)', *Review of English Studies*, 39 (1988), 177–98.

'article desseigne', F 'Article designe', usually emended to 'article designed') at 1.1.93, and the bold 'Go, get thee to the inn' (Q 'Goe get thee in', F 'go, get thee to *Yaughan*') at 5.1.59–60.

A particularly valuable source of information is Thomas L. Berger's guide to 'Press Variants in Substantive Shakespearian Dramatic Quartos'.[31] He describes and documents the work that has been done on the subject. 'Substantive' in his title is used very broadly: his article covers 'any quarto text that may not be derived solely from an earlier quarto' and 'any quarto that *may* have served as copy for the Folio' (p. 232). As Berger says, 'studies of press variants remain integral to the creation of an intelligently edited version of a printed text of a play of the English Renaissance' (p. 241).

M. W. A. Smith has been refining his computer-aided stylometric investigations into authorship problems in Elizabethan–Jacobean drama. His latest two papers analyse word-counts of Acts 1–2 and Acts 3–5 of *Pericles*, with the help of control samples from Chapman, Jonson, Middleton, Shakespeare, Wilkins, Tourneur, and Webster.[32] The results tend to support the theory that Acts 1–2 of *Pericles* were written by Wilkins, whose known work they more closely resemble – as far as their rates of use of certain common words are concerned – than that of the mature Shakespeare. As Smith says, 'the next stage is to perform a more broadly based investigation of *Pericles*, in which the relative claims of the various suggested authors for Acts I and II, that is Day, Heywood, Rowley, Wilkins and both the young and mature Shakespeare, can be examined' (p. 229).

Marvin Spevack works painfully towards the conclusion that 'the copy for *Antony and Cleopatra* was Shakespeare's foul papers, or his fair papers, or a prompt copy, or a producer's copy – in Shakespeare's autograph or in a scribal hand, as the case may be. Conclusive proof is still missing in all instances. And in all likelihood it will never exist.'[33] In fact, although Folio *Antony and Cleopatra* shows

many of the features we might expect in a text set from a Shakespearian autograph that was rather more 'finished' than most, the predominance of the spelling 'Oh' over 'O' for the exclamation is almost decisive evidence – not cited by Spevack – that copy for F was a scribal transcript. Spevack's free-floating scepticism appears to attach itself even to Theobald's admirable emendation of F's 'Anthony' to 'autumn' in the lines:

> For his Bounty,
> There was no winter in't. An *Anthony* it was,
> That grew the more by reaping.
>
> (3304–6; 5.2.85–7)

John Dover Wilson suggested that autograph 'autome' had been misread as 'antonie'. Spevack's objections to Wilson's remarks confuse arguments against his explanation of how the error arose with arguments against the emendation itself.[34] Can anyone who appreciates Shakespeare's way with imagery doubt for one moment that, however he spelt the word, he intended 'autumn' here?

John C. Coldewey argues that in Sonnet 73 the Quarto's 'Bare rn'wd quiers' are primarily 'quires' or gatherings of leaves of a book,

---

[31] *The Library*, 10 (1988), 231–41.

[32] 'The Authorship of *Pericles*: New Evidence for Wilkins', *Literary and Linguistic Computing*, 2 (1987), 221–30; 'The Authorship of Acts I and II of *Pericles*: A New Approach Using First Words of Speeches', *Computers and the Humanities*, 22 (1988), 23–41.

[33] 'On the Copy for *Antony and Cleopatra*', in *'Fanned and Winnowed Opinions': Shakespearean Essays Presented to Harold Jenkins*, ed. John W. Mahon and Thomas A. Pendleton (London and New York: Methuen, 1987), pp. 202–15; p. 213. Spevack touches on the same topic in 'The Editor as Philologist', *Text: Transactions of the Society for Textual Scholarship*, 3 (1987), 91–106.

[34] If it be accepted that Shakespeare is unlikely to have used the spelling 'autome' (with 'o' and without 'n'), then this becomes an argument for F's having been set from scribal rather than autograph copy only if Theobald's emendation is also accepted. Spevack's discussion of the crux is muddied by his use of the word 'written' (twice) when he means 'printed' and his use of the word 'necessarily' when he must mean 'readily' (p. 212).

rather than 'choirs' or the part of the church occupied by choristers.[35] Obviously both meanings are present, and the only question for modernizing editors is which one is best considered dominant.[36] The customary alteration of 'quiers' to 'choirs' is a modernization, not an emendation, as Coldewey assumes. He is wrong to describe 'choirs' as 'a word appropriated from French towards the end of the seventeenth century'; what *OED* shows is simply that the *spelling* 'choir' did not appear in English until that time. Coldewey also sees wordplay in the Q spelling that has the boughs shaking 'against the could': 'the "could/cold" pun is important here, and also in Sonnet 94, where Shakespeare uses it again in a similar way, suggesting unrealized possibilities – the "could" that will never happen' (p. 4). This is most implausible. Shakespeare's was an oral art. Nowhere else did he indulge in purely visual punning (the two words are, and were, phonetically dissimilar) that operated outside the constraints of syntax. What on earth would the line 'Upon those boughs which shake against the *could*' (my italics, spelling modernized) mean? Coldewey is trying to turn Shakespeare into an e. e. cummings.[37]

Among books submitted for review are three in the Garland Shakespeare Bibliographies series, *Pericles: An Annotated Bibliography* (New York and London: Garland Publishing, 1987), compiled by Nancy C. Michael, and *Richard II: An Annotated Bibliography* (New York and London: Garland Publishing, 1988), in two volumes, compiled by Josephine A. Roberts. The compilers appear to miss little of consequence, and their summaries of the articles listed are clear and accurate. Also useful is Linda Woodbridge's compact and inexpensive *Shakespeare: A Selective Bibliography of Modern Criticism* (West Cornwall, Conn.: Locust Hill Press, 1988), which is 'intended for beginning graduate students, senior undergraduate students, and teachers of Shakespeare at the university, college, and/or high school level' (p. vii). It is not annotated. But it fills a niche unoccupied by any competitors, partly

by being up-to-date and hospitable to the new historicism, feminist criticism, and other recent theoretical approaches.

R. V. Holdsworth weighs the competing claims of the usual interpretation of Q's 'vigour' and Stanley Wells's conjecture that it is a rare spelling of 'figure' in Aaron's reference to his child as 'The vigour, and the picture of my youth' in *Titus Andronicus*, 4.2.107.[38] Eric Sams argues that *The Troublesome Reign* preceded *King John* and was, like the Folio play, written by Shakespeare.[39] David Atkinson, in a note on '*Romeo and Juliet* V.i.24', supports Q2's 'denie' against Q1's 'defie' in Romeo's outcry, 'I denie you starres'.[40] And in 'Falstaff's Nose *Was* "A Table of Green Fields": A Footnote to Ephim Fogel's Defense of the Folio Reading', Henry D. Janowitz adds to earlier arguments for a connection between the Hostess's famous lines in *Henry V* and Hippocrates' *Prognostica* the diagnosis that Falstaff's face was 'green with chronic jaundice and terminal liver failure'.[41] Bardolph's execution was a blessing in disguise: at least he died with his nose still glowing![42]

---

35 '"Bare rn'wd quiers"': Sonnet 73 and Poetry, Dying', *Philological Quarterly*, 67 (1988), 1–9.

36 John Kerrigan notes the wordplay in his Penguin edition of *The Sonnets and A Lover's Complaint* (Harmondsworth: Penguin Books, 1986), p. 265.

37 'Could', a very common sixteenth- and seventeenth-century spelling of 'cold', occurs five times in the Sonnets (excluding 'A Lover's Complaint') as against only two instances of 'cold(e)'. The spelling can hardly be supposed to suggest 'unrealized possibilities' on all of these occasions.

38 'A Crux in *Titus Andronicus*', *Notes and Queries*, 35 (1988), 44–5.

39 'The Troublesome Wrangle over *King John*', *Notes and Queries*, 35 (1988), 41–4.

40 *Notes and Queries*, 35 (1988), 49–52.

41 *Cahiers Elisabéthains*, 33 (1988), 53–55.

42 Survey-writers do not normally survey surveys, but R. V. Holdsworth's sections on Shakespearian 'Editions' and 'Textual Matters' in *The Year's Work in English Studies*, 65 (1987 for 1984) and 66 (1988 for 1985), 184–95 and 202–10, deserve mention not only for their carefully considered judgements but for describing several items that my own surveys have ignored or overlooked.

BOOKS RECEIVED

This list includes all books received between 1 September 1987 and 31 August 1988 which are not reviewed in this volume of *Shakespeare Survey*. The appearance of a book in this list does not preclude its review in a subsequent volume.

L'Angleterre et le Monde Méditerranéen. Actes du Centre Aixois de Recherches Anglais (CARA), 7. Université de Provence, 1987.

Beyer, Manfred. *Das Staunen in Shakespeares Dramen: Ursachen, Darstellungswiesen und Wirkungsintentionen*. Anglistische Studien, Band 7. Cologne and Vienna: Böhlau Verlag, 1987.

Elliott, Martin. *Shakespeare's Invention of Othello: A Study in Early Modern English*. Contemporary Interpretations of Shakespeare. Basingstoke and London: Macmillan, 1988.

Homan, Sidney. *Shakespeare and the Triple Play: From Study to Stage to Classroom*. Lewisburg, Penn.: Bucknell University Press; London and Toronto: Associated University Presses, 1988.

Horwich, Richard. *Shakespeare's Dilemmas*. New York: Peter Lang, 1988.

Lamb, Charles and Mary. *Tales from Shakespeare*. Washington, D.C.: Folger Shakespeare Library, 1979.

Redmond, James, ed. *Farce*. Themes in Drama 10. Cambridge: Cambridge University Press, 1988.

INDEX

INDEX

INDEX

INDEX

INDEX

Kean, Sidney, 151
Keats, John, 68
Kemble, Charles, 47
Kemble, John P., 37, 47
Kemble, Roger, 38n
Kemp, Will, 63, 199, 204
Kent, Diana, 155
Kepler, Johannes, 208
Kernan, David, 162
Kerrigan, John, 72n, 74, 210, 213n
Kerrigan, Patricia, 159
Kershaw, David, 158
Kershaw, Noreen, 153, 155
King's Men, The, 188, 194, 202
Kingsford, C. L., 26
Kingsley, Ben, 200
Kinnear, Roy, 92
Kirkpatrick, John, 159
Kiss Me Kate, 157
Kitchen, Michael, 156
Klause, John, 185
Klein, Theodore M., 34n
Knapman, David, 149, 154
Knight, Anderson, 160
Knight, G. Wilson, 165
Knight, Tom, 154
Knightley, Will, 155
Knott, Betty I., 68n
Knowles, James, 186n
Knowles, Richard, 125
Kohler, Estelle, 159
Kott, Jan, 18
Kunz, Simon, 150
Kuriharar, Komaki, 153
Kyd, Thomas, 127
Kyle, Barry, 156, 160, 200

Laing, R. D., 208
Laing, Stewart, 156
Lamb, Charles and Mary, 214
Landor, Gina, 149
Lang, Andrew, 25n
Langworthy, Charles, 206
Lanier, Emilia, 186-7
Lanquet, Thomas, 27n
Larkin, James, 129
Larmour, Brigid, 149
La Rochefoucauld, 96
Laroque, François, 196
Laughton, Charles, 103
Lavin, J. A., 105n
Lawrence, D. H., 3n
Lawson, Aletta, 155
Lazaridis, Stefanos, 158
Leavis, F. R., 165, 181

Ledebur, Ruth F. von, 175
Lee, Sidney, 67n, 70n
Leggatt, Alexander, 10n, 165, 168-9
Legge, Thomas, Dr, 20, 21
Legrand, Julie, 140
Leishman, J. B., 74n
Lerner, Laurence, 196
Lett, Ray, 153
Levenson, Jill L., 199
Lever, J. W., 67n, 75n
Levi, A. H. T., 68n
Levi, Peter, 185-6
Levin, Richard, 168
Levins, Peter, 58n
Levy, F. J., 29
Lewi, Angela, 81n, 82n, 83n
Liberty, Kate, 157
Lincoln, Mary, 149
Linz-Roberts, Jane, 152
Livy, 118
Lloyd, Phyllida, 156
Lloyd-Pack, Roger, 158
Lock, Kate, 160
Lockey, Rowland, 80, 81, 83
Lodge, Thomas, 71n
Long, William B., 202
Longhurst, Derek, 164
Longmore, Wyllie, 149
Lord Admiral's Men, 114
Lord Chamberlain's Men, 63, 64n, 92, 194
Lord Strange's Men, 114
Lowry, Malcolm, 207
Loyd, Lodowicke, 54n
Lucan, 66
Luther, Martin, 176
Lyly, John, 1-13, 106-7
Lynch, Kathryn L., 183
Lynn, Jack, 149

McAleer, Des, 136
MacArthur, David, 155
McAuliffe, Nichola, 157
McCartney, Paul, 160
McClellan, Kenneth, 155
McCreery, Kathleen, 157
McCulloch, Ian, 161
McCullough, Christopher J., 164
McDermott, Phelim, 150
MacDonnell, Chris, 158
McEwan, Geraldine, 129
McGee, Arthur, 176-7
McGowan, Kevin, 151
McGrath, Elizabeth, 157
MacGregor, Joanna, 159

McInnery, Lizzie, 162
MacIntyre, Jean, 112
McKellen, Ian, 162
McKerrow, Ronald B., 15n, 88n
McKillop, Alan D., 99n
Mackinnon, Lachlan, 173
Mackintosh, Steven, 145
Macklin, Charles, 85
McLay, Catherine M., 7n
McMillin, Scott, 77
MacNeil, Colin, 154
MacNeil, Ian, 151
MacPhee, Wendy, 160
Macready, Charles, 39n
McTeer, Janet, 154
Maguire, Nancy K., 197
Mahon, John W., 181, 212n
Mahood, Molly, 181
Manningham, John, 115
Mannion, Tom, 160
Maplethorpe, Bernard G., 158
Marathe, Sudhaker, 181
Marcell, Joseph, 156, 162
Marcus, Paul, 156
Mares, F. H., 203-6
Margolies, David, 164
Marklew, Trudy, 149
Marlowe, Christopher, 33, 55, 56, 65, 66, 80n, 127-8, 196, 208n
Marston, John, 104, 107, 187, 194, 197
Martin, William F., 179
Martindale, Charles, 196n
Mary Stuart, Queen, 33, 34
Massarella, David, 151
Massinger, Philip, 189
Masters, Helen, 153
Maverick, Rik, 152
Maycock, Hazel, 152
Mayhew, A. L., 58n
Meade, Dorothy M., 195
Meadows, Alan, 158
Mercer, Peter, 177
Meres, Francis, 63, 65, 66, 70, 73
Merrison, Clive, 133
Merrix, Robert P., 182
Meth, Jonathan, 158
Methua-Scheller, Maria, 199
Meyrick, Sir Gelly, 193
Michael, Nancy C., 213
Michaels, Kenneth, 154
Michell, Roger, 151, 154
Middleton, Alasdair, 150
Middleton, Juliet and Grenville, 158
Middleton, Thomas, 187, 189, 212

INDEX

Millbank, Elizabeth, 154
Miller, Dave, 158
Miller, Jonathan, 158
Miller, William E., 28n
Mills, Alison, 157
Milton, John, 68
Mincoff, Marco, 3n
Miola, Robert S., 165
Mitchell, John, 157
Molloy, Dearbhla, 130, 131, 153
Monks, Chris, 154
Montgomery, William, 25n, 93n, 202n
Montrose, Louis A., 1n, 6, 191
Mooney, Paul, 153
Moore, Henry, 145
More Light, 162
More, Sir Thomas, 21
Morison, Stanley, 82
Morris, P. E., 89n, 93n
Morris, R., 56n
Morrison, Clive, 148
Morrissey, David, 138–9
Morse, Hayward, 153
Mortimer, Terry, 161
Mossman-Ellis, Jo, 158
Mouffet, Thomas, 53, 61n
Mowat, Barbara A., 197
Mozart, W. Amadeus, 113
Mueller, Michael, 150
Muir, Kenneth, 39, 53, 58, 59, 181, 195n
Muldowney, Dominic, 149
Mullaney, Steven, 191–2
Muller, Heiner, 150
Mullins, Ian, 150, 154
Mulryne, J. R., 199
Mumford, Peter, 156
Munday, Anthony, 77, 79, 83
Munkelt, Marga, 207–8
Murcell, George, 154
Murchison, Ruari, 153
Murphy, Gerard, 154, 160
Murphy, John L., 210n
Murray, Brabham, 154
Mussato, Albertino, 21
Mussolini, 157
Myers, Keith, 153

Nagarajan, S., 181
Nagler, A. M., 100n, 104n
Nash, Pip, 155
Nashe, Thomas, 15n, 27, 87, 88n, 92, 182, 187
Neely, Carol T., 168, 192

Neville, Jenny, 157, 158
Nevo, Ruth, 6n, 170, 181, 201
Newman, Karen, 163
Newton, Isaac, 208
Newton-De Molina, David, 89n
Nicholls, Derek, 151
Nietzsche, Friedrich W., 173
Nims, J. F., 53n, 54n
Ninagawa, Yukio, 153
Noack, Klaus, 159
Noakes, Carol, 156
Noble, Adrian, 137, 152, 157
North, Sir Thomas, 196, 206
Northampton, Earl of, 198
Northey, Christopher, 160
Nunn, Trevor, 136
Nuttall, A. D., 196

O'Callaghan, Richard, 150
O'Connell, Kate, 149
O'Connell, Patrick, 161
O'Connor, Marion F., 163
Odajima, Youshi, 162
Odell, George C. D., 47
Ogden, James, 198
Ogilvy, Rachel, 156
Oliver, Stephen, 158
Olivier, Lord, 86
O'Mara, Kate, 152, 157
O'Meara, Jean M., 19n
Omesco, Ion, 176
O'Neill, Eliza, 39
Oras, Ants, 206
Ordish, T. F., 114
Orgel, Stephen, 58n, 175
Orkin, Martin, 165–6
Ormerod, Nick, 153, 159
Orrell, John, 194
Osborne, John, 181
Otway, Thomas, 85
Ovid, 4, 54–6, 59, 60, 62, 63, 65–76, 182, 196–7
Owen, Geoff, 155
Owens, Steve, 151

Padrin, L., 21n
Palmer, David, 11n
Palmer, Kenneth, 181
Palmer, Richard, 155
Paramour, Thomas, 114
Parfitt, David, 129
Parker, Patricia, 164n
Partridge, Phil, 158
Pasternak, Boris, 150
Paterson, Ronan, 151

Patten, William, 28n
Patterson, Annabel, 190
Peele, George, 55
Pelling, G. B. R., 196
Pember, John, 159
Pendleton, Thomas A., 181, 212n
Pennington, Michael, 129, 161
Petcher, Stephen, 162
Peters, Helen, 195
Peters, John, 155
Petherbridge, Edward, 200
Petherbridge, Jonathan, 155
Petrarch, 4
Pfister, Manfred, 166
Phaer, Thomas, 54n
Piachaud, René-Louis, 181
Pickard, David, 156
Pietschmann, Herbert, 208
Pigott-Smith, Tim, 143–5, 149
Pimlott, Steven, 159
Pirandello, Luigi, 103n
Pitt, Angela, 32n
Plato, 16
Platter, Thomas, 115n, 206n
Plautus, 201
Plutarch, 196
Pollard, A. W., 77, 79, 119
Poole, John, 162
Pope, Alexander, 205, 207
Portacio, Tony, 160
Porter, Cole, 157
Potter, Lois, 197–8
Pound, Ezra, 54
Pownell, David, 162
Prendergast, Shaun, 129, 131
Price, Cecil, 37n, 85n
Price, George R., 209
Price, Hereward, 12
Price, Jonathan, 152
Prior, Roger, 186
Pronko, Leonard C., 103n
Proudfoot, Richard, 161, 181
Pryce, Jonathan, 134, 137
Purcell, Alice, 155
Purcell, John, 151
Puttenham, George, 55, 66, 67, 70, 73, 92, 93
Pythagoras, 67, 72–4

Quarshie, Hugh, 160
Quayle, Anthony, 152
Quint, David, 68n, 164n
Quintilian, 70, 89
Quirk, Sir Randolph, 195

INDEX

INDEX

INDEX